State of the World's Cities 2008/2009

HARMONIOUS CITIES

UN@HABITAT

earthscan

publishing for a sustainable future

London • Sterling, VA

First published by Earthscan in the UK and USA in 2008 for and on behalf of the United Nations Human Settlements Programme (UN-HABITAT).

Copyright © United Nations Human Settlements Programme, 2008.

United Nations Human Settlements Programme (UN-HABITAT)
P.O. Box 30030, Nairobi, Kenya
Tel: +254 20 7621 234
Fax: +254 20 7624 266/7
Website: www.unhabitat.org

DISCLAIMER

The designations employed and the presentation of the material in this report do not imply the expression of any opinion whatsoever on the part of the Secretariet of the United Nations concerning the legal status of any country, territory, city or area, or of its authorities, or concerning delimitation of its frontiers or boundaries, or regarding its economic system or degree of development. The analysis, conclusions and recommendations of this reports do not necessarily reflect the views of the United Nations Human Settlements Programme or its Governing Council.

The Report is produced with official data provided by governments and additional information gathered by the Global Urban Observatory. Cities and countries are invited to update data relevant to them. It is important to acknowledge that data varies according to definition and sources. While UN-HABITAT checks data provided to the fullest extent possible, the responsibility for the accuracy of the information lies with the original providers of the data. Information contained in this Report is provided without warranty of any kind, either express or implied, including, without limitation, warranties of merchantability, fitness for a particular purpose and non-infringement. UN-HABITAT specifically does not make any warranties or representations as to the accuracy or completeness of any such data. Under no circumstances shall UN-HABITAT be liable for any loss, damage, liability or expense incurred or suffered that is claimed to have resulted from the use of this Report, including, without limitation, any fault, error, omission with respect thereto. The use of this Report is at the User's sole risk. Under no circumstances, including, but not limited to, negligence, shall UN-HABITAT or its affiliates be liable for any direct, indirect, incidental, special or consequential damages, even if UN-HABITAT has been advised of the possibility of such damages.

HS/1031/08 E (paperback)
HS/1032/08 E (hardback)

ISBN: 978-1-84407-696-3 (Earthscan paperback)　　ISBN: 978-92-1-132010-7 (UN-HABITAT paperback)
ISBN: 978-1-84407-695-6 (Earthscan hardback)　　ISBN: 978-92-1-132011-4 (UN-HABITAT hardback)

Design and layout by Michael Jones Software, Nairobi, Kenya.
Printed and bound in Malta by Gutenberg Press Ltd.

For a full list of Earthscan publications contact:

Earthscan
Dunstan House
14a St Cross Street
London EC1N 8XA, UK
Tel: +44 (0)20 7841 1930
Fax: +44 (0)20 7242 1474
E-mail: earthinfo@earthscan.co.uk
Website: www.earthscan.co.uk

22883 Quicksilver Drive, Sterling, VA20166-2012, USA

Earthscan publishes in association with the International Institute for Environment and Development.

A catalogue record of this book is available from the British Library.

Library of Congress Cataloging-in-Publications Data has been applied for.

The paper used for this book is FSC-certified. FSC (the Forest Stewardship Council) is an international network to promote responsible management of the world's forests.

Mixed Sources
Product group from well-managed forests, and other controlled sources
www.fsc.org Cert no. TT-CoC-002424
© 1996 Forest Stewardship Council

Foreword

With more than half of the world's population now living in urban areas, this is the urban century. Harmonious urbanization, the theme of this fourth edition of the State of the World's Cities, has never been more important.

Cities embody some of society's most pressing challenges, from pollution and disease to unemployment and lack of adequate shelter. But cities are also venues where rapid, dramatic change is not just possible but expected. Thus they present real opportunities for increasing energy efficiency, reducing disparities in development and improving living conditions in general. National and local governments can promote harmonious urbanization by supporting pro-poor, inclusive and equitable urban development and by strengthening urban governance structures and processes. History demonstrates that integrated urban policy can be a solid path towards development.

Contrary to popular opinion, inequality and the unsustainable use of energy are not inevitable aspects of urban development, nor are they necessary for urbanization and economic growth to occur. Rather, as this report illustrates, cities can advance the prosperity of their inhabitants while achieving equitable social outcomes and fostering the sustainable use of resources. Today, many small, well-managed cities in both the developing and developed worlds are enjoying rapid growth, giving us a chance to stave off entrenched poverty and cultivate healthy environments in which people can thrive.

The data and analysis contained in this report are intended to improve our understanding of how cities function and what we, as a global community, can do to increase their liveability and unity. In that spirit, I commend this report to policymakers, mayors, citizens' groups and all those concerned with the welfare of our urbanizing world.

Ban Ki-moon
Secretary-General
United Nations

Introduction

Half of humanity now lives in cities, and within two decades, nearly 60 per cent of the world's people will be urban dwellers. Urban growth is most rapid in the developing world, where cities gain an average of 5 million residents every month. As cities grow in size and population, harmony among the spatial, social and environmental aspects of a city and between their inhabitants becomes of paramount importance. This harmony hinges on two key pillars: equity and sustainability.

The world has witnessed for the past year some of the social challenges associated with global warming and climate change. The rise in prices of fuel and food has provoked angry reactions worldwide and threatens to eradicate, in many instances, decades of social and economic advancement. This relatively new threat to harmonious urban development is nonetheless directly linked to poorly planned and managed urbanization. Urban sprawl, high dependence on motorized transport and urban lifestyles that generate excessive waste and consume large amounts of energy are some of the major contributors to the global increase in greenhouse gas emissions.

However, data analyzed by UN-HABITAT shows that not all cities contribute to global warming and climate change in the same way. While wealthier cities tend to produce more emissions than less wealthy cities, as higher incomes often translate into higher energy consumption, significant differences in emissions are also found between cities of similar wealth. Some cities in developed countries have, for example, been reducing their per capita energy consumption and emissions through better transport planning and energy conservation. At the same time, other cities in newly industrializing countries are increasing per capita emissions through the combined impact of motorization and increased energy consumption. The findings presented in this report clearly show that policies that promote energy-efficient public transport, that reduce urban sprawl and that encourage the use of environmentally-friendly sources of energy, can reduce a city's ecological footprint and carbon emissions significantly. In fact, cities provide a real opportunity to mitigate and reverse the impact of global climate change. Properly planned cities provide both the economies of scale and the population densities that have the potential to reduce per capita demand for resources such as energy and land.

The world is also confronting the challenge of increasing disparities between the rich and the poor. This edition of the State of the World's Cities shows that spatial and social disparities within cities and between cities and regions within the same country are growing as some areas benefit more than others from public services, infrastructure and other investments. Evidence presented in this report also shows that when cities already have high levels of inequality, spatial and social disparities are likely to become more, and not less, pronounced with economic growth. High levels of urban inequality present a double jeopardy. They have a dampening effect on economic growth and contribute to a less favourable environment for investment.

But just as importantly, urban inequality has a direct impact on all aspects of human development, including health, nutrition, gender equality and education. In cities where spatial and social divisions are stark or extreme, lack of social mobility tends to reduce people's participation in the formal sector of the economy and their integration in society. This exacerbates insecurity and social unrest which, in turn, diverts public and private resources from social services and productive investments to expenditures for safety and security. Pro-poor social programmes, equitable distribution of public resources and balanced spatial and territorial development, particularly through investments in urban and inter-urban infrastructure and services, are among the most effective means for mitigating or reversing the negative consequences of urban inequality.

Many cities and countries are addressing these challenges and opportunities by adopting innovative approaches to urban planning and management that are inclusive, pro-poor and responsive to threats posed by environmental degradation and global warming. From China to Colombia, and everywhere in between, national and local governments are making critical choices that promote equity and sustainability in cities. These governments recognize that cities are not just part of the problem; they are, and must be, part of the solution. Many cities are also coming up with innovative institutional reforms to promote prosperity while minimizing inequity and unsustainable use of energy. Enlightened and committed political leadership combined with effective urban planning, governance and management that promote equity and sustainability are the critical components to the building of harmonious cities.

Anna K. Tibaijuka
Under-Secretary-General and Executive Director
United Nations Human Settlements Programme
(UN-HABITAT)

Acknowledgements

Core Team

Director: Oyebanji Oyeyinka
Coordinator: Nefise Bazoglu
Task Manager: Eduardo López Moreno
Statistical Adviser: Gora Mboup
Editor: Rasna Warah

Principal Author: Eduardo López Moreno
Additional Authors: Nefise Bazoglu, Gora Mboup and Rasna Warah

Support Team

Research: Gianluca Crispi, Yuzuru Tachi, Anne Klen, Maharufa Hossain, Asa Jonsson
Graphs: Yuzuru Tachi
GIS: Maharufa Hossain and Jane Arimah
Statistics: Josephine Gichuhi, George Madara, Julius Majale, Philip Mukungu,
Souleymane N'doye, Omondi Odhiambo, Raymond Otieno
Editorial Support: Darcy Varney
Administrative Assistance: Anne Idukitta and Elizabeth Kahwae

UN-HABITAT Advisory and Technical Support

Sharif Ahmed, Alioune Badiane, Daniel Biau, Mohamed Halfani,
Marco Keiner, Inga Klevby, Anantha Krishnan, Ansa Masaud, Victor Mgendi,
Naison Mutizwa-Mangiza, Jane Nyakairu, Ligia Ramirez, Roman Rollnick,
Wandia Seaforth, Sharad Shankardass, Mohamed El-Sioufi, Paul Taylor, Anna K. Tibaijuka,
Nicholas You

International Advisory Board

A. T. M. Nurul Amin, Perinaz Bhada, Robert Buckley, Naser Faruqi, Paolo Gamba,
Dan Hoornweg, Paola Jiron, Marianne Kjellen, Patricia McCarney, Molly O'Meara
Sheehan, Francisco Perez Arellano, Clara E. Salazar Cruz, David Satterthwaite,
Dina K. Shehayeb, Belinda Yuen

Financial Support

Government of Norway, Kingdom of Bahrain, Government of Italy,
International Development Research Center (Canada), and World Bank, among others

Cover design and page layout: Michael Jones Software
Cover image: ©Mudassar Ahmed Dar/ Shutterstock & Li Wa/Shutterstock

Contributors

Significant contributions in the analysis of data and drafting of background papers:
Adriana Allen for "Addressing Rural-Urban Disparities for Harmonious Development"
Federico Butera for "Cities and Climate Change" and "Energy Consumption in Cities"
Patricia McCarney and Richard Stren for "Metropolitan Governance: Governing in a City of Cities"
Simone Cecchini, Jorge Rodríguez, Maren Jiménez, Daniela González, Ernesto Espindola and Hernan Pizarro of the UN Economic Commission for Latin America and the Caribbean (ECLAC) for collating urban/city Gini coefficients for Latin America and the Caribbean, in consultation with Miguel Ojeda and Lucy Winchester
Jorge Carrillo and Sarah Lowder of UN Economic and Social Commission for Asia and the Pacific (ESCAP) for collating urban/city Gini coefficients for Asia and the Pacific

Additional contributions in the preparation of thematic papers and in the analysis and review of data:
Carmen Bellet and Josep Ma Llop Torne for "The Role of Intermediate Cities"
Jordi Borja, whose ideas were adapted from "La Ciudad Conquistada" (Barcelona, 2007)
Suochen Dong, Marlene Fernandes, Yasser Rajjal, David Schmidt, Maram Tawil, Vinod Tewari for Metropolitan Governance Surveys in China, Brazil, Amman, Cape Town and India
Ali Farzin for "Urban Inequalities in Iran"
Pietro Garau for "Preliminary analysis of surveys on slum upgrading polices"
Padmashree Gehl Sampath for "Institutional Analysis and Innovation" and research on economic policies and migration
Prabha Khosla for "Gender Sensitive Urban Governance" and analysis of gender disaggregated slum data
Enzo Mingione and Serena Vicari for "Inequalities in European Cities"
Afsaneh Moharami for "Drivers of Decline/Growth in Iranian Cities"
Mark Montgomery for analysis and review of global urban data
Ariane Mueller for "Best Practices and Climate Change in Cities"
Maria da Piedade for Gini coefficient data in Brazilian cities
Patricia Romero-Lankao for "Climate Change and Cities – Latin America"
German Solinis "Without harmony, there will be no cities in the urbanized world"
Raquel Szalachman for "Human Settlements and the Environment in Latin America and the Caribbean"
Vinod Tewari for "Urbanization Trends in Asia", "Drivers of City Growth" and Gini coefficients for urban India
Pablo Vaggione for "Planning for Urban Harmony"
Darcy Varney "Inclusive Urban Planning for Harmonious Development"
Luciano Vettoretto for "Regional Planning towards Spatial Strategies: Learning from the European Experience"
Yu Zhu for "Urbanization Trends in China" and "Drivers of City Growth in China"

Input to production of maps and graphs:
Deborah Balk for text and maps on "Cities at Risk in Low Elevation Coastal Zones"
Bangladesh Centre for Advanced Studies for map on "Flood-prone areas in Dhaka"
Centre for Urban Studies (Bangladesh) for map on "Slum settlements in Dhaka"
European Commission Directorate for Regional Policy for map on "Intra-city Differences in Unemployment in London, Berlin, Stockholm and Madrid, 2001"
Kenya Bureau of Statistics for map on "Poverty Incidence in Nairobi, Mombasa and Kisumu"
Rashid Seedat and the South African Cities Network for input to various graphs related to inequality in South African cities
Thailand Department of Land Transport, Pollution Control Department of Thailand and Clean Air Initiative for Asian Cities Centre for text and data on "Air Quality in Bangkok"
World Resources Institute for flowchart on "World GHG Emissions"

Input to boxes:
Suochen Dong, Cristina Martínez Fernández, Padmashree Gehl Sampath, Asa Jonsson, Prabha Khosla, Xue Li, Frederico Neto, Madanmohan Rao, Wandia Seaforth, Deborah Wei Mullin, Xiaojun Zhang

Additional research:
Sai Balakrishnan, Haddy Guisse, Lusungu Kayani, Jennifer Venema

Country information:
Maria Alvarez Gancedo, Wesley Aruga, Kangwa Chama, John Leo Chome, Bharat Dahiya, Suocheng Dong, María D. Franco Delgado, Ali El-Faramawy, Eden Garde, David Houssou, Dodo Juliman, George Kozonguizi, Cecilia Martinez, Alberto Paranhos, Basilisa Sanou, Fole Sherman, Roshan Raj Shrestha, Ileana Ramirez, Tewodros Tigabu, Conrad de Tissera, Merlin Totinon, Pinky Vilakazi

Contents

Part 3: ENVIRONMENTAL HARMONY

Boxes and City Stories

Figures

Tables

Part 4: PLANNING FOR HARMONIOUS CITIES

Boxes and City Stories

Figures

Table

Overview and Key Findings

Cities are perhaps one of humanity's most complex creations, never finished, never definitive. They are like a journey that never ends. Their evolution is determined by their ascent into greatness or their descent into decline. They are the past, the present and the future.

Cities contain both order and chaos. In them reside beauty and ugliness, virtue and vice. They can bring out the best or the worst in humankind. They are the physical manifestation of history and culture and incubators of innovation, industry, technology, entrepreneurship and creativity. Cities are the materialization of humanity's noblest ideas, ambitions and aspirations, but when not planned or governed properly, can be the repository of society's ills. Cities drive national economies by creating wealth, enhancing social development and providing employment but they can also be the breeding grounds for poverty, exclusion and environmental degradation.

Half of humanity now lives in cities, and within the next two decades, 60 per cent of the world's people will reside in urban areas. How can city planners and policymakers harmonize the various interests, diversity and inherent contradictions within cities? What ingredients are needed to create harmony between the physical, social, environmental and cultural aspects of a city and the human beings that inhabit it?

Harmonious Cities

A society cannot claim to be harmonious if large sections of its population are deprived of basic needs while other sections live in opulence. A city cannot be harmonious if some groups concentrate resources and opportunities while others remain impoverished and marginalized. Harmony in cities can not be achieved if the price of urban living is paid by the environment. Reconciling contradictory and complementary elements is critical to creating harmony within cities. A harmonious city promotes unity within diversity. Harmony within cities hinges not only on prosperity and its attendant benefits, but on two pillars that make harmony possible: equity and sustainability.

Harmony is both an ancient social ideal as well as a modern concept. In ancient Chinese philosophy, harmony implied moderation and balance in all things. Today, the concept of harmony encapsulates more modern concepts, such as environmental sustainability, equity, gender parity, inclusiveness and good governance. While the concept of sustainability focuses on ethical and ecological considerations and is focused primarily on protecting the Earth's environmental and natural assets, the concept of harmony also entails the synchronization and integration of all of the Earth's assets, whether they are physical, environmental, cultural, historical, social or human. In this sense, harmony is a broad concept that relies on distinctly human capabilities, such as mutual support, solidarity and cooperation. Harmony has now become the theoretical foundation for deepening understanding of the social, economic, political and environmental fabric of cities in order to create a more balanced society.

Harmony is therefore both a journey and a destination.

This report adopts the concept of Harmonious Cities as a theoretical framework in order to understand today's urban world, and also as an operational tool to confront the most important challenges facing urban areas and their development processes. It recognizes that tolerance, fairness, social justice and good governance, all of which are inter-related, are as important to sustainable urban development as physical planning. It addresses national concerns by searching for solutions at the city level. For that purpose, it focuses on three key areas: spatial or regional harmony; social harmony; and environmental harmony. The report also assesses the various intangible assets within cities that contribute to harmony, such as cultural heritage, sense of place and memory and the complex set of social and symbolic relationships that give cities meaning. It argues that these intangible assets represent the "soul of the city" and are as important for harmonious urban development as tangible assets.

Spatial Harmony

The Century of the City

The 21st century is the Century of the City. Half of the world's population already lives in urban areas and by the middle of this century, most regions of the developing world will be predominantly urban. This report takes a fresh look at existing urban data and delivers a compelling and comprehensive analysis of urbanization trends and the growth of cities in the last two decades. Using a wealth of significant and comparative data on cities, the report analyzes global and regional trends that reflect the pace and scale of urbanization in the developing world and the key drivers of urban growth in the world's fastest growing cities. The purpose of this analysis is to explore the spatial nuances and implications of economic and social policies.

Urban growth rates are highest in the developing world, which absorbs an average of 5 million new urban residents every month and is responsible for 95 per cent of the world's urban population growth. Urban growth is as a result of a combination of factors: geographical location, natural population growth, rural-to-urban migration, infrastructure development, national policies, corporate strategies, and other major political, social and economic forces, including globalization. In the 1990s, cities in the developing world grew at an average annual rate of 2.5 per cent. More than half of the urban areas in the developing world grew at the high annual rate of between 2 and 4 per cent or more during this period, while more than one-third grew at the moderate or slow rate of less than 2 per cent a year. Although urban growth rates are slowing down in most regions of the developing world, levels of urbanization are expected to rise, with the least urbanized regions of Asia and Africa transforming from largely rural societies to predominantly urban regions during the course of this century. By 2050, the urban population of the developing world will be 5.3 billion; Asia alone will host 63 per cent of the world's urban population, or 3.3 billion people, while Africa, with an urban population of 1.2 billion, will host nearly a quarter of the world's urban population.

In sharp contrast, the urban population of the developed world, including countries of the Commonwealth of Independent States, is expected to remain largely unchanged, rising only slightly from just over 900 million in 2005 to 1.1 billion in 2050. Many cities in this region are actually experiencing population loss, largely due to low rates of natural population increase and declining fertility rates. The phenomenon of declining populations is generally associated with the developed world; however, the phenomenon of shrinking urban populations can be observed in some cities in the developing world. There is, therefore, a need to combine new methods and techniques that respond to urban growth and expansion in some cities, while responding to the emerging trend of population and economic decline in others. Smart planning for growth should be combined with smart planning for contraction if more harmonious urban development is to be achieved.

Urban change in the developing world does not always follow identical patterns or trends. Urbanization in Africa is characterized by disproportionately high concentrations of people and investments in the largest city (in most cases, the capital) and by very high annual slum growth rates of more than 4 per cent. Urbanization in the region, especially in sub-Saharan Africa, is therefore characterized by urban primacy and slum formation.

In Asia, an emerging trend is that of metropolitan expansion, which is becoming a prominent feature of large cities. Urban populations are shifting or relocating to suburban locations or satellite towns linked to the main city through commuter networks. This phenomenon is particularly prevalent in large Indian cities, where ring towns or "bedroom communities" have formed around cities such as New Delhi and Mumbai. Urban growth patterns in China, on the other hand, have tended to produce "city regions" along the eastern coastal belt, which are responsible for much of the economic growth experienced by the country in recent years. In countries where urban primacy is still the rule, such as the Philippines and Indonesia, the trend has been to promote the growth of intermediate cities in order to direct migrants away from the largest city.

Urban development in Latin America and the Caribbean, the most urbanized region in the developing world, is also characterized by a high degree of urban primacy with one-fifth of the region's urban residents living in cities with populations of 5 million or more. However, one of the most distinctive features of urbanization in the region is the rapid growth of small cities, which are home to nearly 40 per cent of the region's urban population. Another distinctive characteristic of the region is that urban growth is often the result of people moving from one city to another, and not from rural areas to urban areas.

Central governments play a critical role in determining the prosperity and growth of cities

Geography clearly matters when explaining the economic dynamism and growth of cities and regions (location, comparative advantages, agglomeration factors, proximity etc.). For instance, cities located near the sea, along a river bank or in a delta have historically dominated, and continue to dominate, the urban landscape of countries and regions. Fourteen of the world's 19 largest cities with populations of more than 10 million are located near a large water body that serves to link local economies to regional and global supply chains and trade.

However, geography alone does not determine which cities will grow or prosper. This report shows that the growth of cities is neither random nor entirely organic. National policies, corporate strategies and the comparative advantages that cities offer in global, regional and local markets to a large extent determine which cities will grow and thrive and which will decline in size or economic or political significance. National policies that include pro-urban approaches to economic development play a critical role in the growth of cities, as has been witnessed in China's southern and eastern regions in recent years.

In many cities, national economic policies and investments are mostly the result of government decisions and budget allocations. The State, in its various institutional forms, exerts a critical influence on determining which cities and regions will benefit most from public resources. Governments also promote and/or regulate private or public investments for the construction of infrastructure and other investments that contribute to urban development. Central governments in many countries are concentrating more attention and resources on particular city-regions to redirect regional or national development. They are also using cities to connect to the global space of business and financial flows, while concurrently using such cities to propel social change in particular directions.

In many countries, urban growth is initially driven by national governments, and then further propelled by local authorities and other actors, such as the private sector. This has led to cities competing with each other for resources and for inclusion in regional and national development plans and strategies. The growth of cities through local initiatives reflects a rising trend towards greater urban entrepreneurialism and more intense city competition.

Balanced urban and regional development can be achieved through consistent and targeted investments in transport and communications infrastructure

Cities can no longer be treated as distinct spaces unconnected to the regions surrounding them. Linkages between rural and urban areas and between cities have created new opportunities that rely on connectivity to enable the flow of people and resources from one area to another. Investments in urban, inter-urban and rural-urban transport and communications infrastructure are, therefore, critical for balanced regional development and for enhancing the economic potential of cities and the regions surrounding them.

Central governments play a pivotal role in allocating and mobilizing financial resources either to support urban economic development or to redress regional/territorial disparities. This report shows that targeted investments in transport and communications infrastructure, in particular, are the most significant drivers of urban growth and economic development in the developing world.

A preliminary UN-HABITAT analysis of the fastest growing cities in the developing world shows that more than 40 per cent benefitted from the diversification, expansion or improvement of regional or national transport systems, including roads, airports, urban and inter-urban railway lines and ports. Investment in transport and communications infrastructure not only increases the overall productivity of cities, nations and regions, it also promotes balanced urban and regional development. Policies to promote economic development, including designation of special economic zones or industrial hubs, are also playing an important role in the growth of cities, particularly in Asia.

Social Harmony

Cities are becoming more unequal

In many cities, wealth and poverty coexist in close proximity: rich, well-serviced neighbourhoods and gated residential communities are often situated near dense inner-city or peri-urban slum communities that lack even the most basic of services. This report presents a preliminary global analysis of income and/or consumption distribution at the urban and/or city level. It shows that income distribution varies considerably among less-developed regions with some regions, notably Africa and Latin America, exhibiting extremely high levels of urban inequality compared to Europe and Asia, where urban inequality levels are relatively low.

Latin American and Caribbean cities are among the most unequal in the world, with Brazilian and Colombian cities topping the list, closely followed by some cities in Argentina, Chile, Ecuador, Guatemala and Mexico. Urban inequalities in this highly unequal region are not only increasing, but are becoming more entrenched, which suggests that failures in wealth distribution are largely the result of structural or systemic flaws.

In Africa, urban income inequalities are highest in Southern Africa, with South African and Namibian cities exhibiting levels of urban inequality that rival even those of Latin American cities. Cities in sub-Saharan Africa that have recently emerged from apartheid systems of governance tend to be the most unequal. South Africa stands out as a country that has yet to break out of an economic and political model that concentrates resources, although the adoption of redistributive strategies and policies in recent years have reduced inequalities slightly. Unfortunately, rising economic growth rates in several African countries have not reduced income or consumption disparities; on the contrary, urban inequalities in many African cities, including Maputo, Nairobi and Abidjan, remain high as wealth becomes more concentrated. In general, urban inequalities in African countries tend to be higher than rural inequalities, and Northern African cities tend to be more equal than sub-Saharan African cities.

Asian cities, on the other hand, tend to be more equal than cities in other parts of the developing world, although levels of urban inequality have risen or remain high in some cities, including Hong Kong and Ho Chi Minh City. High levels of urban inequality have also been reported in cities in Thailand and the Philippines. Cities in China tend to be more equal than other Asian cities, with Beijing being among the most equal city in the region, although some Chinese cities, such as Shenzhen, are experiencing relatively high inequality levels similar to those of Bangkok and Manila. China's booming economy has also led to rural-urban and regional disparities, with populations living in cities located on the eastern part of the country enjoying significantly higher per capita incomes than rural populations living in remote western parts of the country. In Bangladesh, India, Pakistan and Indonesia, levels of urban inequality are generally low and are comparable to many cities in Europe, Canada and Australia. However, recent analyses suggest that India will experience rising levels of urban inequality in the future as a result of liberalization and industrialization policies coupled with lack of adequate investment in provision of public goods to the most vulnerable populations.

High levels of urban inequality are socially destabilizing and economically unsustainable

High levels of inequality in cities can lead to negative social, economic and political consequences that have a destabilizing impact on societies. Inequalities create social and political fractures within society that can develop into social unrest. This is particularly true in places experiencing both high levels of inequality and endemic poverty, which increase the risk of political tension and social divisions that can threaten national security and economic development. Social unrest and insecurity, in turn, reduce incentives for investment and force governments to increase the amount of public resources devoted to internal security – resources that might have otherwise been spent on more productive sectors of the economy or on social services and infrastructure.

This report shows that the benefits of economic growth are not realized in societies experiencing extremely high levels of inequality and poverty. In fact, recent evidence shows that societies that have low levels of inequality are more effective in reducing poverty levels than those that are highly unequal. Economic growth benefits larger groups of people and is "absorbed" better by egalitarian societies than by those where disparities between the rich and the poor are very wide, as the former tend to concentrate the benefits of wealth creation, leaving the majority behind. Inequalities also have a dampening effect on economic efficiency as they raise the cost of redistribution and affect the allocation of resources for investment.

A significant conclusion of this report is inequality is not a natural consequence of economic growth and that while the relationship between economic growth and urban income inequality is neither simple nor correlational, levels of inequality can be controlled or reduced by forward-looking mitigation efforts on the part of governments. UN-HABITAT analysis of urban inequalities in 28 developing countries indicates that since the 1980s nearly half of these countries managed to reduce levels of urban inequality while enjoying positive economic growth. Malaysia, for instance, has been steadily reducing levels of urban inequality since the early 1970s through the implementation of pro-poor policies and through human resources and skills development. Similarly, Indonesia's "Growth, Stability and Equity" programme has ensured that income distribution and poverty alleviation are integral components of economic growth and development. Policies promoting equity in Rwanda have also ensured that the high economic growth rates that the country is currently experiencing do not increase inequality levels. These countries have shown that it is possible to grow economically without increasing inequality levels, and that reduction of inequalities is, in fact, a pro-growth strategy.

Focused and targeted investments and interventions can significantly improve the lives of slum dwellers

Slum dwellers in many of the world's poorest cities experience multiple deprivations that are direct expressions of poverty: many of their houses are unfit for habitation and they often lack adequate food, education, health and basic services that the better-off take for granted. Frequently, their neighbourhoods are not recognized by local and central authorities. In many parts of the world, these "invisible", unplanned parts of cities are growing faster than the more visible, planned parts.

In some cities, slum dwellers constitute the majority of the urban population and slums are the most common type of human settlement, giving rise to what this report refers to as "slum cities", while in others, slums are small pockets of deprivation physically isolated from the rest of the city. Slum prevalence is highest in sub-Saharan-Africa (62 per cent), followed by Southern Asia (43 per cent) and Eastern Asia (37 per cent). Northern Africa has the lowest slum prevalence in the developing world (15 per cent).

However, new UN-HABITAT data shows that not all slum dwellers suffer from the same degree or magnitude of deprivation, nor are all slums homogenous. In other words, not all slum dwellers around the world suffer the same fate: some are worse off than others. In general, however, the poorest regions of the world tend to host the largest slum populations that suffer from multiple shelter deprivations, including lack of access to improved water and sanitation, overcrowding, non-durable housing and insecure tenure. For instance, surveys conducted in Angola, the Democratic Republic of the Congo, Guinea Bissau, Sudan and Sierra Leone show that slum dwellers there are likely to experience a combination of shelter deprivations, whereas in countries such as Benin, Burkina Faso, Burundi, Cameroon, Gabon, Kenya, Ghana and Senegal, most slum dwellers tend to suffer from one or two shelter deprivations. The report also shows that woman-headed households suffer disproportionately from multiple shelter deprivations; in Haiti, for instance, nearly 60 per cent of woman-headed households suffer from three shelter deprivations, while in Kenya and Nicaragua, one-third of woman-headed households experience four shelter deprivations.

The report also shows that slum dwellers across regions suffer from similar deprivations: slum dwellers in Colombia, Turkey and Zimbabwe, for instance, suffer mostly from overcrowding, whereas slum dwellers in Egypt and Mexico suffer most from lack of improved sanitation. In many cities, however, living in a non-slum area is no guarantee against poor living conditions. UN-HABITAT data shows that a slum resident in Cairo can be better-off than a non-slum dweller in Lagos, Luanda and many other cities in sub-Saharan Africa in terms of indicators such as health, education or environmental conditions. These differentiated levels of social inequality and exclusion can adversely affect cities and regions' social and economic development.

By identifying the particular deprivation that is prevalent in slums, governments and local authorities can focus public resources for the improvement of slums more effectively. In the case of Benin, for instance, targeted investments in sanitation facilities in slums could easily elevate a quarter of the slum households to non-slum status. By disaggregating the type and level of shelter deprivation in slums (i.e. severe or non-severe), policymakers can be in a better position to devise policy responses that are better focused and targeted. Furthermore, by categorizing slums according to the type or intensity of deprivation they experience, it is possible to better target interventions in cities and even within specific neighbourhoods. This information can be combined with other urban and slum indicators in order to make more informed decisions about how to improve the lives of slum dwellers and build cities that are more socially harmonious.

Environmental Harmony

Cities provide an opportunity to mitigate or even reverse the impact of global climate change as they provide the economies of scale that reduce per capita costs and demand for resources

Cities that are not properly planned or managed can be a burden on natural resources and can easily threaten the quality of the air and water, thereby negatively impacting the natural and living environment. Because of their compact form and economies of scale, cities offer major opportunities to reduce energy demand and to minimize pressures on surrounding land and natural resources. Well-planned and well-regulated cities hold the key not only to minimizing environmental losses, but to generating creative solutions to enhance the quality of the environment and to mitigate the negative consequences of climate change.

However, if cities can harness the inherent advantages that urbanization provides, they can, in fact, be part of the solution to global environmental challenges, including the rise in greenhouse gas emissions brought about by fossil fuel consumption. Although cities and urban-based activities are usually blamed for the increase in greenhouse gas emissions globally, evidence suggests that these emissions are more related to consumption patterns and gross domestic product (GDP) per capita than they are to urbanization levels per se. For instance, the megacity of São Paulo in Brazil produces one-tenth the emissions of San Diego in the United States, even though the latter is one-quarter the size of the former.

This report presents a first general account of how cities consume energy, disaggregating the information in three sectors: industry; residential and commercial buildings; and transport, taking into account the stage of development of countries and their income levels. Although per capita energy consumption tends to be higher in rich industrialized cities, there are significant variations between cities in different regions. For example, cities in Europe, which tend to be compact and which encourage use of public transport, use energy more efficiently than cities in North America, where urban sprawl, high-energy-consuming lifestyles and high dependence on motorized private transport is the norm.

The findings further show that energy use differs between cities in the developed world and those in developing countries. Heating and lighting of residential and commercial buildings consume more than 50 per cent of energy in cities such as New York, London and Tokyo, while transport accounts for more than half of the energy consumed in Hong Kong, Bangkok, Cape Town and Mexico City. In some Chinese cities, such as Beijing and Shanghai, industry is the main consumer of energy. Variations between regions and cities can also be found at the household level. The bulk of energy in low-income households in developing countries is used for cooking, whereas space heating and lighting use up the bulk of energy in households in high-income countries. For urban poor households the climb up the energy ladder – from biomass fuels to cleaner energy sources, such as electricity or natural gas – not only improves their quality of life, but also reduces greenhouse emissions. There is, therefore, a need to introduce new energy-efficient and environmentally-friendly technologies in low-income communities in order to reduce their environmental impact and lessen environmental hazards.

Data on energy consumption at the city, sub-city and household levels is still scant, however, which calls for the need to set up a global monitoring mechanism to measure energy consumption in cities, their impact on greenhouse gas emissions and the mitigation and adaptation solutions that are being implemented.

Evidence shows that compact and well-regulated cities with environmentally-friendly public transport systems have a positive environmental impact

Although the rich generally consume more energy than the poor, the report shows with convincing evidence that urban form and density and environmentally-friendly public transport systems strongly influence energy consumption at the city level and that some cities in developed countries now produce fewer carbon emissions per capita than cities in some less developed countries. Cities that are more compact, use more clean energy and are less dependant on motorized transport are not only more energy-efficient but contribute less to greenhouse gas emissions.

A comparison of transport-related carbon emissions in various regions around the world shows that emissions are highest in North America and Australia. North American cities are suffering from urban sprawl and expansion and increased use of private motorized transport, which contribute to the exceptionally high levels of emissions in this region. Western Europe, on the other hand, produces approximately a quarter of the transport-related emissions of North America, a difference that can be explained by the tendency of European cities to promote the use of clean energy and the more prevalent use of public transport in the region. Increased use of environmentally-friendly public transport systems and halting of urban sprawl in cities can therefore substantially reduce emissions at the city level.

Sea level rise could have a devastating impact on coastal cities

Global mean projections indicate that global warming could lead to a rise in sea levels in the coming decades. Sea level rise brought about by climate change could have a devastating impact on coastal cities and urban populations. Globally, nearly 60 per cent of the world's population living in low elevation coastal zones – the continuous area along coastlines that is less than 10 metres above sea level and which is most vulnerable to sea level rise – is urban. Some regions, such as Asia and Africa, are particularly vulnerable, as many coastal cities in these regions do not have the infrastructure to withstand extreme weather conditions. Parts of cities such as Dhaka in Bangladesh and Alexandria in Egypt could in effect be swept away as the infrastructure to withstand extreme flooding in these and other cities in the developing world is insufficient. Because the urban poor tend to live in hazardous locations, such as flood plains, they are particularly vulnerable in the event of sea level rise as their housing is often of a non-durable nature and their settlements often lack adequate drainage, embankments and other infrastructure. These cities need to urgently adopt mitigation and adaptation strategies in order to avert catastrophic consequences in the future.

Planning for Harmonious Cities

Cities are not just brick and mortar: they symbolize the dreams, aspirations and hopes of societies. The management of a city's human, social, cultural and intellectual assets is, therefore, as important for harmonious urban development as is the management of a city's physical assets.

Urban planning has to go beyond being just a technical exercise to one that is cognizant of a city's various tangible and intangible assets. Innovative approaches to urban planning have to also respond to the following emerging priorities and concerns: regional disparities; urban inequalities; and metropolitan expansion or the growth of "city regions". This report presents some of the elements required to implement innovative planning solutions for sustainable and harmonious urban development with examples of cities that are making a difference.

Commitment to pro-poor, inclusive urban development

Pro-poor social programmes, inclusive governance structures and investment in public goods and services have gone a long way in reducing inequalities in many cities. Investments in infrastructure and basic services for the poorest or most vulnerable groups have not only drastically reduced urban poverty levels, but also bridged the urban income divide.

This report presents the main conclusions of an analysis of the policies and interventions that cities are implementing to achieve more harmonious urban development. The analysis was conducted by UN-HABITAT and the Cities Alliance and covers approximately 52 cities in 21 countries. This study provides a better understanding of what drives city/country's performance in reducing intra-city inequalities by upgrading slums and preventing their formation. The report shows that successful slum improvement or reduction initiatives share six attributes, and when governments harness all or some of them the possibility of success is higher. These attributes

are: i) awareness and political commitment; ii) institutional innovation; iii) policy reforms and institutional strengthening; iv) effective policy implementation; v) setting up monitoring and evaluation mechanisms; and v) scaling up actions.

Political commitment, especially by the top leadership, plays a critical role in reducing urban poverty and slum prevalence. Some of the most successful cities in this regard have benefitted from visionary mayors and political leaders who have radically transformed city landscapes by introducing reforms and strengthening institutions that enhance a city's economic vitality and environmental sustainability while simultaneously reducing poverty levels and slum prevalence. Political commitment coupled with performance monitoring, either from the bottom up or from the top down, have shown to improve the quality of urban services in many cities, and made local authorities more accountable to citizens.

Governing in a city of cities

The report advocates for the need to consider metropolitan and regional governance structures to respond to the growing demands and challenges of urban agglomerations that are expanding outside the traditional city limits. The "city of cities" or "city regions" should be able to respond to issues such as transport, crime, pollution, poverty and exclusion through effective metropolitan governance arrangements. These new structures of governance would address fundamental challenges, such as territorial isolation, fragmentation of technical and political interests, legal restrictions on municipalities to intervene beyond the politico-administrative jurisdictions, and different levels of functionality of the fiscal and administrative systems.

Metropolitan governance arrangements affect the levels of harmony and disharmony in cities. Harmony can be enhanced through effective leadership, efficient financing, effective evaluation mechanisms and forms of citizen participation, and institutional reforms addressing multi-level and inter-jurisdictional challenges to better govern metropolitan areas.

Competitive cooperation between cities that are part of the same urban agglomeration can help to overcome disharmonies related to spatial or territorial disparities and inequalities in the access to housing and basic services. They can also contribute to more balanced development between rich and poor municipalities and between the urban agglomeration and the hinterland. Metropolitan governance structures that coordinate with other levels of government can also put in place mitigation and adaptation measures that can contribute to the improvement of the quality of the environment.

Effective metropolitan governance offers the potential for more harmonious urban development responding to the following fundamental concerns: i) *spatial disparities*, ensuring that government policies promote convergence of leading and lagging regions and cities, supporting further development in the former and dealing with asymmetric growth and regional disparities in the latter; ii) *an increasingly divided urban society*, ensuring that governments adopt pro-poor growth policies and reforms by designing interventions in those sectors and areas in which poor people earn their living and where economic development faces distributional challenges; iii) *increased environmental costs*, ensuring that governments adopt policies to enhance energy efficiency related to the functionally of the city such as public transport and anti-sprawl policies that improve the quality of the environment without impairing economic growth; iv) ensuring that governments adopt policies to protect *intangible assets*, such as cultural heritage, and create social spaces that contribute to "humanizing" cities.

Coordination and collaboration between national, provincial and local authorities can achieve harmonious regional and urban development, provided they share a common vision and demonstrate sufficient political will

Improved coordination between the three levels of government – local, provincial and national – involves a change in the national and urban governance paradigm, in which central governments have the responsibility to put forward legislation, adopt social and economic policies and allocate budgets through a continuous dialogue with regional and local authorities in support of city growth. On their part, local authorities, working with regional authorities, need to develop clear visions and strategies that articulate short- and medium-term responses to enhance economic and social conditions in their cities. When local authorities set up good local governance structures for effective urban management and city development, and when they improve coordination with the other two levels of government, there are more chances to achieve harmonious regional and urban development. Economic and social policies need to address the needs of both cities and the regions in which cities are located, including urban-rural interfaces. If this is not done, it is likely that regional disparities will continue to widen.

▶
Hong Kong
©Xing Zhang

State of the World's
CITIES 2008/9
HARMONIOUS CITIES

Part One

01

Cities and the regions surrounding them have a symbiotic relationship; as long as this relationship is understood and carefully nurtured, both will advance together. Part 1 presents preliminary observations on the spatial identity of the world's cities, going beyond the "one or two cities tell everything approach" that has dominated urban studies so far. It shows with compelling evidence that the growth of cities is experiencing a dramatic bifurcation: while most cities in the developing world are growing, with some doubling in size every 15 to 30 years, some cities are actually experiencing population loss.

These changes are neither random nor organic; urban growth and decline are a result of a combination of factors, including geographical location, natural population growth, infrastructure development, national policies, corporate strategies and globalization. Understanding the determinants of the growth or decline of cities can help planners to support the processes that lead to harmonious urban development and to deal with some of the negative consequences of urban growth, such as asymmetrical regional development and rural-urban disparities.

SPATIAL HARMONY

Downtown Dhaka at night
©Manoocher Deghati/IRIN

1.1

The Spatial Distribution of the World's Cities

▲
Montevideo cityscape from port district
©Sonja Fagnan/iStockphoto

Geography matters

The evolution of cities is intimately linked to geography. Archaeological evidence shows that many of the oldest human settlements were located along the banks of mighty rivers and lakes, in deltas or along coastlines. Locations near water offered opportunities for fishing and agriculture, which helped ensure a steady food supply. Coastal cities and cities located in river deltas also served to link local economies to regional and global supply chains and trade; such cities have continued to provide vital economic links throughout time.

Coastal areas have always been preferred locations for human settlements, both in ancient times and today. Cities located near the sea have an obvious advantage: they provide access to sea trade routes and links.[1] Globally, coastal zones are the most urbanized ecosystems, with 65 per cent of their inhabitants residing in urban areas; Europe, North America, Oceania, and Latin America have the most urbanized coastal areas, with more than 80 per cent of the population along coastlines living in cities.

Settling near large bodies of water has clearly been an important factor in the economic and demographic growth of cities. Inland water ecosystems, like coastal areas, also tend to be highly urbanized. Globally, 55 per cent of the world's population residing in inland water ecosystems was urban in 2000. In Africa, slightly more than 50 per cent of the population residing along the shores of inland lakes and rivers was urban in 2000, while in Asia, the figure was 47 per cent.[2] (Figure 1.1.1)

While coastal zones tend to be the most urbanized ecosystems in all regions of the world, they do not support the largest share of urban populations in countries with coastlines; in all regions of the world, except Oceania, cultivated ecosystems – or agricultural land – support the largest urban populations. In China, for instance, more than 85 per cent of the urban land area and urban population is located in cultivated ecosystems; China's coastal zone, however, represents just 2 per cent of the total land area but is home to 23 per cent of the urban population of the country and 14 per cent of the total population.[3]

Cities located near the sea, along a river bank or in a delta tend to be the largest cities in all regions of the world. Port cities, in particular, continue to dominate the urban landscape of countries and regions. Fourteen of the world's 19 largest cities are port cities located along a coastline or in a river delta. (Fig. 1.1.2) A similar pattern exists at the regional level. Fourteen of the 20 largest cities in both Africa and Latin America and the Caribbean are located on a coastline or along a river bank. In Asia, the dominance of port cities is even greater: 17 of the region's 20 largest cities are either coastal, on a river bank or in a delta. In general, large cities – both coastal and inland – in the developing world tend to be larger and more dense than those in the developed world, as most cities with populations greater than 500,000 are located in low- or middle-income countries, with Asia having the largest number of cities with populations of 1 million or more.[4]

Rivers and delta regions have played an equally important role in the growth of Asian cities as coastlines; half of the largest cities in the region developed along important rivers that serve as gateways to coastal and inland areas. In the developed world (including Japan), 35 of the 40 largest cities are either coastal or situated along a river bank. In Europe, rivers have played a more important role in determining the growth and importance of a city than the sea; more than half of the 20 largest cities in the region developed along river banks. These cities have played, and continue to play, an important role in the economy of the region. As the volume of sea trade has more than doubled in the last 30 years, and is likely to grow, port cities are likely to gain even more economic importance in the future.[5]

Cities in other ecosystems are now growing faster around the world than cities in coastal zones. Globally, cities located in mountainous regions grew at almost the same rate as cities located in coastal zones (approximately 2.5 per cent a year) between 1995 and 2000. Although cultivated and dryland ecosystems supported the largest share of the total urban population of Africa between 1995 and 2000, the urban population in forested and mountainous areas grew the fastest during the same period. Urban growth in these areas, however, could have negative implications for the continent's already fragile environment, and for climate change. In Asia, cities in both coastal and cultivated areas grew at the same rate (3 per cent a year), while in Latin America, cities in dryland, forest and inland water areas grew at the same rate (2.2 per cent a year) during this period. Projections suggest that in the next 15 years, cities in coastal, dryland, inland water, and mountainous ecosystems will grow steadily at an average rate of 2 per cent per year.[6]

FIGURE 1.1.1: **URBANIZATION LEVELS (PERCENTAGE URBAN) BY ECOSYSTEM, 2000**

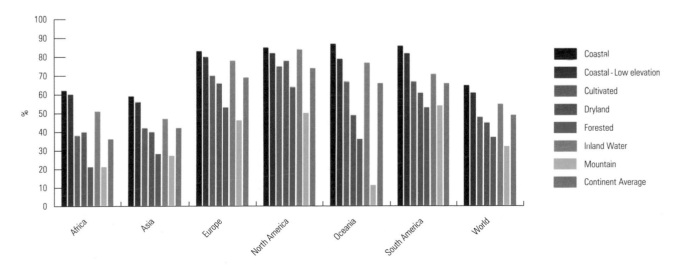

Source: Balk et al., 2008.

National economic and industrial policies make a difference

In the last two decades, some inland cities have taken advantage of the opening up of economies, the elimination of trade restrictions, and the reduction of tariff and transport costs to foster economic and population growth.[7] Other inland cities have used their proximity to larger urban agglomerations to improve their transport and communication systems to become more competitive. Many small cities are developing urban-scale economies, enhancing their ability to manage urbanization with added commuting technology and basic services, and are improving the delivery of social services to attract people and capital. As a consequence, some cities are growing very rapidly, other less rapidly and some not at all; in fact, numerous cities are experiencing a decline in their populations and in their economies.

These changes are neither random nor entirely organic; the growth of cities is determined by a variety of factors, many of which have to do with national policies. Governments and private capital often determine which cities will grow and which will not by deciding on the location of key investments, such as roads, airports, universities, communications, or capital, which influence a range of economic activities that lead to population growth or in-migration.[8] The city of Shenzhen in China, for instance, grew at the astounding annual rate of 20 per cent during the 1990s after it was declared a Special Economic Zone by the Chinese authorities in the 1980s. As an industrial growth pole, the city is now one of the most important transport and industrial hubs in China, and a key driver of the country's economy.

When central authorities implement macroeconomic policies or adopt specific economic or industrial reforms, some areas benefit more than others. The economic reforms have a cumulative impact; they in turn, influence the spatial distribution of new investments and employment in specific regions.[9] To some extent, the movement of rural populations to urban areas and movement of populations between different areas is linked to these spatial influences: people generally migrate to places where they think there are more opportunities, and the concentration of economic activity in cities is a major attractor for people from rural areas. However, rural-to-urban migration is becoming less prevalent in many regions as urban-to-urban migration and natural population growth gain momentum. Mobility from one city to another is becoming one of the predominant types of population movements in Latin America, where half of the people moving from one state to another originate from and end up in cities.[10]

FIGURE 1.1.2: **THE WORLD'S MEGACITIES, 2007 AND 2025**

2007

		Population (Thousands)
1	Tokyo	35,676
2	Mexico City	19,028
3	New York-Newark	19,040
4	São Paulo	18,845
5	Mumbai	18,978
6	Delhi	15,926
7	Shanghai	14,987
8	Kolkata	14,787
9	Buenos Aires	12,795
10	Dhaka	13,485
11	Los Angeles-Long Beach-Santa Ana	12,500
12	Karachi	12,130
13	Rio de Janeiro	11,748
14	Osaka-Kobe	11,294
15	Cairo	11,893
16	Beijing	11,106
17	Manila	11,100
18	Moscow	10,452
19	Istanbul	10,061

▬ : Cities located near a large water body (sea, river or delta)

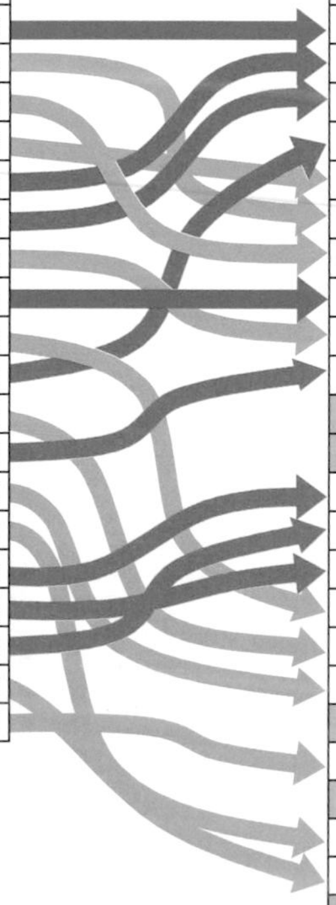

Source: UN-HABITAT 2008
Data from UN Population Division, World Urbanization Prospects 2007.
Figures for 2025 are projections.
Note: Population figures are for urban agglomeration, not city proper.
Megacities are cities with populations of more than 10 million.

2025

		Population (Thousands)
1	Tokyo	36,400
2	Mumbai	26,385
3	Delhi	22,498
4	Dhaka	22,015
5	São Paulo	21,428
6	Mexico City	21,009
7	New York-Newark	20,628
8	Kolkata	20,560
9	Shanghai	19,412
10	Karachi	19,095
11	Kinshasa	16,762
12	Lagos	15,796
13	Cairo	15,561
14	Manila	14,808
15	Beijing	14,545
16	Buenos Aires	13,768
17	Los Angeles-Long Beach-Santa Ana	13,672
18	Rio de Janeiro	13,413
19	Jakarta	12,363
20	Istanbul	12,102
21	Guangzhou, Guangdong	11,835
22	Osaka-Kobe	11,368
23	Moscow	10,526
24	Lahore	10,512
25	Shenzhen	10,196
26	Chennai	10,129

▬ : New megacities

Pyramids along the River Nile: Many of the largest cities in the world have developed along river banks or deltas.
©**Madanmohan Rao**

FIGURE 1.1.3: **URBAN POPULATION (MILLIONS) BY REGION, 2005 AND 2050**

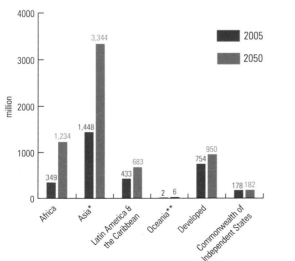

Source: UN-HABITAT, Global Urban Observatory, 2008.
Data from UN Population Division, World Urbanization Prospects, 2007 revision.
*Note: *Asia doesn't include Japan. ** Oceania doesn't include Australia and New Zealand.*

Reconciling geography and economy with policy

Geography and national economic policies alone do not determine which cities will grow and which will decline. In an increasingly globalizing world, countries and cities that take advantage of global, regional and local markets tend to thrive while those that are not part of this marketplace tend to decline in size and significance. The concentration of economic activities and population generates efficiency gains in certain regions and urban centres that benefit from international, national and local factors, while leaving other regions and cities behind. This has led to regional imbalances in the incidence of poverty, on the one hand, and also intra-regional imbalances on the other. Whereas the top one-third of developing countries experienced a relatively large increase in the ratio of trade to Gross Domestic Product over the past twenty years, the remaining two-thirds of developing countries actually trade much less today than twenty years ago.[11]

Spatial and regional disparities have become more visible and have increased in many countries, particularly over the last two decades.[12] In Peru, the incidence of poverty in coastal

▲
Dhaka: This megacity is expected to absorb an additional 9 million inhabitants in the next 15 years.
©Maciej Dakowicz

districts was 46 per cent in 1997, while for districts at an altitude greater than 3,500 meters above sea level it was 63.3 per cent.[13] In Mexico, the poorest areas are mainly in the indigenous and rural south, while the north has benefited from strong investments and economic integration with the United States and Canada.[14] In China, large economic and social gaps exist between the mostly urban coastal areas and inland regions, with coastal areas growing five times as fast as inland areas. Income disparities between rural and urban areas in China are becoming more apparent and are rising. Urban per capita disposable income in 2003 was 3.23 times that of rural per capita net income, while urban per capita consumption was 3.6 times rural per capita consumption.[15]

Concentration of economic activities does not automatically lead to population growth. In Thailand, from 1987 to 1996, the capital city of Bangkok accounted for more than 52 per cent of the rise in GDP, but only 11 per cent of the increase in population. In contrast, the northeast region, which accounted for only 11 per cent of the GDP, experienced a 32 per cent increase in population.[16]

Numerous examples point to an increase in spatial disparities and uneven regional development around the world. What is clear is that these asymmetries are reflected in economic, social and health indicators and in development opportunities. In many developing countries, the average cost of education in a full-time four-year university is equivalent to 30 or 40 years

of income for a poor farmer, meaning that many children raised in rural areas cannot access a full education. Disparities at national and local levels have isolated entire areas and groups, and, in many cases, these inequalities are aligned to political and ethnic divisions. Regional rivalries and disputes have become major concerns of national policy makers, who understand that if sections of a country's population cannot savour the sweetness of economic growth and prosperity, their discontent may eventually spark off social unrest or conflict. Policymakers are becoming increasingly aware that economic growth and prosperity that excludes large portions of a country's population may not pave the way for peace and democratic institutions.

The Chinese authorities have acknowledged that "a most severe social crisis can erupt at the time when an economy reaches its most flourishing stage".[17] Official data corroborates this statement: incidents of social unrest, including strikes, demonstrations and riots, increased in China by nearly 50 per cent in the period from 2003 to 2005.[18] Voices of discontent are also being heard in other countries. In South Africa, for instance, the minister in charge of safety and security acknowledged that in 2005 alone, there were 881 protests in slums, approximately five times the number of any comparable previous period; unofficial sources indicate that at least 50 of these protests turned violent.[19] And in Kenya, many people believe that regional and intra-city disparities and inequitable distribution of resources were the root causes of the ethnic tensions and violent conflicts that engulfed most of the country in January 2008.[20]

In Russia, India, Brazil, and most other developing and transition economies, the spatial dimension of inequalities has begun to attract considerable policy interest.[21] Yet, despite new interest in policy concerns arising from spatial and regional disparities, the dynamics of urban change that lead to spatial disparities in an increasingly urbanized world are not well understood.

Cities that are located near target markets and that have well-developed infrastructure (particularly transport and communications), are physically attractive or have a unique cultural identity are well-positioned to take advantage of regional or national development priorities and globalization. The success or failure of these cities and regions often depends on past or present national policies and historical events that have impacted them in different ways, however, in the vast majority of cases, natural geographical advantages play a more crucial role.[23]

After the widespread application of sectoral and spatial regional strategies during the 1970 and 1980s, recent years have witnessed a progressive disenchantment with the implementation of regional planning strategies.[24] Recent development has largely been based on economic growth strategies and different forms of medium- and long-term redistribution mechanisms – including targeting poor populations, enacting labour-intensive industrialization policies, enforcing employment generation policies, and the like – that do not have a clear spatial dimension.

This report advocates for decision-makers at all levels to become more cognizant of the regional and spatial dimensions of economic and social policies and institutions. Understanding the dynamics of urban growth is critical to propelling further urban development and to dealing with asymmetric growth and regional disparities. Through the analysis of these spatial disparities, the report seeks to raise several policy-relevant issues. The report also highlights the real need for regional and national governments to integrate regional considerations when formulating economic and social

▲
Car manufacturing: National industrial policies have an impact on city growth.
©**Mypokcik/Shutterstock**

policies; otherwise, regional disparities and spatial inequalities may continue to grow.

Governments need to pursue national objectives while implementing a policy of interregional equity. This means that they need to provide continuous support to economically dynamic cities and regions and, at the same time, create conditions to mitigate imbalances. These efforts hinge on governments' ability to identify patterns of spatial organization of both economic activities and population that best combine environmental benefits with economic and social benefits.[25] By doing so, governments will reverse regional polarization and reduce spatial inequalities, thus creating conditions for more harmonious regional development.

NOTES

1 The Coastal Portal, 2007.
2 Balk, McGranahan, & Anderson, 2008.
3 Balk, McGranahan, & Anderson, 2008.
4 Balk, McGranahan, & Anderson, 2008.
5 Organisation for Economic Cooperation and Development (OECD), 2007.
6 Balk, McGranahan, & Anderson, in press.
7 Overman & Venables, 2005.
8 DFID, 2005.
9 Satterthwaite, 2007.
10 Economic Commission for Latin America and the Caribbean (ECLAC), 2000.
11 Rodriguez & Rodrik, 2000.
12 Kanbur & Venables, 2005.
13 Kanbur & Venables, 2005.
14 Jiménez, 2005.

15 UNDP, China 2006.
16 Benn, 2005.
17 Yuanzhu, 2005.
18 Lum, 2006.
19 Wines, 2005.
20 Warah, 2008.
21 Kanbur & Venables, 2005.
22 In order to have a larger time frame of analysis, a new study was conducted from 1980 to 2000 for all the cities in the sample. This study, which has data for four different points in time, permitted a better understanding of trends in a longer perspective.
23 DFID, 2005.
24 Parr, 1999.
25 Martine, 2001.

1.2
Urban Growth Patterns

▲
Shanghai, China.
©**Robert Churchill/iStockphoto**

Methodology

This part of the report aims to provide a preliminary analysis of the spatial and demographic identity of the world's cities, going beyond the "one or two cities tell everything" approach that has tended to dominate most urban studies so far. The chapters analyze population changes in 2,695 cities with populations of more than 100,000 (1,408 cities from the developing countries and 1,287 from the developed countries) from 1990 to 2000. This sample of cities represented nearly 53 per cent of the world's urban population in 1990. Cities, towns and "urban villages" with populations under 100,000 were not included in the analysis because no global database systematically identifies smaller cities, although a rough estimate would suggest that they comprise some 40 per cent of the world's urban population. The data used for this analysis is based primarily on statistics from the United Nations Demographic Yearbooks for various years between 1985 and 2004 (depending on the years for which data was available in each country), published by the United Nations Statistics Division. For the purposes of this analysis, most of the data is roughly for the period between 1990 and 2000. The results of the analysis differ from the UN Population Division's *World Urbanization Prospects* series in two key areas: 1) The analysis is based on "city proper" populations (the single political jurisdiction that contains the city centre) rather than on the populations of urban agglomerations (the built up or densely populated area containing the city proper, suburbs and continuously settled commuter areas) or metropolitan areas (the set of formal local government areas that normally comprise the urban area as a whole and its primary commuter areas); and 2) the cities included in the sample include those with populations under 750,000 – small cities with populations of between 100,000 and 500,000 that are not included in the *World Urbanization Prospects*. Although, the analysis presented here does not cover all cities of the world, as data for many cities is either unavailable or outdated, it does point to general trends. The analysis was undertaken by UN-HABITAT's Global Urban Observatory in 2007.

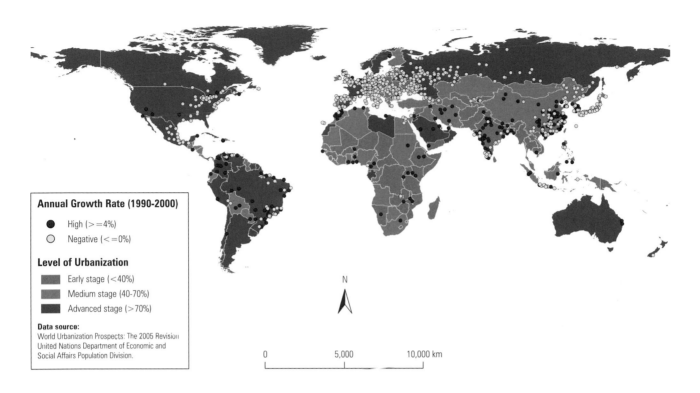

Annual Growth Rate (1990-2000)

● High (>=4%)

○ Negative (<=0%)

Level of Urbanization

Early stage (<40%)

Medium stage (40-70%)

Advanced stage (>70%)

Data source:
World Urbanization Prospects: The 2005 Revision
United Nations Department of Economic and
Social Affairs Population Division.

N

0   5,000   10,000 km

Source: UN-HABITAT Global Urban Observatory

The world is now half urban. Sometime in 2008, humankind achieved a momentous milestone: for the first time in history, half of the world's population, or 3.3 billion people, lived in urban areas.[1]

In some regions of the world, the urban transition occurred decades ago, in the 1950s and 1960s, if not earlier. More than 70 per cent of the populations of Europe, North America and Latin America are already urban; Asia and Africa remain predominately rural, with 40 per cent and 38 per cent of their populations living in urban areas, respectively. However, if current trends continue, half of Africa's population will be urban by 2050. In Asia, the urban transition will occur even earlier, owing to rapid urban growth rates in China, a country that is expected to be more than 70 per cent urban by 2050. Urban growth rates in India will be slower; by 2050, 55 per cent of its population, or 900 million people, will live in cities. Globally, urbanization levels will rise dramatically in the next 40 years to 70 per cent by 2050.[2]

Altogether, small, intermediate and large cities from the global South and North grew at 1.83 per cent from 1990 to 2000. This means that the world's urban population will swell to almost 5 billion in 2030 and 6.4 billion by 2050.

Every day, 193,107 new city dwellers are added to the world's urban population, which translates to slightly more than two people every second. But not all regions are affected by this growth in the same way or on the same scale. In developed nations, the total increase in urban population per month is 500,000, compared to 5 million in the developing world. In terms of absolute numbers, the growth of cities in the developing world is ten times that of cities in the global North. Annually, cities in the developing world grew at a rate of 2.5 per cent in the 1990s, compared to an annual growth rate of 0.3 per cent in the developed world.[3]

While very high urban growth rates characterize urban change in the developing world, moderate growth and decline are the norm in developed nations. UN-HABITAT analyses show that 17 per cent of cities in the developing world experienced very high growth rates of 4 per cent or more, while 36 per cent experienced high growth rates of between 2 to 4 per cent annually. In sharp contrast, nearly half of the cities in the developed world grew at a snail's pace of less than 1 per cent annually. In fact, a staggering 40 per cent of cities in the developed world experienced negative growth and suffered a population loss in the 1990s.

Urban Change in Developed and Transition Countries

The total urban population in the developed world is expected to remain largely unchanged in the next two decades, increasing from nearly 900 million people in 2005 to slightly more than one billion in 2030, and to nearly 1.1 billion by

2050 – growth resulting from in-migration of people from poorer countries, not natural population growth. On average, 2.3 million people migrate into developed countries each year.[4] This means that immigration – both legal and illegal – accounts for approximately one-third of the urban growth in the developed world. Without immigration, the urban population of the developed world would likely decline or remain the same in the coming decades.

Low levels of natural population increase and declining fertility rates are prevailing trends in developed countries. Consequently populations are likely to shrink in dozens of rich nations, sometimes dramatically: projections show that Bulgaria's population will fall by 35 per cent by 2050; Ukraine's will plummet by 33 per cent, Russia's will decline by 25 per cent and Poland's will reduce by 20 per cent. There will be 10 per cent fewer Germans and 7 per cent fewer Italians. The populations of 46 countries, including Germany, Italy, Japan, most of the former Soviet states, and several small island states, are expected to be smaller in 2050 than they are now.[5]

These demographic trends are reflected at the city level, as well. In the last 30 years, more cities in the developed world shrank than grew. From 1990 to 2000, 4 cities out of 10 in the developed regions experienced a population loss. In contrast, only 6 out of 100 cities experienced a rapid growth rate. In Europe – where the number of people aged 60 or older surpassed the number of children under the age of 15 a decade ago – 5 out of 10 cities experienced a decrease in their populations in the same decade and only 3 per cent grew at a rapid rate.

Considering that most countries in the developed world have already attained high levels of urbanization, and given their overall low levels of population growth, they are not expected to experience serious growth in the coming decades. It is also possible that the population decline observed in previous decades will continue.

Despite a certain level of homogeneity and predictability in the rates of urban growth in the developed world, a high degree of variation in city size and patterns of growth and decline exists among the different regions. For instance, Australia and New Zealand have no cities of more than 5 million inhabitants; in Australia, the largest cities have populations of between 1 and 5 million. By far the largest proportion of Europe's total urban population (almost 70 per cent) lives in small cities of fewer than 500,000 inhabitants; Europe is also the only region in the world that does not have any megacities – cities with populations of more than 10 million. In the United States, on the other hand, while 80 per cent of the country's population is classified as living in a metropolitan area, one-third of this population lives in large cities with populations of 5 million or more.[6] In some cases, the greater metropolitan area of a city consists of many small cities, the combined population of which is often larger than the population of the city proper. For instance, the population of the Las Vegas metropolitan area was 1.6 million in 2000, but only 478,000 people lived within the Las Vegas city limits.

Patterns of population growth and decline of cities are largely influenced by the share of population distribution in the different sub-regions and countries. While a quarter of the cities in Australia and New Zealand grew at high growth rates of between 2 and 4 per cent in the 1990s, nearly half of the cities in Europe experienced a decline in their populations; the majority were small cities with populations of between 100,000 and 500,000. In Japan, 25 per cent of cities decreased in size, while 65 per cent grew at the slow pace of less than 1 per cent annually. In North America, the patterns of growth

FIGURE 1.2.2: **CITY GROWTH AND DECLINE BY CITY SIZE IN THE DEVELOPED WORLD, 1990-2000**

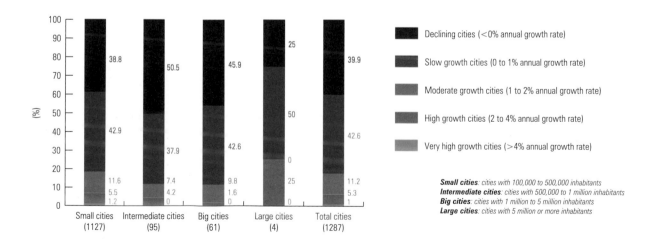

Declining cities (<0% annual growth rate)

Slow growth cities (0 to 1% annual growth rate)

Moderate growth cities (1 to 2% annual growth rate)

High growth cities (2 to 4% annual growth rate)

Very high growth cities (>4% annual growth rate)

Small cities: cities with 100,000 to 500,000 inhabitants
Intermediate cities: cities with 500,000 to 1 million inhabitants
Big cities: cities with 1 million to 5 million inhabitants
Large cities: cities with 5 million or more inhabitants

Source: UN-HABITAT Global Urban Observatory 2008.
Note: UN-HABITAT calculations based on UN Demographic Yearbooks (various years between 1990 and 2003.)
Analysis based on a sample of 1,287 cities with populations of more than 100,000.

A suburb in Madrid, Spain: Increasing suburbanization has led to population decrease in several European cities.
©iStockphoto

and decline are not so homogenous. While one-fifth of cities experienced a decline in population, a similar proportion grew at a high rate from 1990 to 2000; the fastest-growing cities were either small or intermediate cities.

European cities, in general, are not growing any more, including cities in the nations of the Commonwealth of Independent States.[7] The population of urban centres with more than 100,000 inhabitants, taken together, remained stable during the years 1991 to 2001. Among the large cities with populations of more than 5 million, the proportion of inhabitants increased by 1.4 per cent, mainly because of the growth experienced by Moscow, the capital of the Russian Federation, which grew at the rate of 2.1 per cent annually. However, at present, the continent has none of the world's 100 fastest growing large cities with populations of more than 1 million inhabitants.

Large cities in Europe are not growing rapidly, owing in part to relatively low rates of natural population increase in countries, as well as more decentralized patterns of urban development.[8] Larger cities and metropolitan conurbations in the United Kingdom, with the exception of London, are almost all declining in size.[9] In Germany, Italy and Poland, more than half of the cities are decreasing in size. Among the big European urban centers with populations of between 1 and 5 million, all experienced negative growth rates, with the exception of Baku – the largest port city and capital of Azerbaijan – which grew at the rate of approximately 3.5 per cent annually in the 1990s.

Increasing suburbanization may account for population decrease in some cities. The regions surrounding Stockholm, Helsinki, Sofia, Madrid, and inner London all saw their share of the national population increase by more than 5 per cent between 1995 and 2004, while populations within the city limits decreased. The populations of Dublin, Berlin and Budapest also declined, but the populations of cities and regions surrounding them increased during the same period. Population movements between European cities can also be attributed to the relaxing of immigration restrictions in the European Union, which saw populations move from economically less attractive countries to more attractive ones.[10]

Despite the fact that on average, the population of small European cities did not grow between 1990 and 2000, an analysis of individual cities shows that four small urban centers – York, United Kingdom; Ulyanovsk, Russia; Almere, the Netherlands; and Andizhan, Uzbekistan – experienced an annual growth rate of more than 5 per cent. Of the four, the city of York experienced the fastest annual growth rate in Europe (9 per cent) due largely to its successful economic transformation from a manufacturing centre into an information technology and biosciences hub. Ulyanovsk, a small but important industrial city in Russia, and Almere in the Netherlands both grew at the rate of 5.4 per cent a year. Andizhan, an administrative centre in Uzbekistan that is one of the main producers of cotton fibre and an agriculture and industrial development pole in the Eastern part of the

Las Vegas aerial view: North American cities are among the fastest growing cities in the developed world.
©**Valerie Loiseleux/iStockphoto**

country, recorded an annual growth rate of approximately 5 per cent. Twenty-five other cities experienced a high growth rate of more than 2 per cent; 10 of them were located in the United Kingdom, 4 in the Netherlands, 4 in Russia, 3 in Sweden, and the rest in various other countries.

North American cities grew the fastest among all cities in the developed world between 1990 and 2000, particularly cities in the United States, which grew an average of 1 per cent. Small cities of 100,000 to 500,000 inhabitants experienced the highest growth – 1.3 per cent, on average, but as high as 5 per cent or more in some places – of all categories of cities in North America. At the metropolitan level, urban agglomerations with populations of 2 million to 5 million in 2000 grew the fastest, up to 2 per cent per year. The largest and smallest metropolitan area size categories, those with populations of 5 million or more and those with populations of less than 250,000, each grew by about 1.1 per cent annually.[11]

The highest urban growth rates were recorded in small cities, some of which grew at the rate of 5 per cent or more per year. In the United States, Las Vegas – the gambling and tourist resort in the state of Nevada – grew at an annual rate of 6.2 per cent, and the city of Plano on the outskirts of Dallas, Texas, saw growth rates of 5.5 per cent per year; both cities benefitted from migration from other parts of the United States. Another 37 U.S. cities expanded their population at rates of between 2 and 4 per cent annually, and a significant number of them were located in the west and south of the country[12]; two of these cities – Phoenix, Arizona, and San Antonio, Texas – were intermediate cities, with populations of 500,000 to 1 million. On the other hand, cities in rust belt regions such as Detroit, Michigan, Buffalo, New York, and Youngstown, Ohio, the economies of which

were dependent on manufacturing, have suffered. They are enduring population loss, diminished local tax revenue, aging infrastructure, and middle-class flight.[13]

In Canada, small cities also registered the largest growth rates: Halifax, Nova Scotia, grew at a very high rate of 11.4 per cent annually, owing primarily to the economic expansion generated by the city's port. The city of Ottawa, the country's capital, grew at a rate of 9 per cent per year, and Vaughan, the fastest growing municipality in Canada, nearly doubled in population since 1991 as part of the greater Toronto Area. An additional 7 urban areas observed a growth rate above 2 per cent per year; among these, Hamilton, a port city in the province of Ontario, grew at the rate of 4.3 per cent annually in the 1990s, thanks in part to the endurance of competitive steel and heavy manufacturing industries and a successful shift in the last decade towards the service sector. Surrey also grew at the rate of 3.5 per cent annually during this period, mainly owing to the development of residential and commercial suburbs in an area traditionally supported by agriculture and sawmilling.

At the metropolitan level, the city of Calgary experienced the strongest rate of growth by far; its population rose by 15.8 per cent from 1996 to 2001 – from 710,000 people to nearly 1 million. Calgary accounted for 47 per cent of the total growth of Alberta province in the western part of Canada. Edmonton, the capital city of Alberta province, registered the second-highest growth rate in the country. The dynamism of these two metropolitan areas boosted Alberta province's growth to more than three times that of the nation as a whole.[14]

Several metropolitan areas in Canada are also experiencing what is known as "the doughnut effect" – a phenomenon in which the inner core of a city grows more slowly than the areas around it. For instance, the population of the core municipality of Saskatoon grew by 1.6 per cent, while that of the surrounding municipalities grew by 14.6 per cent from 1996 to 2001.[15]

Population decline is also a feature of Canadian cities, and is a reflection of the slow growth rate of the country's total population. According to official data, one-third of all 2,607 municipalities in Canada suffered from population loss in the two decades between 1981 and 2001.[16]

In **Australia and New Zealand**, the pattern underlying urban growth or decline is not as evident as elsewhere in the developed world. Only one city out of 21 showed a decrease in its population. Yet, the overall trend in the two countries is slow urban growth, with nearly half of the cities growing at less than 1 per cent annually.

A large proportion of Australia's population lives in state and territorial capitals (63 per cent), cities with relatively small populations compared to other capital cities of the world. Higher growth in the late 1980s than in the 1990s was a common pattern for most of the country's state capitals.[17] Between 1986 and 1994, the fastest growing cities were Brisbane and Perth, with a total growth of 19 and 18 per cent, respectively. Between the years 1993 and 2003, three non-capital cities – Gold Coast, Sunshine Coast and Townsville – experienced the fastest growth rates in the country, more than 4 per cent per year, mainly resulting from growth in tourism. As coastal cities continue to dominate the Australian urban system, another process at work is the consolidation of the major regional towns that grew at the expense of smaller towns in surrounding areas. Some 245 municipalities lost population, according to the 2001 census, and the process is projected to continue.[18] Along with the loss of population in the small towns and rural areas, other urban regions, particularly mining and manufacturing areas, are experiencing population decline.[19]

In New Zealand, cities in the Auckland metropolitan area all had above average growth rates compared to the rest of the nation: Manukau and Waitakere grew slightly more than 2 per cent per year, and the cities of North Shore and Auckland grew slightly less than 2 per cent annually from 1991 to 2001. High population growth in the Auckland area – the commercial heart of the country – is reflected in various economic indicators: approximately 73 per cent of New Zealand's imports and 40 per cent of its exports pass through Auckland's ports, and 96 of the top 200 business are located in the region.[20] On the other side of the spectrum are cities such as Dunedin, the main urban centre in the Otago region on the South Island, which experienced a population decline between 1996 and 2001, largely due to rising unemployment.[21]

Urban Change in Developing Countries

In the last two decades, the urban population of the developing world has grown by an average of 3 million people per week. By the middle of the 21st century, the total urban population of the developing world will more than double, increasing from 2.3 billion in 2005 to 5.3 billion in 2050. By 2050, Asia will host 63 per cent of the global urban population, or 3.3 billion people; Africa will have an urban population of 1.2 billion, or nearly a quarter of the world's urban population. Altogether, 95 per cent of the world's urban population growth over the next four decades will be absorbed by cities in developing countries.

Since 1950, 30 cities grew more than twenty fold and dozens of major cities, including Kuwait City in Kuwait and Tuxtla Gutierrez in Mexico have grown more than tenfold; some, including Abidjan in Côte d'Ivoire, have expanded their populations by more than twenty times in the last 50 years. These changes reflect major shifts in economic activities and employment structures from agriculture to industry and services, and a diversification of the economy of developing countries.[22]

▲
Calgary business district: Many Canadian cities are experiencing population decline in their inner cores, while their suburbs are expanding in size and population.
©iStockphoto

Although city growth is slowing down in most of the developing world, levels of urbanization within countries are expected to rise, with the least urbanized countries in Africa and Asia achieving an urban transition before 2050. On average, cities of the developing world grew at an estimated annual rate of 2.5 per cent from 1990 to 2000. At this rate, the developing world's urban population will double in 29 years. Some cities are growing faster than others: the populations of 218 cities, including Shanghai, Beijing, Riyadh, Addis Ababa, Nairobi, Lagos, and Khartoum, grew at a very high rate of 4 per cent or more in the 1990s. The exceptionally high population growth rates of some cities in the developing world imply that a city such as Dhaka, the capital of Bangladesh, will take just 12 years to absorb an additional 8 million inhabitants, a feat that took New York City – the world's largest metropolis in 1950 – nearly 150 years.[23]

Large cities in the developing world, with populations of more than 5 million people, on the other hand, did not experience such high growth rates in the 1990s; the average annual growth rate of large cities was 1.8 per cent, with the exception of those in China, which grew at the phenomenally high rate of approximately 4 per cent per year. (Figure 1.2.2) Much of the growth observed in Chinese cities such as Beijing and Shanghai between 1982 and 1998 can be attributed to the expansion of city borders to include populations that lived on the periphery.[24] Chinese cities grew rapidly in the 1990s, and by 2005, 40 per cent of the country's population was classified as urban.

Over the next 10 years, the urban population in many developing countries is expected to grow at an average annual rate of slightly more than 2 per cent, down from 3.8 per cent during the 1980s and 4 per cent during the 1950s and early 1960s.[25] This suggests an inverse relationship between levels of urbanization and urban growth rates.

Urban growth rates vary not only within regions and countries, but also among cities. Only a fraction of 1,408 cities sampled (2 per cent) grew at more than 10 per cent annually from 1990 to 2000. More than one half of the cities grew at very high growth rate of more than 4 per cent a year or high growth rate of between 2 and 4 per cent a year. One third of the cities grew at the moderate rate of 1 to 2 per cent or slow rate of 0 to 1 per cent. Ten per cent of the cities experienced negative growth rates or declining populations.

It may seem paradoxical that regions experiencing high urban growth also have cities with declining populations, but the growth of some cities and contraction of others signals the start of a new urban cycle in the developing world that may lead to closer alignment with trends in developed regions. Out of a sample of 1,408 cities in the developing world, 143 experienced the collective loss of 13 million people from 1990 to 2000. As in Europe and the rest of the developed world, the developing world may experience urban saturation levels, which could lead to slower growth rates.[26] It is still too early, however, to know whether urban contraction will continue and become more pronounced, as the number of cities growing rapidly or moderately far outweighs the number of cities experiencing population decrease; the latter represent just 5 per cent of the total urban population of the developing world.

The most interesting aspect of urban growth in the developing world is not one that has much to do with city size or growth rates, as is commonly believed – though both happen on a greater order of magnitude in the developing world than in the developed world. The real story is the absolute size of the increments of growth, especially in Asia and Africa, and the role that different cities play in this growth.[27] The timing and scope of these changes vary considerably among less-developed regions.

FIGURE 1.2.3: **ANNUAL GROWTH RATE OF THE WORLD'S CITIES BY REGION AND CITY SIZE, 1990-2000**

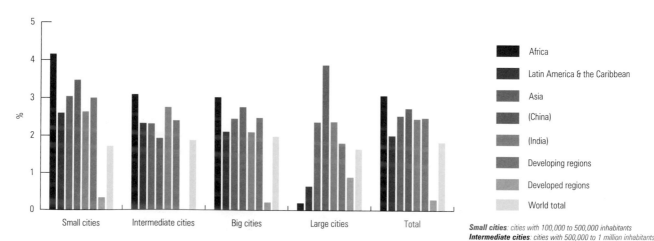

Africa
Latin America & the Caribbean
Asia
(China)
(India)
Developing regions
Developed regions
World total

Small cities: cities with 100,000 to 500,000 inhabitants
Intermediate cities: cities with 500,000 to 1 million inhabitants
Big cities: cities with 1 million to 5 million inhabitants
Large cities: cities with 5 million or more inhabitants

Source: UN-HABITAT Global Urban Observatory, 2008.
Note: UN-HABITAT calculations based on UN Statistics Division, Demographic Year books (1985 - 2004), various years, and UN Population Division, World Urbanization Prospects, 2005 revision. Analysis based on a sample of 2,695 cities with populations of more than 100,000.

Downtown Nairobi: Urban primacy characterizes urban growth in most African countries.
©Peter Miller/iStockphoto

Africa

The rate of change of the urban population in Africa is the highest in the world. Despite some signs that urban growth is slowing down, the potential for further urbanization is still huge: the region is in the early stages of its urban transition, with an estimated 38 per cent of its population classified as urban; urban growth rates in Africa are the highest in the world (3.3 per cent per year between 2000 and 2005) and are expected to remain relatively high; and fertility rates in 2007 were still high (4.7 per cent) compared to the global average (2.5 per cent).[28] The region is thus expected to sustain the highest rate of urban growth in the world for several decades, with underlying rates of natural increase playing an important role.[29] (These city population statistics are based on estimates and projections in the absence of recent census data in some countries.)

The region's most distinguishing urban characteristic is the presence of high concentrations of people and investments in the single largest city of its countries, in most cases, the capital.

FIGURE 1.2.4: **CITY GROWTH AND DECLINE BY CITY SIZE IN THE DEVELOPING WORLD, 1990-2000**

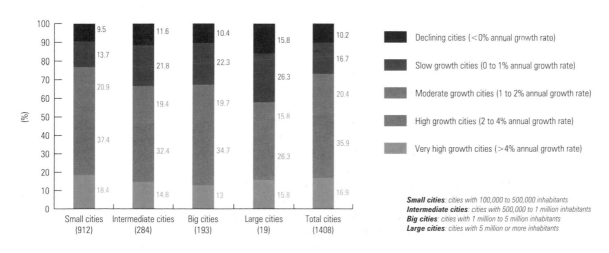

Source: UN-HABITAT Global Urban Observatory, 2008.
Note: UN-HABITAT calculations based on UN Demographic Yearbooks (various years between 1985 and 2004)
Analysis based on a sample of 1,408 cities with populations of more than 100,000.

This phenomenon, known as "urban primacy", characterizes urbanization in Africa today, as it did in Latin America and the Caribbean in past decades. By 1990, approximately half of the 54 countries in Africa concentrated more than 10 per cent of their urban populations in one single primate city.[30] More than half of Africa's urban population lives in big cities with populations of between 1 and 5 million, compared to 26 per cent in Latin America and the Caribbean and 38 per cent in Asia. Between 1990 and 2000, big cities in Africa, including Nairobi, Addis Ababa and Dakar, experienced the fastest annual growth rates among all cities of this size in the developing world, averaging 3.3 per cent, versus an average of 2.5 per cent for the developing world as a whole.[31] Today, the region has 17 of the word's 100 fastest growing cities with populations of more than 1 million.[32] Concomitantly, Africa has a preponderance of smaller cities of fewer than 100,000 inhabitants, meaning that for every big city there exists a multitude of small towns.

In the 1990s, small African cities (with populations of between 100,000 and 500,000) recorded the fastest growth rates (4.16 per cent per year) of all cities in the developing world, followed by Asian small cities (3 per cent).[33]

Urban growth in Africa is a consequence of many factors, including positive factors such as economic growth and negative events such as conflict and disaster. Forced movements of people provoked by drought, famine, ethnic conflicts, civil strife, and war have driven much of the urban growth in the region. Luanda and other important provincial centres of Angola experienced an influx of more than 2 million people in only two years (1992-1994) as a consequence of the armed conflict in that country.[34] Civil conflict also drove the population of Khartoum, Sudan, up from 2.3 million in 1990 to 3.9 million in 2000, and Monrovia, the capital of Liberia, grew from 535,000 inhabitants to 776,000 inhabitants in the same period. The population of the capital of the Democratic Republic of the Congo, Kinshasa, also grew from 3.6 million

to 5 million from 1990 to 2000 for similar reasons. Other war-torn countries, such as Somalia, have also witnessed an increase in their urban populations for similar reasons.

The HIV/AIDS epidemic has also impacted urban growth in various countries. In southern Africa, the sub-region with the highest prevalence of the disease, life expectancy has fallen from an estimated 62 years in 1990 to 49 years in 2005. As a consequence, the growth rate of the population in southern Africa has fallen, from 2.5 per cent annually in the period between 1990 and 2005 to 0.6 per cent annually from 2005 to 2010; it is expected to continue declining in the foreseeable future.[35] In Zambia, for instance, the population of the capital Lusaka has increased by only 0.7 per cent annually from 1990 to 2000, a trend that is prevalent throughout the country's urban centres; the populations of the Zambian cities of Luanshya, Ndola and Mufulira have actually experienced a decline in population in recent years. How much of this decline is directly attributable to the HIV/AIDS pandemic is not clear, but the high prevalence of the disease in the country's urban areas is significant enough to have made an impact on population growth rates. In fact, in Zambia, HIV prevalence among urban populations is twice that of rural populations – a trend that is common in many sub-Saharan African countries, including Tanzania and Burundi.[36]

Africa has been said to have urbanized in the absence of a stable economic basis to sustain its growth. Economic development has recently, however, shown encouraging progress around the continent, particularly in sub-Saharan Africa. Growth has been more resilient in sub-Saharan Africa than in most other parts of the world during the recent global economic downturns, with real gross domestic product (GDP) increasing by more than 3 per cent per year between 2001 and 2003.[37] Recent World Bank reports indicate that 16 countries in the region experienced economic growth rates of 4.5 per cent per year in the last decade and that economic growth in the region as a whole averaged 5.3 per cent in 2006.[38] Yet,

FIGURE 1.2.5: **DISTRIBUTION OF URBAN POPULATION IN THE DEVELOPING WORLD BY CITY SIZE, 2000**

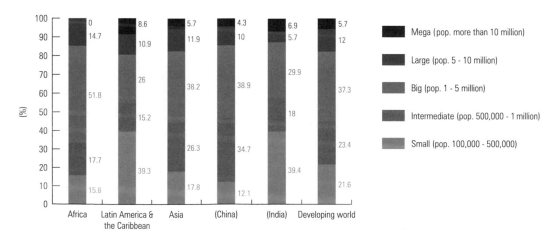

Source: UN-HABITAT Global Urban Observatory, 2008.
Note: UN-HABITAT Global Urban Observatory, 2008. Data from UN-Statistics Division, Demographic Yearbook (various years), UN Population Division, World Urbanization Prospects 2005.
Analysis based on a sample of 1,408 cities. Data for Asia includes China and India.
Data only includes cities with populations of 100,000 + inhabitants.

these achievements are rather fragile, and economic growth in Africa remains below potential. Even growing at 3 per cent per year, it would take more than 50 years for countries in this region to reach the average income levels other developing nations have already achieved.

Poverty lies at the heart of Africa's problems. Most countries in sub-Saharan Africa are in the world's lowest income category as measured by gross national income per capita per year (less than US $765).[39] It is possible that regional and domestic turmoil, weak governance, inappropriate policies, rampant corruption, and insufficient pro-poor structural reforms will make it difficult to ensure steady growth with poverty reduction. Urbanization in Africa will continue to be strongly associated with slum formation, as indicated by urban growth trends: between 1990 and 2000, slum areas grew at a rate of 4.53 per cent, while overall urban growth rates were 4.58 per cent in the same time period.[40] In this context of sharp contrasts between the haves and the have-nots, where inequality in access to resources dominates urban development patterns, it is unlikely that cities in the region will develop harmoniously. This also means that much of the growth of populations in African cities will be associated with growth in the size of their slum populations.

Asia

Asia is urbanizing rapidly, with approximately 40 per cent of its inhabitants now living in urban areas. The region is expected to experience significantly high rates of urbanization over the next 20 years; projections indicate that one out of every two Asians will live in cities sometime before the year 2025.

Although the annual urban growth rate for Asia as a whole has been declining, from 3.8 per cent in the 1960s to 2.6 per cent today, the region will continue to host the largest urban population in the world in the coming years. Asia's urban population increased from approximately 234 million in 1950, to 575 million in 1975, 1 billion in the early 1990s, and 1.5 billion today.[41] Of the 76 million persons added annually to the world population between 2000 and 2005, approximately 46 million (60 per cent) were in Asia, with 8 million in China and 16 million in India alone.[42] An additional 1.25 billion people will be added to the Asian population by 2030, 54 per cent of whom will live in urban areas.[43]

Asia is such a vast heterogeneous region that it defies generalization: the continent is home to some of the world's largest and richest economies and some of its poorest. Despite impressive reductions in family size and high prevalence of contraceptive use, progress in bringing down growth rates and fertility levels has been uneven.

In both South and Central Asia, population growth rates remain high, at about 2 per cent per year.[44] In East Asia as a whole, fertility levels appear to have dropped roughly to the replacement level (1.9 children per woman of child-bearing age), a breathtaking transformation in childbearing patterns in just four decades.[45] In Western Asia, population growth rates remain high, at 4.1 children per woman.[46] These demographic trends, however, only partially explain urban growth rates. In various East Asian countries (including China) population growth rates are declining, yet urban growth rates remain relatively high (2.5 per cent per year). In China alone, the average annual urban growth rate is even higher (2.7 per cent per year). Furthermore, many cities in China are growing at staggeringly high growth rates of more than 10 per cent per year, including Chongqing, Xiamen and Shenzhen. This can be attributed to a variety of factors, including the adoption of a pro-urban approach to economic development by the government of China, shifting from a state-directed process under a planned economy to a state-guided process within a market system; administrative reclassification of predominantly rural settlements as cities; and in-migration. Together, these processes have opened doors for city growth in the eastern coastal part of the country and have dramatically transformed the urban and regional landscape of the system of cities in the country.[47]

▲
Skyscraper in Shenzhen, China's youngest and fastest growing metropolis
© **Liugen Cheng/iStockphoto**

A housing complex in Delhi, India.
©**Maciej Dakowicz**

Metropolitan growth: a prominent feature of Asian cities

The majority of the largest cities in the developing world are located in Asia. In 2000, the region contained 227 cities with 1 million or more residents and 21 cities with 5 million or more inhabitants. Of every 10 big or large cities from the global South, more than 7 are located in Asia. Moreover, of the 100 fastest growing cities with populations of more than 1 million inhabitants in the world, 66 are in Asia. Among these fastest growing cities, 33 are Chinese. In fact, China hosts half of the urban population of the developing world that lives in big cities. The potential of urban growth of large Chinese cities is tremendous: on average, they grew at the rate of 3.9 per cent each year from 1990 to 2000 – more than two times faster than the world's average.

In sharp contrast, India's large cities are a surprising minority, representing only 10 per cent of all Asian cities of this size. Big Indian cities (those with populations of between 1 and 5 million) are growing fast (at the rate of 2.5 per cent annually), however, since the 1980s, their pace of growth has slowed slightly.[48] In fact, the six largest metropolitan areas in the country have shown a decline in their growth rates, while secondary metropolitan areas such as Indore, Kanpur, Jaipur,

Patna, Pune, and Surat have maintained their fast pace of urban growth.

The slowing down of growth in large cities in India could be explained by the "doughnut effect", whereby the inner city grows at a slower pace than the surrounding metropolitan areas. For example, the growth rate of the city of Mumbai was 1.5 per cent annually from 1991 to 2001, but the brand new satellite city of Navi Mumbai grew at the rate of 6.9 per cent annually. A survey released in the year 2000 revealed that 43 per cent of the families currently settled in Navi Mumbai migrated from Mumbai and that the percentage of migrants has most likely gone up since then because of improved mass transport links with the main city, as well as improvements in infrastructure.[49] Similarly, while India's capital city, New Delhi (not including the whole metropolitan area), experienced negative population growth (-0.2 per cent annually) between 1991 and 2001, the neighbouring city of Noida grew at the rate of 5.8 per cent per year. Other ring towns forming part of the Delhi metropolitan region, such as Ghaziabad, Loni, Gurgaon, Bahadurgarh, and Faridabad, have also been experiencing high growth rates in the past two decades. This indicates a growing trend among Indian metropolitan areas in which populations are moving to suburban locations or satellite towns as commuter networks improve. The development of second-tier metropolitan cities is a response to the improved economies of Indian cities and increasing congestion in the primary metropolitan areas.[50]

Countering metropolitan growth by unleashing the potential of intermediate cities

A distinct characteristic of urbanization in Asia is that with varying degrees of success or failure – and quite often total failure or limited impact – intermediate cities (with populations of between 500,000 and 1 million) have been used as mechanisms of population redistribution and regional development to slow down metropolitan growth. Government officials often assumed that development of intermediate cities would stimulate rural economies by providing linkages between rural and urban areas and that they would increase rural employment and incomes as a way to provide economic opportunities to neglected or impoverished areas. The planning of intermediate cities has often served to promote spatial integration via a more dispersed population.

Although a relatively small share (18 per cent) of its population lives in intermediate-sized cities, India's urbanization is being fueled by the growth of cities in the intermediate range. This is a distinctive pattern of urban growth in the country. A large share of India's population lives in small cities – 39 per cent, compared to 12 per cent in China and 18 per cent in the rest of Asia. The country's small cities may be experiencing a level of saturation, as their growth has begun to slow significantly. From 1991 to 2001, 41 per cent of India's small cities experienced a moderate or slow growth rate, and 7 per cent experienced a decline in population. This pattern of slow or no growth in the 1990s may indicate that Indians from large and small cities are migrating to intermediate cities for better opportunities. These findings run counter the conventional assumption that all Indian cities are growing rapidly, a pattern that is noticeable in intermediate and big cities.

In countries in which urban primacy is the rule, such as the Philippines, Thailand, the Republic of Korea, and Indonesia, the role of intermediate cities has been to gradually redirect the flow of migrants away from the primate city. In the more industrialized nations, such as the Republic of Korea, medium-sized cities are viewed as instruments for bringing about a more balanced distribution of population and the amelioration of income inequalities within and between sub-national regions. In the less industrialized nations, such as Indonesia and the Philippines, intermediate cities have been perceived as a bridge, promoting the growth of rural industries based on the processing of farm products for export.[51]

In sharp contrast, population growth in China is now taking place in the two extreme poles: small and large cities, which are experiencing the fastest annual growth rates in the country (3.47 per cent and 3.89 per cent, respectively). The country's efforts to sustain the population growth of medium-sized cities and to settle "floating populations" through the

reform of the household registration (*Hukou*) system have not yielded the expected results.[52]

Asia's economic growth in the last two decades has been phenomenal. The region now constitutes one-third of the world's economy. Its economic dynamism has contributed to the reduction of income poverty[53] and also to the expansion of cities and towns. Of the 140 new big and large cities that emerged in the world after 1990, 111 were located in Asia. This trend is not consistent across the continent. On the one hand, the emerging economies of India and China are likely to represent 50 per cent of global GDP in the next decade. On the other hand, the region is also home to the majority of the world's most impoverished people.[54] In Southern Asia and Western Asia, urban growth over the last 15 years has been accompanied by a commensurate growth in slums. In both sub-regions, annual slum and urban growth rates are quite similar (2.2 and 2.9 per cent in Southern Asia, and 2.7 and 2.96 per cent in Western Asia from 1990 to 2000).[55] Disparities in Asia are not only between sub-regions and countries, but also among and within human settlements of growing economies. Some urban areas are expanding and have become economic powerhouses; other areas, often less dynamic cities or remote rural areas, are lagging behind.[56] Even China – the GDP of which is growing at the dazzling rate of 9.5 per cent annually, and which accounts for 75 per cent of global poverty reduction – recognizes that "GDP growth does not necessarily indicate corresponding social development… and economic growth is achieved at the expense of social harmony".[57] While the balance between urban growth and social and economic development in various Asian countries seems elusive to achieve in the short- or mid-term, it is conceivable that policy change can usher in such harmony in the foreseeable future. Achieving harmonious cities depends largely on how well and how fast countries are able to achieve this balance.

Latin America and the Caribbean

Latin America and the Caribbean is the most urbanized region in the developing world, with 77 per cent of its population living in urban areas. The region will continue urbanizing over the next two decades, when the proportion of the urban population will reach 85 per cent. Urban growth in this region started in the early 1940s and reached its peak during the 1960s, at 4.6 per cent per year. Urban growth began to slow down in the 1980s, declining to 3.0 per cent per year, and reduced even further, to 1.7 per cent per year in 2005. Urban growth in the region took place despite economic instability, social and institutional crises and clear anti-urban policies.[58]

The slowing of urban growth in Latin America and the Caribbean is concomitant with declining population growth rates, which have fallen consistently over the last three decades. Although countries in the region span all stages of the demographic transition,[59] most of the region's population is contracting; the mean number of children born to women has fallen from 6 to 3,[60] average life expectancy is comparable to that of North America, and infant mortality is the lowest among developing regions. On the other hand, income and consumption inequalities in the region are the highest in the world, and there are expanding pockets of poverty in nearly every Latin American country.

Urban development in Latin America and the Caribbean has been characterized by a high degree of urban primacy, with a large proportion of the urban population residing in the largest cities. In 2000, one-fifth of the region's total urban population lived in large cities of 5 million people or more, most of which were national capitals (compared with 18 per cent in Asia or 15 per cent in Africa). Moreover, among the 14 most populated urban agglomerations in the world, four are located in this region (São Paulo, Mexico City, Buenos Aires, and Rio de Janeiro).

While large cities are home to most of the population of the region, they are no longer growing rapidly. In fact, all of the large cities in Latin America and the Caribbean have shown a steady trend of slow growth, and projections indicate that by 2015 they will experience growth rates of less than 0.8 per cent annually.

Perhaps one of the most distinctive features of urbanization in the region is the growth of small cities (with between 100,000 and 500,000 inhabitants). Small cities not only experienced the fastest urban growth in the region (2.6 per cent per year), but also were home to nearly half of all new urban residents from 1990 to 2000. Small cities such as Barcelona in Venezuela and Itaquaquecetuba in Brazil experienced growth rates in excess of 10 per cent per year in the 1990s. Today, small cities are home to a greater proportion of the population of Latin America and the Caribbean than any other region in the developing world (39 per cent, compared to 18 per cent in Asia and 16 per cent in Africa).

The progressive reduction of the share of the population living in Latin America's primate cities is likely an outgrowth of the expansion of small urban centres and the relative growth of big cities. Indeed, even if big cities (with populations of between 1 and 5 million) are not growing as fast as in previous years, when rates of more than 4 per cent per year were common, they are still experiencing significant growth, with more than 40 per cent growing at a rate of 2 to 4 per cent per year. Many big cities are playing active roles as core urban centres, promoting socio-economic development through the accumulation of population and technology, economies of scale and improved infrastructure. Small cities, in turn, are diversifying the urban system in the region, growing as an alternative to the social and environmental consequences of excessive concentration and physical congestion of primate cities, and offering new opportunities for economic development.

The growth and concentration of populations in small and big cities, and population decline in large agglomerations, has generated self-limiting mechanisms of urban growth in the region as it has transitioned away from urban primacy. These self-limiting mechanisms may have been induced by decentralization policies, regional planning programmes, industrial delocalization strategies, and governmental actions channeling investments to specific regions and cities. The consensus among scholars, however, is that regional planning efforts in Latin America and the Caribbean region have not been a great success. With the exception of a few countries and programmes – Mexico's deconcentration of its system of cities; the "Marcha hacia el Este" in Paraguay and Bolivia that reoriented migratory flows towards Santa Cruz and Ciudad del Este; and Cuba's decentralization policies that reduced growth in the capital, Havana – government interventions have not

▲
Teenagers playing street soccer in Mexico City: A large proportion of the urban population in Latin America resides in large cities.
©Milan Klusacek/iStockphoto

managed to reorient growth to secondary cities. Governments and programmes have also not succeeded, for the most part, in stimulating growth in poor regions, or helping the poor, even in regions in which economic growth has occurred.

In Latin America and the Caribbean, per capita GDP grew on average by 1.1 per cent per year in the 1990s and by a mere 0.7 per cent per year in the four years from 2000 to 2004. Since the beginning of the 21st century, poverty levels in absolute terms have increased, particularly in urban areas, revealing a lack of improvement in the living conditions of the population at large.[61] Clearly, the region's economic growth and social development have not happened as expected, at least in the last 10 years. Slum growth and slum prevalence declined in some countries in the late 1980s and 1990s, when the process of re-democratization resulted in the adoption of progressive policies aimed at promoting more inclusive governance and reducing inequalities. However, one consistent factor in the region's tumultuous economic and political history is the persistence of mass poverty in the face of enormous wealth. The region continues to have the greatest income inequality in the world,[62] which hampers its potential to achieve harmonious urban development.

NOTES

1. UNFPA, 2007, p. 1. Earlier UN estimates indicated that this urban transition would occur in 2007.
2. UN Population Division, 2007.
3. This growth rate considers cities with more than 100,000 inhabitants in the period 1990-2000. Urban growth of the total urban population has been estimated at 2.67 per cent for the developing world and 0.54 per cent for the developed world for the years 2000-2005.
4. U.N. Department of Economic and Social Affairs Population Division, 2007.
5. U.N. Department of Economic and Social Affairs Population Division, 2007.
6. Metropolitan areas with populations between 2 and 5 million contained 14 per cent of the population. Cities with populations between 1 and 2 million contained 13 per cent, and those with populations between 250,000 and 1 million and less than 250,000 contained 16 and 7 per cent, respectively. United Nations Census Bureau, 2007.
7. The Commonwealth of Independent States (CIS) consists of 11 former Soviet Republics: Armenia, Azerbaijan, Belarus, Georgia, Kazakhstan, Kyrgyzstan, Moldova, Russia, Tajikstan, Ukraine and Uzbekistan.
8. Satterthwaite, 2007.
9. Lupton & Power, 2004.
10. European Commission, 2007.
11. United States Census Bureau, 2007.
12. Population growth varied significantly by region in the 1990s, with higher rates in the west (19.7 per cent) and south (17.3 per cent) and much lower rates in the midwest (7.9 per cent) and northeast (5.5 per cent), U.S Census Bureau, 2007.
13. Innovations for an Urban World Summit, Bellagio Italy, July 2007.
14. Statistics Canada, 2007.
15. Ibid.
16. Statistics Canada, 2007.
17. Between 1986 and 1994, the population living in capital cities grew by 10 per cent, and since then the annual rate of growth has been decreasing. Australian Bureau of Statistics, 1996.
18. Martinez-Fernandez & Wu, 2007.
19. Australian Bureau of Statistics, 1996.
20. Statistics New Zealand, 1999a.
21. Statistics New Zealand, 1999b.
22. Satterthwaite, 2007.
23. Kasarda & Crenshaw, 1991, p. 467-501.
24. Municipality of Shanghai, n.d.
25. UN DESA, 2007.
26. The trend of urban population decrease is well known and largely associated with cities in the western world, especially in Europe and some parts of North America, where the number of shrinking cities has increased faster in the last 50 years than the numbers of expanding ones.
27. UNFPA, 2007, p. 8.
28. In some parts of sub-Saharan Africa, fertility rates are even higher. Central Africa, for instance, had a fertility rate of 6.1 in 2007.
29. UNFPA, 2007, p. 11.
30. UN-HABITAT, in press.
31. The average growth rate for cities in the developing world is 2.58 per cent.
32. The fastest growth observed during the years 1990 to 2000. Refer to database used by UN-HABITAT in this Report. In the study, "The Transition to a Predominantly Urban World and Its Underpinnings", David Satterthwaite indicates that Africa has 25 such cities, considering a longer period starting in 1950.
33. Interestingly, around 10 per cent of small cities in the region experienced a population loss.
34. OCHA, 2003.
35. UN DESA, 2007.
36. Demographic and Health Surveys, various years between 2000 and 2004.
37. This growth is important if compared with about 1.5 per cent in the advanced economies. Only countries in Asia and countries in transition grew faster than SSA. BBC News, n.d.
38. BBC News, n.d.
39. World Bank, 2003
40. UN-HABITAT, 2006a.
41. UN DESA, 2007.
42. Ibid. UN-HABITAT estimations, 2007.
43. Cohen, 2004.
44. UNFPA, n.d.
45. Eberstadt, 1998.
46. United Nations Economic and Social Council, 1997.
47. Zhu, 2006.
48. The growth rate of big and large Indian cities declined from 36 per cent during the years 1981-1991 to 34 per cent in the next decade. Cited in Bhagat, 2005.
49. Survey done by the Tata Institute of Social Sciences in 2000.
50. Bangalore is the only big metropolitan area with positive growth rates. Secondary metro cities are Pune, Surat, Patna, Kanpur, Jaipur, and Indore. Congested primary cities are Mumbai, Chennai, Kolkota and Delhi. Cited in Bhagat, 2005.
51. This rural-based development strategy is designed to provide non-agricultural employment and thus prevent a mass migration to primate and regional cities already undersupplied with essential services. Asian Urban Center of Kobe, 1987.
52. Wang, 2003.
53. The percentage of people living on less than one dollar a day declined from 35 per cent in 1990 to about 20 per cent in 2003. ADB, DFID and World Bank, 2006.
54. ADB, DFID and World Bank, 2006.
55. UN-HABITAT, 2006a, p. 20.
56. Blair, 2006.
57. Government of China, 11th Five-Year Plan period (2006-2010).
58. Rodriguez, 2007. In only 50 years, the percentage of the total population living in urban areas rose from 42 per cent in 1950 to 75 per cent in 2000.
59. Bolivia and Haiti: incipient transition. El Salvador, Guatemala, Honduras, Nicaragua, and Paraguay: moderate transition. Brazil, Colombia, Costa Rica, Ecuador, Mexico, Panama, Peru, the Dominican Republic, and Venezuela: transition in progress. Cuba, Argentina, Chile, and Uruguay: advanced transition.
60. ECLAC, UNFPA, PAHO, 1999.
61. The number of poor grew by 3 million persons between 1990 and 2001, about 7 million in 2000-2001, and 17 million in 2002. ECLAC, 2002.
62. Cohen, 2004.

1.3

Which Cities are Growing and Why

Urban growth is a result of a combination of factors: geographical location, natural population growth, rural-to-urban migration, infrastructure development, government policies, corporate strategies, and other major political and economic forces, including globalization.[1] In some regions, such as Latin America, urban growth is, in fact, largely a result of urban-to-urban migration. And in many Asian countries, including China, national economic policies often play a significant role in determining which cities will grow in size and importance.

Demographic factors

Contrary to common perception, migration from rural to urban areas is no longer the dominant determinant of urban growth in developing countries. In demographic terms, the main cause of urban growth in most countries is natural increase – when births in cities outpace deaths. United Nations estimates indicate that natural increase accounts for some 60 per cent of urban growth.[2] Several demographic dynamics interact in most cities to influence growth or contraction. In Iran, for instance, the population of urban areas has increased over the past five decades as a result of both high natural population growth rates and rapid rural-urban migration. In contrast, cities in the State of Kerala in India experienced a decline in population over the past 50 years, as Keralites migrated to other states and literacy rates among women increased, impacting fertility rates.[3] In Cuba, the country with the lowest birth rate in Latin America and the Caribbean, urban growth has leveled off as the population has aged. A country's demographic patterns are, therefore, an important determinant of urban growth. Yet, countries with similar demographic patterns may experience different patterns of urban change, with some cities growing faster than others.

Demographic determinants that account for the remaining 40 per cent of urban growth are migration, both intra-national (rural to urban and urban to urban) and international, and the transformation of rural settlements into urban places, a process known as "reclassification". Overall, for every 60 million new urban dwellers added every year to the cities of the global South, approximately 36 million are born there,

12 million migrate in and the remaining 12 million become urban residents by virtue of the reclassification of their rural lands to urban areas.

These demographic factors are influenced by a country's stage of development and its level of urbanization. In countries with low levels of urbanization, migration is often the primary engine driving city growth, as is the case in various countries in Africa and Asia. For instance, the net migration rate into Ho Chi Minh City in Viet Nam was twice that of the natural increase rate between 1999 and 2004.[4] Studies have also shown that more than 60 per cent of population increase in Dhaka, Bangladesh, is due to in-migration.[5] But even in such a case, immigration is driven by industrial policies that centre development in the capital city.

As the urban base grows, the patterns reverse, with natural increase becoming responsible for a higher proportion of urban growth.[6] For instance, in Latin America and the Caribbean, where almost 80 per cent of the population lives in cities, natural growth accounted for more than 60 per cent of urban growth in 2005, despite steep declines in fertility rates, while migration accounted for less than 20 per cent of urban growth that year. In countries with youthful populations, natural increase is a big contributor to urban growth. In India, for instance, where 35 per cent of the population is under 15 years old, natural increase accounted for 56 per cent of urban growth in 2001, while net migration accounted for 23 per cent.[7]

In contrast, in China, where two-fifths of the population is urban and fertility rates are extremely low (an outcome of the one-child policy),[8] rural-to-urban migration was the main cause of population growth, accounting for 55 per cent of growth in 1990, while natural increase accounted for only 23 per cent of growth. In Shanghai – and possibly in other major Chinese cities – natural increase has played a limited role in urban growth since then. Of the 16.4 million people counted in the 2000 population census for Shanghai, 5.5 million were migrants.[9]

In many countries, the largest movements of population are taking place between cities and not from rural to urban areas. In Latin America and the Caribbean, half of all migrations originate and end in cities.[10] In São Paulo, for instance, one-third of all urban growth can be attributed to urban-to-urban

Economic policies and migration: The case of Dhaka

The domestic economy of Bangladesh is characterized largely by low technology endowments and dominance in trade and services in the absence of significant natural resource assets. Problems of low economic growth, low savings and investments, mounting foreign debts and fiscal and current account deficits and rising inflation characterize the microeconomic climate. The country's traditional dependence on agriculture and its low level of industrial development due to lack of human resources and scientific and technological infrastructure has meant that most of the economy has relied on the agricultural sector for job creation.

The inability of the low-tech, low-output agriculture sector to cater to this led to the adoption of liberal economic policies in an effort to alleviate poverty, and an increased emphasis on labour-intensive manufacturing industries and agro-based industrial production. The Industrial Development Policy of 1999 has been the most consequential economic policy in the country that promotes export-oriented industrialization and led to growth in three sectors: ready-made garments; food processing and pharmaceutical production.

Employment in the garments sector, which concentrated in and around the capital city Dhaka, was preferred by women who either worked in the informal sector, or who had to deal with the vagaries of agricultural production as a result of extreme weather. Employment of women and men in this sector and others has been the main driving force for the massive rural-to-urban migration witnessed in Bangladesh in the last two decades. However, lack of appropriate city planning, redistributive mechanisms and protective labour laws have increased the vulnerability of the poorest groups in the city and led to increasing social divisions.

▲
A labourer in Dhaka: Urban growth in Bangladesh is driven by labour-intensive manufacturing industries that have intensified rural-to-urban migration.
©**IRIN**

Sources: Hossain & Karunarathne 2004; Gehl Sampath 2007; UNCTAD 2007; UNIDO 2007.

FIGURE 1.3.1: **NET MIGRATION RATE AND NATURAL GROWTH RATE IN SHANGHAI, 1995 - 2006**

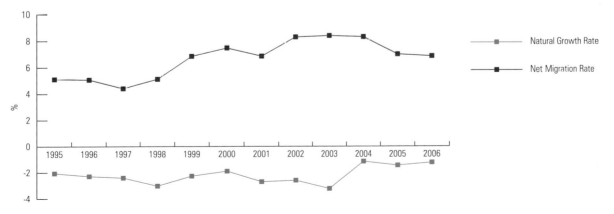

Source: Data from Shanghai Municipal Statistics Bureau, Shanghai Statistical Yearbook 2007.
Note: Net migration rate = in-migration rate minus out-migration rate.
Natural growth rate = birth rate minus death rate.

migrations. Urban-to-urban migration is also becoming more common in African cities. In South Africa, approximately 3 million urban residents have migrated from one district or metropolitan municipality to another in the last five years.[11]

Urban primacy

A common historic pattern observed in virtually all developing countries is urban primacy: the concentration of a significant proportion of the national urban population, and the control of flows of capital, financial transactions, industrial production, national revenue, and other similar indicators in one city. This typically happens at the early stages of a country's development. Cities such as Mogadishu in Somalia, Lomé in Togo, Phnom Penh in Cambodia, Ulaanbaatar in Mongolia, Kuwait City in Kuwait, Port-au-Prince in Haiti, Panama City in Panama, and San Juan in Puerto Rico were home to more than half of the total urban population of their respective countries in 2005. Other cities such as Dakar in Senegal, Ouagadougou in Burkina Faso, Kampala in Uganda, Tel-Aviv in Israel, Santiago in Chile, San José in Costa Rica and Montevideo in Uruguay hosted more than 40 per cent of their respective national urban populations in 2005. The demographic dominance of primate cities frequently results in economic, social, and political dominance over all other cities within an urban system. This was the case until recently in many Latin America and Caribbean cities that concentrated people, resources and investments.

Urban primacy is the norm in most developing countries that are in the early stages of the urban transition. But urban primacy is also bad for business – it distorts the economy, creates imbalances in the distribution of populations and resources and gives rise to different forms of socio-economic disarticulation.[12] All this, in turn, generates regional asymmetries in development and weak political integration, both of which place structural constraints on harmonious development.

However, from a more pragmatic viewpoint, based on historic evidence of urbanization patterns, it seems that the growth of primate cities has been a function of development that helped nations concentrate and maximize their limited financial and human resources more efficiently until a time when resources and growth allowed deconcentration and regional spread.[13] Primate cities, therefore, played – and are still playing – an important role as engines of national and regional economic development, institutional building, cultural progress and, in some countries, political integration by creating national centres of governance. This explains why in most countries primate cities are capital cities or state capitals.

Primate cities[14] altogether grew at the average rate of 3.11 per cent per year from 1990 to 2000, compared to an average of 2.5 per cent for all types of cities. The highest growth rates were recorded in African primate cities (3.65 per cent per year), including in Nairobi, Kenya; Niamey, Niger; Dar es Salaam, Tanzania; and Lomé, Togo, all of which grew at an annual rate of 4 per cent or more. Kigali, the capital of

▲
A street in Cairo: Investments in information technology have boosted urban growth in several cities.
©Madanmohan Rao

Rwanda, is the only primate city that experienced soaring annual population growth of 8.6 per cent from 2000 to 2005. Even if the growth of primate cities in Africa is slowing down, in general, most African countries are still dominated by a single city rather than a network of cities.

Asian primate cities are growing at the same pace as the developing world average (3.11 per cent per year), which is extremely high, considering that the average growth rate of Asian cities is 2.5 per cent annually. Cities such as Phonon Penh, Kathmandu, Dubai, Sana'a, and Dhaka grew at an annual rate of more than 4 per cent between 1990 and 2000. Dhaka, the capital of Bangladesh, is the fastest growing megacity in the world, with an annual growth rate of 4.4 per cent per year. In Latin America and the Caribbean, only two primate cities grew at a rate higher than 4 per cent: Port-au-Prince in Haiti and Asuncion in Paraguay. The overwhelming concentration of the population in one or two urban centres was a trend in this region from 1960 to 1980, but since then, the urban landscape has diversified.

In the second stage of the urban transition, as countries move from low to intermediate levels of development, the role of primate cities diminishes, or in some cases, starts to decline. Small and intermediate cities that were somehow overshadowed by the dynamism of the primate city start to emerge, diversifying the system of cities and reducing the attractiveness of the capital or primate city. This process can accelerate when new development priorities emerge, decentralization policies are put into practice, infrastructure is expanded to different regions, or different forms of globalization come into view in specific locations. The process can also be hastened by problems of governance or when primate cities generate significant negative externalities, such as high costs of living, transport and pollution problems, increased crime, and the like.

How governments are propelling urban growth

UN-HABITAT analysis of 245 cities that are experiencing the fastest growth in the developing world shows very clearly that spatial influences of macroeconomic and industrial policies and related investments (or economic development), are the main drivers of city growth in 78 per cent of the cities analyzed. Investments in transport infrastructure (roads, ports, airports) were by and large the most important contributor to city growth. Forty per cent of the cities analyzed experienced high growth rates as a direct result of the diversification, expansion or improvement of regional or urban transport infrastructure. The designation of regions or cities as special economic zones contributed to the rapid growth of one-fifth of these cities. The development of information and services-related sectors, such as banking and financial systems, including different forms of trade, was the third most important contributor to city growth, representing 16 per cent of the cities.

In a large number of these cities, economic policies and investments are mostly the result of national government decisions and allocations. The State, in its various institutional forms, exerts a critical influence in the growth of these cities. For instance, decisions to designate cities or regions as free trade areas or special economic zones are made at the central government level; likewise, the mobilization and allocation of huge public (and often private) investments for the construction of transport and communication infrastructure and the improvement of these services is usually a central government responsibility. This suggests that urban growth in many countries is initially driven by national governments, and then further propelled by local authorities and the private sector. In this scenario, central governments quite often determine which cities will benefit from investments and macroeconomic decisions.

National governments in a number of countries, including Thailand, the Philippines, South Korea, Mexico and Brazil, are concentrating more attention and resources on particular city-regions. Others, like Malaysia and China, are using cities to connect the nation to the global space of business flows, while concurrently using such cities to propel social change in particular directions. It is clear that the growth of the fastest cities in the developing world cannot be adequately understood without an examination of the matrices of state territorial organization within and through which it occurs.

This does not mean that local authorities are not

▲
Crowd of people crossing the street at a busy intersection in Central District, Hong Kong
©**Christine Gonsalves/iStockphoto**

playing an important role in economic and urban growth. Local authorities, in conjunction with political and economic local and regional elites, are transforming their cities into dynamic economic areas oriented towards global, regional and local growth sectors. Cities such as Salem, Pimpri, Chinchawad and Pune in India, Guadalajara and Ensenada in Mexico, Maracay in Venezuela, Cuenca in Ecuador and Zambaoanga in the Philippines, to name just a few cities, are all growing at the annual rate of 3 per cent or more by adopting pro-growth strategies through place marketing and promotion, focusing on high-potential economic sectors. Major urban centres in South Africa have also adopted different forms of economic development strategies as part of integrated development plans, which were implemented through local economic development units. As a consequence of this, economic growth in these cities was higher than population growth by slightly more than 1 percentage point over the 1996-2001 period.

The growth of cities through local initiatives reflects a rising trend towards greater urban entrepreneurialism and more intense city competition. However, many cities in the developing world, particularly in the small and intermediate ranks, do not have adequate financial and human resources to conceive and implement medium- and long-term development strategies. These cities, and many other large agglomerations, often compete with each other to gain recognition as important urban centres and to be included in regional and national development plans and strategies, which gives them the authority to be considered in the allocation of budgets and to be part of strategic alliances that combine private and public resources etc.

This articulation of local initiatives with central government economic and political decisions is bringing about changes in the governance paradigm in which the private sector is also involved in specific plans and funding. At the national or regional level, the central government decides on macroeconomic policies with clear spatial implications, implements institutional reforms and mobilizes huge domestic resources to support infrastructure and communication development. On their part local authorities design local development strategies or refashion their policies, programmes and projects in order to link up with wider initiatives that mobilize public and private investments at a larger scale.

However, while developing countries are using macro and microeconomic policies to jump-start economic development, they often lack the regulatory competence and strategic focus to enact policies for infrastructure and other public goods to promote regional balance. Moreover, there is a lack of policies and institutions that focus on more equitable distribution of the gains of economic development, not only between regions or cities, but within cities. Cities in countries that do relatively well to balance their needs and create spheres of harmony not only have strategic industrial and innovation policies that cater to the need for better infrastructure to achieve economies of scale; they also have the institutional mechanisms that distribute the gains of economic growth more evenly. Often, developing countries' focus on economic development is not accompanied by concomitant policies to improve the quality of rural life. This leads to a widening rural-urban divide in employment, schooling and medical services, among others, which fuels further migration to cities, and worsens the divide.

Analysis by UN-HABITAT Global Urban Observatory 2008. Data and other information on the 245 fastest growing cities derived from various sources, including Wai-Chung et al. 2004, South African Cities Network 2006 and Harvey 1989.

Cities in the developing world that are not primate cities showed quite diverse patterns of urban change from 1990 to 2000. While some grew very fast, at the annual rate of 10 per cent or more, the vast majority experienced an annual growth rate of between 2 and 4 per cent, and a considerable number grew at a moderate pace, while a relatively small number experienced population decline. This differentiated level of urban growth can be explained by the particular attributes that a city may have had in the past or that it has developed more recently: Cuautla in Mexico grew from a small market town to a city of more than 120,000 inhabitants because of tourism; Chungju in South Korea doubled in size with the establishment of the National University of Industry; the small city of Annaba in Algeria increased its population by more than 130,000 inhabitants as a result of the improvement of transport infrastructure; Cochabamba in Bolivia grew from 282,000 to 404,000 inhabitants between 1982 and 1989, as the area prospered from agricultural exports.

New drivers of growth

UN-HABITAT's analysis of the causes and effects of population growth in a sample of 245[15] of the fastest growing cities in the developing world (cities growing at an average annual growth rate of more than 2 per cent per year) between

1990 and 2000[16] shows that the driving forces behind urban growth are often complex and overlapping. However, the analysis led to the identification of the three most significant drivers of urban growth in Africa, Asia and Latin America and the Caribbean:

1. Economic and industrial policies (i.e., creation of special economic zones, industrialization and export promotion areas, etc.) and related strategic investments in two key areas — transport infrastructure and communications and trade service sectors;
2. Improvements in the quality of life in cities (basic services, transport, green areas, public amenities, etc.); and
3. Changes in the legal and/or administrative status of urban areas.

National economic policies and investments in infrastructure

Economic and industrial policies and related infrastructure investments play a critical role in determining which cities will grow and which will decline. UN-HABITAT analysis of 245 cities that are experiencing the fastest growth in the developing world shows very clearly that macroeconomic

---

TABLE 1.3.1: **DRIVERS OF GROWTH IN THE DEVELOPING WORLD'S FASTEST GROWING CITIES**

UN-HABITAT's State of the World's Cities report team adopted a range of research methods to estimate the new drivers of population growth in cities of the developing world. First, the team conducted a statistical analysis, based on data from the United Nations Demographic Yearbooks, to identify those cities experiencing very high urban growth rates. A maximum of 10 cities per country were selected taking into account different city-sizes. A conceptual framework for possible reasons of city growth was created and presented to an internal advisory group for revision/modification. Second, the team hired a number of international urban experts in different regions as research advisers. In the case of Asia, two additional experts were engaged at the country level, one for India and the other for China. The report team commissioned local experts to carry out fieldwork to identify the drivers of growth in selected cities using a combination of quantitative and qualitative research methods based on the agreed framework. Local experts were identified through the network of urban observatories (approximately 300 around the world), UN-HABITAT's programme managers in some 40 countries and well-known academics and practitioners. Qualitative analysis included focus group discussions and expert group meetings in selected cities. Quantitative analysis included an examination of changes

in the city's labour force; variations in local economic product; changes in income and in investments in cities; and in - and out-migration. Third, local experts, supported by international urban experts and UN-HABITAT's Global Urban Observatory, determined the main reason driving population growth in these cities. When causality was not clear or when there were several factors contributing to growth or it was difficult to determine the main contributory factor, the city was eliminated from the list of cities analyzed. (The final list comprised 37 cities in Africa, 57 cities in Latin American and the Caribbean and 151 cities in Asia and the Pacific.) Fourth, the team validated the results of the analysis by undertaking further literature research of information published by national statistical offices, local authorities etc. and through consultations with experts at the UN Economic Commissions in the different regions. The resulting findings are preliminary and should be considered as a first step towards a more detailed qualitative and quantitative research analysis of the drivers of city growth in the developing world.

The preliminary results of the UN-HABITAT analysis are presented in the table below.

New drivers of growth in the fastest cities of the developing world

	Africa		Latin America & Caribbean		Asia		Total	
Economic reasons (total)	29	78.4%	48	85.7%	113	74.3%	190	77.6%
Designation of economic zone	4	10.8%	12	21.4%	35	23.0%	51	20.8%
Investment in transport infrastructure	19	51.4%	14	25.0%	67	44.1%	100	40.8%
Information and services	6	16.2%	22	39.3%	11	7.2%	39	15.9%
Improvement in quality of life	8	21.6%	5	8.9%	12	7.9%	25	10.2%
Administrative change	0	0.0%	3	5.4%	27	17.8%	30	12.2%
Total	37	100.0%	56	100.0%	152	100.0%	245	100.0%

Source: UN-HABITAT Global Urban Observatory, 2008.

Bangkok's advanced transport infrastructure: In many Asian cities, investment in urban infrastructure has boosted urban growth.
©iStockphoto

policies and related investments, or economic development, were the main drivers of city growth in 78 per cent of the cities analyzed. More than half of the cities that grew because of economic reasons did so because of investment in transport infrastructure (roads, ports, airports, and the like). The designation of regions or cities as special economic zones contributed to the development of one-fifth of these cities. The development of information technology and financial services related sectors, such as banking and financial systems, including different forms of trade, was the third most important contributor to city growth, representing 16 per cent of cities that were driven by economic factors.

Cities that are oriented towards global or national growth sectors that specialize in industrial development, or are transport hubs and markets, are experiencing the fastest urban and economic growth. In general terms, these cities have more infrastructure investments, more robust labour markets, more employment opportunities and higher incomes than other cities. All of these factors make the fastest growing cities attractive to potential migrants in search of economic opportunities. The reasons for growth vary according to regions. While in Asia the designation of economic zones and investments in infrastructure appear to be the most important contributors to urban growth, in Latin America and the Caribbean, service sector development appears to play a larger role. In Africa, improvements in quality of life appear to be an important factor of city growth, particularly in the cities of North Africa.

The pathways of growth for cities driven by economic development are diverse: economic reforms that facilitate access to capital markets and foreign investment; political changes that make possible greater local fiscal autonomy and permit import and export licenses; government and corporate strategies that increase investments in strategic economic sectors; and national or local initiatives that position cities in global, regional or local spaces of economic flows.

The growth of these cities is not random; very often, they benefit from economic policies because of where they are located geographically. In modern economic urban growth analysis, geography continues to play a key role in determining the economic policies and related investments in cities. Proximity to various geographic features or political entities that facilitate trade often explains the rationale for deciding which city will benefit the most from economic policies and investments: proximity to coastlines and navigable rivers with the consequent reduction of transport costs[17]; proximity to major cities and important urban agglomerations; proximity to markets, infrastructure and transport systems; proximity to natural resources, including water, minerals, hydrocarbon deposits, and the like; and proximity to transnational borders.[18] For example, Gaborone, the capital of Botswana and one of Africa's fastest growing cities, has experienced an annual growth rate of 3.3 per cent as a result of its strategic location at the frontier of the South African border. This city is becoming a thriving financial, industrial, administrative and educational hub for the region, attracting investments and generating opportunities that are magnets for accelerated migration.[19] Many other cities across the developing world experienced important population growth by taking advantage of their strategic geographic location for trade activities: General Santos in the Philippines; Ensenada and Nuevo Laredo in Mexico; Barquisimeto, Ciudad Bolivar and Maracay in Venezuela; Teresina and Fortaleza in Brazil, to name just a few.

Geography is not the only deciding factor in the growth of such cities. A city that might have emerged because of geographic comparative advantages can continue to thrive as a result of agglomeration economies and good urban management. It is also possible to find cities that prosper and grow without a clear geographic advantage, mainly because of their capacity to develop self-organizing spatial patterns of development that are based on agglomeration effects and effective governance and urban management structures.

Construction cranes doing ground work for a light rail system in Shenzhen, a special economic zone in China.
©**Hector Joseph Lumang/iStockphoto**

Creation of special economic zones

In a number of rapidly growing cities, economic policies and investments grow primarily from national government decisions and allocations. The state, in its various institutional forms, exerts a critical influence on the growth of these cities. For instance, decisions to designate cities or regions as free trade areas or special economic zones are made at the central government level; likewise, the mobilization and allocation of huge public (and often private) investments for the construction of transport and communication infrastructure and the improvement of these services is often a central government responsibility.

The designation of special economic zones covers a wide range of economic activities, from custom-bonded warehouses, factories and export processing zones to free trade ports or areas. In 2002, there were approximately 3,000 variations of special economic zones (SEZs) in 116 countries.[20] Rapid urban growth that accompanies the creation of a SEZ is largely an Asian phenomenon: 35 SEZ Asian cities experienced the fastest urban growth among all cities in the developing world from 1990 to 2000; 11 were in China, 9 were in India, 5 were in South Korea and the rest were distributed among other Asian countries. In Latin America and the Caribbean, 12 cities in 5 countries – 8 in Mexico, 1 in Dominican Republic, 1 in Chile, 1 in Peru, and 1 in Paraguay – grew rapidly as a result of designation as SEZs. In Africa, SEZs contributed to rapid urban growth in only two countries: Egypt (Suez and Port Said cities) and Libya (Tripoli and Banghazi).

China's eastern and southern coastal areas have experienced rapid population growth, making them among the fastest growing cities in Asia. The establishment of SEZs in the 1980s, and the further expansion of the coastal belt in the beginning of the 1990s, led to high economic and population growth. The SEZs were originally set up in four cities along the southern coast – Shenzhen, Zhuhai, Shantou and Xiamen – to attract foreign capital and advanced technology and management systems, in line with China's economic reforms. Globalization and the outsourcing of production to these cities helped to accelerate their growth. The Chinese policy was also strategic in terms of foreign direct investment. For example, investment in the computer manufacturing sector, one of China's highest growing hi-tech sectors in recent times, were planned and concentrated around the Pearl River Delta, Yangzi River and the Look BoSea Region. As a result, intermediate-size cities such as Yantai and Qinhuangdao grew at approximately 5 per cent per year, and Wenzhou and Xiamen grew at an impressive rate of more than 11 per cent per year, while the city of Shenzhen, located in the heart of Pearl River Delta, experienced a phenomenal annual growth rate of 20.8 per cent, slightly more than the city's economic growth rate of 16.3 per cent in the 1990s.[21] Shenzhen's population grew from fewer than 1 million inhabitants in 1990 to 7 million by 2000, and the GDP of 15 SEZs along China's coastline accounted for nearly 21 per cent of the national total.[22]

These cities are not only engines of China's economic growth, but also of the country's transformation from a predominantly rural society to one that is increasingly becoming urban-based.[23] Designated economic zones in other countries have also helped accelerate urban growth; for instance, the Iranian city of Sirjan and the Indian urban agglomeration of Nashik grew rapidly in the 1990s, at the rate of 6 and 4 per cent, respectively, owing to their designation as special economic zones.

In South Korea, the implementation of industrialization and export promotion policies in the late 1970s led to rapid growth rates in urban areas, but with significant regional imbalances. As a result, the government adopted a regional policy of placing industrial parks in areas that were lagging behind, and implemented the so-called "three coastal areas development strategies".[24] These policies helped redress spatial inequalities by boosting urban growth in various coastal cities, particularly in Yeosu, Gyeonan and Cheonan, which grew at approximately 6 to 7 per cent per year, and Gimhae city, which experienced the highest annual population growth rate of 11.6 per cent on average.

In Mexico, export processing zones, known as "Maquiladoras", which are given special incentives to attract industrial foreign investors through infrastructural development, tax exemptions, and the like, boosted the development of nine cities along the Mexico-U.S. border: Ensenada, Reynosa, Matamoros, Nogales, Nuevo Laredo, Chihuahua, Ciudad Juarez, and Tijuana. The outcome of the border's dynamic maquiladora growth has not only improved job creation, exports and foreign exchange in Mexico,[25] but has also resulted in remarkable population growth in all of these border cities, which grew at an annual rate greater than 3 per cent from 1990 to 2000[26] – two times faster than the national average.

In Libya, an overwhelming concentration of the population lives along the northern coast, principally in the Gafara and Benghazi Plains, which are more favourable for agricultural productivity and living conditions than elsewhere in the country. A 2002 study reports that urban centres such as Benghazi, Misurata, Tripoli and Zawia, all coastal cities, are growing at a rate twice that of the national average. Favourable state policies promoting open boundaries and economic opportunities followed by huge public investments will continue to encourage migration to these coastal cities.[27]

These patterns suggest that urban growth in many countries is initially driven by national governments, and then further propelled by local authorities. In this scenario, central governments quite often determine which cities will benefit from investments and macroeconomic decisions. National governments of countries as diverse as Thailand, the Philippines, South Korea, Mexico, and Brazil are concentrating more attention and resources on particular city-regions. Others, like Malaysia and China, are using cities to connect the nation to the global space of business and trade, while concurrently propelling social change in desired directions.[28] It is clear that the growth of the fastest growing cities in the developing world cannot be adequately understood without an examination of the matrices of state territorial organization within and through which it occurs.[29]

This does not mean that local authorities are not playing an important role in economic and urban growth. Local authorities, in conjunction with political and economic local and regional elites, are transforming their cities into dynamic economic areas oriented towards global, regional and local growth sectors. Indian cities such as Salem, Pimpri, Chinchawad and Pune; the Mexican cities of Guadalajara and Ensenada; and Maracay, Venezuela, Cuenca, Ecuador, and Zambaoanga, the Philippines, to name just a few cities, are all growing at the annual rate of 3 per cent or more by adopting pro-growth strategies through place marketing and promotion, focusing on high-potential economic sectors. Major urban centres in South Africa have also adopted different forms of economic development strategies as part of city-integrated development plans, which have been implemented through local economic development units. As a result, economic growth in these cities (3.2 per cent) was higher than population growth by slightly more than 1 percentage point between 1996 and 2001.[30]

The growth of cities through local initiatives reflects a rising trend toward greater urban entrepreneurialism and more intense city competition. However, many cities in the developing world, particularly in the small and intermediate ranks, do not have adequate financial and human resources to conceive and implement medium- and long-term development strategies. These cities, and many other large agglomerations, often compete with each other to gain recognition as important urban centres and to be included in regional and national development plans and strategies, which gives them the authority to be considered in the allocation of budgets and to be part of strategic alliances that combine private and public resources.

This articulation of local initiatives with central government economic and political decisions is bringing about changes in the governance paradigm, in which the private sector is often involved with specific plans and funds. At the national or regional level, the central government decides on macroeconomic policies with clear spatial implications, implements institutional reforms and mobilizes domestic resources to support infrastructure and communication development. On the other hand, local authorities design local development strategies or refashion their policies, programmes and projects to link up with wider initiatives that mobilize public and private investments at a larger scale.[31]

Transport and communications infrastructure

Transport and communications systems are fundamental to development. The construction and maintenance of roads, highways, ports, airports, urban and inter-urban railways, and other forms of transport systems determine, to a large extent, whether or not cities and countries will succeed economically.[32]

> Proximity to geographical features or political entities that facilitate trade often explains which cities will benefit from investments

Investments in transport infrastructure and related reforms in the sector, including finance and regulations, deliver major economic development benefits,[33] contribute to poverty alleviation, and improve the quality of life of citizens.

Transport connectivity is the most important driver of city growth in developing regions, particularly in Asia and Africa. Two-fifths of the 245 cities in the UN-HABITAT sample of the developing world's fastest growing cities have benefitted from diversification and improvement of regional transport systems, in terms of infrastructure and technology. Investments in transport not only increase the overall productivity of nations' and regions' economies, but they can also contribute to the maintenance of balanced regional development and the reduction of socio-economic disparities across space and people. Transport connects areas with economic potential to isolated places that otherwise would be left far behind.

Many countries improve their transport and technology systems when they open or liberalize their economies to reduce tariff and transport costs. These related initiatives have opened an array of markets and fostered growth in individual cities. Transport connectivity is integral to the economic growth of second and third-tier inland cities that have a functional connection to coastal settlements, transnational borders and other larger cities. As a result of transport and communication investments, inland urban centres are growing both economically and demographically. A study on population change from 1995 to 2000 shows that cities in coastal areas are not the fastest growing cities any more; in fact, cities in almost all ecosystems are growing at roughly the same of rate of 2.2 per cent per year. In Africa, cities in mountainous and forested areas grew the fastest, at the rate of 3.6 and 3.7 per cent annually, compared to the growth rate of 3.3 per cent per year for cities in coastal zones. In Latin America and the Caribbean, cities in dryland, forest and inland water ecosystems grew equally at the rate of 2.2 per cent per year, which is higher than the growth rate of coastal cities during this period (2.0 per cent per year).[34] Better transport and communications infrastructure in several countries has made these cities more attractive destinations for economic activities, contributing to high rates of growth.

For similar reasons, inland Chinese cities such as Xinyang and Nanyang grew at an impressive rate of 15 per cent per year as a result of national efforts to develop transport infrastructure and communication technology in central China. New urban centres are also developing some 200 kilometres from the coastline in the eastern part of the country; these cities are already creating a new wave of urban settlements in the interior with strong linkages to the coastal region.[35] In other Asian countries, coastal cities are receiving a new boost; for instance, the cities of Tirunelveli and Tiruchirappalli in the southern part of India, and Sirjan in the Islamic Republic of Iran, experienced growth rates of around 5 per cent per year, mainly because they have developed into important transport hubs.

In the Philippines, cities such as Mandaue, Davao and Cebu experienced significant urban and economic population growth as a result of the implementation of the Local Productivity and Performance Measurement System (LPPMS), which promoted the development of cities conducive to business, industry and entrepreneurship, and in which infrastructure development played a key role.[36]

Investments in transport facilities in various transnational border cities that combine large transport and distribution functions with trade activities have also boosted urban growth. In many cases, the strategic border location has been enhanced by industrial development, tourism or the development of a port: the Iraqi city of Basra, the country's main port, located close to the Kuwaiti and Iranian borders in the southeast part of the country, experienced population growth of 4.5 per cent per year in the 1990s; Nuevo Laredo, a small city of only 300,000 people that accounts for 70 per cent of all Mexican goods exported to the United States by road, expanded its population at a rate of 3.4 per cent per year; and the Venezuelan city of San Cristobal on the Colombian border grew at 2.6 per cent per year. In addition to these cities, many other urban centres that are positioned at the convergence of land or sea border transport systems experienced accelerated economic and population growth between 1990 and 2000.

In many other cases, the expansion of regional transport networks boosted the development of urban centres located along railways and roads lines, often as trade and tourism places. This has been the case with the Latin America and Caribbean cities of Bayamo in Cuba, Chiclayo in Peru and San Cristobal in Venezuela, all of which grew at a rate of between 1 and 2 per cent annually following the development of provincial transport networks that were linked to national railway and roadway systems. In Africa, the expansion of transport infrastructure in the 1990s contributed to the growth of dozens of cities, both on the coastline and in the interior. Cities such as Annaba and Tebessa in Algeria grew at an annual rate of 3 per cent or more because a national railway line passed through them, and the city of Tiaret grew at a similar rate as a result of the construction of a high plateau line. Populations in the cities of Kaduna and Maiduguri in Nigeria also expanded with the improvement of the road and railway systems, the former for industrial development and the latter for transport services.

Connectivity through the development of infrastructure has been vital for the growth of cities in close proximity to larger urban centres. A considerable number of small and intermediate cities grew as bedroom communities, residential suburbs or satellite cities, offering the amenities of urban life – proximity, convenience and diversity – without the disadvantages, such as air pollution, congestion and crime. Investments in transport have effectively reduced the "commuter territory" in many places, linking metropolitan and sub-regional spaces and interconnecting various urban settlements in neighboring geographic locations.

In Asia, the development of better commuter systems has led to the growth of new cities, such as Ghaziabad, Noida, Faridabad, and Meerut, which have boomed as satellite cities of New Delhi, each with annual urban growth rates of between 3 and 6 per cent. The planned city of Navi Mumbai grew at a staggering pace of 7 per cent per year

Subway in Seoul, Korea; Transport connectivity is one of the most important drivers of urban growth in developing countries.
©Juergen Sack/iStockphoto

in the 1990s as part of the deconcentration strategy of the megacity of Mumbai; two other cities in the vicinity, Kalyan-Dombivli and Thane, experienced more spontaneous growth by offering more affordable housing solutions and adequate transport facilities. Information technology (IT) hubs, such as Bangalore and Hyderabad, are also experiencing growth driven by the establishment of international software companies that attract young professionals to the IT sector.

In South Korea, various cities have been experiencing rapid urban growth as part of the greater Seoul Metropolitan Area: Seongnam, which grew as a residential city; Suwon and Puchon, which became satellite cities that share the same subway line; and Incheon, which in 2001 built its own international airport. In Iran, the metropolitan areas of Isfahan and Tehran gave a boost to well-connected neighbouring cities: Khomeini-Shahr city, which grew at the rate of approximately 4 per cent per year, boosted by infrastructure development and the relocation of various companies from Isfahan; and Karaj city, which grew at an impressive rate of 8 per cent per year from 1994 to 2003, benefited from the commuter surface connection Teheran-Karaj, Mehrshahar Express Line and a privileged geographic location at the crossroads of the western and northern routes of the country.

Proximity to a large urban agglomeration is an important determinant of growth in many small and intermediate

Latin American cities. Between 1990 and 2000, small and intermediate cities grew faster when transport and communication infrastructure was extended to them or substantially improved. Better connectivity allowed them to exploit the employment opportunities, improved access to public amenities, and recreational and cultural services offered by big cities. Simultaneously, the small and intermediate cities were in a better position to offer land, housing and labour at a fraction of what they would cost in a big city, sometimes with a higher quality of life. They were also in a better position to offer specialized services around tourist attractions and scenic natural environments with comparative advantages. Alajuela city in the vicinity of San Jose, the capital of Costa Rica, experienced rapid urban growth, at a rate of 4 per cent per year, by hosting the main airport serving the country. The location of an international airport in the small city of São José dos Pinhais in Curitiba, Brazil, combined with good road infrastructure and industrial development, propelled the growth of the city at an annual rate of more than 9 per cent. San Bernardo in the Santiago Metropolitan Region in Chile saw growth of approximately 3 per cent per year as a result of the construction of a new highway that attracted industrial development. Likewise, the city of Cabimas in Venezuela grew at a rate of 3 per cent per year as a result of its oil production and its reliable highway connection to the city of Maracaibo.

Luxurious residential buildings in Dubai Marina: The city's remarkable growth has been propelled by a combination of innovative real estate projects, financial services and development of the tourism industry.
©Shao Weiwei/iStockphoto

Information technology and financial services sectors

The development of economic infrastructure related to information technology and financial services was identified as the third most important economic driver of city growth in the developing world in the UN-HABITAT analysis. Investments in information and communication technology (telephone, cellular and radio services, and electronic communication), and related communication services, such as financial, banking, insurance, and other various forms of trade, were the primary boosters of growth in 39 of the 245 fastest growing cities in the developing world.

In addition to the already well-known urban centres that experienced significant economic and population growth in recent years as a result of financial trade and communication services, such as Singapore, Kuala Lumpur, Beijing, and Hong Kong, other cities in countries from India to Venezuela, Pakistan to Mexico, Cameroon to Puerto Rico also witnessed rapid growth as a result of public and private investments in communication technology and related services, including various other forms of trade. Hyderabad in India was transformed into a dynamic economic region oriented toward global growth sectors, inspired by the infrastructure-led growth model, focusing on industrial development, particularly in the information technology (IT) sector.[37] Likewise, the city of Bangalore has become a major centre of information technology and software services in the country with an annual population growth rate of 2.2 per cent from 1991 to 2001. The city of Gumi, known as the Korean Silicon Valley, and the Chinese cities of Xian and Changsha, two high-tech

industrial development zones, grew at the annual rate of 5 per cent. The coastal city of Karachi in Pakistan increased its population by more than 3 million people from 1990 to 2000, mainly as a result of high fertility rates, national and international in-migrations, trade activities related to the port, and the growth of information and communication technology industries. Dubai in the United Arab Emirates experienced a remarkable growth rate of 7 per cent per year during the 1990s by combining innovative real estate projects with IT, industrial and finance services, free trade zones and the development of the tourism industry.

Improvement in the quality of life

Of the 245 sample cities, 25 experienced rapid urban growth principally by improving the quality of life and well-being of their citizens. Some cities developed clear visions and strategies for their potential futures, articulating short- and medium-term responses that contributed to enhancing social, economic and, in some cases, environmental conditions, including personal safety and health, transport and other public services.

Cities such as Curitiba, Goiania and Fortaleza in Brazil and Gaziantep in Turkey grew at a rate of more than 2 per cent per year, largely by setting up good governance structures that enabled them to bring benefits to their inhabitants by expanding their connection to infrastructure, piped water, sewerage, electricity, and telephone, and by developing social amenities such as schools and health centres.[38] The small city of Rishon LeZion in Israel doubled its population in

20 years, starting in the mid 1980s, through the creation of employment opportunities, high-quality schools and services –including innovative urban transport – open spaces and green areas within the city. Today, Rishon LeZion is the fastest growing metropolitan area in the country, growing at 3.3 per cent per year, with the highest average per capita income and a record number of square metres of park space per resident.[39]

A similar situation has been observed in the city of Bacolod in the Philippines: despite experiencing a rapid growth rate of 2.4 per cent per year in the 1990s, it was ranked first in the country's quality of life assessment in 2006.[40] In China, the city of Yantai in the eastern part of the country grew at an accelerated annual rate of more than 7 per cent from 1990 to 2000 following its complete transformation into a "safer, greener and better serviced city". This award-winning city has successfully competed with large Asian cities for new investments by embracing sustainable development principles that combine strategies to create a more conducive environment for business and good-quality housing solutions. The city of Dubai in the United Arab Emirates is a first-class example of economic and urban development based on risk-taking and profit-oriented strategies that are boosting economic and urban growth based on the concept of a "quality of life city". Many other cities in developing countries are enhancing their attractiveness through the development of high-quality services in various sectors, including the city of Davao in the Philippines, which is considered one of the most competitive and liveable cities in the country.[41]

In the 1990s, quality of life was an important driver of growth in cities that implemented place-specific development strategies, raising living standards by building economic infrastructure and social amenities. These cities boosted their economic and urban growth by exploring natural advantages, often in the tourism and leisure industries. Good examples of this are the Chilean cities of Temuco, La Serena and Villa del Mar and Rishon LeZion in Israel. The Moroccan cities of Saîda, Taghazout, Mogador and El Haouzia implemented a "Sustainable Development of Coastal Tourism Programme", which provides water, electricity, roads, and telecommunication infrastructure to new real estate developments along the coasts. Similarly, various South Korean cities have developed the "Corporate Cities" concept, merging business, research, tourism, and residential areas in new urban developments.[42]

An important driver of city growth related to quality of life is the construction of a prominent public or private institution, often a university or research institute. The Algerian cities of Blida, Tlemcen, Sidi-bel-Abbès and Setif, the city of Bobo Dioulasso in Burkina Fasso and Concepción in Chile grew, to a large extent, as a result of the attraction of their institutes of higher learning.

Administrative and/or legal changes in city status

Between 1990 and 2000, 30 cities in the UN-HABITAT sample of 245 rapidly growing cities experienced administrative and political changes, often absorbing large populations that were not previously part of the city. This form of urban growth – of urban change, in fact – is largely influenced by governments' decisions to modify the legal and administrative status of urban areas very often as a response to economic growth or as a way to induce economic development. These modifications involve changes in the size of cities, their boundaries, forms of classification and definition.

Another dimension of change in administrative designation is the reclassification of rural areas into cities. Reclassification accounts for approximately a quarter of urban population increase in the developing world. Scholars have pointed out that in most parts of the world where reclassification occurs, it tends to be in areas that have experienced, or are experiencing, the fastest economic growth. In China, for instance, 25 per cent of urban growth in the country has been attributed to reclassification; this phenomenon is particularly prevalent in the eastern part of the country.[43]

An obvious form of urban growth resulting from geopolitical decisions is the transfer of capital cities to other small cities or to new, previously undeveloped locations. Other cities were designated capitals of their provinces or departments, and by virtue of this change experienced significant population growth, as was the case in Samarinda, Indonesia.

The change of administrative and legal status is an important driver of many cities' growth; 12 per cent of the 245 cities analyzed by UN-HABITAT recorded administrative changes as the most significant factor in their growth between 1990 and 2000. Twenty-seven of the 30 cities that experienced an administrative or legal change in their status were in Asia, while the remaining 3 were in Latin America and the Caribbean; no city sampled in Africa grew as a result of change in status. In Asia, more than half of the legal and administrative city definitional changes occurred in China (8), South Korea (9) and Indonesia (3). In China, contrary to the policies restricting urban development before the era of economic reforms, the government adopted a more positive attitude toward the designation of cities and towns in the 1990s[44]; this not only increased the number of cities, but also led to a population increase in cities. Cities such as Lu'an, Xinyang and Nanyang grew at an astounding annual rate of more than 15 per cent following their changed ranking from county-level cities to prefecture-level cities and the expansion of the urban area.[45] A similar situation occurred in the small South Korean cities of Gyeongiu, Yeosu, Gumi, and Pohang, which merged with other counties in 1995, precipitating population growth of approximately 5 per cent in each of the cities. In Indonesia, the cities of Sukabumi and Bogor grew at a rate of more than 10 per cent every year as a result of the expansion of the administrative area.

New entrants in the league of cities

Between 1990 and 2000, urbanization in developing regions was characterized by the entry of new cities that did not exist as such in 1990. This constellation of 694 new cities started out as rural towns and became urban areas by virtue of changes in their administrative status, natural growth or in-migration.

These significant changes took place mostly in Asia, where more than 295 settlements became small cities, followed by 171 new small cities in Latin America and the Caribbean. More than 90 per cent of the cities in which populations grew from fewer than 100,000 to more than 1 million people were also in Asia, owing to a variety of factors, including changes in administrative and legal boundaries and changes in political status of settlements.

Among the cities that emerged after 1990, 73 per cent joined the category of small cities, 19 per cent became intermediate cities and 7.5 per cent developed into big cities.

Not only did the number of cities increase, but many of the cities that existed in 1990 also became larger: 122 small cities (13 per cent) became intermediate or big cities; 66 intermediate cities (23 per cent) became big or large cities; and 10 big cities (5 per cent) developed into large cities. On the other hand, 17 cities contracted, changing from big to intermediate or from intermediate to small.

These changes are not only a matter of numbers – they also represent a qualitative change in what the world perceives to be "small", "intermediate" and "large" in terms of city size over time. The emergence of "hyper-large" or "meta-city" urban agglomerations with more than 20 million inhabitants has led to a fundamental shift in conceptions of city size.

TABLE 1.3.2: **NUMBER AND TOTAL POPULATION OF NEW CITIES ESTABLISHED SINCE 1990**

	New small cities		New intermediate cities		New big cities		Total	
	Number	Population	Number	Population	Number	Population	Number	Population
Africa	44	6,335,094	1	523,265	0	0	45	6,858,359
Latin America & Caribbean	171	27,138,867	6	3,930,127	2	3,008,885	179	34,077,879
Asia	295	60,825,858	125	86,595,611	50	65,491,865	470	212,913,334
excluding China & India	72	13,374,321	5	3,109,207	0	0	77	16,483,528
China	78	26,331,991	119	82,966,103	49	64,485,448	246	173,783,542
India	145	21,119,546	1	520,301	1	1,006,417	147	22,646,264
TOTAL	510	94,299,819	132	91,049,003	52	68,500,750	694	253,849,572

Source: UN-HABITAT Global Urban Observatory 2008
Data source: UN Demographic Yearbooks, various years (1985 - 2004)

FIGURE 1.3.2: **NUMBER OF NEW CITIES AFTER 1990 IN THE DEVELOPING WORLD**

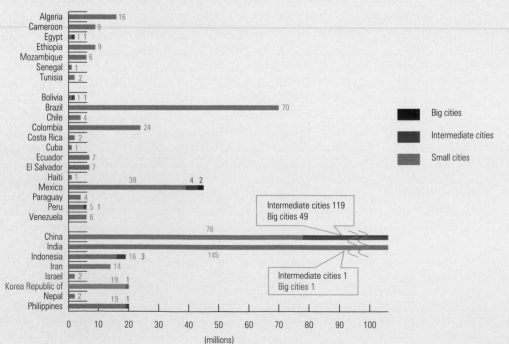

Source: UN-HABITAT Global Urban Observatory 2008
Data source: UN Demographic Yearbooks, various years (1985 - 2004)

Chengdu city in China
©Mikko Pitkänen/Shutterstock

Bangalore: India's Silicon Plateau

As recently as the late 1980s, Bangalore, a quiet hillside city in southern India blessed with lush greenery, was known primarily as a "pensioner's paradise". All this changed in the 1990s when Bangalore emerged as India's first "technopolis".

Described as India's "Silicon Plateau", in reference to the city's high altitude and the concentration of high-technology companies in its environs, Bangalore is a city that has achieved remarkable success as a result of national policies that encouraged the development of an information technology (IT) services industry. The city's emergence as an IT hub began in the early 1990s, when the Government of India began pursuing an "informationization strategy" that hinged on the development and export of computer software. The strategy led to several policies and programmes aimed at boosting information technology, including the establishment of a national Information Technology Task Force in 1998. The adoption of this strategy saw Indian computer software exports rise from US$100 million in 1990 to nearly US$10 billion in 2004 (more than 2 per cent of India's GDP). Growth is still in excess of 25 per cent for the industry as a whole, and is projected to reach $50 billion by the end of this decade. In India today, more than half a million people are employed by almost 3,500 companies in this industry.

Bangalore now hosts more than 500 high-tech companies that produce computer hardware and software. Large multinational software companies have established bases in Bangalore as have leading Indian high-tech companies. Silicon Valley "micro-multinationals" are also tapping into the city, which is seen as an innovation and support hub. A lot of the software work was, until recently, project-based, involving a mix of on-site and offshore programming. A second wave of development has been in research and development (R&D), innovation and intellectual property, particularly along the United States-India technology corridor.

Domestically, huge markets are growing in sectors such as mobile communications, with India adding a steady 8 million new subscribers every month. A mindset change is also being observed in academic institutes where a new crop of students are more entrepreneurially-driven and globally-oriented than before. In the late 1990s, a new growth driver emerged for the Indian IT services industry: the IT-enabled services sector or ITES. This term referred to the business process outsourcing (BPO) and call centre services. Young, educated, English-speaking Indians deliver remote services – made possible by low-cost communication technology – to clients in the United States and Europe in areas as diverse as processing credit card applications, human resources benefits administration, insurance claims processing, telesales and telemarketing, and customer support.

Bangalore's strengths as an IT centre include widespread English skills, sheer numbers of lower-wage "techies", experience in managing global software and services projects, growth in multinational company development centres, and connections with non-resident Indians (NRIs) in California's Silicon Valley who are excelling there. In addition, Bangalore's evolution as an IT hub was facilitated by the presence of a large state-run industrial technology sector (especially in aeronautics), a cluster of the country's leading scientific research institutes (such as the Indian Institute of Science) and a pool of highly qualified technical manpower. The city has been compared to the Silicon Valley phenomenon in major technology hotspots of the world: Cambridge in England, Helsinki in Finland, Tel Aviv in Israel, Singapore, and the HsinChu-Taipei belt in the Taiwan province of China. These cities share many success factors: low taxes, venture capital (VC), risk-taking start-up culture, business webs, physical infrastructure, IT-savvy local population, local "living laboratories," good local markets, networking skills, activities and organizations for communities of interest, co-location of companies in various stages of development, flexible organizational structure, legal/accounting services, mergers and acquisitions activity for flow of skilled labour and intellectual property, local academic and research institutes, commercial partnerships between academia and industry, activist government policy via research funding and small business debt assistance, speed of business activity, presence of role models, human talent in innovation, serial entrepreneurs, marketers, and managers.

A recent UN Human Development Report ranked Bangalore as the only city among the top ten centres of technological innovation to be located in a developing country. However, while Bangalore gets a high ranking as a major technology hotspot, it faces several challenges and obstacles, including poor infrastructure, a massive digital divide, government bureaucracy, presence of just a few higher educational institutes, low research and development spending by IT companies, and high employee attrition especially at the level of team leaders. Cultural divides have also grown between locals and outsiders, including non-resident Indians from abroad, who have flocked to the city's hi-tech industry. (In 2007 the city was officially renamed "Bengaluru" to reflect the concerns of the local language movement, but the name Bangalore is still commonly used.)

Bangalore's global ambitions are thus threatened by its crumbling infrastructure, according to analysts and even ordinary citizens. Scores of tall, massive apartments now dominate Bangalore's skyline, a testimony to the real estate boom and expanding horizons of the IT spectrum, but many of them have inadequate water and power supplies and poor access roads. Many companies use generators to compensate for power outages.

A study by the Asian Development Bank found that among Indian cities with 5 million or more residents, Bangalore is the second fastest growing in terms of population, experiencing a population growth rate of 2.8 per cent a year. The study projects the population of Bangalore to increase from the current 6 million to nearly 10 million in 2020. Among Asia-Pacific cities with 5 million or more residents, Bangalore stands eighth in terms of rate of population growth. (Dhaka, with an annual increase of 3.8%, tops the Asia-Pacific list.)

In order to deal with the problems associated with the rapid expansion of the city, State governments have been trying to obtain "Metropolitan City" status for Bangalore in order to become eligible for more central government funds. A separate fund for infrastructure has also been established, not only to attract more investments to the city, but also to overcome the congestion caused by traffic. Upcoming projects include the Bangalore Metro Rail Project, Bangalore Mysore Expressway, and a number of ring roads, elevated expressways and underpasses.

TECH HOTSPOTS AND THEIR RATING (ON A SCALE OF 1-5)

	Startup Activity	Human Talent	Venture Capital	Global links	Univs. /R&D	Taxes/ Regul.	Total
Britain/Cambridge	3	4	4	2	4	4	3.45
Finland/Helsinki	3	4	3	3	5	3	3.45
India/Bangalore	4	3	2	4	2	2	3.05
Taiwan province of China/ HsinChu-Taipei	4	4	4	5	5	5	4.35

Source: Rosenberg, 2002.

Sources: Anandram, 2004; Rosenberg, 2002; Singhal & Rogers, 2001; Asian Development Bank, 2008. Text and analysis by Madanmohan Rao.

1 Ofori-Amoah, 2007.
2 UN Department of Economic and Social Affairs (DESA), 2006.
3 Veni 2005.
4 Thanh, 2006.
5 Pantelic, 2000.
6 UN DESA, 2006.
7 Census of India, 1991.
8 UNFPA, 2007.
9 Zhu 2004.
10 ECLAC 2007
11 South African Cities Network, 2006.
12 Kasarda & Crenshaw, 1991
13 Ibid.
14 Urban primacy exists where the largest city has a size that exceeds the expected size under the rank-size rule. In an ideal system of cities, there is a lognormal frequency distribution by size, which forms a rank-size distribution. There are several ways to measure "urban primacy". Some define it as a ratio of twice or three times the population size of the second-largest city. Others use the ratio of twice the size of the combined second and third-largest cities. In this Report, primate cities are considered as concentrations of more than 20 per cent of the country's urban population.
15 The sample comprised 37 cities in Africa, 57 cities in Latin America and the Caribbean and 151 cities in Asia.
16 A maximum of 10 cities experiencing the fastest population growth per category of city size were selected in each country, using a matrix with various possible reasons for population growth. Based on the results and frequencies of different factors, a table was prepared with the most frequent three factors: 1) administrative change; 2) economic reasons separated into three indicators: a) designation of economic zone; b) investments in infrastructure; c) service sector development; and 3) improvements in quality of life. For each city, only one factor was taken into account (i.e., designation of economic zone) despite the fact that in reality, more than one factor contributes to city growth (designation of economic zone plus infrastructure investments). In combination with economic reasons, quality of life was not selected as a main reason for growth. Some cities with fast growth were not included in the analysis, either because they were not clear enough or not confirmed. This method should be considered as a preliminary qualitative approach to city growth analysis. The sources of information were consultation with experts in cities or regions, advice from ECLAC and ESCAP professionals in the area, UN-HABITAT programme managers in a number of countries, two special advisers for China and India, city council web sites, specialized articles, national statistical web sites, and the like.
17 Some academicians argue that coastal areas, and particularly port cities, are no longer playing the same determinant role as in the past in the economic development of cities. However, leading thinkers note that the core coastal region has a mere 10 per cent of the world's population but produces at least 35 per cent of the world gross national project. See Gallup, Sachs & Mellinger, 1998.
18 In this sense, it is interesting to note that countries located in disadvantageous geographic areas, such as landlocked nations, are in typically poor, with the exception of a handful of countries in Western Europe that are deeply integrated into the regional European market and connected by different transport means. See Gallup, Sachs & Mellinger, 1998.

19 Urban growth in Gaborone is also explained by the reclassification of traditional villages and urban towns as "urban villages". This administrative process is a key factor in urban growth. The share of "urban villages" in the urban population has increased from 10 per cent in 1981 to 60 per cent in 2001. Botswana, Central Statistics Office, website accessed in November 2007.
20 Changwon, 2005.
21 Shenzhen's economy grew also at the fast rate of 16.3 per cent. China Statistical Yearbook 2002-2006, National Bureau of Statistics of China – 2002-2006 editions.
22 National Bureau of Statistics of China (2002 - 2006), China Statistical Yearbook 2002 - 2006, Beijing.
23 Hu & Yueng, 1992.
24 East Coast Development, South Coast Development, and West Coast Development.
25 From 1983 to 2000, annual growth in maquiladora employment and exports averaged almost 14 per cent and 21 per cent, respectively. At about 1.3 million workers, maquiladora employment represented 29 per cent of Mexico's manufacturing jobs in 2000, up from slightly more than 7 per cent in 1983. Vargas, 2001.
26 Except the city of Chihuahua, which grew at 2 per cent.
27 Antipolis, 2002.
28 Henry, 2004.
29 Olds & Yeung, 2004.
30 South African Cities Network, 2006.
31 Harvey, 1989.
32 World Bank, 2004b.
33 A 1 per cent increase in the stock of infrastructure is associated with a 1 per cent increase in GDP. World Bank, 2004.
34 Balk, McGranahan & Anderson, forthcoming.
35 Small-sized cities concentrated 18.6 per cent of foreign direct investment in 1990, and most of these cities (95 per cent) are located in the Eastern region. Moreover, foreign investment from Hong Kong is mainly located in rural settlements of the Pearl River Delta that will contribute to the rapid rural urbanization of this area. China Urban Statistical Yearbook, 1991.
36 Department of the Interior and Local Government, the Philippines, UN-HABITAT & UNDP, 2007.
37 Kennedy, 2007.
38 Bazoglu, 2007.
39 The city enjoys the best quality of life, with 17 square metres of parks per resident compared to the national average of 5 sq. m. http://duns100.dundb.co.il/companies.
40 This assessment included criteria such as incidence of theft and murder, number of hospital beds, length of life expectancy, cleanliness of roads and public open spaces, and competitiveness of the economy. Bacolod, 2007.
41 Davao city, 2007.
42 Quote by Lim Byoung-Soo, Assistant Ministry of Culture and Tourism.
43 The People's Government of Lu'an, n.d.
44 Zhu, 2003.
45 Lu'an City remained at county level until September 1999, when the Lu'an Prefecture was removed and the City of Lu'an was promoted to the prefecture level. The former area of the county level Lu'an City was divided into two parts and became Jin'an and Yu'an districts of the prefecture level Lu'an City. In March of 2000, Lu'an City was put under the direct administration of Anhui Provincial Government. The People's Government of Lu'an, n.d.

1.4

Shrinking Cities

The history of cities has not been dictated exclusively by urban growth; a long-term perspective on demographic and economic changes, particularly in the developed world, shows that, historically, cities have experienced boom and bust cycles over time, and in some places, decline and population contraction result in permanent alterations to city structures.

Cities may expand or contract in size and importance; their growth and decline is dependent on a variety of historical, economic, political, and demographic factors. While some cities are growing more rapidly than others, the widespread assumption that increasing global urbanization means that all cities are growing is false; in fact, evidence shows that in all regions of the world, and especially in the developed regions, many cities are actually shrinking in size.

Although slow or negative urban growth is overwhelmingly a developed-world phenomenon, it is also occurring in developing countries. A UN-HABITAT analysis of 1,408 cities[1] in the developing world showed that 143 cities, or 10.2 per cent of the sample, experienced a reduction in population (i.e., recorded negative growth rates) between 1990 and 2000. Rapid or accelerated urban growth is still the norm in most regions of the developing world, however: more than half of the cities in the sample (53 per cent) have been growing at an accelerated or rapid pace since the 1990s[2]; 17 per cent of these cities experienced an accelerated growth rate of more than 4 per cent per year, while 36 per cent saw rapid annual growth rates of between 2 and 4 per cent).

It may seem paradoxical that in a period of rapid urban growth, some cities in the developing world are actually shrinking. The negative growth trend is largely associated with cities in North America and Europe, where the number of shrinking cities has increased faster in the last 50 years than the number of expanding cities. In the United States alone, 39 cities have endured population loss, while in the United Kingdom, Germany and Italy, 49, 48 and 34 cities, respectively, shrank in size between 1990 and 2000. Another recently observed trend is the increase in the number of cities

FIGURE 1.4.1: **PROPORTION OF CITIES EXPERIENCING ACCELERATED, RAPID, MODERATE, SLOW AND NEGATIVE GROWTH RATES IN THE DEVELOPING AND DEVELOPED WORLD IN THE 1990s.**

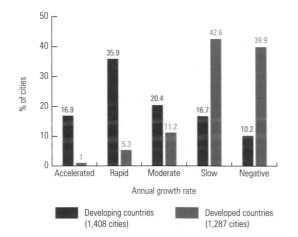

Source: UN-HABITAT, Global Urban Observatory, 2008
Data are from UN Statistics Division, Demographic Yearbook, 1990-2005, and UN Population Division, World Urbanization Prospects, 2005

TABLE 1.4.1: **DECLINING CITIES IN THE DEVELOPING WORLD (1990-2000)**

Region	No. of cities experiencing declining populations (from 1990 to 2000)	Population loss (millions) (1990-2000)
Africa	11	0.37
Latin America and the Caribbean	46	2.8
Asia	86	9.7
China	50	6.8
India	16	0.7
Total	143	13

Source: UN-HABITAT, Global Urban Observatory, 2008.
Data from United Nations Statistical Division, Demographic Yearbook, various years (various years, 1985 and 2004)
Note: Data refers to cities of more than 100,000 inhabitants experiencing a real decline in their populations and not just a slowing down of urban growth rates.

Kiev, Ukraine: A number of cities in transition countries are suffering from population loss.
©Tissa/IStockphoto

losing population in countries of the former Soviet bloc. Nearly 100 Russian cities experienced negative growth in the 1990s; in Ukraine, 40 cities experienced population loss.

The phenomenon of declining populations in cities of the developing world is relatively new, an emerging trend that is not yet as prevalent as it is in the developed world. Population loss may be, however, a prelude to a new urban trend that is starting to unfold in the developing world, signaled by the fact that 143 cities experienced the loss of 13 million people from 1990 to 2000. More than half of this population loss (6.8 million people) occurred in Chinese cities, while roughly 16 per cent (2.1 million people) of the population loss occurred in other Asian countries. In Latin America and the Caribbean, the total population loss between 1990 and 2000 amounted to 2.8 million people, while in Africa the figure was 370,000.[3]

The paradox of shrinking cities in regions where urban growth rates are generally high could be explained by a variety of factors. In some cases, cities start to experience population loss when they cease serving as primate cities; others may lose populations to more dynamic cities that offer more opportunities and attract more residents. Deteriorating living conditions and urban decay may also contribute to population loss as residents seek opportunities in other cities that offer a higher quality of life. In some countries, the core of the declining city begins to contract or to become economically disassociated from the satellite cities emerging around it – a phenomenon known as "the doughnut effect". Jakarta, the capital city of Indonesia, experienced annual growth rates of -0.7 per cent per year from 1995 to 2003, while the population of suburban areas – commonly known as Bodetabek – increased dramatically. The neighbouring city of Bogor, for instance, experienced a phenomenal growth rate of 13.2 per cent per year during the same period. People with sufficient money, jobs and energy to move outside of the city were attracted by the better living environments provided by suburban enclave housing; simultaneously, the poor in Jakarta were relocated to the fringe areas to make room for the expansion of the formal sector in the central city.[4]

A similar phenomenon is evident in Seoul, which grew from a small, unknown capital of the Republic of Korea to one of the world's large-population cities. Seoul started experiencing negative growth at a rate of -0.7 per cent per year in the 1990s. This transformation came about in a context of intensive suburbanization and sprawl into the neighbouring Gyeongii Province, which received 64 per cent of Seoul's emigrants in 2005.[5] In other cities, such as Shanghai in China, in-migration is responsible for much of the growth of the city, as natural population growth has been declining since 1995. In China, rapid urban growth rates in one part of the country are accompanied by slow or negative urban growth rates in other parts of the country. This is not only an outcome of demographic changes and population mobility, but in many cases is associated with uneven regional development.

Understanding which cities are experiencing a boom in terms of economic and demographic growth, and which cities are going through economic and population decline, is important for maximizing gains, locating or relocating investments and opportunities, and for planning for more sustainable and balanced regional development. Knowing which cities, parts of cities, metropolitan areas, and even regions are not growing – or are experiencing population loss – is essential for policymakers and urban planners, who need accurate data to anticipate trends, design recovery policies and rethink strategies for bringing opportunities to cities and preventing excessive out-migration.[6]

Growth and contraction are not two different phenomena; they are two sides of the same coin of urban change.[7] Evidence about how these dual trends are changing urban areas today can help shift thinking from a broad assumption that all cities are growing in order to understand the dynamics of city growth for improving quality of life in all cities.[8] City and regional planning requires new methods and techniques that respond to urban development, expansion and growth management, but also new methods and techniques that respond to decline or out-migration. "Smart planning for growth" should be combined with "smart planning for contraction" if more harmonious urban and regional development is to be achieved.

The phenomenon of shrinking urban populations can be perceived as a sign of a new era in the history of some cities, in which the initial impulse of all-embracing and ever-accelerating urbanization gives way to a more complex, subtle and ambivalent process.[9]

Shrinking cities are often associated with economic and political failure. Until recently, many European cities were reluctant to even admit that they were shrinking in size.[10] The primary assumption was that people who move out of cities "vote with their feet", making judgments about the quality of life in the cities they leave behind. This is true to some extent: when a city shrinks in size, the reasons are usually economic. In most shrinking cities, unemployment is high and business opportunities are either unexploited or unavailable.[11]

Yet, urban decline occurs even in regions that prospering. In some cases, the reasons have to do with urban environmental degradation, inner-city decay and suburbanization. The reality today is that not even big urban centers are protected from population loss. They are also threatened by some of the urban and environmental manifestations of economic and population decline, such as abandonment of residential areas and obsolete industrial areas, wastage of infrastructure and deterioration of the inner city, among others.

Years of civil war in Afghanistan led to abandonment of residential and commercial areas in cities such as Kabul.
©**Rasna Warah**

Planning for growth while anticipating decline

In order to arrest out-migration from cities, policymakers and urban planners should consider the following:

- Management of shrinking cities requires innovative skills and strategies for "keeping people", or containing population flight.

- Flexible design and placement of assets (such as industrial infrastructure, commercial buildings, and infrastructure for water, sewage, electricity, and industrial land) facilitate transformation into new uses when necessary.

- Regional connectivity and networking schemes aid cooperative public policy in changing urban areas.

- Public-private partnerships allow for innovation, renewal and for adapting fiscal bases of cities.

- Knowledge transfer and economic diversification assist regions in moving from outdated economic activities to new businesses and sources of revenue.

- Urban policies should facilitate planning for industrial environmental impacts in the declining phases of cities, and for management of the environmental legacy of industrial activities.

- Issues surrounding the environmental legacy of shrinking cities are a global phenomenon: planners and policymakers need to be aware of the environmental changes that lead to shrinkage (drought, climate change); and the ways in which shrinkage leads to environmental changes (mining, heavy industry).

Martinez-Fernandez, MC and C-T Wu (2007) Urban Development in a Different Reality, Berlin 2006.

Shrinking cities in the developing world

In 2000, nearly 100 million people were living in cities whose populations were declining, representing 8.3 per cent of the total urban population in developing nations. Half of the population loss in shrinking cities took place in big cities of between 1 and 5 million, and almost one-fourth in intermediate cities of 500,000 to 1 million. These cities are not only experiencing a dramatic decline in their populations, but also in their economic and social bases.

Asian cities are the most affected by population decline; they account for 60 per cent of all shrinking cities in the developing world. Most of these cities are in China; Indian cities account for approximately 20 per cent. The cities experiencing population decline in the two countries differ in terms of size: in China, urban contraction concerns intermediate and big cities, and in India, it occurs mostly in small urban centers. In some cities, population loss is seasonal, often related to harvesting or planting seasons. Many rural migrants find temporary work in cities and return to their villages or small towns in time for the harvesting season. In these cases, urban population sizes of both the cities and the villages grow or contract, depending on the time of year and the season.

In the cities of **Latin America and the Caribbean**, growth slowed considerably in the late 1980s – a trend that has been amply documented. The reality of urban population loss in the region, however, still goes largely unrecognized, with the exception of some studies that find urban sprawl and increasing suburbanization are responsible for population decline in specific parts of cities. UN-HABITAT's analysis shows that some 46 cities in the region, mainly in Brazil, Mexico and Venezuela, experienced population loss in the 1990s.

In **African cities**, signs of decline are almost negligible. Some urban areas, however, are either experiencing slow growth or are suffering from population loss. This phenomenon is confined mainly to small towns and cities. The UN-HABITAT analysis of urban growth from 1990 to 2000 reveals that of the 11 African cities that experienced declining populations, 10 were small cities.[12] It is possible that some cities lost populations as a result of war, disasters or civil conflicts, but in most cases, population loss has been a transitory process. Recent studies on migration and urbanization in Africa have produced empirical evidence demonstrating new patterns of return migration from urban to rural areas that may have an impact on population decline in the future. These patterns are more visible in once-booming economies such as Côte d'Ivoire, Cameroon and Zimbabwe and are apparently fuelled by the high cost of living in urban areas, unemployment and the relatively low cost of food, education and housing in rural areas.[13] In many African countries, migration to a city is often temporary, as many migrants retain their rural roots even while working in the city. This also explains why the majority of woman-headed households in Africa are found in rural areas, as males tend to migrate to cities, leaving their wives and children behind.[14]

Why are some cities in developing countries shrinking?

The UN-HABITAT analysis of 143 cities with declining populations in the developing world provides a preliminary overview of the causes behind these changes, which can be grouped into four types.[15]

Suburbanization and the growth of nucleations

This process involves the systematic rapid growth of areas on the outskirts of cities, while growth in the inner core slows down, remains stagnant or declines. Suburbanization is associated more with urban sprawl than with urban decline per se. However, the movement of populations out of a city's borders may not always mean that residents are moving to peri-urban municipalities or to the countryside; their movement may also be to neighbouring cities with different politico-administrative structures. Many formerly monocentric cities in the developing world are becoming increasingly polycentric, developing urban nucleations with their own downtowns, employment centres and other features of independent cities. These adjacent urban areas expand their populations, often at the expense of the original city that experiences a decline in population, accompanied by a decline in economic activities and opportunities. In other cases, economic growth provokes land use changes promoted by business ventures that inflate land values in some parts of the city; this process ends up displacing poor and middle-income residents to neighbouring cities, thereby leading to a reduction in the number of inhabitants in the original city.

Migration from the central city to suburban areas or neighbouring cities generates simultaneous growth and decline, known as the "doughnut effect". This type of outward sprawl is often precipitated by middle- or high-income families who move out of the inner city to less-dense neighbouring cities that have better amenities.

Urban sprawl does not always generate low-density suburban areas and new urban nucleations. The City of La Paz in Bolivia, for instance, lost an average of 10,000 people every year from 1989 to 2003 to the nearby El Alto settlement, owing to lack of affordable housing in the capital city and the difficulties of expanding a city that is located in a small, steep basin. Those who moved were mostly poor urban residents. Urban contraction is expected to continue in La Paz, as the city has been experiencing a negative annual growth rate of approximately -1.1 per cent since the 1990s.

Studies of urbanization patterns in the developing world show that urban sprawl, suburbanization and the growth of nucleations will continue as the globalization of consumption patterns produces increasing homogeneity in the cities of the South. This trend will be further exacerbated by improvements in commuting technology and infrastructure, and the development of behaviours that drastically affect the dynamics of population distribution in various cities.

Economic decline

A number of cities are experiencing dramatic declines in their economic and social bases, which is related to a far-reaching structural crisis. Others are affected by long-term economic depressions or lack of economic impetus. These cities have lost or are losing significant numbers of people as a result of economic changes. The Indonesian cities of Pekalongan and Tegal experienced negative urban growth of -1.3 and -2.2 per cent, respectively, from 1995 to 2003, owing to the decline of processing industries; in both cases, the labour force migrated to the nearby larger cities of Semarang and Jakarta.

In most cases, depopulation is provoked by obsolete industries and incremental declines in single factory-based industries, as evident in the small cities of Linhares, Brazil, and Valera, Venezuela, where the number of residents decreased by 2 per cent in the 1990s as a result of the decline of the main agricultural industry. The closing of a brick factory in Orizaba, Mexico, and the difficulties in reactivating the economy through new industries, explains the dramatic decline of population in this city that witnessed a reduction of more than 100,000 inhabitants at an annual growth rate of -6.5 per cent from 1990 to 2000. Likewise, the Chinese cities of Fuxin and Kaiyuan were affected by over-mining of coal that caused internal migrations to other cities; the cities subsequently lost 1.7 and 1 per cent of their populations, respectively. The copper mining city of Mufulira in Zambia experienced a massive economic decline in the late 1980s and 1990s and a progressive reduction of inhabitants in the same decade; population decrease in this city was largely a result of investments that halted production and drastically reduced social benefits and to mine workers, impacting their well-being.

Economic decline in one city can also lead to prosperity in another as capital and infrastructure investments move between regions and cities. This was the case in the city of São Caetano do Sul, part of the São Paulo metro area in Brazil. The city, selected as an industrial development pole by the federal government, benefited from the government's infrastructural and industrial development during the second half of the 20th century, but was negatively affected by the building of a new highway in the neighbouring district of San Bernando and the transfer of many businesses to a new industrial park located along the highway in the 1990s. The resulting economic decline has had a devastating effect on São Caetano in terms of physical decay, social problems and population loss, as the city experienced a negative growth rate of -3.4 per cent during this period.

A similar simultaneous loss of economic dynamism, disinvestment and increasing unemployment in one city and prosperous development in nearby agglomerations or other competitive cities in the region are observed in Barra Mansa, Brazil, the port of Coatzacoalcos, and the cities of Tampico and Torreon in Mexico that lost population by -2.1, -6.5, -3.8 and -3 per cent, respectively, in the 1990s. In these, as in other cities, urban decline is prompted by a loss of employment opportunities, leading to an exodus of both high- and low-income residents, which leaves the city and its region with very few resources in terms of employment and fiscal base. In many cases, the decline – and possible renewal – of cities cannot be divorced from their wider regional contexts. Declining cities are almost always concentrated in declining regions. The decay of a cluster of four coal-mining cities located in the Taeback Mountain Region in South Korea (Taeback, Jeongsun, Samcheok, and Youngwol) further illustrates this point. The import of cheaper oil and coal from international markets and the rationalization in

> Many formerly mono-centric cities in the developing world are becoming increasingly polycentric, developing urban nucleations with their own downtowns, employment centres and other features of independent cities.

▲
A conveyor belt feeds broken rock into a stockpile at sunset at an open-pit copper mine in Zambia. High concentrations of sulphur dioxide emitted by its smelter and continuous water pollution from the mines has led to population loss in the city of Mufulira.
©Michael Fuller/iStockphoto

environmental policies between 1988 and 1993 led to a massive closure of mines that affected the entire Gangwon Province, which lost 11 per cent of its urban population from 1985 to 2002.[16]

Selective decline

There is no doubt that economic decline and the loss of employment opportunities are the primary causes of urban contraction. Other factors are intimately linked to the demographic decline of cities, as well: political decisions involving change of city status and reduction of investments, and the entrenchment of poor-quality urban environments, have led to selective decline in some cities.

The city of Nkongasamba in Cameroon experienced a population decline (-1.3 per cent per year) from 1986 to 1998, mainly because of the progressive loss of its political importance over the last three decades, which has negatively affected investments and has reduced political and economic support from the province and the central government. The difficulties in generating adequate infrastructure and public amenities, and the diversion of the highway and related economic activities, exacerbated the outward migration from Nkongasamba. Other forms of social and economic

segregation, combined with local conflicts and increased tensions partially explain the depopulation of some cities, including Ambon, Indonesia, which reduced its population by -1.3 per cent, and the Venezuelan cities of Guarenas and Catia la Mar, which lost population at a annual rate of -1.2 and -1.9 per cent, respectively.

Other cities lose populations because of serious environmental problems that overlap with other economic and social factors. This is the case, for instance, in the Indian city of Singrauli, the country's energy capital. The city has seven coal mines and 11 thermal plants; many Singrauli residents were relocated when the government built a reservoir and power plants nearby, and when poisonously high levels of mercury pollution were discovered. As a result, Singrauli experienced negative growth, at a rate of -1.3 per cent, between 1990 and 2000. A similar situation exists in the city of Minatitlan, Mexico, the population of which contracted at an annual pace of -2.6 per cent between 1990 and 2000 as a consequence of the local decline in the oil industry and the contamination associated with oil exploration. Likewise, the Zambian city of Mufulira has experienced population loss because of high concentrations of sulphur dioxide emitted by its smelter and continuous water pollution from the mines, in addition to political and economic problems.

Reclassification of cities

Cities in the developing world grow through natural increase, migrations and the reclassification of rural areas as urban centres. Through reclassification, the city's boundaries are redefined, villages abolished and towns established. In recent years, the annexation of surrounding areas by cities has become one of the main determinants of urban growth and urbanization.

In some cases, the opposite happens: adoption of new administrative rules and settlement definitions can lead to urban contraction, simply as a consequence of boundary drawing. As cities are divided into smaller administrative urban areas, their physical space and number of inhabitants shrinks. This has happened in several Chinese cities – namely, Chaozhou, Yancheng, Jingmen, Pingxiang, Xiaogan, and Yulin–Guangxi – which were reduced from a prefecture level, with a population of more than 1 million inhabitants, to county-level cities and counties with populations of approximately half a million people. Other intermediate Chinese cities with populations of between 500,000 and 1 million residents were also divided into smaller urban administrative units, leading to population

losses that varied from 9 to 1 per cent, particularly in the cities of Heyuan, Jincheng, Qingyuan, Yangiiang, Quijing, Deyang, and Huaihua. In other cases, the creation of new political regions and municipalities near a city provokes loss of population in the existing city, as happened with Nova Iguaçu in Brazil, which reduced its population by -6.2 per cent with the creation of Belford Roxo, Querimados, Japeri, and Mesquita municipalities in the beginning of the 1990s.

Is urban contraction a trend of the future?

While debate on the consequences of shrinking cities is intense in North America and Western and Central Europe, it is not yet a well-recognized issue in the developing world. The problem of shrinking cities in developing regions is woefully underrepresented in international comparative research despite the links between urban population growth and decline. This report provides a first insight into the scope of the urban contraction process in the developing world and also explores some of the different possible causes for it, producing a preliminary typology aimed at better understanding this phenomenon.

▲
An abandoned building in Philadelphia, U.S.A.: Economic decline often leads to population decline in cities.
©iStockphoto

Urban regeneration halts population decline in a European town

The municipality of Leinefelde-Worbis in the former East Germany has succeeded in addressing the problems faced by shrinking cities through an innovative and integrated participatory approach to urban regeneration. The living environment has been significantly upgraded, with redundant housing stock demolished and more than 2,500 apartments refurbished to high environmental standards. As a result of the project, the economy has revitalized and depopulation trends have gradually been reversed.

The "ZukunftsWerkStadt" project aimed to achieve sustainable urban development in the context of the dramatic changes in East Germany after reunification. It sought to dramatically improve living conditions, urban infrastructure and the urban environment; create new job opportunities; promote affordable and attractive housing opportunities in a diversified and balanced housing market; improve social and economic stability; and encourage active community life.

The creation of employment has been a key aspect of the approach, as has the revitalization of infrastructure, both physical and social. The

improved living conditions and resurgent local economy have created a base for social and financial stability. High-quality public services and infrastructure, including access to good schools, an efficient and convenient public transport system and facilities for sports and leisure pursuits, have made the city attractive to new migrants and encouraged residents to stay. The municipality's integrated approach and work with private partners created essential conditions for sustainable private investment in the locality, and the new urban environment is attracting new residents.

A range of options were developed to deal with the municipality's various housing problems. With growing unemployment rates, many inhabitants of this small town, comprising just 20,000 inhabitants, had left for other more prosperous regions in Germany. The low-quality, standardized prefabricated units they left behind made up the bulk of the housing stock. Architectural competitions were held for all key projects and high environmental standards were applied throughout, whether for new construction, refurbishment or demolition of surplus apartments.

The project strategy has given residents, landlords, businesses and the municipality a positive economic outlook. The spatial anonymity of socialist urbanism has been replaced with clear distinctions between private and public spaces. Different housing types and sizes have been developed to encourage diversity.

The investment has been largely absorbed by the local building trade and the job market, which has been advantageous to the local community. Leinefelde-Worbis currently hosts 1,200 businesses, and its unemployment figure of 15.1 per cent is significantly lower than the regional (Thuringia) average of 18.1 per cent. The municipal debt is one-third lower than the regional average, despite its below-average per capita tax income. Families with young children are taking advantage of the improved schooling and living environment, and elderly and retired people are utilizing the improved local services. In addition, 1,300 people commute regularly into the town, and the 6 per cent increase in population in 2006 indicates that people are returning to the area.

Source: Building and Social Housing Foundation, 2008.

At present, it is difficult to predict whether the trend of urban decline in the cities of the developing world will continue into the future. It may be that contraction represents a broader phenomenon of an urban life cycle that is only emerging now. Declining fertility rates coupled with changes in rural-to-urban migration flows may contribute to the decline of populations in some towns and cities. From a physical perspective, shrinking cities are characterized by abandoned or vacant commercial sites, deserted or unoccupied houses, wasted infrastructure, and neighbourhoods in physical decay. This phenomenon could be arrested through strategies that enhance the liveability and economic viability of cities, and through diversification of economic activities to attract people and investments.

NOTES

[1] The rationale for choosing this sample of cities is explained in Chapter 1.2.
[2] Calculations based on years for which data exists.
[3] Data on the decline of population in the city refers to the entire city or a part of the city in a metropolitan region.
[4] Indonesia's Urban Studies, 2007 and Rustiadi & Panuju, n.d.
[5] National Statistics Office South Korea, 2005.
[6] Refer to various documents of the Shrinking Cities Association.
[7] Martinez Fernandez & Chung-Tong, 2007.
[8] Ibid.
[9] Sitar & Sverdlov.
[10] In the last five years, the situation has changed significantly. The term "shrinkage" has become common across Europe. Today, for instance, innumerable activities and events in Germany deal with the shrinkage issue.

Refer to Thorsten, 2006.
[11] Delken, 2007.
[12] Yet, data in this region is quite questionable not only because of the lack of consistent definitions and problems of city boundaries that are common to other regions, but also because of the structural weakness of the statistical systems.
[13] Beauchemin & Bocquier, 2004.
[14] UN-HABITAT, 2006a.
[15] Wiechmann Thorsten suggests a typology based on four types: suburbanization, industrial transformation, selective collapses, and political strategies. Refer to the Thorsten, 2006.
[16] Shin, 2006.

Part Two

02

SOCIAL HARMONY

In many cities, wealth and poverty co-exist in close proximity: rich, well-serviced neighbourhoods are often located next to dense inner-city or peri-urban slum settlements that lack basic services and adequate shelter. A city cannot claim to be harmonious if some groups concentrate resources and opportunities while others remain impoverished and deprived. Income inequalities and shelter deprivations within cities not only threaten the harmony of cities, but of countries as well, as they create social and political fractures within society that fuel social unrest.

Part 2 presents preliminary findings of a global analysis of income and consumption inequality at the city level. The overall conclusion drawn from the findings is that inequality within cities is high in the developing world, especially in Latin America and sub-Saharan Africa, and in some cities, it is actually rising. Part 2 also looks at levels of shelter deprivation in various cities and concludes that not all slum dwellers suffer from the same degree or magnitude of deprivation and not all slums are homogenous. However, inequalities and levels of deprivation vary widely among regions and countries. These differentiated levels of social inequality and exclusion can adversely affect cities' and regions' social and economic development.

▶
Artist's impression
©**Moshi**

2.1
Why Urban Inequality Matters

Over the past few decades, the world has witnessed an increase in income inequalities. Rising inequalities in the latter half of the 20th century have been recorded in all regions of both developed and developing countries. Between 1990 and 2004, the share of national consumption by the poorest fifth of the population in developing regions dropped from 4.6 to 3.9 per cent. In the high-growth economies of East Asia, notably China and Viet Nam, inequalities have risen steadily since the late 1980s. Inequalities have also increased in low-income countries such as Bangladesh, Nepal and Sri Lanka, and in middle-income countries such as Argentina. Regionally, Africa and Latin America have the world's highest levels of inequality, with many countries and cities experiencing widening disparities between the rich and the poor. In both regions, the poorest fifth of the population accounts for only 3 per cent of national consumption.[1]

Although social and economic disparities exist in every society, and relative inequalities – which depend on a variety of factors, including natural endowments, cultural norms, individual capacities, and the like – will always exist, extreme inequalities have historically been less tolerated by societies over time. Often, it is not the actual degree of inequality that matters, but rather perceptions of it. When people perceive inequalities to be the result of unfair processes and unequal distribution of opportunities, they are less likely to accept them than if inequalities are perceived to be the result of differences in individual effort.[2] These perceptions often create conditions in which social unrest or conflict can flourish, as gross inequalities are associated with unjust systems that perpetuate poverty, hamper upward mobility and exclude the majority. Quite often it is not inequalities per se that fuel conflict, but rising expectations. Individuals and groups are more likely to engage in violence or generate social unrest if they perceive a gap between what they have and what they believe they deserve.

Inequalities take various forms, ranging from different levels of human capabilities and opportunities, participation in political life, consumption, and income, to disparities in living standards and access to resources, basic services and utilities.[3] Although the traditional causes of inequality – such as spatial segregation, unequal access to education and control of resources and labour markets – have persisted, new causes of inequality have emerged, such as inequalities in access to communication technologies and skills, among others. "Digital exclusion", for instance, has exacerbated inequalities within sub-Saharan Africa and resulted in the further marginalization of the region within a globalizing economy.[4]

A society cannot claim to be harmonious if large portions of its population are deprived of basic needs while others live in opulence. A city cannot be harmonious if some groups concentrate resources and opportunities while others remain impoverished and deprived. Income inequalities not only threaten the harmony of cities, but also put the harmony and stability of countries at risk, as they create social and political fractures within society that threaten to develop into social unrest or full-blown conflicts. An excessive distributive polarization of income and wealth challenges social cohesion in many parts of the world, and the demands for narrowing social distance are in fact demands for social inclusion, social mobility and equal opportunities; in short they are demands for human dignity.

Equality versus equity

"Equality" refers to having the same status in all aspects of life, including income. Equal distribution of income or resources, however, may not always be desirable or possible, as when incomes are generally low or when equal distribution would not produce desirable development outcomes or incentives for growth. "Equity", or the distribution of opportunities such as equal access health care and education in a manner that is fair and just, is therefore seen as a more appropriate response to growing disparities in societies around the world. Equity concerns levelling the playing field so that disadvantaged groups benefit from a larger share of public resources than the rest of the population until they "catch up", after which they can share more equally in the overall pool of resources. Equity can be difficult to measure, so for the purposes of this report, income and access to shelter are used to determine levels of equality. The solutions proposed in this report for reducing inequalities are based on the concept of equity.

Measuring inequality at the city level

The Gini coefficient is a useful metric for understanding the state of cities with regard to distribution of income or consumption. It is the most widely used measure to determine the extent to which the distribution of income or consumption among individuals or households deviates from a perfectly equal distribution. Other less commonly used measures of inequality include the decile dispersion ratio, which presents the average income or consumption of the richest 10 per cent of a population divided by that of the poorest 10 per cent; the share of income or consumption of the poorest; and the Theil index. This report uses the Gini coefficient. Data on distribution of income and consumption is derived primarily from national household surveys and censuses.

A Gini coefficient of 0 indicates perfect equality, whereas a Gini coefficient of 1 indicates perfect inequality. Higher values, therefore, denote greater inequality, but the correspondence of the ratio to specific conditions is complicated. Generally, cities and countries with a Gini coefficient of between 0.2 and 0.39 have relatively equitable distribution of resources; they typically enjoy social stability and high levels of economic development. A Gini coefficient of 0.4 denotes moderately unequal distributions of income or consumption; it is the threshold at which cities and countries should address inequality as a matter of urgency. Cities and countries with a Gini coefficient of 0.6 or higher suffer from extremely high levels of inequality as a result of inadequately functioning labour markets, sluggish economies, or structural problems of wealth distribution or institutional failure, which put them at high risk of instability.

Levels of inequality should not be confused with levels of poverty. While poverty corresponds to degrees of specific deprivations, measurements of inequality capture the entire distribution of income, or the intensity of concentration of income.

Income or consumption inequality is usually measured at the country or regional level; few studies or surveys examine these inequalities at the city level. The findings presented in this report are the first to compare levels of inequality in a relatively large sample of cities in the developing world. Using a dataset of Gini coefficients in 94 cities from 47 countries, an additional 68 countries with data aggregated at the overall national urban level, and 61 provinces with data at the urban level, the findings present urban inequalities in a total of 72 countries. The years for which changes in urban inequalities at the national or city level are calculated range from 1983 to 2005.

The Gini coefficient data for Latin America and the Caribbean was produced especially for this report by the statistical and social development division of the UN Economic Commission for Latin America and the Caribbean (ECLAC), which calculated the Gini coefficients for all selected cities using household surveys from 1989 to 2006. All these surveys have a module on income and the method of estimation is explained in the document by Cfr. F. Medina, "Consideraciones sobre el índice de Gini para medir la concentración del ingreso", Serie Estudios Estadísticos y Prospectivos, No. 9, CEPAL, Santiago de Chile, marzo de 2001.

To obtain Gini coefficient data for Asia, UN-HABITAT's Monitoring and Research Division worked with the statistical division in the UN Economic and Social Commission for Asia and the Pacific (ESCAP), which calculated Gini coefficients for Asian cities and urban areas using different sources, including national surveys, censuses and data produced by national statistics offices in various countries.

The Gini coefficient data for African cities and urban areas was more difficult to obtain as there is no central depository of such data in the region, and also because many countries do not conduct surveys or censuses that collect information at the city or urban level. Where such information exists, UN-HABITAT worked with various partners, mostly national statistics offices, to obtain and analyze the data. Additional data was obtained through literature research that cites Gini coefficient data produced by national or international organizations in various countries. For instance, the Gini coefficient data for South African cities was obtained from the South African Cities Network; data for Kenyan cities and urban areas was derived from a recently-published integrated household budget survey, while the Gini coefficient data for Kenyan, Tanzanian and Ugandan cities and towns within the Lake Victoria region was produced by UN-HABITAT using its own urban inequities surveys.

The table below provides a general guide to the social causes and consequences associated with different values of the Gini coefficient. It is important to note, however, that not all societies respond to inequalities in the same way; perceptions, belief systems, cultural norms, and collective modes of action often play a role in determining which societies have a higher level of "tolerance" for inequalities than others.

Gini coefficient value	What it means
0.6 or above	Extremely high levels of inequality, not only among individuals, but also among social groups (known as "horizontal inequality"). Wealth concentrated among certain groups at the exclusion of the majority. High risk of social unrest or civil conflict.
0.5-0.59	Relatively high levels of inequality, reflecting institutional and structural failures in income distribution.
0.45-0.49	Inequality approaching dangerously high levels. If no remedial actions are taken, could discourage investment and lead to sporadic protests and riots. Often denotes weak functioning of labour markets or inadequate investment in public services and lack of pro-poor social programmes.
0.40	International alert line – inequality threshold
0.3-0.39	Moderate levels of inequality. Healthy economic expansion accompanied by political stability and civil society participation. However, could also mean that society is relatively homogenous – that all groups are generally rich or poor – and, therefore, disparities are not reflected in income or consumption levels.
0.25-0.29	Low levels of inequality. Egalitarian society often characterized by universal access to public goods and services, alongside political stability and social cohesion.

Source: UN-HABITAT Monitoring and Research Division, 2008.

Cities can grow economically without increasing inequalities

In the last few years, there has been intense debate about whether or not inequalities are a natural consequence of economic growth and development. Since the 1950s, economists and researchers (notably, W. Arthur Lewis and Simon Kuznets), have stipulated that in the early stages of a country's development, inequalities intensify up to a certain stage as low-wage agricultural labour migrates to the higher-wage industrial sector. As aggregate incomes increase and as a country develops, inequalities decrease in the long term.[5]

Inequalities have thus been viewed as "good" for economic growth and development in the initial stages of a country's development, as they allow industries to take advantage of cheap labour in order to reinvest profits. Capital accumulation has also been seen as a positive outcome of inequality because it allows investments in sectors that would reduce poverty and inequality in the long term. Others have also argued that inequalities are an unavoidable side effect of liberalization and globalization and that inequality is the price countries need to pay for economic growth.

Previously accepted views are increasingly being challenged, however. Recent evidence[6] shows that the benefits of economic growth are not realized in societies experiencing extreme levels of inequality and poverty. In fact, when inequality and poverty levels are very high, as they are in many cities of the developing world, economic growth does not benefit all groups, and can actually increase levels of poverty in a country. Evidence also suggests that economic growth benefits larger groups of people when it occurs in egalitarian societies. The benefits of growth are "absorbed" better by equal societies than unequal ones, as the latter tend to concentrate the benefits of economic growth among select groups, leaving the majority behind. It is thus argued that reducing levels of inequality permits people at the lower end of the wealth or income scale to fully exploit their capabilities and contribute to human capital development that in turn has positive impacts on overall labour productivity and contributes to accelerated economic growth. This part of the report validates the idea that equality and economic development are not conflicting variables, but in fact maintain a relationship that is mutually reinforcing. Cities can grow without generating further inequalities, and can thus be sites of opportunity for more harmonious development.

The relationship between economic growth and urban income inequality is neither simple nor correlational, and it depends to a large extent on forward-looking planning or mitigation efforts on the part of governments and other actors. Evidence shows that in many cities and countries, rising economic growth rates do not automatically lead to higher levels of inequality. UN-HABITAT analysis of urban inequalities in 28 developing countries[7] showed that while positive economic growth since the early 1980s has been accompanied by a rise in urban income inequalities in 43 per cent of the countries, 46 per cent of the countries managed to reduce urban income inequalities in an environment of positive economic growth, as measured by the Gini coefficient for each country. And in 7 per cent of the sample, positive economic growth had virtually no impact on urban inequality levels[8] (Fig. 2.1.1). Interesting findings were also reflected at the city level. UN-HABITAT analyses of 94 cities in 47 developing countries show that while some cities, such as Beijing, Accra, Maputo and Dar es Salaam, experienced rising inequalities in an environment of positive economic growth, in other cities, such as Phnom Penh and Kigali, inequalities remained constant in an environment of high economic growth – their Gini coefficients did not change.

Malaysia provides useful lessons in managing high levels of economic growth while reducing poverty and inequality. In Malaysia, urban income inequalities have decreased steadily since 1979, although the levels of inequality in this country are generally higher than in many other Asian countries. Rapid economic growth has also helped reduce levels of urban poverty, which fell from 18.7 per cent of the urban population in 1979 to 2.4 per cent in 1997.[9] Reductions in inequality and poverty were achieved through social programmes for the poor in the short term and investment in human capital and infrastructure, including skills development and gender equity, in the long term.

Changes in levels of urban inequality should also be understood in the context in which they occur. As Figure 2.1.1 indicates, unprecedented economic growth rates in China, India and Malaysia in the last two decades have had different outcomes in urban areas. For instance, even though India experienced high economic growth throughout most of the 1990s, urban inequalities in the country remained more or less constant and there was no dramatic reduction in levels of poverty. In China, urban inequalities have been rising since the 1990s, but gross domestic product (GDP) per capita has quadrupled and poverty levels have dropped drastically. Urban inequalities in China are tempered, however, by the fact that until recently, urban residents had access to public housing subsidies, private housing imputed rent, pension, free medical care and educational subsidies that were not so easily available to rural populations. Of more concern to the Chinese authorities is the income gap between rural and urban populations: in 2003, per capita disposable income of urban residents was more than three times that of rural residents, making China one of the countries with the highest rural-urban inequalities in the world.[10] On the other hand, Malaysia, which has levels of urban inequality that are higher than those of both India and China, has managed to reduce both inequality and poverty levels in the last 30 years, largely owing to systematic implementation of pro-poor policies since the 1970s.

It is important at this point to move beyond the relationship between economic growth and income inequality towards a closer examination of key emerging economies that suggest the positive welfare effects of accelerated economic

Kuala Lumpur: Urban inequality and poverty levels in Malaysia have been decreasing since the 1980s.
©**Loke Yek Mang/Shutterstock**

growth could outweigh the negative effects of rising relative inequality. Furthermore, aggregate welfare gains can be maximized by prioritizing the provision of basic services to lower income groups.

China and India, which have been experiencing staggeringly high economic growth rates since the 1990s, provide useful lessons in this regard. Interestingly, both India and China see their cities as engines of export- and services-oriented economic growth from which they can draw maximum benefits.[11] However, the consequences of urban expansion and growth have been quite different in both countries. China, which had extremely low levels of inequality in the 1980s and 1990s, was able to lift more

than 500 million people out of $1-a-day poverty between 1981 and 2004.[12] On the other hand, India, which had higher levels of inequality during this period, only managed to raise 60 million people above the poverty line between 1983 and 2000, although it has been suggested that access to subsidized food and other subsidies substantially reduced levels of vulnerability among the urban poor.[13] This suggests that countries that have low levels of income inequality to begin with have a better chance of reducing poverty than those in which inequalities are relatively high. World Bank analyses show that on average, for countries with low levels of income inequality, a 1 percentage point growth in mean incomes could lead to a 4 percentage point reduction in the

TABLE 2.1.1: **CHANGE IN URBAN INEQUALITIES (GINI COEFFICIENT) AND GDP PER CAPITA (PPP) IN SELECTED COUNTRIES**

Country	Urban Gini coefficient						GDP per capita (PPP, current US$, country data)					
	year	Gini	year	Gini	% change per annum		year	GDP per capita	year	GDP per capita	% change per annum	
Algeria*	1988	0.39	1995	0.35	-1.64%	-	1988	4110	1995	4531	1.39%	+
Egypt**	1990	0.34	1997	0.39	1.78%	+	1990	2284	1997	3061	4.18%	+
Morocco**	1990	0.377	1998	0.377	0.00%		1990	2724	1998	3502	3.14%	+
Benin**	1999	0.48	2002	0.45	-1.87%	-	1999	929	2002	1046	3.95%	+
Botswana*	1985	0.54	1993	0.54	0.00%		1985	2598	1993	5195	8.66%	+
Côte d'Ivoire*	1993	0.489	1998	0.487	-0.07%	-	1993	1334	1998	1633	4.04%	+
Cameroon*	1983	0.45	1996	0.47	0.33%	+	1983	1616	1996	1600	-0.08%	-
Ethiopia**	1994	0.46	2000	0.43	-0.93%	-	1994	651	2000	814	3.72%	+
China*	1988	0.23	2002	0.32	2.36%	+	1988	1173	2002	4782	10.04%	+
Bangladesh**	1991	0.31	2000	0.37	2.01%	+	1991	1020	2000	1543	4.60%	+
Nepal*	1985	0.26	1996	0.43	4.57%	+	1985	651	1996	1138	5.08%	+
Sri Lanka*	1990	0.37	2002	0.42	1.06%	+	1990	1922	2002	3739	5.55%	+
Pakistan**	2000	0.32	2004	0.34	1.22%	+	2000	1880	2004	2187	3.78%	+
India**	1993/4	0.35	1999/2000	0.34	-0.05%	-	1994	1659	2000	2364	5.90%	+
Cambodia**	1994	0.47	2004	0.43	-0.74%	-	1995	1253	2004	2381	6.42%	+
Viet Nam*	1993	0.35	2002	0.41	1.76%	+	1993	1192	2002	2348	7.53%	+
Brazil*	1990	0.61	2005	0.60	-0.07%	-	1990	5,241	2005	8,402	3.15%	+
Chile*	1990	0.54	2006	0.52	-0.24%	-	1990	4,686	2005	12,027	6.28%	+
Colombia*	1999	0.56	2005	0.59	0.87%	+	1999	5,750	2005	7,304	3.99%	+
Ecuador*	1990	0.46	2005	0.51	0.69%	+	1990	2,639	1999	3,419	1.73%	+
Guatemala*	1989	0.56	2004	0.53	-0.37%	-	1989	2,647	2004	4,401	3.39%	+
Mexico*	1992	0.51	2005	0.50	-0.15%	-	1992	6,920	2005	10,751	3.39%	+
Uruguay*	1990	0.51	2005	0.45	-0.83%	-	1990	5,723	2005	9,962	3.70%	+
Venezuela*	1990	0.46	1994	0.48	0.30%	+	1990	4,702	2002	5,449	1.23%	+
El Salvador*	1991	0.495	2000	0.503	0.18%	+	1991	3,092	2000	4,597	4.41%	+
Honduras*	1990	0.55	1999	0.50	-1.06%	-	1990	2,239	1999	2,725	2.18%	+
Nicaragua*	1993	0.525	1998	0.530	0.19%	+	1993	2,284	1998	2,802	4.09%	+
Peru*	1991	0.43	1997	0.45	0.76%	+	1991	3,228	1997	4,589	5.86%	+

Source: UN-HABITAT Global Urban Observatory, 2008.
Data from various sources, mostly national surveys between 1983 and 2005.
*Note: * Urban Gini coefficient for income*
*** Urban Gini coefficient for consumption*

FIGURE 2.1.1: **URBAN INEQUALITIES IN CHINA, INDIA AND MALAYSIA, 1969-2002**

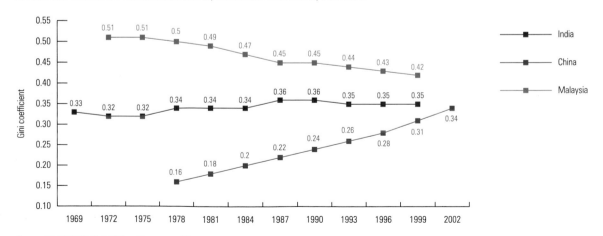

Source: UN-HABITAT, Global Urban Observatory, 2008.
Data for India is from Raghbendra Jha, "Reducing and Inequality in India: Has Liberalization Helped" which was prepared for the WIDER project by UNU.
Data for China is from UNDP, National Human Development Report in China, 2005.
Data for Malaysia is from Ragayah Haji Mat Zin, "Improving Quality of Life after the Crisis: New Dilemmas" Malaysian Journal of Economic Studies; Jun-Dec 2001.
Note: India's Urban Gini coefficient is for consumption, while Urban Gini coefficients for China and Malaysia are for income.

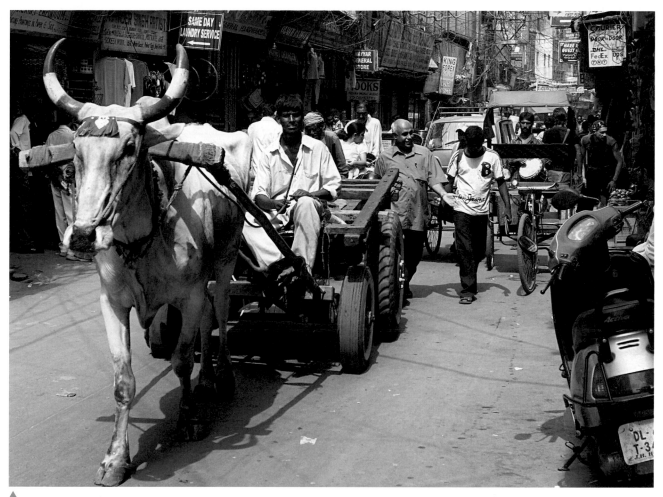

A bazaar in Delhi: Urban inequalities in India are relatively low, but poverty remains a perennial problem.
©**Galina Mikhalishina/Shutterstock**

incidence of $1-a-day poverty. In countries in which income inequalities are high, the same level of growth could result in little or no reduction in poverty.[14] However, while China has been successful in reducing poverty levels on a large scale, it has been unable to bridge the rising inequalities between rural and urban residents, which suggests that the benefits of economic growth have tended to favour urban populations.

The limited impact of economic growth on poverty reduction in India could also be partly explained by the fact that India assigns a relatively low priority to enforcement of policies for the provision of public goods, while industrial policies are given high priority status; China, on the other hand, emphasizes both, at least in urban areas.[15] In China, the strong influence of the state in determining policies has been influential in managing the country's urbanization process, whereas in India, the influence of local institutions, including non-governmental organizations and the private sector, have led to a kind of "spontaneous" urbanization associated with liberalization and consensual decision-making.[16] China's sharp drop in poverty levels, for instance, have been attributed to deliberate agrarian reforms, lower taxes on farmers, investment in urban infrastructure and macroeconomic stability[17]; in India, on the other hand, the role of the state has been comparatively weak in terms of infrastructure development, regulation and enterprise control.

As China increasingly moves toward a market-based economy, however, inequalities in cities and between rural and urban areas may continue to rise. Meanwhile, the Government of India is tackling poverty and inequality in its cities through the National Urban Renewal Mission, which was launched in 2005 and which aims to reduce poverty in 63 Indian cities. Implementation of this seven-year programme may help to bring about large-scale improvements in service delivery and infrastructure in Indian cities, which could impact urban poverty and inequality levels.[18]

Inequalities also have a dampening effect on economic efficiency: they raise the cost of redistribution and affect the allocation of investments, while also creating an unfavourable environment for economic growth and development. Income inequalities impact education and health care outcomes and reduce economic opportunities. In some cases, extreme inequalities can create social and political fractures within society that have the potential to increase social unrest or develop into full-blown conflicts, which discourage investment and induce greater government spending on non-productive sectors, both of which impact economic growth.[19]

The social consequences of inequality in cities

High levels of inequality do not just hamper poverty reduction and economic growth – they impact all aspects of human development. Abundant empirical evidence demonstrates that inequalities affect a host of human development outcomes, including health and education. In cities and countries where inequalities abound and persist, there is a chronic dearth of non-monetary resources for the urban poor, including limited access to opportunities and social mobility. The poor themselves perceive these cities as places with limited prospects, as advantages accrue to a few at the expense of the majority. This is even more evident in places where endemic poverty and high levels of inequality persist alongside visible signs of wealth, creating risks of local tensions, social and political fracturing, forms of violent redistribution of property and widespread social explosion of unpredictable consequences.

Thus, in addition to creating greater social vulnerability by limiting access to basic services, public amenities and opportunities, inequalities are also increasingly associated with social tensions, conflict and different forms of social unrest. Conflicts of this nature cause destruction of infrastructure and property and significant human capital losses through death, displacement and forced migration. In short, conflicts turn back the development clock by several years.

Social unrest, in turn, forces governments to increase the amount of public resources devoted to internal security –

Youths in Kibera slum in Nairobi carry crude weapons ready to fight youths from a rival side. Rising inequalities have been blamed for the violence that engulfed the country after the General Elections in 2007.
©Julius Mwelu/IRIN

resources that might have otherwise been invested in more productive sectors of the economy or in social services. As inequalities rise, the poor and disenfranchised are likely to engage in behaviours that the state perceives as leading to instability, forcing the political and economic elite to resort to different forms of repression, using resources that were designated for redistribution. This scenario risks the formation of "bandit" economies, in which the few who have access to state resources and security benefit at the expense of the majority.

Gross inequalities also substantially reduce incentives to participate in the formal labour force, as those outside of it often perceive few or no prospects for upward mobility in formal-economy jobs. Lack of opportunity in the legitimate labour force may motivate the poor and marginalized to engage in illegal activities and to divert their resources away from formal, productive activities into informal activities that are not subject to taxation, and which may have negative social consequences.

In cities, inequalities manifest themselves physically, as wealth and poverty are often spatially concentrated. In many cities, rich, well-serviced neighbourhoods and gated residential communities are often located near dense inner-city or peri-urban slum communities that lack even the most basic services. This form of spatial inequality can often have more serious consequences than income inequality, as the poor and the rich are physically separated in enclaves that generate mistrust and alienation, eventually triggering various forms of social discontent. In many cases, slums become the sites of riots and violent protests. In 2005, South Africa reported 881 protests in urban slums, at least 50 of which turned violent[20]; three years later, in 2008, slums in Johannesburg became the sites of more violence as unemployed South Africans vented their anger at immigrants from other African countries, while rising food prices sparked protests in several other cities in Africa, Asia and Latin America. In China, increasing disparities between rural and urban populations and among regions have also been accompanied by protests, sit-ins, group petitions and public order disturbances,[21] which have prompted the Chinese government to implement reforms allowing for a smoother transition from a planned economy to a market-based economy with the aim of "building a harmonious society".[22]

Inequalities also have psychological costs. New empirical evidence shows that inequalities have negative effects on happiness where signs of persistent unfairness and unrelenting disadvantages for the urban poor exist.[23] Although most of the studies linking inequality and happiness have taken place in developed countries, evidence is conclusive that socio-economic phenomena, such as unemployment and income inequality, negatively effect subjective well-being. For instance, a study in 23 European countries found that people most directly affected by inequalities are unhappy because of their lower social mobility.[24] Similar studies have found that inequality has a significant negative impact on happiness, particularly when individuals perceive that opportunities for upward mobility are limited.

Inequalities in society can have serious political repercussions. Social and economic inequalities can awaken a host of negative sentiments among the poor and dispossessed and lead to mass action, or worse, civil strife, either because disparities are not acknowledged and thus not remedied, or because corrective measures such as laws and redistribution policies attempt to entrench the status quo or seek to placate those mired in a highly unequal system. Inequalities can also reduce the base of social and political support for fundamental structural reforms necessary to embark on a path of high growth with more equity; basically because some groups may perceive that the gains of the reform may not be equitably distributed.[25] In all of these cases, the cost of maintaining inequalities is much higher than the cost of reducing them.

Acting now to prevent tomorrow's urban rebellion

The ancient Greek philosopher Plato argued that "if a state is to avoid … civil disintegration … extreme poverty and wealth must not be allowed to rise in any section of the citizen-body because both lead to disasters".[26] When the disadvantaged realize that economic growth and development do not benefit them directly, or when they perceive that they will never attain their desired living standard and expected personal outcomes despite contributing to economic growth with their labour, it is likely that they will react to perceived or real unfairness through protest, violence or apathy, depending on prevailing cultural and political norms. The responses driven by indignation can entail different forms of rebellion that can range from simple protests to full-blown civil war as the disadvantaged seek more equal relationships or punish those they perceive to have behaved unfairly by violently transforming the status quo.[27]

In view of the political, economic and social costs of inequality, cities and countries need to act now to reduce income and consumption inequalities and other forms of social injustice. The risks of not addressing deep inequalities are social unrest and possibly conflict. The situation can become particularly explosive when inequalities are associated with individual ethnic, religious or minority groups and not just individuals. The cultural, social or political conditions that create different forms of horizontal inequality are primed for political instability and high risks of generalized civil conflict.[28]

Many countries have started to address inequalities before they erupt into a political or social crisis. For instance, the "Grow with Equity" policy in Iran brought greater equality to urban residents at the end of the 1990s. In Indonesia, under the "Growth, Stability and Equity" programme, economic and social policies on income distribution and poverty alleviation were important determinants of growth and economic development. The Indonesian policies led to reductions in income inequality in urban areas by 8.3 per cent from 1976 to 1993.[29] Despite the financial crises that affected many Asian countries in the second half of the 1990s, and despite

City landscape, Yogyakarta, Java: Economic and social policies on income distribution and poverty reduction have led to a reduction in urban inequalities in Indonesia.
©**Morozova Tatyana/Shutterstock**

registering negative economic growth from 1996 to 2002, Indonesia has managed to reduce urban income inequalities by 4 points: the Gini coefficient dropped from 0.36 to 0.32. Similarly, pro-poor policies helped reduce inequalities in the Philippines, where a decrease in income was proportionally less, on average, among poor households than among non-poor households in a period of economic recession, leading to a reduction in the country's urban Gini coefficient from 0.46 to 0.41 from 1997 to 2003.

The reduction of inequality is not simply a matter of providing better distribution of wealth or income. In many cases, more equitable distribution of monetary resources must also be accompanied by better health care, nutrition and education for larger portions of the population. Several studies have abundantly verified that cities that have high levels of inequality have lower human development indicators than cities that have low levels of inequality.[30] Similar studies have found a clear relationship between a country or city's level of inequality and the degree of intergenerational socioeconomic mobility i.e. children of parents who are poor

are likely to also be poor. Some countries have addressed intergenerational inequality by enforcing laws that specifically address past injustices. South Africa, for instance, introduced subsidies and social reforms after the dismantling of the apartheid system in the early 1990s, which led to a decrease in income inequality by 1 per cent per annum between 2001 and 2005.[31] This positive development should, however, be tempered by the fact that inequality in South African cities remains significantly high.

In all of the countries mentioned above, social institutions were created or reinforced when the countries experienced rapid growth, with the aim of improving the lives of the urban poor and reducing levels of inequality. These successful experiences show that institutional reforms and government interventions can efficiently maintain or reduce income disparities during periods of high-speed growth. They also demonstrate that it is possible to realize equity in the distribution of income through market mechanisms and distributive government policies. In other words, they show that market efficiency and equity can go hand in hand.

Bhutan's Gross National Happiness Index

For many years, the international development community has struggled to define what constitutes human progress and well-being. The conventional approach – reflected in the United Nations Human Development Index – has been to measure human development within countries through measurable quantitative indicators, such as life expectancy, literacy and Gross Domestic Product (GDP) per capita.

However, long before demographers, economists and development experts had started to think about how to measure prosperity and development, the tiny land-locked Himalayan kingdom of Bhutan began a serious discourse on whether quantitative indicators accurately reflected levels of well-being in society. In 1972, concerned about the negative effects of unrestrained economic growth, Bhutan's newly-crowned leader, H.M. King Jigme Wangchuk, introduced the concept of Gross National Happiness (GNH), which is based in the premise that true development of human society takes place when material and spiritual development occur side by side and complement and reinforce each other. The four key pillars of Bhutan's Gross National Happiness are: promotion of equitable and sustainable socio-economic development; preservation and promotion of cultural values; conservation of the natural environment; and establishment of good governance.

Bhutan's National Human Development Report 2000 states that the country considers GNH to be far more important than GDP because its focus is on "enriching people's lives, improving their standard of living, and augmenting people's economic, spiritual and emotional well-being". The report further argues that economic indicators do not adequately capture many aspects of Bhutan's largely rural economy, which is non-monetised, and fail to reflect the kingdom's vast and diverse natural resources and its rich cultural and religious heritage.

Bhutan 2020, the country's long-term development blueprint, notes that Bhutan's approach to development is firmly rooted in its rich tradition of Mahayana Buddhism that stresses "individual development, sanctity of life, compassion for others, respect for nature, social harmony, and the importance of compromise". The Vision also cautions that while modernization and urbanization have their benefits, they may erode the values and assets that Bhutan has built over the centuries and may lead to negative consequences, such as high levels of urban poverty and environmental degradation.

However, although Bhutan has accepted GNH as the basic tool for measuring its level of development, measuring "happiness" remains an elusive quest. Most studies on happiness are conducted using self-reporting techniques, and are therefore, highly subjective.

Nonetheless, Bhutan's outlook on development is increasingly being adopted by other countries in the region and elsewhere.

In 2006, for instance, the Chinese government endorsed the new doctrine of "building a harmonious society" that emphasizes balance, moderation, social equity, justice, cultural harmony and coordinated development. The doctrine is being implemented to mitigate some of the negative effects of unrestrained economic growth, including rising inequalities and environmental degradation. While recognizing that a harmonious society needs to be relatively wealthy and needs to meet its basic needs, China is also realizing that rising inequalities in society can contribute to social disharmony.

Like China, many countries are now beginning to wonder whether they got it all wrong when they assumed that rapid economic growth and high per capita incomes would boost overall well-being in their countries. Researchers, such as Martin Seligman, credited for launching the positive psychology movement in 1998, and Ruut Veenhooven, who created the World Database of Happiness in 1999, are also encouraging policymakers to consider more than economic development in their planning and to examine ways in which governments can boost national contentment levels.

Sources: Royal Government of Bhutan, 2000; Xinhua News Agency, 2006

FIGURE 2.1.2: **SOCIAL MOBILITY AND EQUITY IN SOUTH AFRICAN CITIES – CLASS COMPOSITION**

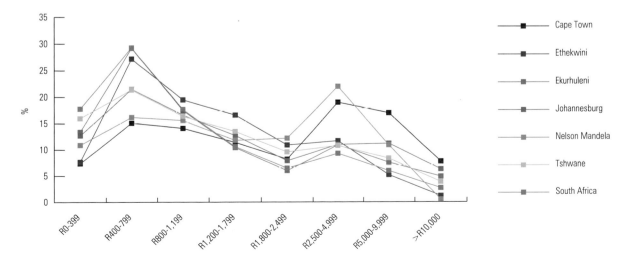

Income (South African Rand)

Source: Statistics South Africa: General Household Survey, 2006.

New dimensions of inequality in emerging economies: Recent evidence from China, India and Brazil

The recent economic experience of major developing economies shows that rising per capita income is often accompanied by greater income inequality. Despite the increasing global economic influence of emerging economies, such as China, India and Brazil, recent research suggests that they are increasingly reluctant "to challenge the contemporary world order and the widening income and wealth inequalities within their borders." It is further argued, however, that growing inequalities can lead to socio-political instability and thus eventually compromise economic growth.

There are many reasons for rising income inequality, ranging from "traditional" causes – such as concentration of land ownership and unequal access to education – to "new" causes, such as technological change and associated wage differentials. For example, unequal access to land is closely linked to income inequality and poverty in both China and India, whereas access to education by household head is a critical determinant of economic status in India, though not in China, where fewer are illiterate.

Strong evidence also exists that increasing wage and income inequality in India is attributed to skill-biased technological change and greater wage differentials within key urban economic sectors. Further evidence shows that rising income inequality in both developing and developed countries is closely associated with the rising capital share of total income and, conversely, the declining labour share. In the case of India, the share of total income accruing to the top one per cent of income and dividend earners in the 1990s increased from 4 per cent to almost 11 per cent.

This has generated an intense, and so far inconclusive, debate about whether the positive welfare effects of accelerated economic growth are outweighed by the negative effects of rising relative inequality. Part of the problem surrounding this debate is that per capita income (as a measure of economic growth) and relative income inequality (as measured by the Gini coefficient) are often examined in isolation from each other.

Recent comparative research on Brazil and China has attempted to find relationships between the two by evaluating the overall welfare effects of per capita income growth and relative inequality in the distribution of income simultaneously. It concludes that while inequality has worsened in

A slum settlement in Mumbai: Unequal access to land and skill biased technological change has led to greater wage differentials in key urban economic sectors.
©**Rasna Warah**

both countries over the past two decades, economic welfare in Brazil actually increased following implementation of a programme launched in 1994 that contained a set of drastic fiscal and monetary measures to stabilize the Brazilian economy. As the researchers discovered, "the rise in income ... was sufficient to overcome the negative effects of a slight worsening of inequality over the whole period".

In China, economic welfare rose even more spectacularly over the past two decades, as the rapid increase in per capita income was more than sufficient to counteract the negative effects of increased relative inequality. New evidence incorporating spatial price deflators also suggests that the magnitude of income inequality in China, as well as the role played by regional and urban-rural differences in the recent inequality rise, tends to be overstated. On the other hand, since consumption inequality (arguably a better indication of economic welfare than income inequality) in both urban and rural areas rose significantly between 1985 and 2001, the overall welfare increase in the country may be smaller than previously estimated.

The overall welfare increase in both Brazil and China is thus more complex when disaggregated by its urban-rural dimension or by levels of income. For example, contrary to frequent assumptions, evidence suggests that rural incomes are less equally distributed than urban incomes in China. Urban inequality was thus lower than rural inequality between 1985 and 2001, although it has been rising much faster as urbanization accelerates in the country.

A closer look at the welfare gains caused by fast economic growth in large emerging countries shows that higher-income groups have benefited far more than lower-income groups, particularly in urban areas, even if overall welfare has increased across the board. Furthermore, when there is a serious downturn in the economy, as Brazil experienced during the 1980s, it is the poor who suffer most.

One key policy implication for fast-growing emerging economies is that priority in the provision of basic urban services should be given to lower-income groups, as they tend to experience greater welfare effects than higher-income groups with the same expenditure of public resources. Increased public expenditure on primary schools, basic health services and provision of water supply and sanitation for poor urban districts thus improves the lives of more people than equal expenditures on universities, advanced medical services or increased piped water for the swimming pools and manicured lawns of wealthy neighbourhoods.

Sources: Palat, in press; Borooah, Gustafsson & Li, 2006; Kijima, 2006; Cornia, 2005; Cloes, 2008; Demurger, Fournier & Li, 2006; Wu & Perloff, 2004.

Slum in Rio de Janeiro: Healthy economic indicators in Brazil have had little impact on inequality levels.
©Ceiso Pupo/Shutterstock

NOTES

1. World Bank, 2006 and United Nations 2007.
2. World Bank, 2006.
3. This report analyses inequality in income and consumption, as these are the most commonly used variables in inequality surveys.
4. World Bank, 2007a.
5. Williamson, 1965. This work elaborated on earlier work done by S. Kuznets (1955), whose inverted "U" hypothesis made a strong link between inequality and economic growth.
6. Refer among other studies to Tony & Giovanni, 2001; Franco, 2002; and Kanbur, 2000.
7. These countries were: (Africa) Algeria, Benin, Botswana, Cameroon, Cote d'Ivoire, Egypt, Ethiopia, and Morocco; (Asia) Bangladesh, Cambodia, China, India, Nepal, Pakistan, Sri Lanka, and Viet Nam; and (Latin America and the Caribbean) Brazil, Chile, Colombia, Ecuador, El Salvador, Guatemala, Honduras, Mexico, Nicaragua, Peru, Uruguay, and Venezuela.
8. Analysis by UN-HABITAT in 2008.
9. Zin, 2001.
10. UNDP and China Development Research Foundation, 2005.
11. Biau, 2007
12. World Bank, 2007.
13. UNDP National Human Development Report (India), 2001. Data from Planning Commission, Government of India.
14. "Low" and "high" inequality refers to Gini coefficients of 0.3 and 0.6, respectively.
15. Oyelaran-Oyeyinka, & Gehl Sampath, in press.
16. Biau, 2007
17. World Bank, 2008.
18. Biau, 2007. The National Urban Renewal Mission is supported by a central government budget of US$12.5 billion over seven years.
19. Persson, & Tabellini, 1994.
20. Wines, 2005.
21. Lum, 2006.
22. Xinhua News Agency, 2006. The resolution on social harmony, published in October 2006, highlights "coordinated development" and "social equity and justice", among other goals and principles.
23. Graham & Felton, 2006.
24. Alesina, Di Tella & MacCulloch, 2001.
25. Rodriguez, 2002.
26. Quoted in World Bank, 2005.
27. Ullmann-Margalit, & Sunstein, 2001.
28. Addison & Cornia, 2001.
29. Akita & Lukman, 1999.
30. Messias, 2003. This study found that for each 0.01 increase in the Gini coefficient, life expectancy declined by 0.6 years in an analysis conducted in all the Brazilian federal states.
31. South African Cities Network, 2006.

2.2
Urban Inequalities:
Regional Trends

▲
Homeless in New York
©Emin Kuliyev/Shutterstock

Methodology

This chapter provides preliminary results of an analysis of income and consumption/expenditure inequality at the urban or city level undertaken by UN-HABITAT's Global Urban Observatory in 2007/2008. Although income and expenditure variables do not represent a holistic view of the entire range of inequalities experienced by populations, such as inequalities in access to land or education, they are the most commonly collected measures in national household surveys and are useful for standardizing and comparing inequalities across regions and cities. Using a relatively large dataset of Gini coefficients for 94 cities in 47 countries, an additional 68 countries with data aggregated at the national urban level and 61 provinces with urban data, the findings described in this chapter reflect urban inequalities in a total of 72 countries. The years for which changes in urban inequalities at the national or city level are calculated range from 1983 to 2005. The data used in this analysis is derived mainly from official statistics and national household surveys.

The findings on urban income distribution not only provide information on levels of stratification of household earnings in selected cities, but also provide some information on economic and social welfare at the city level. The analysis details income distribution in selected cities as a way to understand local urban dynamics and to measure the success or failure of local policies and development strategies that do not necessarily mirror what is happening on the national scene. The findings of the analysis are intended to help policymakers, urban planners and others gain some insight into the possible causes of urban inequality and deepen their understanding of intra-city differentials.

Income Inequalities and Urban Development: Understanding New Patterns and Trends to Reshape Policies

A growing number of statisticians, demographers, economists, and policymakers are recognizing that country-level calculations of inequalities often mask the degree of inequality across regions and locations. Evidence shows that national trends cannot explain what is happening in all cities and regions in the same country because the drivers of growth and the reasons for inequality vary in each location. Studies at the local level demonstrate that it is possible to find huge variations in income distribution in different cities and regions of the same country. National aggregates thus hide more than they reveal. For instance, the level of income inequality in Beijing is exactly half of the national index of income distribution, making it one of the most egalitarian cities in China. Conversely, income inequality in Maputo, the capital of Mozambique, is significantly higher than the national average, making it the most unequal city in the country.

National calculations of inequality also mask differences between rural and urban areas. In rural Kenya, for example, inequalities are declining, while urban inequalities are rising; the Gini coefficient of expenditure in rural areas fell from 0.417 in 1997 to 0.38 in 2006, while the urban Gini coefficient of expenditure rose from 0.426 to 0.447 during the same period. Interestingly, the proportion of people living in poverty in urban areas fell from 49.2 per cent in 1997 to 33.7 per cent in 2006, which could be a result of the significant rise in economic growth after 2003, which may have impacted some sections of low-income urban populations positively.[1] Similarly, in Chile, a study on income inequality at the county level shows huge differences in levels of inequality among various counties; the Gini coefficient for counties ranged from 0.41 to 0.61 (A Gini coefficient value above 0.4 generally denotes relatively high levels of inequality while a Gini coefficient value between 0.2 and 0.39 denotes moderate or low levels of inequality).[2]

Over the last two decades, international development efforts have increasingly focused on poverty reduction rather than on inequality. Yet, as discussed in the previous chapter, rising inequalities can hamper socio-economic development, poverty reduction efforts and economic growth. Gross inequalities can also create conditions conducive to social unrest and conflict.

Inequality levels have risen since the 1980s, especially in transition countries and some emerging economies of the developing world.[3] At the global level, on average, the most egalitarian cities in the world are located in Western Europe. Income inequalities are also low in most urban areas of Eastern Europe, with the exception of Moldova, followed by cities in the countries of the Commonwealth of Independent States (CIS) region, excluding Russia, Azerbaijan and Turkmenistan, where income inequalities are relatively high. In other developed countries, such as Japan, Australia and Canada, inequalities in cities are also relatively low.

In the developing world, on the other hand, income inequalities in cities are generally high, with some regions, notably Latin America and Africa, exhibiting exceptionally high levels of urban inequality. Latin American and African countries in which cities exhibit extremely high levels of inequality include Brazil, Colombia, Kenya, Namibia, South Africa, and Zimbabwe. Conversely, Asian cities tend to reflect moderate or relatively low levels of inequality.

FIGURE 2.2.1: **AVERAGE GINI COEFFICIENT OF SELECTED CITIES BY REGION**

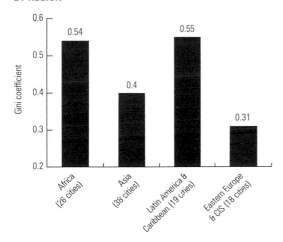

Source: UN-HABITAT, Global Urban Observatory, 2008.
Data from UN-ECLAC, UN-ESCAP, UNU and other sources.
Note: Gini data is a mix of income and consumption. Africa (income: 15 cities, consumption: 11 cities), Asia (income: 37 cities, consumption: 2 cities), LAC (all data are on income), Eastern Europe and CIS (all data are on income) Years of data are various.

FIGURE 2.2.2: **AVERAGE URBAN GINI COEFFICIENT BY REGION**

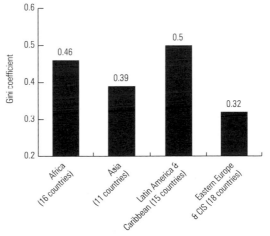

Source: UN-HABITAT, Global Urban Observatory, 2008.
Data from UN-ECLAC, UN-ESCAP, UNU and other sources.
Note: Gini data is a mix of income and consumption. Africa (income: 8 countries, consumption: 8 countries), Asia (income: 6 countries, consumption: 5 countries), LAC (all data are on income), Eastern Europe and CIS (all data are on income) Years of data are various.

Inequalities in cities of the developed world

European countries, particularly Denmark, Finland, the Netherlands, and Slovenia, exhibit relatively low levels of inequality (Gini coefficient below 0.25, the lowest in the world). Inequalities are also low in Austria, Belgium, France, Germany, Luxemburg, Norway, Sweden, and Switzerland, where the Gini coefficents range from between 0.25 and 0.3. Low levels of inequality reflect the performance of national and regional economies in these countries and the regulatory, distributive and redistributive capacity of the national and local welfare states.[4] Countries with relatively high inequalities by European standards are Greece, Ireland and Italy, (Gini coefficients between 0.32 and 0.33); Portugal (0.363); the United Kingdom (0.343); and Spain (0.34).

Within cities, however, significant differences in unemployment rates have been observed among neighbourhoods, illustrating clear income inequalities. An urban audit of 258 cities in the European Union found that the highest inter-neighbourhood differences were recorded in cities with high overall unemployment. Neighbourhood disparities in unemployment are particularly noticeable in France, Belgium and southern Italy, countries with high unemployment rates in general but are also significant in the cities of Eastern Germany, larger Spanish cities and the north of England. Long-term unemployment rates among elderly workers (aged between 55 and 64) is very high in Belgium, while youth unemployment is particularly high in Central

FIGURE 2.2.3: **INTRA-CITY DIFFERENCES IN UNEMPLOYMENT IN LONDON, BERLIN, STOCKHOLM AND MADRID, 2001**

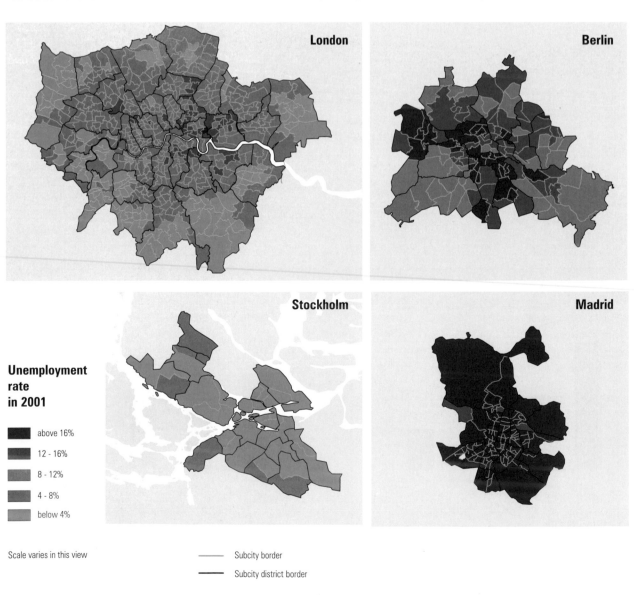

Unemployment rate in 2001

- above 16%
- 12 - 16%
- 8 - 12%
- 4 - 8%
- below 4%

Scale varies in this view

—— Subcity border

—— Subcity district border

Source: Urban Audit Data Base, State of European Cities Report 2007 - European Community, Directorate General for Regional Policy.

and Eastern European and French cities.[5] Differences in levels of employment among various neighbourhoods within the same city could affect the social cohesion of these cities.

The Gini coefficient in *Australia's* urban areas ranges from 0.332 in major cities to 0.31 in small cities in remote parts of the country.[6] In Tokyo, the capital of Japan, the Gini coefficient is 0.33, and is likely to increase[7] as emerging economies of other Asian countries deprive Japanese blue-collar workers of highly remunerated employment. Inequality is likely to grow, too, as the service sector grows, particularly in information technology, a market that is bringing disproportionate rewards to the most highly skilled workers.[8]

Although cities in the *United States of America* have relatively lower levels of poverty than many other cities in the developed world, levels of income inequality are quite high, and have risen above the international alert line of 0.4.[9] Large cities in the United States tend to be more unequal than small cities. Major metropolitan areas, such as Atlanta, New Orleans, Washington D.C., Miami, and New York, have the highest levels of inequality in the country,[10] similar to those of Abidjan, Nairobi, Buenos Aires, and Santiago (Gini coefficient of more than 0.50).

Canada's, Gini coefficient is approximately 0.35. However, inequalities are increasing in most of the country's urban areas. In Toronto, for example, median family income in the poorest 10 per cent of neighbourhoods has risen by 0.2 per cent since 1980. In the richest 10 per cent, on the other hand, family incomes rose by 24 per cent. This increasing difference is observed in all large metropolitan areas in Canada.[11]

In Australia, Canada and the United States, one of the most important factors determining levels of inequality is race. In western New York state, for instance, nearly 40 per cent of the black, Hispanic, and mixed-race households earned less than US $15,000 in 1999, compared with 15 per cent of non-Hispanic white households.[12] The life expectancy of African Americans in the United States is about the same as that of people living in China and some states of India, despite the fact that the United States is far richer than the other two countries.[13] Racial inequalities in Canada are also significant. In Winnipeg, for instance, the employment rate of Aboriginal people was 65 per cent in 2001, compared with 85 per cent among non-Aboriginal people; the same year, the annual employment income of Aboriginal people in Canada was only 68 per cent of that of their non-Aboriginal counterparts.[14] These countries are not only witnessing income polarization, but spatial polarization as well; in Canada and the United States, the urban poor are often clustered together, particularly in the inner core of cities.[15]

Inequalities in transition countries

Perhaps nowhere has poverty and inequality spread so rapidly during the last decade than in the transition economies of Eastern Europe and the former Soviet Union, which were hit by unprecedented declines in gross domestic product (GDP) per capita and a marked increase in income inequality

in the 1990s.[16] Studies suggest that the introduction of market reforms led to income polarization in various transition countries.[17] In Uzbekistan, for instance, between 1991 and 1995 and between 1996 and 2000, the bottom 10 per cent of the population earned only 5 per cent of the country's total income, while the income share of the richest 10 per cent rose from 24 to 29 per cent, and the ratio of the income shares of the two groups grew from 9.7 per cent to 11.6 per cent in the same years.[18] Inequality has also increased in the Baltic republics of Estonia and Lithuania, which have witnessed rapid economic growth in recent years.[19] Increases in urban poverty and different forms of inequality were also registered

▲
Tallinn city, Estonia: Income inequalities have risen in several transition economies of Eastern Europe.
© **Marek Slusarczyk/iStockphoto**

in Hungary and Poland, two nations that have long been characterized by low Gini coefficients (0.29) but where social safety nets that kept inequality levels low, are being eroded.

Despite a positive sign of income inequalities declining in Georgia and Russia at the national level in the late 1990s (suggesting that households with below average income had benefitted from recent economic growth,[20] particularly in

▲
Housing in Macau city.
©**Sam D Cruz/Shutterstock**

rural areas), studies at the city level in Russia show that the distribution of income is, in fact, becoming more unequal. An analysis of the small city of Taganrog near the Black Sea showed that the Gini coefficient increased from 0.22 in 1989 to 0.382 in 2000, an increase that is reflected in other Russian cities.[21] Inequality in urban Russia, as in other former Soviet republics emerging from a centralized planned economy to a market economy, has been accompanied by a rapid decline in production that causes real wages to decrease substantially, which, along with growing unemployment, has increased uncertainty and volatility in urban areas.

It is clear that the burden of the economic transition in these countries has not been shared equally. It has even been suggested that income inequalities in urban areas may be higher and growing faster than what is reported because the method of estimation systematically over-samples the rich and under-reports the poor. The prevalence of high levels of inequality and worsening conditions are further demonstrated by a surprising increase in morbidity and mortality rates in these countries, which can be attributed not only to the sharp decline in public expenditure, but also to rising unemployment, low salaries and increased marginalization of the urban poor.

Inequalities in cities of the developing world

Levels of income distribution and consumption vary considerably among less-developed regions. Many countries in the developing world are enjoying rapid, positive economic growth, but a large majority of their populations are not benefitting from the new wealth. On the other hand, in countries that are experiencing negative economic growth or recessions, low-income populations are becoming more marginalized. For instance, the share of national income of the wealthiest 10 per cent of the population in India in 2004 and 2005 – when the country's economy was growing at more than 7 per cent – was nearly ten times that of the poorest 10 per cent. Deep income inequalities were even more evident in Brazil, where the wealthiest 10 per cent of the population enjoyed 45 per cent of the national income in 2005, while the poorest 10 per cent received only 0.9 per cent the same year. In some rapidly growing Asian economies, the prevalence of poverty has decreased in an environment of rising inequalities, while in some poorly performing economies in Latin America and Africa, levels of both urban poverty and inequality have increased. The booming Chinese economy, which was growing at a remarkable 9.5 per cent a year in 2004, has dramatically reduced levels of poverty in the country, but inequalities between rural and urban areas have increased. This suggests that growth processes at the national and global levels have not had the same effect in all countries, and that they depend very much on how wealth is distributed nationally. In most countries, the rich or the skilled tend to capture a much larger share of the national income than the poor; there are, however, significant regional and local variations with different outcomes.

Latin America and the Caribbean

Latin America and the Caribbean is the land of inequality: Gini coefficients in urban areas and several cities in the region are among the highest in the world. Moreover, a mere 5 per cent of the population receives a quarter of all national income, compared to South-Eastern Asian countries, where the wealthiest 5 per cent receive 16 per cent of all national income, and developed countries, where the richest 5 per cent receive 13 per cent. Meanwhile, the poorest 30 per cent of the population in Latin America and the Caribbean receives only 7.5 per cent of the national income, a figure that is not comparable to any other part of the world; in even the most unequal societies, the poorest groups typically receive at least 10 per cent of the national income.[22]

The high levels of inequality in the region are accompanied by slow-growing or volatile economies; per capita GDP in 2002 was below the level recorded in 1997.[23] Even in countries that are experiencing high economic growth rates, such as Brazil and Mexico, urban inequalities remain a persistent problem. UN-HABITAT analysis shows that the average Gini coefficient for urban areas of 15 countries in the region is 0.50 and the average Gini coefficient for 19 selected cities is 0.55,[24] which is extremely high when compared with urban India, where the average Gini coefficient for expenditure was 0.37 in 2005.

Latin America is the only region in the developing world where inequalities between urban and rural areas are similar

FIGURE 2.2.4: **URBAN INEQUALITIES IN LATIN AMERICA AND THE CARIBBEAN**

Urban Gini Coefficient

- No Data
- 0.25 - 0.29
- 0.30 - 0.39
- 0.40 - 0.49
- 0.50 - 0.59
- 0.60 & Above

City Gini Coefficient

- 0.25 - 0.29
- 0.30 - 0.39
- 0.40 - 0.49
- 0.50 - 0.59
- 0.60 & Above

Note: Urban Gini Coefficients denote Gini Coefficients for the total urban population of a country

City Gini Coefficients denote Gini Coefficients at the city level

0   1,500 km   3,000 km

N

Source: UN-HABITAT Global Urban Observatory, 2008

(0.5 in 15 countries).[25] In four of these countries – Bolivia, Honduras, Guatemala, and Nicaragua – inequalities are higher in rural areas, exhibiting the highest difference of up to 15 points. These countries are characterized by very low urbanization levels (53.5 per cent versus 80.2 per cent in most other countries in the region); low per capita gross national income (GNI) (US $1,370 versus US $4,205); relatively low levels of industrial development and an important agricultural base that represented just less than one-fifth of the national structure of outputs by sectors in 2005, twice that of other countries in the region.[26] In only two countries – Chile and Mexico – are levels of urban and rural inequality practically identical, with average Gini values of approximately 0.52 and 0.50, respectively.

At the city level, the most unequal cities in this region include the Brazilian cities of Goiania, Brasilia, Belo Horizonte, Fortaleza, and São Paulo, and the Colombian city of Bogota – all with a Gini coefficient of above 0.60, which is considered extremely high by international standards. These are very closely followed by Rio de Janeiro and Curitiba in Brazil, which have Gini coefficients of just below 0.60, Buenos Aires and Catamarca in Argentina, Santiago in Chile, Quito in Ecuador, and Guatemala and Mexico City (the capital cities of Guatemala and Mexico, respectively), where the Gini coefficients ranged from 0.50 to 0.56 in 2005. Cities that have relatively low levels of inequality compared to the regional average include Caracas in Venezuela, Montevideo in Uruguay, and the city of Guadalajara in Mexico, where the Gini coefficient was below 0.45 in 2002.[27]

Despite progress in some countries, the data and analysis show that levels of income concentration are exceptionally high in Latin America and the Caribbean and have remained so since the 1990s. It is clear that the path to development in the region has not lessened inequalities. The cumulative effect of unequal distribution stretching over various phases of development – from post-war industrial-led growth to structural adjustment, liberalization and reforms – has been a deep and lasting division between the rich and poor. The macroeconomic policies adopted since the 1990s have apparently had negative distributional effects because they have not brought about structural changes in distribution. A study conducted by the Economic Commission for Latin America and the Caribbean (ECLAC) in nine countries in the region shows that the adoption of reforms in favour of unregulated markets, private investments and a greater integration in the international economy produced an abrupt and significant deterioration in income distribution both in rural and urban areas.[28] Unlike some Asian countries, trade liberalization or provision of public goods and infrastructure did not bring about expected benefits in the reduction of income polarization in cities. In Mexico, for instance, the urban Gini coefficient has fluctuated from 0.5 to 0.56,[29] even though the country has made important progress in health, education and other development indicators. This suggests that improved access to basic services does not always translate into increased income for the urban poor; sometimes it is necessary to introduce structural changes that would distribute incomes more evenly.[30]

FIGURE 2.2.5: **URBAN AND RURAL GINI COEFFICIENTS FOR SELECTED DEVELOPING COUNTRIES**

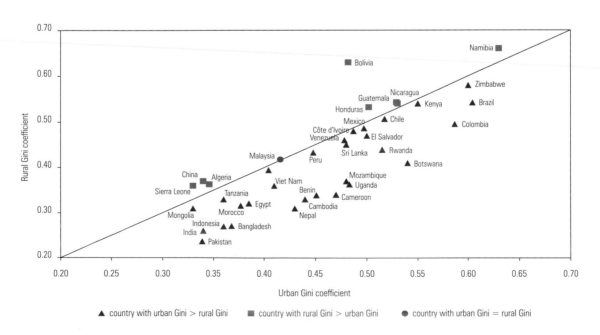

Source: UN-HABITAT Global Urban Observatory, 2008.
Note: Data is from UN-ECLAC, UN-ESCAP, UNU and other sources, various years.
Gini data are mix of income and consumption. Africa (income: 8 countries, consumption: 8 countries), Asia (income: 6 countries, consumption: 5 countries), Latin America and the Caribbean (all for income).

São Paulo, Brazil.
©**iStockphoto**

FIGURE 2.2.6: **GINI COEFFICIENT FOR SELECTED CITIES IN LATIN AMERICA AND THE CARIBBEAN**

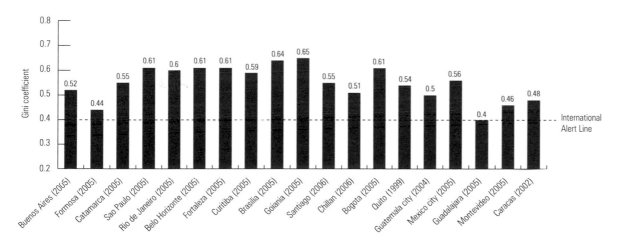

Source: UN-HABITAT, Global Urban Observatory, 2008.
Data from UN-ECLAC, for various years.
Note: All Gini coefficients are for income.
International alert line denotes Gini coefficient value above which inequalities can have negative social, economic and political consequences. The alert line was established by UN-HABITAT in consultation with its partners.

Inequalities in the region can also be partially explained by the adoption of industrialization processes based on capital-intensive industries that contributed to exacerbating the negative effects of sluggish GDP growth. For instance, in Brazil, unemployment rose from 4.3 per cent in 1990 to 12.3 per cent in 2003, and average wages of employees in the formal industrial sector fell by 4.3 per cent in 2003. Unemployment and declining wages in urban areas have polarized income distribution in urban areas.[31] For this and other historical reasons, Brazilian cities today have the greatest disparities in income distribution in the world. Inequalities in this country are rooted in structural causes, such as poor educational attainment among certain groups, land ownership patterns, inappropriate economic policies and, paradoxically, distributional policies.[32] Surprisingly, democratic processes that involve citizens' participation – which have created more opportunities for lower-income groups to influence institutions and policies that lead to greater redistribution of income – have had little or no impact on income inequalities; in fact, inequalities have grown. For instance, the metropolitan area of Porto Alegre, which is lauded for its participatory budgeting and inclusive policies,[33] registered a significant increase in levels of inequality, with the Gini coefficient increasing from 0.473 in 1991 to 0.495, in 2000.[34] However, it is possible that without participatory budgeting, this Brazilian city would have recorded even higher inequality levels.

Income inequalities in most cities and countries in this highly unequal region have not only increased in general, but have also grown in the places considered to be the most progressive in the region.[35] Buenos Aires, the capital of Argentina, for instance, has experienced a steadily unequal trend in the distribution of household income since the 1970s, resulting in an exacerbation of inequality, as evidenced by a rise in the Gini coefficient from 0.360 in 1974 to 0.510 in 2001.[36] Likewise, urban Costa Rica, which had one of the lowest levels of inequality in the region in 1990 (0.39) has since experienced a significant increase in inequality, with the Gini coefficient rising to 0.404 in 2006.[37] These alarming trends indicate that despite progressive policies and practices in recent years, the region still has a long way to go toward addressing some of the root causes of inequality, including the structural and systemic flaws that favour some groups in relation to income and opportunities at the expense of others.

Africa

Sub-Saharan African countries have the highest levels of urban poverty in the world. Although rural poverty is pervasive in the region, more than 50 per cent of the urban population in the poorest countries lives below the poverty line.[38] Poverty often manifests itself in inequality in access to adequate housing. In 2005, six out of every ten urban residents in the region were slum dwellers – nearly double the proportion of the rest of the developing world, and four times that of Northern Africa, where slum prevalence is approximately 15 per cent, and where slum growth is slowing.[39]

Sub-Saharan Africa is also the most unequal region in the world in terms of educational attainment. The Gini coefficient for education in the region is 0.59, much higher than that of Latin America and the Caribbean (0.34) and Europe, the most egalitarian region in the world, where the Gini coefficient for education is 0.19, denoting near-universal access to education.[40]

Educational inequalities are an important factor in the perpetuation of other types of inequality because they are strongly linked to opportunities and occupational mobility. In Africa, they are also associated with ***social origin***. A study in 6 African countries shows that social origin –understood as region of birth, education of parents and place of residence – is a contributing factor in inequality levels. In Uganda, for instance, despite a certain level of democratization in access to schooling, a ratio of 1 to 7 still separated the sons of educated fathers from the sons of non-educated fathers. In Guinea, 64

FIGURE 2.2.7: **URBAN INEQUALITIES IN SELECTED COUNTRIES IN LATIN AMERICA AND THE CARIBBEAN, 1989 - 2006**

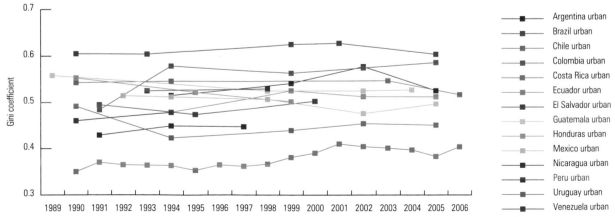

Source: UN-HABITAT, Global Urban Observatory, 2008
Data are from UN-ECLAC, UNU and other sources.

per cent of children who never attended school had parents who were farmers or never went to school themselves.[41]

In terms of urban income inequality, however, sub-Saharan Africa ranks second after Latin America and the Caribbean for the highest levels of disparity between the urban rich and the urban poor; the average Gini coefficient for urban Africa is 0.46 compared to 0.50 for urban Latin America and the Caribbean and 0.39 for urban Asia. Income is concentrated among certain groups and areas in both urban and rural areas of the continent. With the exception of Algeria, Namibia, and Sierra Leone, where inequality levels are higher in the countryside than in cities, in all other countries for which data is available, average Gini coefficients are higher in urban areas than in rural areas.

Northern Africa, on the other hand, shows a relatively egalitarian pattern of income distribution. The differences in urban poverty and slum prevalence between Northern Africa and sub-Saharan Africa are reflected in the distribution of income, with the former having a moderate urban Gini coefficient of 0.37, compared with urban sub-Saharan Africa, where the Gini coefficient has an average value of 0.46. Indices of income inequality in urban and rural zones are also less pronounced in Northern Africa, with only a four-point difference between them, whereas in sub-Saharan Africa there is an eight-point difference between urban and rural values.[42]

In many countries, economic growth is often accompanied by rising inequalities. In fact, Africa's average economic growth rate of 5.4 per cent in the last decade[43] has exacerbated disparities between the rich and the poor; these disparities are likely to become more entrenched unless active steps are taken to provide lower-income groups with subsidies and other public goods, including schools and infrastructure.

Countries such as Ghana, Mozambique and Tanzania, which have been experiencing rapid economic growth in

FIGURE 2.2.8: **URBAN INEQUALITIES IN AFRICA**

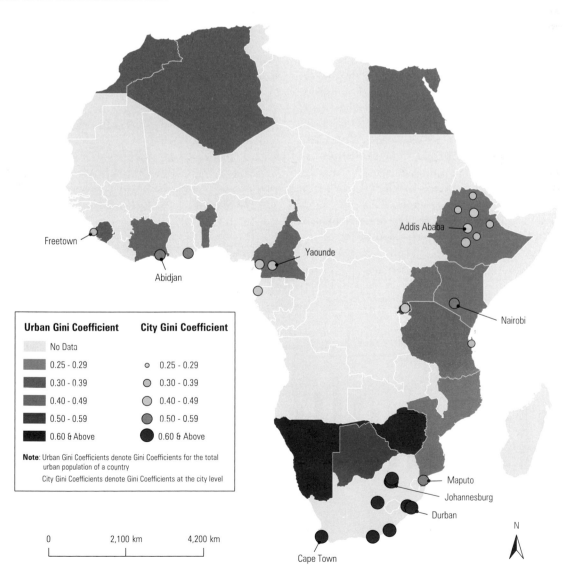

Source: UN-HABITAT Global Urban Observatory, 2008

recent years, are also experiencing rising urban inequalities. However, economic growth is not the only impetus of rising inequalities in the region – countries experiencing slow growth, such as Cameroon and Côte d'Ivoire, have also recorded rising urban inequalities. In Kenya, on the other hand, economic growth in recent years has been accompanied by rising urban inequalities but declining rural inequalities.[44]

Income inequalities are high in most cities of the region, and in some cities they are rising. In South African and Namibian cities, inequalities are most pronounced and extraordinarily high, despite the dismantling of apartheid in the early 1990s. In fact, urban inequalities in these two countries are even higher than those of Latin American cities. The average Gini coefficient for South African cities is 0.73, while that of Namibian cities is 0.62, compared to the average of 0.5 for urban Latin America.[45] Maputo, the capital of Mozambique, also stands out as a city with high levels of consumption inequality, with a Gini coefficient of 0.52. The economic growth and general increase in consumption ratios registered in Mozambique have not benefitted the population that lives below the poverty line.[46]

Kenya also exhibits relatively high levels of urban inequality; the Gini coefficient of expenditure in urban areas recorded in 2006 was 0.447, compared to 0.38 in rural areas.[47] However, the introduction of free primary education in 2003 and the recent decision to allocate public resources directly to districts and communities could reduce inequality levels in the country in the future as both programmes aim to increase disposable incomes of the both the rural and the urban poor. More recent surveys conducted by UN-HABITAT in 17 small cities and towns around Lake Victoria in the three East African countries of Kenya, Tanzania and Uganda show that levels of inequality in these towns are almost the same as those of big cities, largely because of high urban growth rates that are not accompanied by increased provision of infrastructure and basic services, such as water and sanitation. The Gini coefficient for income

▲
A street in Lagos, Nigeria: Sub-Saharan Africa cities suffer from high levels of poverty and inequality.
©**Tiggy Ridley/IRIN**

FIGURE 2.2.9: **GINI COEFFICIENT IN SELECTED AFRICAN CITIES**

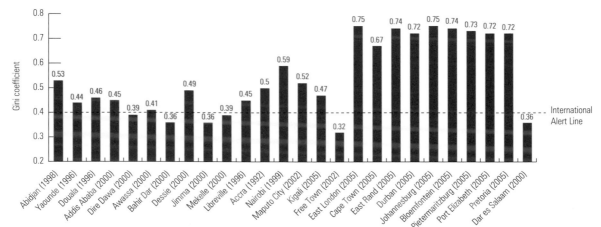

Source: UN-HABITAT Global Urban Observatory, 2008 .
Note: Data from various official sources, including national statistics offices and National Surveys.
Data for South African cities from South African Cities Network, 2006.
International alert line denotes Gini coefficient value above which inequalities have negative social, economic and political consequences. Alert line established by UN-HABITAT in consultations with its partners.

in these towns did not vary much between countries (0.56 for the Kenyan towns, 0.57 for the Tanzanian towns and 0.55 for the Ugandan towns).[48] Inequalities in these and other Eastern African countries are often related to inequality in access to land and assets distribution, both in rural and urban areas.[49]

Freetown in Sierra Leone, Dire Dawa in Ethiopia and Dar es Salaam in Tanzania are among the most equal cities in sub-Saharan Africa, with Gini coefficients of 0.32, 0.39 and 0.36, respectively. While urban inequalities are relatively higher in cities such as Yaoundé, Douala, Addis Ababa, Accra, and Kigali, levels of inequality in these cities – each of which has a Gini coefficient below 0.5 – are still lower than their respective national averages, and are also much lower than those of highly unequal South African cities, where Gini coefficients range from a "low" of 0.67 in Cape Town to a high of 0.75 in Johannesburg.[50] Despite important economic and social progress, particularly in social wage measures with subsidized rates in basic service delivery, education and housing,[51] South Africa has not yet succeeded in breaking out of the apartheid-era economic model that concentrated wealth and opportunities;[52] inequalities continue to be highly "racialized", gendered and geographically localized. In fact, the average black African household experienced a 19 per cent drop in income between 1995 and 2000, while the average white household experienced a 15 per cent increase in income.[53] However, recent data shows that inequality levels have reduced slightly in most South African cities since 2001 when most cities had a Gini coefficient of 0.75 or above, with cities such as Buffalo city having extremely high levels of inequality reaching 0.8.

Positive economic indicators in many African cities, including South Africa, coupled with higher expenditures by the state as part of redistribution strategies, are showing some positive signs of a turnaround on urban poverty, unemployment and income inequality in some countries, although the impact of rapid economic growth on poverty reduction and levels of inequality are yet to be felt in many cities.

Income inequalities in African cities are rooted in their colonial past, but are also reinforced by post-colonial institutions. Corruption, despotism, nepotism and other forms of unequal and exploitative relations have contributed to Africa's poor record of wealth distribution. Income inequalities are also an outgrowth of fragile and ineffective local governments, poor governance and monopolized access to assets, particularly land, which is often in the hands of the political and economic elite. Structural adjustment programmes (SAPs), which removed subsidies for basic services, especially in urban areas, have been unsuccessful in alleviating poverty in cities, and in some countries, SAPs have actually contributed to exacerbating both urban poverty and inequality.[54] In urban Kenya, for instance, the Gini coefficient rose from 0.47 in the 1980s to 0.575 in the 1990s largely as a result of SAPs, poor governance and other factors that adversely affected the urban poor.[55] In Nigeria, the urban Gini coefficient increased from 0.37 to 0.416 for similar reasons,[56] and in Abidjan, adverse economic conditions culminating in the devaluation of the currency provoked an increase in the income Gini coefficient from 0.497 in 1992 to 0.529 in 1998.[57] Furthermore, a relatively new generation of poverty alleviation programmes in many African countries have yet to prove their effectiveness in reducing poverty, as many programmes merely address the symptoms of deep-rooted inequalities, not the structural causes underlying them.

The continent has also been ravaged by different types of calamities, which have exacerbated inequalities. Human-made and natural disasters not only turn back the development clock in countries where they occur, but they also accentuate disparities between social groups and regions. The Gini coefficient in war-torn Angola, for instance, increased from 0.45 in 1995 to 0.51 in 2000[58]. In many countries experiencing conflict or environmental catastrophe, the number of people

FIGURE 2.2.10: **URBAN AND RURAL GINI COEFFICIENTS FOR SELECTED AFRICAN COUNTRIES**

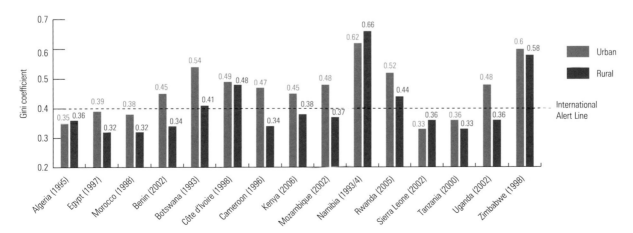

Source: UN-HABITAT Global Urban Observatory, 2008
Note: Data from various sources, and for various years.
International alert line denotes Gini coefficient value above which inequalities have negative social, economic and political consequences. Alert line established by UN-HABITAT in consultations with its partners.

living in poverty in urban areas also tends to increase as fleeing rural populations seek refuge in urban areas, where they join the lowest rung of society as internally displaced persons.

The global AIDS epidemic is another factor that impacts inequality levels on the continent. In addition to exacerbating poverty and hunger, it also affects the economy of the urban poor, contributing to further polarization of income. A study conducted in Botswana – a country with one of the highest rates of HIV prevalence on the planet, with approximately 25 per cent of adults infected with the virus – shows that more than one-quarter of the poorest households are expected to lose an income earner in the next 10 years to HIV/AIDS. Half of the poorest households will incur additional expenditures to treat at least one infected member, while other households will gain four dependents after the death of an infected member, multiplying needs that must be met with the same or fewer resources.[59] This trend is also prevalent in other Southern and Eastern African countries that have high HIV/AIDS prevalence, and must be considered when measuring levels of inequality in cities.

Asia

Asia is the most equal region in the developing world: the urban Gini coefficient is 0.39, slightly below the inequality threshold of 0.4, above which levels of inequality are considered unacceptably high. It is also the region with the greatest variations in income distribution, with some countries maintaining low levels of inequality or reducing them further, and others experiencing a rise in levels of inequality. Inequalities in Asian countries – measured by income or consumption Gini coefficients[60] – are generally higher in urban than in rural areas, with the exception of China, which is the only country in the region with higher Gini coefficients in the countryside than in urban areas.[61] Malaysia is the only country in the region where levels of inequality are more or less equal in urban and rural areas.

In 2005, approximately one in three Asians were poor, representing close to 900 million people or roughly two-thirds of the world's population living below the poverty line; most of them lived in rural areas.[62] UN-HABITAT estimates that globally, approximately one-third of the world's urban inhabitants lived in urban slum conditions in 2005; of these, more than half, or 515 million people, lived in Asia.[63] In general terms, the region has made impressive advances in poverty reduction and in the improvement of living standards as a result of accelerated economic growth, yet, income inequality has not decreased in many countries, and in some cases, has increased considerably.

Income inequalities in Asian cities are at a fairly low level compared to other developing regions. Data from 39 cities in 8 Asian countries shows an average Gini coefficient of 0.40, roughly the average national urban income inequality rating in these countries. However, there are significant income distribution differences among cities, even within the same country, which shows that national aggregates are not necessarily reflected at the local level. For instance, Beijing, the capital of China, is the most equal city in Asia; its Gini coefficient is not only the lowest among Asian cities, but is the lowest in the world (0.22), whereas Hong Kong, the Special Administrative Region of China, has the highest Gini coefficient among all Asian cities, and a relatively high value by international standards (0.53). Hong Kong has witnessed a steady increase in income inequality over the past three decades, with the Gini coefficient increasing from 0.45 in 1981 to 0.476 in 1991 and 0.525 in 2001.[64] The other most unequal cities in Asia are Ho Chi Minh City in the southern part of Viet Nam, with a Gini coefficient of 0.53, and the

FIGURE 2.2.11: **RELATIONSHIP BETWEEN ECONOMIC GROWTH AND CHANGE OF GINI COEFFICIENT IN SELECTED AFRICAN CITIES**

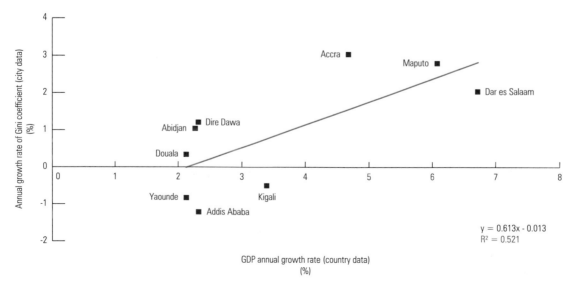

$y = 0.613x - 0.013$
$R^2 = 0.521$

Source: UN-HABITAT Global Urban Observatory
Data from various sources, collected between 1989 and 2005

Floating market in Bangkok: Thai cities have relatively high levels of inequality compared to other Asian cities.
© Kate Shephard/iStockphoto

Thai cities of Nakhon Ratchasima and Songkhla (0.49), closely followed by the capital, Bangkok (0.48). Inequalities are also high in the Philippines, in Metropolitan Manila (0.41), particularly in the cities of Quezon and Pasay, two populated suburbs that in 2003 had a Gini coefficient of 0.44. The rapidly growing Chinese city of Shenzhen in the Pearl River Delta has a high income Gini coefficient (0.49), as do the cities of Yichan (0.42) and Daquin (0.41). Inequalities have been widening in other urban centres in China since the mid-1980s, coinciding with the early stage of urban economic reforms that have increased China's Gini coefficient to 0.32, 9 points higher than it was in 1988.

Colombo in Sri Lanka, is also quite unequal, with a Gini coefficient of 0.46 in 2002. However, Sri Lanka merits a mention as a positive example of income inequality reduction. The country managed to reverse increasing inequalities in urban areas; in the 1990s, the Gini coefficient in urban areas fell from an extreme average high of 0.62 in the 1990s to a moderate high of 0.48 in 2002. Indonesia has also successfully managed to reduce both poverty and inequality levels in cities. Official statistics indicate that the incidence of poverty in the country declined from 40 per cent in 1976 to 13 per cent in 1993.[65] Assuming that there are no data comparability problems, the country also recorded a decline in income inequality in urban areas of approximately 8.3 per cent over the same years. Urban inequalities also remained fairly low during the period of high economic growth in the early 1990s and subsequent financial crisis in the late 1990s, which mainly affected high-income groups dealing with urban real estate and financial markets. For instance, the Gini coefficient in the capital city of Jakarta remained steady during this volatile period, ranging from 0.363 in 1996 to 0.322 in 2002.[66]

Iran is another good example of a country that managed to reduce poverty and inequality levels after its tumultuous post-revolutionary period in the 1980s. Iran's Gini coefficient is 0.40, much lower than other middle-income countries, such

FIGURE 2.2.12: **GINI COEFFICIENTS FOR SELECTED ASIAN CITIES**

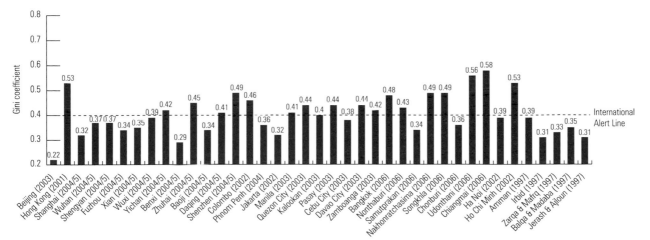

Source: UN-HABITAT Global Urban Observatory, 2008
Note: Data compiled by ESCAP for various years between 1990 and 2006
International alert line denotes Gini coefficient value above which inequalities have negative social, economic and political consequences. Alert line established by UN-HABITAT in consultation with its partners.

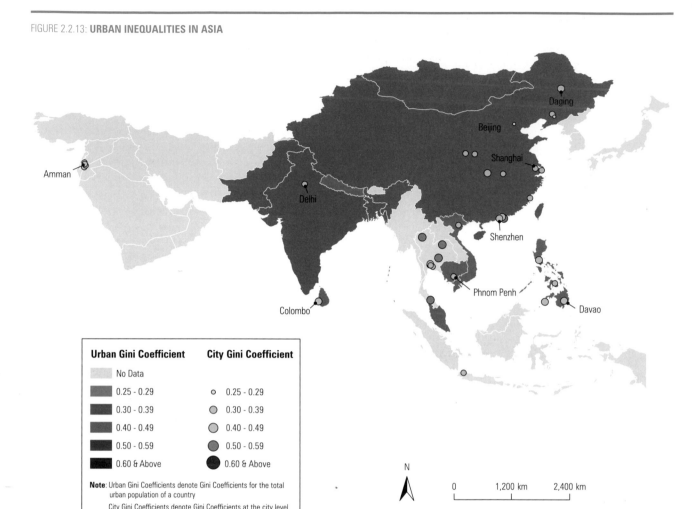

Daqing

Beijing

Shanghai

Amman

Delhi

Shenzhen

Phnom Penh

Colombo

Davao

Urban Gini Coefficient	City Gini Coefficient
No Data	
0.25 - 0.29	○ 0.25 - 0.29
0.30 - 0.39	○ 0.30 - 0.39
0.40 - 0.49	○ 0.40 - 0.49
0.50 - 0.59	○ 0.50 - 0.59
0.60 & Above	● 0.60 & Above

Note: Urban Gini Coefficients denote Gini Coefficients for the total urban population of a country

City Gini Coefficients denote Gini Coefficients at the city level

N

0   1,200 km   2,400 km

Source: UN-HABITAT Global Urban Observatory, 2008

as Malaysia (0.49).[67] In addition, the share of the 20 richest population deciles in terms of per capita expenditures has remained constant since the mid-1980s relative to the poorest population deciles. Unlike in other oil-producing countries, Iran's recent oil boom (from 1994 to 2004) brought greater equality to urban residents, and sustained lower levels of inequality in urban areas than in rural areas, a phenomenon that has characterized this country for at least two decades. However, other studies show that economic growth in Iran is not income-inequality neutral; on the contrary, they show a general pro-rich and inequality-sustaining outcome, resulting from significant distortions in the relationship between institutional settings and the functioning of markets such that the income growth process does not generate sufficient employment, generating inflation.[68] In provincial capital cities such as Bushehr, Ilam, ShahrKord, and Semnan, which have lower than average population growth rates but higher than average economic growth rates, it is very likely, however, that economic growth will be spread more evenly.

Inequalities in Asian cities have often increased in the context of accelerated economic growth. For instance, in China and Viet Nam, which experienced high economic growth rates of 11.5 per cent and 7.5 per cent annually in the 1990s, the cities of Beijing and Hanoi generated Gini coefficient increases of approximately 2.5 per cent.[69] A similar situation has been observed in Hong Kong and other Chinese cities, where increasing per capita incomes led to increased inequality. However, economic growth does not always translate into greater inequality in many Asian cities. Urban inequalities have remained constant or have declined in some countries experiencing positive economic growth.

As economies grow, however, regional disparities become more apparent. In China, for instance, the eastern coastal cities have attracted a remarkable amount of foreign direct investments and have generated large export flows, while inland cities and the country's western regions have fallen behind as a result of several disadvantages, such as a low-skilled workforce, inefficient agglomeration economies and other geographic location factors.[70] Inequalities in urban incomes are reflected regionally, manifested most strikingly in wage disparities among different provinces. Regional inequalities in access to education and other indicators are also of concern: in general, the highly urbanized eastern part of the country has better human development indicators than remote rural areas in the interior of the country. For instance, levels of illiteracy in China's western region of Tibet are more than 60 per cent among girls and more than 40 per cent among boys over the age of 15 – levels comparable to those of less-developed countries in the Asia region and much higher than China's national average.[71]

Many countries in the region, particularly China, are also grappling with income disparities between rural and urban areas. This type of rural-urban inequality has increased in the last two decades mainly as a result of economic liberalization and concentration of economic activities in urban areas or city regions. Prior to the economic transition, these countries had a fairly egalitarian income distribution, with national Gini coefficients of approximately 0.25. Today, China has one of the widest income gaps between rural and urban areas of any country in the world. In 2003, urban per capita disposable income was 3.2 times that of rural per capita income.[72] Studies suggest that the contribution of rural-urban inequalities to the nationwide income distribution may be higher than that regional disparities. The indices of income inequality within rural China are also higher than those in urban areas; this is primarily a result of changes in the agricultural economy, as more rural labourers move to non-farm sectors or migrate to urban areas, thereby widening rural income inequality.[73] Inequalities are also higher in rural areas than in urban settings because of distribution systems that guarantee only a limited level of access to certain services among rural populations, whereas in urban areas, residents have more access to a variety of public goods that help to reduce levels of inequality.[74]

> Today, China has one of the widest income gaps between rural and urban areas of any country in the world

In India, on the other hand, as in other Asian countries, inequalities have increased faster in urban areas than in rural areas as a consequence of a general shift from labour-intensive to capital-intensive economic activities and the growth in manufacturing exports and imports that are demanding skill-intensive jobs with higher wages.[75] In India, rural consumption inequalities declined in the 1990s, from a Gini coefficient of 0.282 in 1993 to 0.258 in 2000. Consumption inequalities in urban India, on the other hand, increased marginally; In urban India, consumption inequalities remained stable and relatively low from 1993 to 2000, and are comparable to many cities in Europe, Canada and Australia. The Gini coefficient for expenditure in urban India has not changed dramatically in the last 25 years, rising only slightly from 0.33 in 1983 to 0.34 in 2000, however, inequality-adjusted monthly per capita consumption expenditure has increased in real terms in urban areas at the national level by nearly 29 per cent. Analysis of the urban Gini coefficient at the state level, however, shows significant variations. Punjab, Rajasthan and Jammu and Kashmir, for instance, had lower urban gini coefficients than the national urban average in 2000, while Maharashra recorded a slightly higher urban Gini coefficient than the national average in 2000. Urban Kerala recorded a significant decline in consumption inequality in the period 1993-2000, while urban Tamil Nadu showed a significant increase during the same period.[76] Tamil Nadu and Maharashtra also achieved a significant decline in urban poverty during this period; the proportion of people living below the poverty line in urban areas in Tamil Nadu declined from 40 per cent in 1993 to 22 per cent in 2000, while in Maharashtra, the proportion fell from 35 per cent to 27 per cent during the same period.[77]

FIGURE 2.2.14: **GINI COEFFICIENTS FOR URBAN AND RURAL AREAS IN ASIA**

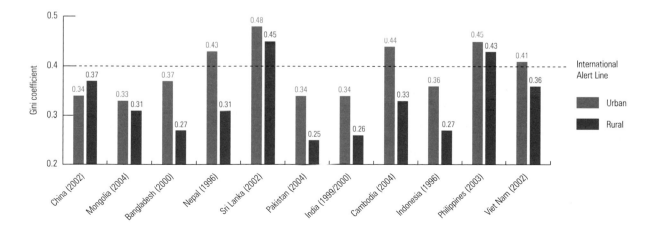

Source: UN-HABITAT Global Urban Observatory, 2008
Note: Data from various sources, and for various years.
International alert line denotes Gini coefficient value above which inequalities have negative social, economic and political consequences. Alert line established by UN-HABITAT in consultation with its partners.

China's urban transition

The word **transition** perhaps best describes China: the world's most populous country is transitioning from a predominantly rural society to an urban one. China's urbanization process in the last two decades has been extraordinary: the urbanization level in the country has nearly doubled from 25 per cent in 1987 to roughly 42 per cent in 2007; it is estimated that by 2030, 60 per cent of the country's population will be urban.

China is also transitioning from a centralized planned economy to a market economy, which has led to another important transition from relative social egalitarianism to a new era of individualism and competition. All of China's recent changes are also leading it to transition, almost within one generation, from a developing country to a developed one.

These changes have brought positive outcomes: China has experienced rapid economic growth for more than 15 years, and the country has been able to lift half a billion people out of poverty in the last 30 years – a remarkable achievement that no other nation has accomplished at the same speed or scale. The country has also improved the quality of life of hundreds of thousands of inhabitants, particularly in urban areas.

China's transitions began with the implementation of a set of progressive policy reforms that started with the restructuring of the agricultural sector at the end of the 1970s, in a period usually referred to as the "agricultural reform" that spanned eight years. It was followed by a second period known as the "urban reform" that started in 1985 and is still continuing. This second period has been characterized by rapid industrialization, the reorganization of state enterprises, increased trade openness, enactment of subsidies and tax exemptions in the export sector, and the gradual liberalization of the country's financial markets.

The changes in China have also had negative effects: decreases in rural-urban inequalities during the agricultural reform rose again because priority was given to coastal and urban areas. China has now attained some of the deepest disparities between rural and urban areas in the world, with urban per capita incomes three times those of rural areas. Regional inequalities are also growing, often among towns and cities within in the same region, as rural non-agricultural opportunities become concentrated in a

Shanghai's skyline at sunset
©**Claudio Zaccherini/Shutterstock**

few areas, and as some urban areas grow more rapidly than others. As a result, China's national Gini coefficient has increased rapidly in recent decades, growing from 0.30 in 1978, the year the reforms began, to 0.38 in 1988 and 0.45 in 2002, reflecting increased inequalities between rural and urban areas and among regions. Today, China has the highest level of consumption inequality in the Asia region, higher than Pakistan (0.298), Bangladesh (0.318), India (0.325), and Indonesia (0.343), among others.

At the urban level, income inequalities are growing as a result of a combination of factors: increases in manufacturing activity, and growth in the service industry and high tech

sectors, bringing disproportionate rewards to the most skilled workers; the adoption of capital-intensive industrial development that is creating a limited number of well-paid new jobs; and the emergence of real estate, insurance and communication sectors that are creating highly remunerated jobs. At the same time, the decline of state-owned enterprises has resulted in layoffs and an increase in the number of unemployed people, who, together with informal workers and rural residents, are facing serious problems in joining the new urban labour market. Cities with high levels of income inequality include Shenzhen (0.49), Zhuhai (0.45), Yichan (0.42), Daquin (0.41), and above all, Hong Kong, a Special

of the city's total income, while 25 per cent was drawn from subsidies in housing, health care and education, and 10 per cent from irregular economic benefits such as second jobs, business sidelines and illegal forms of income. The opportunities for rent seeking, or gray income, widen the gap between the privileged and underprivileged and erode the resource base of the state welfare distribution. In addition, new mechanisms of housing allocation through real estate companies are creating new forms of spatial or area-based marginalization that further accentuate income and social inequalities.

Most studies on income inequality in China also include only those urban populations that are registered under the **Hukou** household registration system, which excludes rural migrants (commonly referred to as "floating populations") who only have temporary residential status in cities The migrant population in China is roughly 150 million, and is considered not only the biggest migrant population in the world, but also the most mobile. Most migrants come to cities in search of jobs, which are often unstable, and live under temporary and inadequate housing conditions.

Ignoring migrants in the studies of overall income distribution therefore distorts levels of urban inequality in China. For instance, a study in the capital city of Beijing – a key destination in recent domestic migration flows – shows that the migrant population increased from 0.32 million in 1985 to 1 million in 1995 and 3.3 million in 2003, representing approximately one-third of the capital's total population. One of the few studies of the Gini coefficient in Beijing found that the coefficient values increase from 0.22 to 0.33 when migrants are included. Similar variances of approximately 12 points are found in other cities that are destinations of recent domestic migrations, with the Gini coefficient increasing from 0.402 to 0.418 when rural migrants are included. In these cities, the migrant population accounts for some 12 per cent of all urban employees and represents nearly one-fifth of the urban population.

Rural-urban and intra-city disparities, are therefore, emerging as consequences of China's urban and economic transition.

Sources: Xue, 1997; Kanbur, Venables & Wan, 2006. Wu, 2004; Meng, Gregory & Wang, 2005;Dai, 2005; Park, Wang & Cai, 2006; Zhu, 2007.

Administrative Region of China, which has the highest Gini coefficient not only in China, but in all of Asia (0.53). In general, however, urban inequalities within Chinese cities tend to be relatively low compared with rural areas and with other cities in Asia.

In modern China, lack of full-time employment means not only the loss of a job and income; in many cases, it also means exclusion from social services, such as education, health, retirement benefits and social security. Less than 15 years ago, social services were provided free of charge by the state or at highly subsidized rates, but now the government is abandoning work-protective policies that are impacting vulnerable populations. For instance, the state

paid 66 per cent of all individual health-care costs in 1988; in 2002, the state paid just 22 per cent. The allocation of social housing has also been dramatically reduced. As a consequence, the proportion of expenditures related to education and health has more than doubled for both mean-income households and the poorest 20 per cent of households.

China's new economic reality impacts both income and social inequality throughout the country. In China, urban incomes do not accurately reflect levels of inequality, as urban residents have access to a variety of services that are not as easily accessible to rural residents.[78] In Shanghai, for example, salary-based income accounted only for 65 per cent

However, recent analyses suggest that India is undergoing an inequality trend somewhat similar to that of China as a result of economic liberalization and globalization.[79] Recent studies have found that economic growth in the country has involved mainly the formal economy and that the decline in manufacturing and the rise of the services sector have also affected the distribution of income among skilled and non-skilled workers. This differentiation of workers has been further aggravated by an increase in the number of people employed in managerial and professional occupations, including those holding new jobs in the banking and financial sectors. All of these changes in the occupational structure of the country are affecting levels of inequality. In 2002, for instance, the income gain of the richest 10 per cent of the population was about 4 times higher than the gain of the poorest 10 per cent.[80]

Between 1993 and 2005, there was an overall increase of about 9 per cent in the consumption Gini coefficient in urban India. At the same time, two of the most economically developed states in the country, Tamil Nadu and Maharashtra, have been able to cap the increase in inequalities at less than 6 per cent.

In Thailand, the provinces of Udonthani and Chiangmai in the northeast and northern part of the country have the highest income disparities among social groups, with very high Gini coefficients of 0.56 and 0.58, respectively – approximately 22 points higher than the national average and 10 points more than the capital city of Bangkok. These provinces are experiencing a significant increase in population, but they have among the lowest GDP growth in the country. The capital cities of these provinces have the highest levels of inequality in all of Asia.

In Viet Nam, the Gini coefficient for the country as a whole increased from 0.356 in 1995 to approximately 0.407 in 1999, owing primarily to the collapse of commodity prices, especially rice and coffee. Inequality appears to have increased significantly in almost all provinces, with more than half experiencing an increase of at least 10 points.[81] These provinces are mainly located in the Red River Delta, Mekong River Delta and Southeast Region, which are the most prosperous and urbanized regions of the country.

In the Philippines, overall income distribution increased in the 1990s, with a change in Gini coefficient from 0.45 in 1994 to 0.487 in 1997, after which it remained stable. Inequalities are much higher in the southern part of the country, where poverty incidence is also higher, particularly in the most unequal region, Zamboanga Peninsula (0.52); followed by Northern Mindano (0.48); and Central and Eastern Visayas (0.47). The regions with the lowest income gaps are Llocos (0.39) and Central Luzon (0.35), which are also among the wealthiest regions in the country.

In war-torn countries and regions, inequalities seem to rise rapidly, owing to disruption in the economy and changes in socio-economic status and earnings. In Nepal, for instance, the urban Gini coefficient increased from 0.26 in 1991 to 0.37 in 2000 as the Maoist insurgency in that country developed. In Iraq, inequalities have been increasing dramatically in recent years in both urban and rural areas; in just one year, the country's Gini coefficient rose from 0.351 in 2003 to 0.415 in 2004.[82] War not only affects labour income, it also damages capital income, thereby exacerbating differences and reshaping the social stratification system. The Iraq Living Conditions Survey 2004, for instance, found that approximately 35 per cent of Baghdad's workers live in poverty and that roughly half of the residents of Mosul, Hilla, Najaf, Nassiriya, and Basra cannot afford to keep their dwellings warm in the winter.[83] Inequalities are likely to increase in some Asian countries in the near future, particularly in regions beset by internal tensions, political transitions and other unresolved territorial issues, which have worsened human development indicators in some countries and made residents more vulnerable.

▲
Cycle taxis in China.
©**Stanislas Komogorov/Shutterstock**

NOTES

1. Government of Kenya, 2007.
2. Agostini & Brown, 2007.
3. Addision & Giovanni, 2001.
4. Mingione & Haddock, 2008.
5. European Community Directorate General for Regional Policy, 2007.
6. Australian Bureau of Statistics, 2003.
7. Tokyo Metropolitan Government, 2003.
8. Tachibanaki, 2005.
9. US Census Bureau, 2006.
10. Ibid.
11. Heisz, 2005.
12. U.S Census Bureau 2000
13. World Bank, 2000.
14. Heisz, 2005.
15. A study of 14 American cities shows that central-city areas have a higher level of inequality than suburban areas, which means that the very rich and the very poor live in the central part of the city. Jargowsky, 1997.
16. UNDP and Center for Economic Research, 2005.
17. Real consumption was affected by chronic rationing of most goods, dual distribution systems, parallel markets and regional differences in the supply. UNDP, op cit.
18. UNDP, op cit.
19. UN Economic Commission for Europe, 2004.
20. UN Economic Commission for Europe, 2004.
21. Gustafsson & Nivorzhkina, 2005.
22. Inter-American Development Bank, 2000.
23. López-Moreno, 2002a.
24. Data produced by ECLAC on 19 selected cities in 9 countries, commissioned for this report, 2008.
25. Gini coefficient data for urban Latin America and the Caribbean was compiled by ECLAC especially for this report.
26. UN-HABITAT Global Urban Observatory 2008, derived from ECLAC data.
27. UN-HABITAT Global Urban Observatory 2008, derived from ECLAC data.
28. Altimir, 2002
29. UN-HABITAT Global Urban Observatory 2008, derived from ECLAC data.
30. UN-DESA, 2007a.
31. UN DESA, 2007b.
32. Clements, 1997.
33. Some recent studies have suggested that participatory budgeting and other innovative governance processes in Brazil have had a minimum impact on inequality levels because they do not benefit the poorest of the poor and tend to be most beneficial to those low-income groups that are able to access governance structures within municipalities. Moreover, as the budget assigned to participatory processes is only a small proportion of the total city budget, its impact is limited.
34. IPEA, 2007
35. Altimir, 2002. Poverty incidence grew from 5 per cent in 1974 to 21 per cent in 2001, and unemployment rose from 3 per cent in the 1980s to around 17 per cent in 2001.
36. Altimir, 2002.
37. Instituto Nacional de Estadistica y Censos, 2008
38. World Bank 2002 estimates indicate that the highest levels of urban poverty in the region are found in Chad, Niger and Sierra Leone, and that rural and urban poverty prevalence is almost the same in many countries, including Nigeria.
39. UN-HABITAT, Global Urban Observatory, 2008.
40. Africa is followed by the Middle East (0.55) and East Asia and the Pacific (0.41). Refer to Cogneau Denis et al, 2006.
41. Cogneau Denis et al., 2006.
42. UN-HABITAT, Global Urban Observatory, 2008.
43. According to the World Bank's Africa Development Indicators 2007, 16 African countries grew by more than 4.5 per cent a year between 1996 and 2006.
44. Government of Kenya, 2007.
45. Cogneau Denis et al, 2006.
46. James, Arndt & Simler, 2005.
47. Kenya Central Bureau of Statistics, 2006.
48. UN-HABITAT Lake Victoria Region Water and Sanitation Initiative, unpublished document.
49. Society for International Development, 2006.
50. South African Cities Network, 2006.
51. Subsidies have brought clear achievements, such as access to water (79 to 83 per cent) and formal housing (66 to 73 per cent). Statistics South Africa, 2001.
52. Southern African Regional Poverty Network, 2008.
53. Statistics South Africa, 2002.
54. López-Moreno, 2002a.
55. Kayizzi-Mugerwa, 2001.
56. Kayizzi-Mugerwa, 2001.
57. Poverty rose four-fold during the same period, from 5 per cent to 20 per cent. Refer to Grimm, 2001.
58. Government of Angola, 2008.
59. Greener, Jefferis & Siphambe, 2000.
60. Note that five countries measure inequalities in consumption differentials and another five countries measure inequalities in income distribution.
61. China intra-urban inequality has been smaller than intra-rural inequality: 0.18 to 0.28 in 1985 and 0.24 to 0.33 in 1995, respectively.
62. López-Moreno, 2002.
63. UN-HABITAT, Global Urban Observatory, database 2008.
64. Zhao & Zhang, 2005.
65. Akita, Lukman &Yamada, 1999.
66. World Bank, 2006.
67. Salehi-Isfahani, 2006.
68. Farzin Ali, economist at UNDP Iran, communication with UN-HABITAT on 13 March 2008.
69. UN-HABITAT, Global Urban Observatory Database, 2008.
70. UN-DESA, 2007.
71. UNDP & China Development Research Foundation, 2005.
72. UNDP & China Development Research Foundation, 2005
73. Changes in the rural economy contribute to the total income inequality up to 36 per cent. UNDP & China Development Research Foundation, 2005.
74. UNDP & China Development Research Foundation, 2005.
75. For instance, in India, the agriculture sector increased wages by 2.5 per cent in the 1990s, while in urban areas, the public sector doubled wages, and the private sector increased wages by several times more.
76. Government of India, 2002.
77. UNDP, 2003.
78. Xue, 1997.
79. Ravallion & Chaudhuri, 2006.
80. Gaurav & Ravallion, 2002.
81. UNDP, 2001.
82. Republic of Iraq/UN-HABITAT, 2007.
83. Data based on UNDP/Ministry of Planning and Development Cooperation's Iraq Living Conditions Survey 2005 and UN-HABITAT Urban Indicators Surveys conducted under a United Nations Development Group (UNDG) Trust Fund Project in cooperation with Iraq's Ministry of Municipalities and Public Works, Global Urban Research Unit, Newcastle University, and UN-HABITAT.

2.3
Education, Employment and City Size

▲
Children in a crowded class in Molo town, Kenya
©**Allan Gichigi/IRIN**

Harmonious urbanization depends upon the progressive growth of access to life-enriching educational opportunities and sustainable employment options for all. Education – a fundamental human right and an essential precursor to informed civic participation – contributes to many important dimensions of well-being and prepares citizens for gaining employment and making healthy life choices. Cities foster healthy human development by providing easier access to education, health care and employment for young men and women than villages can, but not all cities are alike in their accommodation of young people's education and employment needs.

In this chapter, UN-HABITAT presents a preliminary analysis of education and employment indicators based on city size and on whether the settlement is urban or rural. As the analysis in this chapter shows, in some countries, such as Lesotho and Uganda, small cities and towns can, in some cases, provide more access to educational institutions and resources per capita than do bigger cities; however, in general, big metropolitan areas provide more educational facilities than small towns and villages.

Unequal access to education

School enrolment rates are generally much higher in urban than in rural areas, and cities have more educational infrastructure than villages or small towns. Children's access to school in cities, however, is more often determined by the ability of families to pay school fees than by the physical proximity of school buildings and programmes. Economic needs often supersede educational goals among poor urban families, who must choose between paying for basic services – including food, water and housing – and funding their children's education. Particularly in capital cities and large cities in which income and social inequalities are dramatic, many poor urban families cannot afford to ensure their children receive a basic education. Girls are especially likely to miss out on educational opportunities, as parents often rely on girls to assist with domestic work, while they send boys to school.

Causes of social inequality in basic education vary from country to country, but a common set of constraints exists, including: poverty; the embedded costs of education, including school uniforms, books and materials; shortage of school facilities; unsafe school environments, especially in poor urban neighborhoods; and cultural and social practices that discriminate against girls, including requirements that they provide domestic labour, marry and have families at a young age, and limit their independent movement to proscribed areas. More barriers to education exist for girls than for boys around the world. Where resources are limited and school systems are less responsive to the needs of girls than boys, girls risk losing important opportunities to fulfill their potential and improve their lives.

In general, children from poor families, whether urban or rural, are less likely to attend or complete school.[1] The lack of school affordability is more pronounced in large cities than in small cities, owing to higher overall costs of living than in small cities and towns, but governments of large cities more often fail to address all of the barriers children face to attending school. In Kenya and several other countries in the developing world, free primary education policies have helped bolster school enrolment rates; however, lack of a sufficient number of places in overcrowded schools often means that some school-aged children cannot be accommodated. School enrolment is still higher in urban areas than in rural areas, but in terms of progress and trends, there has been a steady decline in enrolment in cities, while more and more rural children become enrolled.

School access and enrolment in Latin America and the Caribbean

In some countries of Latin America and the Caribbean, a higher proportion of children in small cities than in large cities receive a basic education. This gap is particularly evident in Bolivia, where 93 per cent of children in small cities and towns are enrolled in primary education, compared with 68 per cent in the capital and other large cities, and 72 per cent in rural areas. This disparity cannot be seen when analyzing the overall urban average, which shows that enrolment is higher in cities than in rural areas in general: 86 per cent versus 72 per cent, respectively. The disparity between large and small cities can be explained in part by the deep inequalities in the distribution of resources within large cities that leave parents little money for food and housing needs, ruling out paying school expenses for their children. The same situation is evident in Colombia to a lesser degree, with 82 per cent of children in small cities attending school, compared with 73 per cent of children in large cities – the same percentage of rural children enrolled in school. In the Dominican Republic, large cities also have smaller proportions of children enrolled in school than small cities. In Guatemala, this is the case only for boys; in the capital city, 64 per cent of boys are enrolled

FIGURE 2.3.1: **PROPORTION OF CHILDREN ENROLLED IN PRIMARY EDUCATION IN LATIN AMERICAN CITIES AND RURAL AREAS**

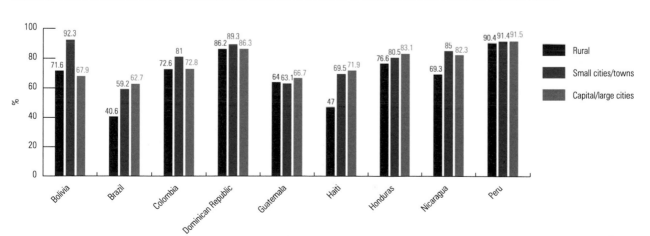

Source: UN-HABITAT Global Urban Observatory 2008

in primary school, compared with 68 per cent in small cities and towns. For Guatemalan girls, the situation is reversed: 69 per cent of girls in the capital city are enrolled in primary school, compared with 58 per cent in small cities and towns. On the positive side, the enrolment rates in Latin America as a whole tend to be generalized compared to sub-Saharan Africa, where there are large disparities in enrolment rates between urban and rural areas and between large and small cities, and to Asia, where there are large disparities between boys and girls.

School access and enrolment in Asia

In Asia, gender plays an important role in determining whether or not a child will be sent to school. For instance, on average, more boys who live in small cities and towns in the region attend school than those who live in capital and large cities. Conversely, girls who live in small cities and towns generally still lag behind their peers who live in capital and large cities. In the Philippines, for example, the school enrolment rate of boys is lower in large cities, at 75 per cent, than in small cities, at 89 per cent, while the differential for girls is in favour of large cities, where 95 per cent are enrolled, versus 89 per cent in small cities and towns. Clearly, both girls and boys in the Philippines are enrolled in school at a high level in small cities.

In the Central Asian country of Uzbekistan, a different pattern exists: a smaller percentage of boys are enrolled in school in small cities (55 per cent) than in large cities (61 per cent) and even rural areas (60 per cent). Only 55 per cent of girls in small cities and rural areas are enrolled, with a greater proportion enrolled in large cities. In Kazakhstan, a greater percentage of boys in small cities are enrolled than in large cities, while no differential exists for girls. In Kyrgyzstan, however, the opposite is the case: more boys in large cities are enrolled than their peers in small cities.

School access and enrolment in Africa

In many sub-Saharan African countries, living in an urban area provides a clear advantage for access to education, regardless of whether one is rich or poor. Inequalities in access to school facilities can partly explain this urban-rural differential. In sub-Saharan African countries, schooling is more readily accessible in cities, where most schools are built; rural communities are often left without public educational infrastructure, and often rely on non-governmental or community institutions for schooling, which are often unable to meet demand. This is true in several of the countries included in UN-HABITAT's analysis, especially in Western and Central Africa: Benin, Burkina Faso, Central African Republic, Chad, Comoros, Cote d'Ivoire, Ethiopia, Guinea, Mali, Mozambique, Niger, and Senegal. In all of the countries analyzed here, more than 75 per cent of the children of primary school age in large cities attend school, but in rural areas, the proportion drops to less than 50 per cent. This pattern is most pronounced in Niger, where 73 per cent of children in the capital city attend school, compared with 17 per cent in rural areas; in Niger's small cities and towns, 53 per cent of children of primary school age are enrolled.

In some countries in sub-Saharan Africa, schooling is quasi-generalized, with small disparities across cities and villages. This is the case in the Eastern and Southern African countries of Cameroon, Congo, Kenya, Lesotho, Madagascar, Malawi, Namibia, Rwanda, South Africa, Tanzania, Togo, Uganda, and Zambia, and in the two North African countries covered in this study, Egypt and Morocco. In Egypt, school attendance rates vary little across different places, with enrolment rates of 86 per cent in the capital and large cities, 89 per cent in small cities and towns and 84 per cent in rural areas. A similar pattern is evident in Morocco, with school enrolment levels of 91 per cent in the capital and large cities, 92 per cent in small cities and towns, and 84 per cent in rural areas.

FIGURE 2.3.2: **PROPORTION OF CHILDREN ENROLLED IN PRIMARY EDUCATION IN ASIAN CITIES AND RURAL AREAS**

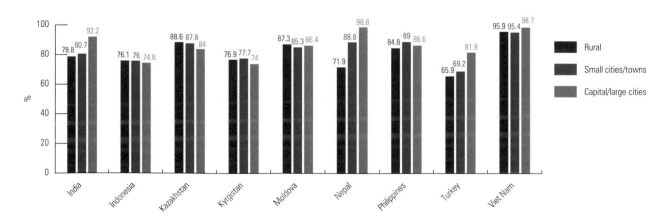

Source: UN-HABITAT Global Urban Observatory 2008

In poverty-stricken areas of many African cities, primary school enrolment is actually decreasing. In Eastern and Southern Africa, the most significant progress in school enrolment in the late 1990s was concentrated in rural areas. In Tanzania, net enrolment ratios increased in both rural and urban areas, but actually decreased in the poorest areas of cities.

The persistent gender gap in access to education

The gender gap in school enrolment narrowed during the 1990s in all regions of the world, and parity in gender representation in school enrolment continues to grow. Progress has been uneven within regions, however, and in a number of countries, girls are still at a significant disadvantage. Countries in which resources and school facilities are limited and enrolment is altogether low exhibit the greatest disparities; in many such countries, less than 50 per cent of girls of primary school age are enrolled in school. Female illiteracy rates remain high in urban poor and rural areas where many girls remain out of school or drop out too early to be able to acquire the necessary skills to acquire literacy skills.

In Benin, more girls attend primary school in the capital and large cities than in small cities and rural areas, but the gap between girls and boys is narrower in small cities than it is in large cities and rural areas: the ratio of girls to boys enrolled in school in small cities and towns is 0.81, versus 0.76 and 0.75 in large cities and rural areas, respectively. In contrast, in Burkina Faso, the capital and large cities have the highest level of school enrolment and the smallest gap between girls and boys, with a gender ratio of 0.95, compared with 0.87 in small cities and 0.74 in rural areas. This is also the case in the Central African Republic, Chad, Guinea, Mali, Mozambique, Niger, and the small island nation of Comoros, where boys and girls are enrolled equally. In Cote d'Ivoire, less of a gender gap exists in rural areas than in small cities and large cities,

FIGURE 2.3.3: **PROPORTION OF CHILDREN ENROLLED IN PRIMARY SCHOOL IN SUB-SAHARAN AFRICAN COUNTRIES EXPERIENCING HUGE RURAL-URBAN DISPARITIES IN ACCESS TO EDUCATION**

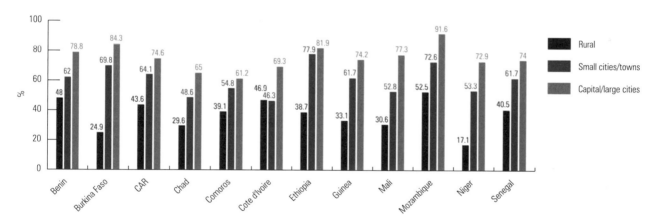

Source: UN-HABITAT Global Urban Observatory, 2008

FIGURE 2.3.4 **PROPORTION OF CHILDREN ENROLLED IN SCHOOL IN SUB-SAHARAN AFRICAN COUNTRIES WHERE ACCESS TO EDUCATION IS GENERALIZED ACROSS URBAN AND RURAL AREAS**

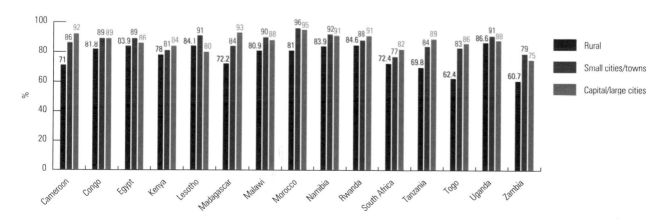

Source: UN-HABITAT Global Urban Observatory, 2008

with ratios of 0.91, 0.80 and 0.85, respectively. The same is true in Ghana, where the ratio of girls to boys in school in rural areas is 0.98, versus 0.95 in small cities and 0.93 in large cities. For girls and boys in Niger, the opposite situation exists: the gender gap has narrowed significantly in large cities and small cities, with ratios of 0.91 and 0.83, respectively, but in rural areas, girls are lagging far behind, with a ratio of 0.52. In Senegal, Congo and Egypt, girls and boys are enrolled equally in all three environments. Similarly, in Cameroon, boys and girls are enrolled equally in cities, and nearly so in rural areas (0.94). In countries in which education is quasi-universal, boys and girls have equal access to education, and in some countries, even more girls are enrolled in primary school than boys.

From education to employment: Trends and opportunities

Basic education is a fundamental human right that affords young people healthy, productive lives, but, clearly, in many of the world's largest cities with the greatest numbers of people in poverty, education remains inaccessible for a significant percentage of the population. As the cost of living in major cities increases with rising food and commodity prices, education becomes more important than ever in the quest for good jobs that pay a living wage. Education, however, does not always guarantee a decent job and a successful future. A study in India, for example, found that schooling can reproduce existing inequalities: many young people from marginalized communities often remain poor and unemployed, even after receiving a secondary education, while privileged families reap the benefits of political and social ties to employers.[2]

In a globalized world, the links between education and employment are increasingly unpredictable and uncertain. Today, huge numbers of young people remain unemployed in the developing world: out of the world's 1.1 billion young people between the ages of 15 and 24, only about 3.8 per cent, or 548 million, are employed. Youth are more than three times as likely as adults to be unemployed; despite the fact that the global population of youth grew by 13.2 per cent between 1995 and 2005, youth employment grew by only 3.8 per cent.[3] Young women in particular are likely to miss out on opportunities for decent, sustainable paid employment, as they often are expected to marry and bear children at a young age; in many places, young women's role as unpaid caregivers of children and other family members prevents them from joining the paid labour force. Those women who do work in the developing world tend to do so in the informal economy, owing to lack of formal job opportunities in many regions. In several countries, the informal sector is thriving in small cities and towns and rural areas. The following UN-HABITAT analysis of employment patterns focuses on young women's opportunities for paid work as an indicator of inequality in the developing world's cities.[4]

Youth non-employment

Youth non-employment, defined as the proportion of youth neither in education nor in employment, almost doubles the level of youth unemployment rates, particularly in Eastern and Southern African countries, where more than 40 per cent of young women are unemployed. In several Western African countries, on the other hand, more than 60 per cent of young women are in school or employed, particularly in Togo and Benin, where 85 and 76 per cent of young women are engaged in educational and productive activities, respectively. Youth non-employment rates remain much higher for women than for men.

Youth non-employment is high in small cities and towns, as well as in capital and large cities of most African countries. In some countries, a large number of children are neither working nor attending school in small cities and towns. In countries such as Tanzania, Malawi and Rwanda, there are more opportunities for young people in capital and large cities than in small cities and towns. For example, in small cities and towns in Tanzania, 41 per cent of young women are neither going to school nor working, while in the capital and other large cities, the non-employment rate is only 26 per cent. In Malawi, young women's non-employment is 52 per cent in small cities and towns and 39 per cent in large cities, and in Rwanda, the rate is 31 per cent in small cities and 22 per cent in large cities.

In some countries, however, the opposite is true: youth non-employment is particularly high in the capital and large cities. In countries such as Senegal, Mozambique and Niger, there are more jobs and schooling opportunities in small cities and towns than in large cities. For example, in Senegal's large cities, 41 per cent of young women are neither working nor attending school, compared with 33 per cent in small cities and towns. The non-employment rates are 30 per cent in large cities and 21 per cent in small cities and towns in Mozambique, and 51 per cent and 40 per cent, respectively, in Niger.

Only in a few countries are youth non-employment rates low overall, in large cities, small cities and towns and rural areas. Among the countries with overall low youth non-employment are Burkina Faso (14 per cent in large and small cities, and 1 per cent in rural areas); Chad (13 per cent in large cities, 10 per cent in small cities and 1 per cent in rural areas); Mali (7 per cent in large cities, 8 per cent in small cities and 3 per cent in rural areas); and Togo (14 per cent in large cities, 15 per cent in small cities and 16 per cent in rural areas). In general, youth in rural areas are working, primarily in the agricultural sector, despite low levels of school attendance.

Women in the informal sector in Africa

In many sub-Saharan African countries, young women from impoverished urban areas find employment in the informal sector. In the absence of an organized labour market, only a few women have access to formal employment with social

▲
Street harber in Dhaka.
©Golam Monowar Kamal

▲
Youth washing cars by Lake Victoria, Kenya.
©Golam Monowar Kamal

Street vendors, Kisumu, Kenya: Most women in Kenya's urban areas are employed in the informal sector.
©**Golam Monowar Kamal**

security coverage, paid and parental leave, retirement, and unemployment benefits; most women are instead dependent upon the informal economy for their own and their family's survival. In sub-Saharan Africa, 84 per cent of women's non-agricultural employment is informal. The informal sector remains important in capital and large cities, but informal employment is actually higher in small cities and towns and rural areas. In Kenya, 58 per cent of young women who are employed in Nairobi and the country's other large cities work in the informal sector, compared with 73 per cent of their counterparts in small cities and towns and rural areas. In Nigeria, where few job opportunities exist in the formal sector, more than two-thirds of employed women work in the informal sector.

In general, few women are employed in the formal labour markets in sub-Saharan Africa. Those who do find formal jobs are often confined to traditionally female, or "pink collar", jobs with low status, low job security and low pay that men typically do not want. In some areas, however, women and men are competing for such low-status jobs in categories such as sales and service activities. Women may be confined to low-paid jobs through discriminatory stereotyping or because they are less available for full-time work owing to family responsibilities.

In Lesotho, 29 per cent of young women in large cities are employed in the informal sector, mostly in sales and service activities, compared with 48 per cent in small cities and towns,

and 58 per cent in rural areas. While the capital and large cities offer young women more formal job opportunities than small cities and towns and rural areas, only a few sub-Saharan African capital and large cities offer regular access to formal jobs for young people; South Africa and Namibia provide the greatest access to formal-sector jobs, where 71 per cent and 61 per cent of women aged 15 to 24, respectively, hold a formal job. In North African countries, most young people attend school, and those who are not attending school are working in a formal-sector job. In Egypt and Morocco, 75 per cent and 60 per cent of young people, respectively, hold formal-sector jobs. Egypt offers a unique situation: in the country's small cities and towns, as well as in its rural areas, the majority of young women are employed in the formal sector (80 per cent and 73 per cent, respectively). In South Africa, the formal sector is also developed in small cities and towns, with 61 per cent of young women employed in it.

Youth non-employment and the informal sector in Latin America and the Caribbean

Among countries in Latin America and the Caribbean, youth non-employment is particularly high in Guatemala, where 58 per cent of young women in rural areas, 44 per cent in small cities and towns, and 22 per cent in large cities are neither attending a school nor working. The situation is similar in Nicaragua, where 58 per cent of young women in rural areas, 27 per cent in small cities and towns, and 22 per cent in large cities are non-employed. The large cities of Haiti have particularly high rates of youth non-employment – averaging 79 per cent – while small cities and towns and rural areas offer more opportunities for young people, with only 27 per cent and 34 per cent of young women neither attending school or nor working, respectively. Colombia provides accessible educational opportunities, as most of its young people attend school. In the large and small cities of Colombia, only 8 per cent and 9 per cent of young women, respectively, are neither attending school nor working. This is also the case in several other Latin American countries, including Brazil, Dominican Republic, Mexico, Chile, and Peru, where young people have more opportunities for schooling or employment than in other countries. Colombia, Brazil and Chile also offer their young people more opportunities in the formal sector than do the Dominican Republic and Peru. For example, while less than 20 per cent of young women in the capital and large cities, as well as small cities and towns, in Colombia are employed in the informal sector, the majority of young Peruvian women are employed in the informal sector (50 per cent and 64 per cent in large cities and small cities, respectively). The informal sector is particularly developed in Haiti and Bolivia, two countries that provide fewer schooling and job opportunities to their young people than even most sub-Saharan African countries.

Youth non-employment and the informal sector in Asia

The youth education and employment figures for Asia are diverse – some Asian countries offer excellent schooling and job opportunities for their young people and others do not. For example, in Armenia, less than 20 per cent of young women are neither attending school nor employed, and most of the employed women are in the formal sector. In Armenia's large cities, only 8 per cent of employed young women are in the informal sector, compared with 15 per cent in small cities and towns and 20 per cent in rural areas. In the capital and large cities of Nepal, 30 per cent of young women are neither attending school nor employed, and among those who are employed, 65 per cent work in the informal sector. The situation is similar in the Philippines, where more than 25 per cent of young women in the capital and large cities, as well as in small cities and towns, are neither attending school nor working. Half of all employed young women work in the informal sector in the Philippines. In Metro Manila, 25 per cent of young women are neither working nor attending school, and among those who are working, 45 per cent are employed in the informal sector. In the small city of Bacolod, 27 per cent of young women are neither working nor attending school, and 40 per cent of working young women employed in the informal sector.

Consequences of youth unemployment

The high rate of non-employment of young people in the developing world is reason for concern; the lack of decent, sustainable jobs promotes a sense of displacement in the general youth population and often leads to crime, under-development, and a cycle of poverty. Frustrations accompanying long-term unemployment among groups of urban young men may feed political and ideological unrest and provoke violence.[5] Many countries have experienced "youth bulges", which occur when young people comprise at least 40 per cent of the population, and it has been argued that in such a context, the large numbers of unemployed and idle youth may challenge the authority of governments and endanger their stability. More importantly, there is no doubt that investing in youth is investing in society at large.

To better address youth unemployment, it is important to consider young people's employability, equal opportunities for jobs, entrepreneurship opportunities, and employment creation strategies. Employability is an outgrowth of education and economic development; measures promoting equity should investigate whether young women and young men have the same opportunities; and efforts to encourage youth-run enterprises can ensure that young people grow in their skills and contributions to their communities. Public policies that lead to new employment opportunities for youth are also essential for creating jobs and ensuring access. Investing in youth requires not just better-skilled youth, but also a commitment by public and private sector partners to keep job creation as a central concern of their investment strategies.

NOTES

1 Birdsall, Levine, & Ibrahim, 2005.
2 Jeffery, Jeffery, & Jeffery, 2008.
3 International Labour Organization, 2006.
4 Data for this section is from UN-HABITAT's Global Urban Observatory, based on data collected from multiple sources.
5 Commission for Africa, 2005.

2.4
Slums: The Good, the Bad and the Ugly

A boy plays with mud pistols in Mathare slum of Nairobi, Kenya
©**Manoocher Deghati/IRIN**

One out of every three people living in cities of the developing world lives in a slum. UN-HABITAT estimates indicate that in 2005, more than half of the world's slum population resided in Asia, followed by sub-Saharan Africa and Latin America and the Caribbean. Slum prevalence – or the proportion of people living in slum conditions in urban areas – is highest in sub-Saharan Africa; 62 per cent of the region's urban population lives in a slum or suffers from one or more of the five shelter deprivations that define a slum. In Asia, slum prevalence varies from a high of 43 per cent in Southern Asia to a low of 24 per cent in Western Asia, while in Latin America and the Caribbean, 27 per cent of the urban population was classified as living in slum conditions in 2005.[1]

Not all slum dwellers suffer the same degree or magnitude of deprivation, however, nor are all slums homogeneous – some, in fact, provide better living conditions than others. The degree of deprivation depends on how many of the five shelter deprivations used to measure slums – lack of access to improved water, lack of access to sanitation, non-durable housing, insufficient living area, and security of tenure – are associated with a particular slum household.

TABLE 2.4.1: **PROPORTION OF URBAN POPULATION LIVING IN SLUMS 2005**

Major area or region	Urban population (thousands) 2005 a	Percentage of Urban Population living in Slum 2005 b	Slum population (thousands) 2005 c
Developing world	2,219,811	36.5	810,441
Northern Africa	82,809	14.5	12,003
Sub-Saharan Africa	264,355	62.2	164,531
Latin America and the Caribbean	434,432	27.0	117,439
Eastern Asia	593,301	36.5	216,436
Southern Asia	468,668	42.9	201,185
South-Eastern Asia	243,724	27.5	67,074
Western Asia	130,368	24.0	31,254
Oceania	2,153	24.1	519

Source: UN-HABITAT Global Urban Observatory, 2008.
Notes: a: United Nations Population Division, World Urbanization Prospects: The 2005 Revision
b: Population living in households that lack either improved water, improved sanitation, sufficient living area (more than three persons per room), or durable housing.
c: This revised 2005 estimate is based on a change in the definition of adequate sanitation, as defined by WHO and UNICEF in 2005, and endorsed by members of the Slum Peer Review, whose members include UN-HABITAT, the World Bank, UNFPA, UN Statistics Division and various universities. These revised figures therefore show an improvement compared to 2001 estimates as the new definition of improved sanitation now includes pit latrines with slabs. The change affects estimates mostly in those regions where the pit latrine is more widespread as in Africa. In 2005, only a portion of households using pit latrines were considered slum households, whereas in 1990 and 2001 all households using pit latrines were counted as slum households.

Kibera slum in Nairobi.
©Josh Webb/iStockphoto

FIGURE 2.4.1: **PROPORTION OF URBAN POPULATIONS LIVING IN SLUMS BY REGION, 2005**

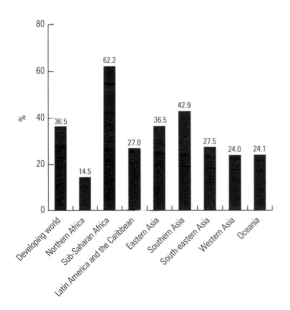

FIGURE 2.4.2: **SLUM POPULATION BY REGION (MILLIONS), 2005**

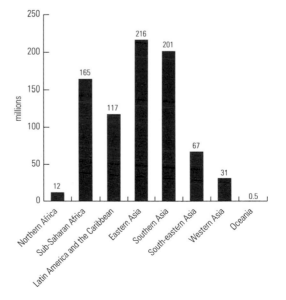

Source: UN-HABITAT, Global Urban Observatory, 2008

Source: UN-HABITAT, Global Urban Observatory, 2008

Slum households and shelter deprivations: degrees and characteristics

A street in the slums of Dhaka, Bangladesh
©**Manoocher Deghati/IRIN**

A slum household is defined as a group of individuals living under the same roof lacking **one or more** of the following conditions: **access to improved water; access to improved sanitation facilities; sufficient living area (not more than three people sharing the same room); structural quality and durability of dwellings; and security of tenure**. Four out of five of the slum definition indicators measure physical expressions of slum conditions: lack of water, lack of sanitation, overcrowded conditions, and non-durable housing structures. These indicators focus attention on the circumstances that surround slum life, depicting deficiencies and casting poverty as an attribute of the environments in which slum dwellers live. The fifth indicator – security of tenure – has to do with legality, which is not as easy to measure or monitor, as the tenure status of slum dwellers often

depends on **de facto** or **de jure** rights – or lack of them. This indicator has special relevance for measuring the denial and violation of housing rights, as well as the progressive fulfillment of these rights.

Defining slums by household-level shelter deprivations, however, does not fully capture the degree of deprivation experienced by a given household or slum community, or the specific needs of that community – a dimension that is important for policymakers. The current definition masks which specific deprivations households experience, as well as the severity of combined deprivations, and creates a challenge for monitoring, as the proportion of slum dwellers may remain the same in any given country, while the type of deprivation experienced by households may change over time. Furthermore, only the elimination of all deprivations in a given

household now registers as an improvement in the incidence of slums.

A simple alternative approach is to group slum households into categories that can be aggregated into moderately deprived (one shelter deprivation), severely deprived (two shelter deprivations) and extremely deprived (three or more shelter deprivations). By studying the prevalence of slum households in categories of severity, changes in household deprivations can be tracked more accurately; a reduction in one shelter deprivation for a severely deprived household, for example, could still leave it with a deficiency, but would move it out of the ranks of the severely deprived. Addressing programmes and policies to geographic areas in which households experience combinations of deprivations also allows for more effective upgrading and improvement.

Source: UN-HABITAT Global Urban Observatory, 2008

As the classification of slum households currently stands, it is not possible to fully appreciate the degree of deprivation experienced by a given household or slum area, or the specific needs of people living in that area – a dimension that is important for policymakers. Slum households are classified as such based only on the presence of *one or more* of the five shelter deprivations; this masks which specific deprivations different households experience, as well as the severity of combined deprivations. Noting only the presence of one or more deprivations also creates a challenge for monitoring, as the proportion of slum dwellers may remain the same in any given country, while the type of deprivation experienced by households may change over time. Programmes and policies required for providing improved water are not the same as those required for improving sanitation or housing, but the prevailing classification system does not make it possible to understand how specific deprivations are distributed or combined in a given area. Furthermore, only the elimination of all deprivations in a particular household currently registers as an improvement.

A simple alternative approach is to group slum households into categories that can be aggregated into moderately deprived (one shelter deprivation), severely deprived (two shelter deprivations) and extremely severely deprived (three or more shelter deprivations). By studying the prevalence of slum households in categories of severity, changes in household deprivations can be tracked more accurately; a reduction in one shelter deprivation for a severely deprived household, for example, could still leave it with a deficiency, but would move it out of the ranks of the severely deprived.

While the common unit of measurement used to define slums is the household, slums may be better defined as geographic areas. It is easier to target programmes and policies that aid slum communities to specific areas than to individual households, and focusing on a geographic area is likely to capture those families who can be assisted in a more cost-effective way by improving the spatial characteristics of an entire area. Categorizing slums as moderately, severely or extremely deprived and linking specific deprivations to each category for each slum area allows for the development of better-informed policies, programmes and urban planning measures to improve living conditions.

Cities differ on a variety of dimensions, from administration of economic and political systems to provision of basic services, that impact the way slums develop and how they change over time. The magnitude and type of shelter deprivations experienced in slums may vary across and within cities and can be addressed in terms of specific cities or in city-size categories. This section analyses slum concentrations in cities of similar sizes, for several reasons: as presented in Part 1, the size of a city is a determinant of its growth, and data associating slum concentration and city size are available for a significant number of countries. Intra-city differentials can be also addressed in many ways. This section adopts a geographic area cluster approach, studying clusters of dwellings that comprise the next standard census unit after the household. It presents data for developing-world regions on the three dimensions of slums – magnitude, specific deprivations and area – in terms of two city sizes: small cities and towns, and capital or large cities.

Sub-Saharan Africa

Nearly two-thirds (62 per cent) of city dwellers in sub-Saharan Africa live in a slum. The proportion of urban dwellers living in slums is particularly high in countries such as Ethiopia, Angola, Central African Republic, Chad, Guinea-Bissau, Madagascar, Mozambique, Niger, Sierra Leone, and Sudan, where slum households are likely to lack clean water, improved sanitation, durable housing or sufficient living space; in many cases, slum dwellers in these countries not only suffer from one shelter deprivation, but from three or more. The Multiple Indicators Cluster Surveys conducted in Angola, the Democratic Republic of the Congo, Guinea-Bissau, Sudan, and Sierra Leone reveal that more than 60 per cent of slum households in these countries experience at least two shelter deprivations, while more than 25 per cent are extremely deprived, with more than three shelter deprivations. Improving the lives of these slum dwellers requires investing in basic services to overcome the multiple shelter deprivations experienced by so many slum households.

In the surveyed countries, the problem of slum conditions, characterized by substandard and inadequate housing, extends beyond informal settlements; it is associated with general poverty, instability, inefficiency or absence of housing institutions, and other factors. Even in planned settlements, many households in the region lack access to basic services and adequate housing, but municipal authorities often refuse outright to extend essential services to unplanned neighbourhoods, putting untold thousands of families at risk. The problem is emblematic of general poverty stemming from chronically low incomes, high unemployment rates and lack of essential services related to health and education.

A second group of countries in sub-Saharan Africa has large slum concentrations but fewer instances of multiple shelter deprivations. Among these countries, are Benin, Burkina Faso, Burundi, Cameroon, Gabon, Kenya, Ghana, and Senegal. Although the majority of urban households in these countries can be classified as slums, most suffer from only one shelter deprivation. This means that a simple programme tackling the lack of improved water, sanitation or housing can contribute significantly to improving the lives of slum dwellers. For countries such as Benin, Burkina Faso, Cameroon, and Ghana, a sanitation programme would be enough to significantly improve the lives of most slum dwellers. For example, in Benin, 25 per cent of households could be reclassified as non-slum households if they gained improved sanitation facilities, because they are already enjoying improved water and sufficient living area in a durable house. UN-HABITAT analysis has also shown that in some countries such as Cote d'Ivoire, a simple housing programme to increase the living area of households and reduce overcrowding could move households from slum to non-slum status. A housing programme, however, can be more complex to implement than a sanitation programme.

FIGURE 2.4.3 A: **DISTRIBUTION OF SLUM DWELLERS BY DEGREE OF SHELTER DEPRIVATION (%), AFRICA**

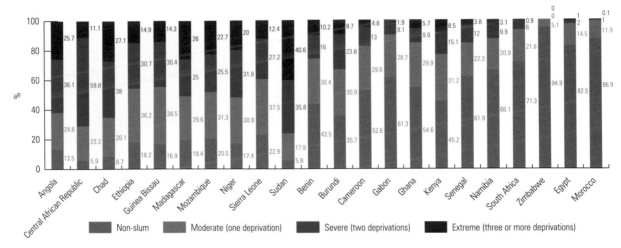

Source: UN-HABITAT, Global Urban Observatory, 2008

FIGURE 2.4.3 B: **DISTRIBUTION OF MODERATELY DEPRIVED SLUM DWELLERS (ONE DEPRIVATION) BY TYPE OF DEPRIVATION (%), AFRICA**

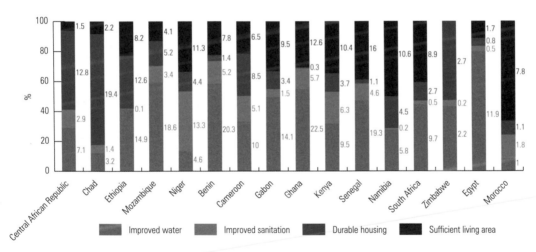

Source: UN-HABITAT, Global Urban Observatory, 2008

FIGURE 2.4.3 C: **DISTRIBUTION OF SEVERELY DEPRIVED SLUM DWELLERS (TWO DEPRIVATIONS) BY TYPE OF DEPRIVATION (%), AFRICA**

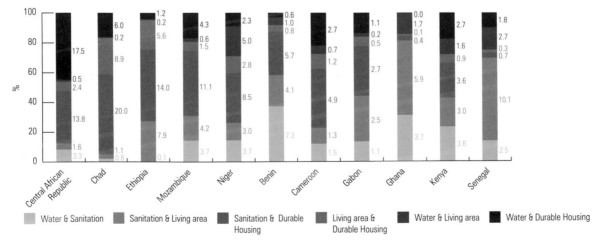

Source: UN-HABITAT, Global Urban Observatory, 2008

Residents of the Boa Vista informal settlement in Luanda, Angola, queue for water
©Jaspreet Kindra/**IRIN**

FIGURE 2.4.3 D: **DISTRIBUTION OF EXTREMELY DEPRIVED SLUM DWELLERS (THREE+ DEPRIVATIONS) BY TYPE OF DEPRIVATION (%), AFRICA**

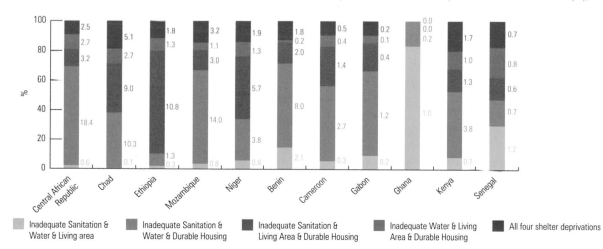

Source: *UN-HABITAT, Global Urban Observatory, 2008*

Urban poor adversely affected by Zimbabwe's political crisis

The prolonged political crisis in Zimbabwe, which began in the late 1990s and escalated in 2007/8, has significantly impacted living conditions in urban areas. Prior to the crisis, Zimbabwe was considered one of the most developed countries in Africa, with most of the country's urban inhabitants having access to basic services and adequate shelter. UN-HABITAT estimates show that in 2001, only 3.4 per cent of the urban population lived in slum conditions, the lowest slum prevalence in sub-Saharan African, where most countries have more than half of their urban populations living in slums. By 2006, however, the figure had risen to 18 per cent, with overcrowding emerging as a key problem in urban areas.

The deterioration of living conditions in urban Zimbabwe have been largely a result of rising unemployment and significant increases in food, medical, and transport costs, which reached unprecedented heights in the last few years. Between 1990 and 1995 food prices increased 516 per cent while education and transport costs grew 300 per cent, making 62 per cent of families in urban areas unable to afford these basic necessities. By 1996, real wages had also declined by 36 per cent of their 1990 value. Political instability during this period saw the economy decline; in 1998, the Zimbabwe economy grew a mere 0.9 per cent, then 0.5 per cent in 1999 before entering negative growth in 2000 and 2001. Today, unemployment is estimated to be between 75-80 per cent and 70 per cent of the population is estimated to be living below the poverty line.

Despite rising poverty levels and hyperinflation, slum prevalence in Zimbabwe defies commonly-held assumptions. Low levels of slum development in Zimbabwe's urban areas could be attributed to a history of policy decisions to maintain elite interests, included overly-high housing standards and colonial by-laws, which ensured that the country's urban areas remained slum- and squatter-free. The relatively low slum prevalence in Zimbabwe can thus be attributed in part to policies that marginalize the urban poor from the standards of the elite. Operation Murambatsvina, a mass slum eviction programme implemented by the government in May 2005, is a clear example of this agenda. By July 2005, some 700,000 urban residents had lost their homes, their source of livelihood or both. Today, the effects of the demolition are still being felt by Zimbabwe's urban poor; 114,000 Zimbabweans are still without shelter and another 20 per cent of urban residents have been forced to rural areas. The evictions forced 170,000 residents to move in with family or friends and an equal number to live in temporary housing provided by churches or other community organizations.

An improved political climate may bring down inflation and reduce poverty and unemployment levels, but experience of other countries shows that once living conditions begin to deteriorate, only dramatic improvements in governance and economic performance can reverse the situation. For Zimbabweans, it seems, the long journey to recovery has not yet begun.

Sources: Tibaijuka, 2005; Dansereau & Zamponi, 2005; UN-HABITAT Global Urban Observatory 2008.

It is important to note that living conditions for people in housing classified as slums are not alarming everywhere in the sub-Saharan Africa region. Indeed, some countries are effectively improving living conditions that have prompted concern in the past.[2] Some countries have moderate slum concentrations and others, including the Southern African countries of Namibia and Zimbabwe, have relatively low slum concentrations similar to those observed in the middle-income countries of Asia and Latin America and the Caribbean. In the Southern Africa region, a simple programme targeting housing or sanitation could help many families to move out of slum life and fully enjoy urban life with all of their basic shelter needs met. In South Africa, for example, 3 out of 10 urban households are slum households and 22 per cent of households suffer from only one shelter deprivation, primarily lack of improved sanitation (10 per cent) or lack of sufficient living area (9 per cent). Only 7 per cent of urban households in the country suffer from multiple shelter deprivations; where multiple deprivations are present, they tend to be lack of improved sanitation in combination with either lack of durable housing or sufficient living area (2.3 per cent and 2.1 per cent, respectively). A programme that provides access to improved sanitation – a flush toilet, improved latrine or pit latrine with slab – could reduce the slum concentration to 19 per cent, two-thirds of its current value of 29 per cent. Along with providing improved sanitation, expanding living area to reduce the number of persons per room would further help reduce the slum concentration to 10 per cent, one third of

▲
Slums in Addis Ababa, Ethiopia: Slum growth rates in Africa are the highest in the world.
©**Jan Martin Will/Shutterstock**

its current value. Reducing overcrowding, however, is more complex than providing sanitation facilities: it requires either a reduction of the household size or an increase in the number of rooms, or both. The ability to do so depends on the state of the housing market as well as on demographic factors and family structures.

One shelter deprivation is also common among slum dwellers in Namibia, where the slum concentration is 34 per cent. The simple lack of sufficient living space is the leading problem in Namibia, with 11 per cent of urban households lacking sufficient living area only and 5 per cent lacking durable housing only. Multiple shelter deprivations are mainly attributable to lack of durable housing in combination with lack of improved sanitation.

Northern Africa

The Northern Africa region has the lowest concentration of slums in Africa, with slum households comprising 15 per cent of all urban households. In this region, nine out of 10 slum households suffer from only one shelter deprivation. The specific concentration of slums and the type of shelter deprivations experienced vary across countries, from Egypt, where urban slum households suffer primarily from lack of improved sanitation, to Morocco, where urban slum households mostly lack sufficient living area. Simple, low-cost interventions could help the countries in Northern Africa to create "cities without slums" – a goal they have been working long before the Millennium Declaration was adopted in the year 2000.[3] As mentioned previously, programmes that promote access to improved sanitation tend to be less complex

FIGURE 2.4.4: **SLUM PREVALENCE IN AFRICA, 2005**

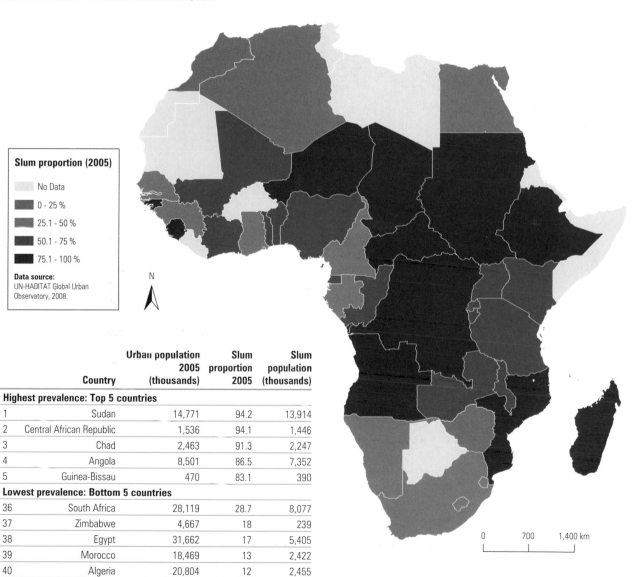

Slum proportion (2005)

	No Data
	0 - 25 %
	25.1 - 50 %
	50.1 - 75 %
	75.1 - 100 %

Data source:
UN-HABITAT Global Urban Observatory, 2008.

N

	Country	Urban population 2005 (thousands)	Slum proportion 2005	Slum population (thousands)
Highest prevalence: Top 5 countries				
1	Sudan	14,771	94.2	13,914
2	Central African Republic	1,536	94.1	1,446
3	Chad	2,463	91.3	2,247
4	Angola	8,501	86.5	7,352
5	Guinea-Bissau	470	83.1	390
Lowest prevalence: Bottom 5 countries				
36	South Africa	28,119	28.7	8,077
37	Zimbabwe	4,667	18	239
38	Egypt	31,662	17	5,405
39	Morocco	18,469	13	2,422
40	Algeria	20,804	12	2,455

0   700   1,400 km

Source: UN-HABITAT Global Urban Observatory, 2008.

Formal and informal areas in Cairo, Egypt
©**Timur Kulgarin/Shutterstock**

and costly than those that aim to reduce overcrowding, and thus must be supported in order to reduce slum prevalence in cities.

In the case of Egypt, near-universal access to improved water and electricity indicate that households classified as slums are not part of non-serviced informal settlements, but are rather households that cannot afford to live in places that have all of the adequate shelter amenities, including access to improved sanitation and sufficient living area. Households make choices and tradeoffs regarding their expenditures to maximize their contentment – or utility – within the options available to

them. Increasing those options so that more households can afford to live in decent housing with all of the amenities they need is important. In this regard, homeowners may have an advantage over renters, in that owners can improve their housing as their income increases, while renters must move to access more amenities. The Urban Inequities Survey conducted in Casablanca and Cairo in 2006 found that owners are more likely to pay for maintenance and repairs on their house than renters; in Casablanca, 20 per cent of owners reported that their houses had been repaired in the three months preceding the survey, compared with 5 per cent of renters.

Asia

Slum concentrations throughout Asia vary widely, from an average of 43 per cent in Southern Asia and 37 per cent in Eastern Asia, to 24 per cent in Western Asia and 28 per cent in South-Eastern Asia. The high concentration of slum households in Southern Asia can be associated with a variety of factors, including lack of investment in the sub-region's housing sector, poverty and instability. Bangladesh and Nepal have the highest slum prevalence in Southern Asia, with 69 per cent and 68 per cent, respectively. In Bangladesh, a significant proportion of urban households lack either durable housing or sufficient living area (19 per cent and 10 per cent, respectively); a further 11 per cent of households lack durable housing and sufficient living area combined, and 13 per cent lack both durable housing and improved sanitation. In India, 44 per cent of all urban households are classified as slums; there, 16 per cent of households lack improved sanitation.

This indicates clearly that there is no universal pattern of slum typology and scheme of shelter deprivation, and there is no universal prescription for slum improvement. The Southern Asian region also comprises countries, such as Afghanistan, where slum prevalence is exacerbated due to factors such as political instability and conflict, among others factors, which have adversely affected basic services provision and shelter conditions in cities.

Although Western Asia has a relatively low average slum concentration, it is important to note that within the sub-region, several countries, including Israel, Kuwait, Qatar, Saudi Arabia, Turkey, and United Arab Emirates, have low slum prevalence while other countries, such as Yemen, Lebanon and Iraq, have large proportions of urban dwellers living in slum conditions. In the first category of countries, slum households typically lack one basic element of adequate

FIGURE 2.4.5: **SLUM PREVALENCE IN ASIA, 2005**

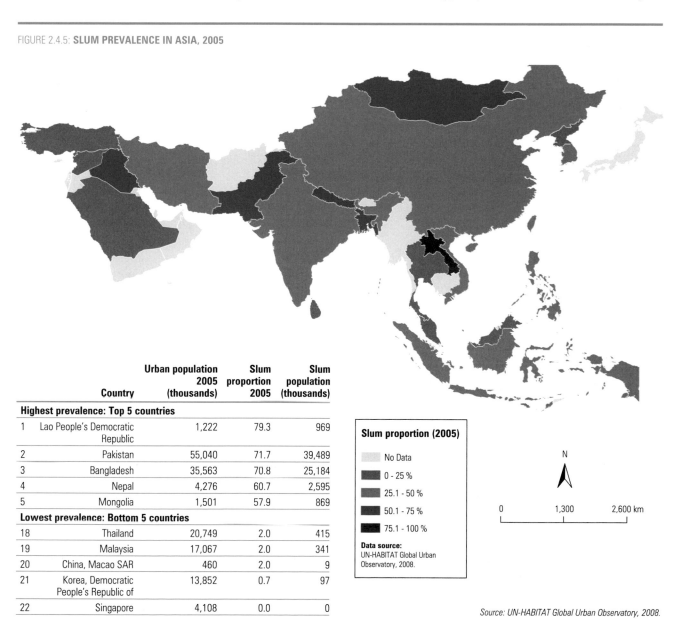

	Country	Urban population 2005 (thousands)	Slum proportion 2005	Slum population (thousands)
Highest prevalence: Top 5 countries				
1	Lao People's Democratic Republic	1,222	79.3	969
2	Pakistan	55,040	71.7	39,489
3	Bangladesh	35,563	70.8	25,184
4	Nepal	4,276	60.7	2,595
5	Mongolia	1,501	57.9	869
Lowest prevalence: Bottom 5 countries				
18	Thailand	20,749	2.0	415
19	Malaysia	17,067	2.0	341
20	China, Macao SAR	460	2.0	9
21	Korea, Democratic People's Republic of	13,852	0.7	97
22	Singapore	4,108	0.0	0

Slum proportion (2005)

No Data
0 - 25 %
25.1 - 50 %
50.1 - 75 %
75.1 - 100 %

Data source:
UN-HABITAT Global Urban Observatory, 2008.

N

0   1,300   2,600 km

Source: UN-HABITAT Global Urban Observatory, 2008.

Old Sanaa: More than a quarter of Yemen's urban households suffer from multiple shelter deprivations.
©**Vladimir Meinik/Shutterstock**

housing, as in Turkey, where 9 per cent of households are overcrowded. In countries with high concentrations of slum households, many suffer from multiple shelter deprivations, as in Iraq, where housing conditions have been deteriorating since the 1990s due to political and social turmoil. Instability in Lebanon has also contributed to increased numbers of slum households, and the situation in both Lebanon and Iraq has been compounded by an influx of refugees and internally displaced persons into cities. The Republic of Yemen has the highest proportion of people in the region living below the national poverty line, at 41 per cent. There, 65 per cent of urban households are classified as slums, and 26.4 per cent suffer from multiple shelter deprivations.

The prevalence of slum households in South-Eastern Asia is similar to that of Western Asia, at 27 per cent. As in the rest of Asia, the magnitude and diversity of shelter deprivations vary around the South-Eastern sub-region. Indonesia hosts 41 per cent of the sub-region's urban population, and there, 31 per cent of urban households are classified as slums, owing primarily to lack of sanitation (10 per cent) and lack of durable housing (9 per cent). Lack of durable housing is the main shelter deprivation in the Philippines. In Viet Nam, 59 per cent of households are classified as slums. Lack of improved water is the leading shelter deprivation, and for 11 per cent of households, water is the only amenity needed to improve their living situation significantly. For a further 8 per cent of households, improved water is one of two or more shelter needs, with many also lacking sufficient living area and improved sanitation. The South-Eastern Asian countries of Malaysia and Thailand have the lowest slum prevalence, at less than 10 per cent, owing to equitable housing policies and significant economic growth in recent years.

FIGURE 2.4.6 A: **DISTRIBUTION OF SLUM DWELLERS BY DEGREE OF SHELTER DEPRIVATION (%) ASIA**

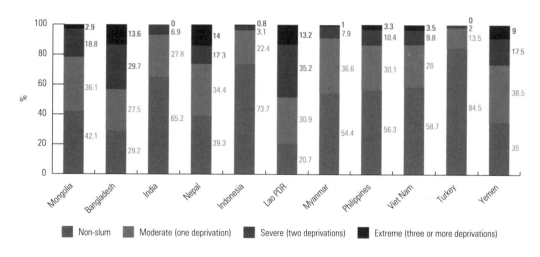

Source: UN-HABITAT, Global Urban Observatory, 2008

FIGURE 2.4.6 B: **DISTRIBUTION OF MODERATELY DEPRIVED SLUM DWELLERS (ONE DEPRIVATION) BY TYPE OF DEPRIVATION (%), ASIA**

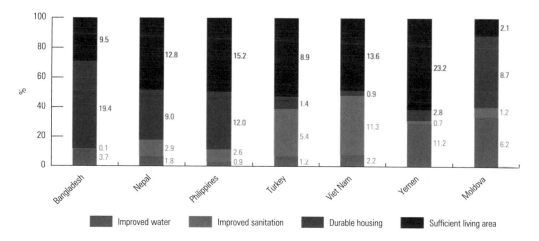

Source: UN-HABITAT, Global Urban Observatory, 2008

Latin America and the Caribbean

The average slum prevalence in Latin America and the Caribbean cities, at 27 per cent, is similar to that of South-Eastern Asia and Western Asia, but higher than that of North Africa. As in every region, slums throughout Latin American and the Caribbean are characterized by a great deal of diversity: the concentration of slum households is relatively low in Chile and Colombia; moderate in Brazil, Mexico and Peru; and dramatically high in Guatemala, Haiti, Nicaragua, and Bolivia.

Brazil and Mexico together are home to 54 per cent of the region's urban population. In Brazil, 34 per cent of households are classified as slums, and most suffer from only one shelter deprivation: of these, 12 per cent lack of improved sanitation; 6 per cent lack of improved water; and 7 per cent lack of sufficient living area. Lack of sufficient living area is the leading shelter deprivation in Colombia and the Dominican Republic. In Colombia, half of the slum households lack only sufficient living area, and one-quarter of slum households lack durable housing. Similarly, in the Dominican Republic, six out of 10 slum households lack sufficient living area.

FIGURE 2.4.7: **SLUM PREVALENCE IN LATIN AMERICA AND THE CARIBBEAN, 2005**

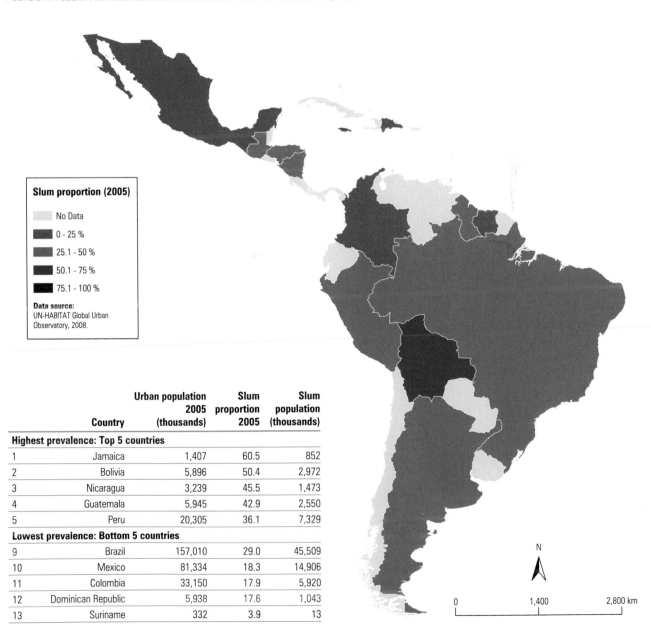

Slum proportion (2005)

	No Data
	0 - 25 %
	25.1 - 50 %
	50.1 - 75 %
	75.1 - 100 %

Data source:
UN-HABITAT Global Urban Observatory, 2008.

	Country	Urban population 2005 (thousands)	Slum proportion 2005	Slum population (thousands)
Highest prevalence: Top 5 countries				
1	Jamaica	1,407	60.5	852
2	Bolivia	5,896	50.4	2,972
3	Nicaragua	3,239	45.5	1,473
4	Guatemala	5,945	42.9	2,550
5	Peru	20,305	36.1	7,329
Lowest prevalence: Bottom 5 countries				
9	Brazil	157,010	29.0	45,509
10	Mexico	81,334	18.3	14,906
11	Colombia	33,150	17.9	5,920
12	Dominican Republic	5,938	17.6	1,043
13	Suriname	332	3.9	13

Source: UN-HABITAT, Global Urban Observatory, 2008

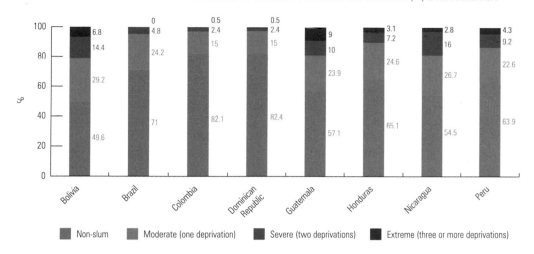

■ Non-slum   ■ Moderate (one deprivation)   ■ Severe (two deprivations)   ■ Extreme (three or more deprivations)

Source: UN-HABITAT, Global Urban Observatory, 2008

FIGURE 2.4.8 B: **DISTRIBUTION OF MODERATELY DEPRIVED SLUM DWELLERS (ONE DEPRIVATION) BY TYPE OF DEPRIVATION (%), LATIN AMERICA**

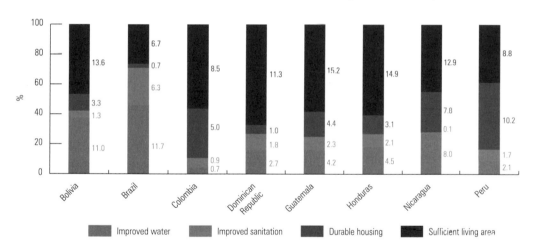

■ Improved water   ■ Improved sanitation   ■ Durable housing   ■ Sufficient living area

Source: UN-HABITAT, Global Urban Observatory, 2008

In most Latin American countries, access to improved water and improved sanitation is quasi-universal. Lack of improved sanitation constitutes a concern only in Guatemala, Haiti, Nicaragua, and Bolivia, each of which have significant concentrations of slum households with multiple shelter deprivations. In Haiti, the proportion of slum households is 76 per cent, with more than half suffering from multiple shelter deprivations. Similarly, in Bolivia, the slum prevalence is 61 per cent, with more than half of slum households suffering from multiple shelter deprivations. In both Bolivia and Haiti, lack of sanitation and lack of sufficient living area are the main shelter deprivations experienced by slum households. In Haiti, 15 per cent of urban households lack sufficient living area, 9 per cent lack improved sanitation, and 8 per cent lack both sufficient living area and improved sanitation.[4]

▶

Boy on bike, Nicaragua
©Charles Taylor/Shutterstock

Woman-headed households suffer disproportionately from inadequate housing

Turkish women taking a lunch break in Ankara
©**Kobby Dagan/iStockphoto**

A recent report released by the Centre on Housing Rights and Evictions notes that while previous studies found that women who migrate to cities do so to join family members – mostly husbands – in the city, this trend appears to be changing: an increasing number of women are migrating to cities on their own, often to escape domestic violence or discrimination in rural areas, or because they have been disinherited. In some sub-Saharan African countries, stigmatization due to HIV/AIDS has also forced women to move to cities. In Kenya, for instance, many rural women who are infected with HIV, or who have lost a husband to the disease, are sent away from the marital home along with their children. Many of these women end up in urban slums, while their children, who are presumed to be infected with the virus, are often denied a share of the father's property.

While poor women and men in urban centres both face insecurity of land tenure and shelter,

women are especially disadvantaged because they are often excluded from secure tenure as a consequence of cultural norms and unequal legal rights in legislative and policy frameworks of political systems. Women who become single heads of households, particularly in Africa, are particularly vulnerable, as in many countries in the region, they can still only access land through husbands or fathers. Where women's land ownership is relationship-based, they risk losing access to land after widowhood, divorce, desertion or male migration, which can lead to destitution. Women who experience violence in their relationships are often not able to secure a safe home for themselves and their children because they lack rights to land, property and shelter, particularly when marital property is only in the husband's name.

The organization, management and cost of land and transport systems have implications for poor

women's land ownership, security of tenure and housing, as well. Many poor women live in slums and informal urban settlements, which are characterized by an array of shelter deprivations: lack of secure tenure, non-durable housing, insufficient living space, and lack of access to basic services such as clean water and improved toilets. Life in slums is difficult and precarious, fraught with ill-health and lack of employment and income-generating opportunities. According to the UN-HABITAT Urban Indicators database (2006 version), these high-density neighbourhoods with limited means of livelihoods are increasingly the homes of woman-headed households. Approximately 20 per cent of households in the 160 sample cities included in the Urban Indicators database are headed by women. In the cities of Central Asia, woman-headed households are almost the norm, rather than the exception. In the cities of Viet Nam, Ethiopia, South Africa, and Colombia, more than one in three households are headed by women.

The table below illustrates that between 15 and 57 per cent of the families living in houses with three combined shelter deprivations are headed by women in the urban areas of selected countries. Woman-headed households in the urban areas of Haiti, Ghana and Nicaragua are specially affected. In Kenya and Nicaragua, one-third of woman-headed households suffer from four shelter deprivations. While more research into the links between gender and urban poverty is needed, this preliminary data suggests that in some countries, woman-headed households disproportionately suffer from inadequate housing in poor urban neighbourhoods.

Sources: UN-HABITAT, 2006 ; Bazoglu & Mboup, 2007; Centre on Housing Rights and Evictions (COHRE), 2008.

PERCENTAGE OF URBAN HOUSEHOLDS HEADED BY WOMEN WITH DIFFERENT DEGREES OF SHELTER DEPRIVATION IN SELECTED COUNTRIES

Country	% one shelter deprivation	% two shelter deprivations	% three shelter deprivations	% four shelter deprivations
Ghana (2003)	38	34	51	-
Kenya (2003	23	24	28	31
Madagascar(1997)	28	24	29	14
Senegal (1997)	27	23	25	14
Tanzania (1999)	28	28	15	
Nicaragua (2001)	40	37	39	33
Haiti (2000)	52	50	57	
Indonesia (2002)	13	14	17	
Nepal ((2001)	20	14	19	
Armenia	30	38	17	

Source: UN-HABITAT (2006) Urban Indicators Database, 2006. Additional analysis by Prabha Khosla.
Note: Shelter deprivations are defined as the absence of the following conditions: durable housing, sufficient living area, access to improved water, access to sanitation, or secure tenure.

High- and low-income housing in Rio de Janeiro, Brazil
©**Jose Miguel Hernandez Leon**

NOTES

1 Slum percentages and populations reflect revised estimates by UN-HABITAT in 2005 after a change in the definition of what constitutes adequate sanitation in urban areas. The decrease in figures from the 2001 estimates reflected in UN-HABITAT's *State of the World's Cities Report 2006/7* is primarily a result of a change in the definition of adequate sanitation. In 2005, only a proportion of households using pit latrines were considered slum households, whereas in 1990 and 2001, all households using pit latrines were counted as slum households. The change affects estimates mostly in those areas where the use of pit latrines is more widespread, as in sub-Saharan Africa.

2 Refer to the global scorecard on slums in the *State of the World's Cities Report 2006/7*, pages 38 to 45.

3 UN-HABITAT, 2006.

4 A similar situation has been also observed in Bolivia and Nicaragua. In Bolivia, 14 per cent of urban households lack only sufficient living area, 11 per cent lack only improved sanitation and 7 per cent lack both. In Nicaragua, with a slum concentration of 57 per cent, 13 per cent lack only sufficient living area, and 8 per cent lack either improved sanitation or durable housing.

2.5
Slum Cities and Cities with Slums

The prevalence of slum households varies dramatically across cities of the developing world. In some cities, a relatively small percentage of households experience shelter deprivations, or many experience only one barrier to adequate housing. In other cities, a majority of dwellings suffer from two or more shelter deprivations, threatening the health, safety and well-being of their inhabitants. This section magnifies the impact of slums on cities, focusing on the spatial component of slum prevalence. It reveals the existence of entire "slum cities", where urban services are either inadequate for rich and poor alike, or where slum households comprise a significantly large majority of households in the city.

In the analysis of slum areas, UN-HABITAT defines any specific place, whether a whole city or a neighbourhood, as a slum area if half or more of all households lack improved water, improved sanitation, sufficient living area, durable housing, secure tenure, or combinations thereof. An area or neighbourhood deprived of improved sanitation alone may experience a lesser degree of deprivation than an area that lacks any adequate services at all, but both are considered slums in this definition. Understanding the spatial components of shelter deprivation and the dynamics of slum development within cities is fundamental to improving the lives of slum dwellers and building urban harmony.

Slums in many cities are no longer just marginalized neighbourhoods housing a relatively small proportion of the urban population: in some cities, particularly in Southern Asia and sub-Saharan Africa, slums are home to significantly large proportions of the urban population and slum growth is as high as urban growth. The increasing prevalence – and even dominance – of poor-quality, underserved housing calls for new ways of looking at cities and the slums within them.

Slum households with the most shelter deprivations are highly visible in most African cities, as many are clustered within geographically contiguous high-density neighbourhoods, either in the centre or on the periphery of cities. In general, if a neighbourhood reflects slum characteristics, so do most of the individual households within that neighbourhood. Variations in the geographic distribution of slums tend to correspond at the highest level with a three-part typology: countries in which both poor families and rich families live in slum areas and non-slum urban areas are virtually absent; countries in which slum areas are distinct settlements only in capital and large cities; and countries in which non-slum areas are predominant and are home to both high- and low-income families.

Methodology

This section focuses on analyzing the geographical prevalence of slums and shelter deprivations according to city size. It is based on data from 49 countries in Africa, Asia and Latin America collected through Demographic and Health Surveys (DHS). DHS collects information on various aspects of housing as well as the place of residence: capital city, large city, small city, town, or village. It is important to note that the DHS definition of city size does not follow the criteria used in Part 1 of this report, but uses instead city sizes determined by the national implementing agency within each country. A city may be considered large at the country level but small at the international level according to its population size. The DHS data analysis reveals four types of variation of slum concentration by city size, each of which is detailed in the following text:

- Slum incidence is very high in small cities and towns, as well as in the capital and large cities (in 11 countries, 22 per cent)

- Slum incidence is high in small cities and towns but relatively low in the capital and large cities (in 17 countries, 35 per cent)

- Slum incidence is relatively low in the capital and large cities, as well as in small cities and towns (in 17 countries, 35 per cent)

- Slum incidence is higher in capital and large cities than in small cities and towns (in 4 countries, 8 per cent)

Locating slums: Geographic concentration and clustering

"Tin city" Kibera, Kenya
© **J Norman Reid/Shutterstock**

The number of slum dwellers in any given city can be discerned from data that enumerates general housing types and characteristics, but to efficiently implement programmes to deliver water, sanitation and durable housing, slum dwellers and shelter deprivations must be associated with specific geographic locations. Doing so can be a challenge, especially when census data and household surveys only distinguish urban from rural households, failing to disaggregate different types and sizes of urban areas.

Some countries have tried to differentiate urban slum and urban non-slum settlements using their own administrative definitions or through income-based indicators, such as poverty levels. This technique has a tendency to underestimate the slum population, as definitions and data collection are not always consistent and accurate. With the development of satellite imagery and geographic information systems, slums can be more easily identified and incorporated to censuses and surveys, but this approach is not yet fully implemented to allow global measurement and comparison of slums.

A different approach is to align the definitions of slum areas or neighbourhoods with census enumeration areas – small areas comprising one or more city blocks, typically canvassed by one census representative. Enumeration areas represent the smallest household aggregation in many countries' census methodologies;

population and housing characteristics within one enumeration area tend to be relatively homogeneous, making them powerful tools for localizing slums.

Slum enumeration areas take as their basis the concentration of slum households, initially disregarding the specific degree of deprivation experienced by households in the area. Recognizing that the threshold of slum household concentration for a slum enumeration area may vary from country to country according to cultural, economic and political factors, UN-HABITAT has opted for a threshold of 50 per cent: a neighbourhood is classified as a slum if more than half of the households in the area suffer from one or more shelter deprivation. (For cities in the developed world, however, the threshold may be lower, while for cities in the developing world, the threshold may be higher.)

Some limitations are inherent in the household concentration method used here: it does not uniformly consider characteristics specific to the settlement, such as the condition of the roads, availability of drainage systems, management of solid waste, and the like, nor does it consider whether the settlement is near a steep slope or in or near a flood plain, toxic waste area, industrial area, or other hazardous site. However, where such environmental information has been collected through Urban Inequities Surveys, preliminary results show that households with multiple

shelter deprivations are more likely to be located in neighbourhoods with poor road conditions, open drains or other inadequate drainage systems, poor management of solid waste, and where air and water pollution are prevalent. Where land and building materials are expensive, low-income families tend to use cheap materials and build fewer rooms to accommodate their households, resulting in lack of durability and overcrowding.

Slums are often viewed as the result of poor population growth management on the part of major cities, but cities of all sizes struggle with the inability to provide adequate affordable housing and the extended water supplies and sanitation facilities needed to serve growing populations. Slums can be easier to improve in small cities than in large cities, as small cities often present fewer social, cultural and economic barriers to urban development. In small cities, developing master plans and engaging in urban planning processes with the participation of families and communities is often more straightforward than in large cities, and institutions can be more easily coordinated to carry out service implementation. In cities of all sizes, improving the lives of slum dwellers depends on the increased development of non-agriculture sectors, services and industries for sustainable urbanization, and creating access to well-paid jobs and formal housing policies with structured mortgage systems.

Countries with generalized slums: Slum incidence is very high in small cities and towns as well as in the capital and large cities

Generalized slums are prevalent throughout least-developed countries. In Africa, slum incidence is very high in both big and small cities of Burkina Faso, Central African Republic, Chad, Ethiopia, Malawi, Niger, Tanzania, and Togo. High slum incidence in all types of cities has also been recorded in Yemen; and Haiti. In each of these countries, poverty is endemic, with populations lacking basic services in shelter, health and social services across city types and sizes. Rapid urban growth without needed urban infrastructure development has resulted in a high proportion of slum households in capital and large cities – urbanization and urban growth have led to increased slum growth. In these countries, slum households are deprived of multiple basic shelter needs; nearly one-quarter of slum households suffer from one or two shelter deprivations, and almost half suffer from *at least* two shelter deprivations.

In the Central African Republic, the prevalence of slums is high in small cities and towns as well as in the capital of Bangui and other large cities, but it is important to note that the incidence of multiple deprivations is much higher in small cities and towns, where 82 per cent of households lack at least two basic services: 27 per cent lack both improved water and sanitation, and 27 per cent lack water, sanitation and durable housing. In the capital and large cities, the leading shelter deprivations are improved sanitation and durable housing; 16 per cent of households lack both. In Chad, while slums comprise 97 per cent of households in small cities and towns, and 96 per cent in the capital and large cities, shelter deprivations experienced by different cities vary. In the capital

of Ndjamena and other large cities, durable housing is the leading deprivation; 18 per cent of households lack durable housing and improved sanitation together, and 12 per cent lack both durable housing and sufficient living space. In small cities and towns, although durable housing is a concern, it is more often combined with other shelter deprivations than in large cities: 22 per cent of households lack durable housing and improved sanitation, and 16 per cent are without durable housing, improved sanitation and improved water combined, constituting an extremely severe deprivation. The situation is similar in Ethiopia and other countries with the same level of slum prevalence.

Countries with high slum prevalence in small cities and towns and relatively low slum prevalence in the capital and large cities

In countries with high rates of slum prevalence in small cities and towns and lower slum prevalence in the capital and large cities, families in small cities and towns typically bear the burden of multiple shelter deprivations. Some small cities and towns are administratively and politically created without basic urban planning systems, adequate shelter and basic infrastructure, while capital and large cities in the same country benefit from urban infrastructure and services. In Benin, for example, the slum prevalence in the capital city of Cotonou and other large cities is relatively low, at 49 per

FIGURE 2.5.1 A: **PERCENTAGE OF SLUM HOUSEHOLDS BY SIZE OF CITY**
COUNTRIES WITH HIGH CONCENTRATION OF SLUMS IN SMALL CITIES/TOWNS AS WELL AS IN CAPITAL/LARGE CITIES

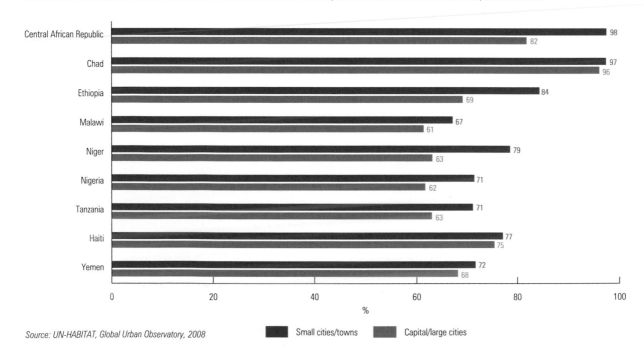

Source: UN-HABITAT, Global Urban Observatory, 2008

Small cities/towns   Capital/large cities

Street market in Benin
©**Peeter Viisimaa/iStockphoto**

cent; in small cities, however, slums comprise the majority of households, at 78 per cent, 30 per cent higher than the prevalence of slums in the capital and large cities. In Benin's small cities and towns, 29 per cent of slum households lack improved sanitation; 12 per cent lack both sanitation and improved water; 11 per cent lack both sanitation and durable housing; and 15 per cent go without sanitation, water or durable housing combined. In the capital and large cities, access to improved water, sufficient living area and durable housing is quasi-general; only 20 per cent of households lack improved sanitation, classifying them as slums.

A similar, but less dramatic, situation exists in Cote d'Ivoire: 69 per cent of households in small cities and towns are classified as slums; 25 per cent lack improved sanitation facilities, 13 per cent lack improved water, and 14 per cent go without either service. In the capital of Abidjan and large other cities, the slum prevalence is 45 per cent, but most of these households have only one shelter deprivation – improved sanitation.

The high prevalence of slum households in the small cities and towns of these countries can be attributed primarily to the lack of urban planning. Hence, while these settlements qualify as "cities" due to their population size, they do not provide the infrastructure and economic activities that make cities liveable and viable. In many countries, "cities" are actually urban agglomerations that encompass a contiguous territory inhabited at urban density levels, without regard to administrative boundaries. In other places, population size is all that matters for classification as a city, as in Mali and Madagascar, where any place with a population of 5,000 inhabitants qualifies as urban. In most of these places, rural activities are predominant, with the exception of some

FIGURE 2.5.1 B: **PERCENTAGE OF SLUM HOUSEHOLDS BY SIZE OF CITY**
COUNTRIES WITH HIGH CONCENTRATION OF SLUMS IN SMALL CITIES/TOWNS AND LOW OR MODERATE CONCENTRATION OF SLUMS IN CAPITAL/LARGE CITIES

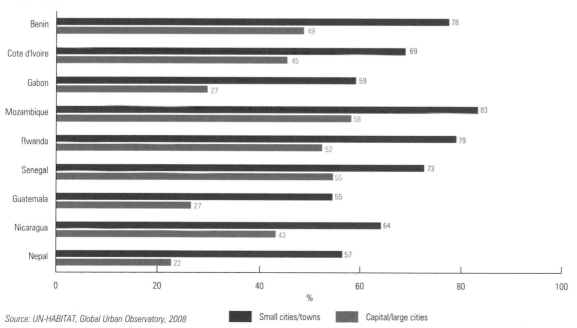

Source: UN-HABITAT, Global Urban Observatory, 2008

■ Small cities/towns   ■ Capital/large cities

Countries with relatively low slum prevalence in capital and large cities, as well as in small cities and towns

administrative services. The reclassification of a location from rural area to city or town can imply the presence of administrative institutions, such as a city council that has the responsibility to develop a city plan, to distribute lands and provide basic services. Water and electricity provision are the primary services that follow such a reclassification. However, development of sewerage systems and a housing scheme to ensure access to adequate dwellings often do not follow, leaving small cities and towns *de facto* villages or rural communities.

Creating "urban" places without adequate urban infrastructure is a recipe for slum cities. Newly provided improved water attracts migrants from neighbouring villages, while the lack of improved sanitation and durable housing remain issues for everyone, including natives and new migrants. In these small cities and towns, the most common improved water supply is from a public tap or borehole; households are rarely connected to piped water. There are no sewerage systems and the management of solid waste is often infrequent or nonexistent. In the capital and large cities of countries where small cities and towns have the highest prevalence of slums, most families have access to improved water and improved sanitation. There, lack of durable housing and sufficient living area are the primary shelter deprivations, reflecting a poor housing market that prevents the attainment of enough equity to make house repairs and extensions. Mortgage markets and other housing finance mechanisms are poor or nonexistent, preventing many residents from accessing affordable houses.

In countries with low prevalence of slums in both large and small cities, multiple shelter deprivations are rare. In Egypt, for example, slum households in the capital Cairo and other large cities, as well as in small cities and towns, tend to lack improved sanitation only. Only 13 per cent of households in the capital, and 21 per cent in small cities, experience shelter deprivations. In Brazil and Colombia, lack of sufficient living area is the main shelter deprivation in the capital and other large cities, while lack of improved sanitation is the leading shelter issue in small cities and towns. Data from the Dominican Republic and Honduras indicate similar conditions, with overcrowding dominating shelter deprivations in large cities and lack of improved sanitation comprising the main shelter issue in small cities. In parts of Asia, too, overall slum prevalence is generally low, with most slum households experiencing only one shelter deprivation. In Turkey and Krygyzstan, for instance, the leading shelter deprivations in small cities and towns are similar to those observed in the capital and large cities. In Turkey, where the prevalence of slums is 10 per cent in the capital city of Ankara and other large cities and 25 per cent in small cities, lack of improved water and sufficient living area are the primary shelter deprivations. In Kyrgyzstan, where prevalence of slums is 19 per cent in the capital and large cities and 39 per cent in small cities and towns, lack of improved sanitation is the leading shelter deprivation factor: 28 per cent of large city households and 14 per cent of small city households lack improved sanitation. South Africa has a similar pattern: multiple shelter deprivations are significant only in small

FIGURE 2.5.1 C: **PERCENTAGE OF SLUM HOUSEHOLDS BY CITY SIZE**
COUNTRIES WITH LOW OR MODERATE CONCENTRATION OF SLUMS IN CAPITAL/LARGE CITIES AS WELL AS IN SMALL CITIES AND TOWNS

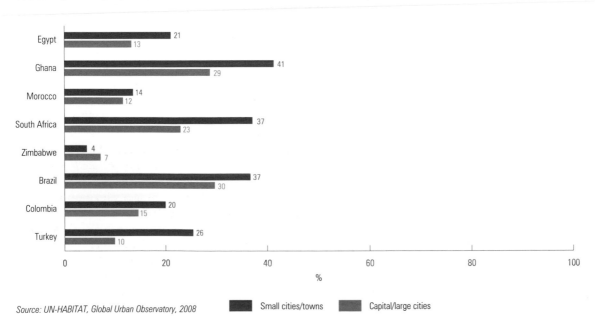

Source: UN-HABITAT, Global Urban Observatory, 2008

■ Small cities/towns ■ Capital/large cities

▲
A slum settlement in Brazil.
©Gustavo Miguol Machado da Caridade Fernandes/Shutterstock

cities and towns, with 10 per cent of households experiencing multiple deprivations, compared with a total slum prevalence of 37 per cent. In the capital city of Pretoria and other large cities, one shelter deprivation is more common: 7 per cent of households lack improved sanitation and 8 per cent lack sufficient living area, where the overall slum prevalence is 23 per cent.

The countries with relatively low slum prevalence across different types and sizes of cities seem to have anticipated needs for basic infrastructure as they grew. In most of these cities, a vast majority of slum households suffer from only one shelter deprivation. Simple, low-cost interventions are all that are needed to help most of these countries to create "cities without slums".

Slum incidence is higher in capital and large cities than in small cities and towns

The prevalence of slums is greater in large cities than in small ones in only four countries in this analysis: Namibia, Bolivia, Bangladesh, and the Philippines.

Namibia is among the few African countries with only a moderate prevalence of slums, at 34 per cent of all households, compared with 66 per cent in the sub-Saharan African region as a whole. Contrary to the general trend, however, slum households in the country are slightly more prevalent in the capital and its large cities (36 per cent) than in its small cities (32 per cent). Clearly, Namibia has taken steps to provide adequate housing for its urban residents, but small cities and towns appear to be providing housing that meets the needs of their residents better than the capital and other large cities. Use of improved water is quasi-universal throughout the country, however sufficient living space is lacking in the capital and other large cities.

Overcrowding typically correlates with urban growth in the absence of adequate housing supplies to satisfy demand generated by additional households. The governments of many capital cities have responded to urban growth by reducing the amount of land available to each household, leading to inflation in the housing market. Land prices have skyrocketed over the last several years in many African cities, where a black market in real estate has also developed to meet demand. The cost of building materials has not followed the inflation in the land market and the market in general, allowing families to afford building materials, but not enough land to provide a home of suitable size for their households.

Many residents of Namibia's cities are also deprived of adequate sanitation facilities, particularly in the capital and other large cities, where 76 per cent of households have access to improved sanitation, compared with 80 per cent in small cities and towns. The gap in sanitation coverage between large and small cities has grown in recent years: from 1992 to 2000, the prevalence of slums in the capital and other large cities grew from 24 per cent to 36 per cent, owing primarily to deterioration in improved sanitation coverage, while slums decreased from 39 per cent to 32 per cent in small cities and towns.

Bolivia is among the countries in Latin America and the Caribbean with a high general prevalence of slum households, particularly in the capital and other large cities, where 60 per cent of households are slums, compared with 47 per cent in small cities and towns. Households in Bolivia's small cities and towns have fewer overall shelter deprivations than those in the capital and large cities. This is especially the case concerning access to improved sanitation and access to durable housing: in small cities, 74.2 per cent have access to sanitation, compared with 62.3 per cent in large cities; and 89.4 per cent of households in small cities have durable housing, versus

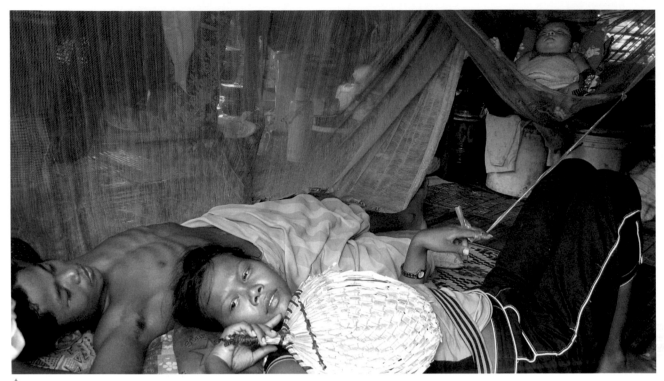

▲
Overcrowded house, Phnom Penh
©**Keisuke Ikeda**

78.3 per cent in large cities. Bolivia's large cities have clearly grown in the absence of sufficient basic shelter services – a longitudinal perspective shows that they once had adequate infrastructure for their populations, but they have not been able to keep up with population growth.

Bangladesh, like several Asian countries, has a high general prevalence of slum households, but unlike many others, slum prevalence in its capital Dhaka and other large cities is higher than in its small cities and towns. In Bangladesh's large cities, 80 per cent of households are classified as slums, compared with 67 per cent in small cities and towns. While access to improved water is quasi-universal and availability of sufficient living area is roughly the same in cities of different sizes, people who live in small cities and towns have better access to improved

sanitation than those in the capital and large cities: 72 per cent of households in small cities have improved sanitation, versus 66.5 per cent in large cities. This is also the case with durable housing, available to 48.6 per cent of households in small cities, compared with 33.8 per cent in large cities.

The Philippines has a moderate prevalence of slum households compared with the rest of Asia, with 40 per cent of households in the capital and large cities classified as slums, compared with 29.1 per cent in small cities. In small cities, 94.6 per cent of households have access to improved sanitation and 74.1 per cent have access to durable housing, while in large cities, 87 per cent of households have access to improved sanitation and 71.6 per cent have access to durable housing.

FIGURE 2.5.1 D: **PERCENTAGE OF SLUM HOUSEHOLDS BY SIZE OF CITY**
COUNTRIES WITH SLUM CONCENTRATION HIGHER IN CAPITAL/LARGE CITIES THAN IN SMALL CITIES AND TOWNS

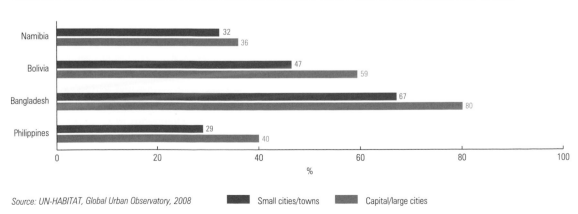

Source: UN-HABITAT, Global Urban Observatory, 2008   ███ Small cities/towns   ███ Capital/large cities

Clustering of slum dwellers within cities

Type 1: Countries with high overall slum prevalence, giving rise to "slum cities"

Where the prevalence of slums is dramatically high in both large and small cities, they become the common form of human settlement, with both poor and rich households lacking at least one element of adequate shelter or where households that have adequate shelter are located in areas that are generally deprived. Most such cities are in countries in which poverty is endemic, urban infrastructure is absent, and housing is inadequate overall. In such "slum cities", the wealthy are able to access improved water and sanitation in durable houses with sufficient living space, but these households comprise a very small proportion of the population, and they are typically subject to the same larger environmental conditions from which the city suffers: lack of solid waste management, excessive pollution and other hazards.

Slum cities are prevalent throughout sub-Saharan Africa, where poor households experience multiple shelter deprivations. In Burkina Faso, for example, 93 per cent of slum households live in a concentrated slum area, with 71 per cent living in an extremely deprived area in which three out of four households lack basic shelter services. Even 65 per cent of households that do not have any shelter deprivations – non-slum households – live in a slum area, while 35 per cent of non-slum households live in a mildly deprived area. In total, 87 per cent of all households live in a slum area – more than the total proportion of slum households, which is 79 per cent.

In the Central African Republic, Chad and Ethiopia, slum cities are more entrenched and underserved, with as much as 91 per cent of even non-slum households living in extremely deprived settlements. Estimations of slum prevalence in Central African Republic, Chad and Ethiopia are the same at both the household and area level of analysis, meaning that they are characterized by slum cities in which rich and poor families live alongside each other. The same situation prevails in Niger, Nigeria, Tanzania, and Togo. The lack of basic services in slum cities cannot be attributed only to the informality of the settlements – indeed, entire cities cannot comprise "informal" settlements – but are rather an outgrowth of inadequate planning, construction and social services. Where governments have not provided adequate urban infrastructure, cities may become more and more deeply mired in the pollution, disease and social ills emanating from underserved areas.

In countries where the urban landscape is dominated by slums, improvement in the lives of slum dwellers first requires the implementation of macro-level programmes, including housing infrastructure and finance, improved water, improved sanitation, and durable housing units with adequate living space. However, macro-level programmes must be associated with micro-level programmes, including micro-financing, self-help, education, and employment. Housing services may exist, but families will use them only if they are affordable.

FIGURE 2.5.2: **PERCENTAGE OF NON-SLUM OR SLUM HOUSEHOLDS LIVING IN SLUM AREAS**

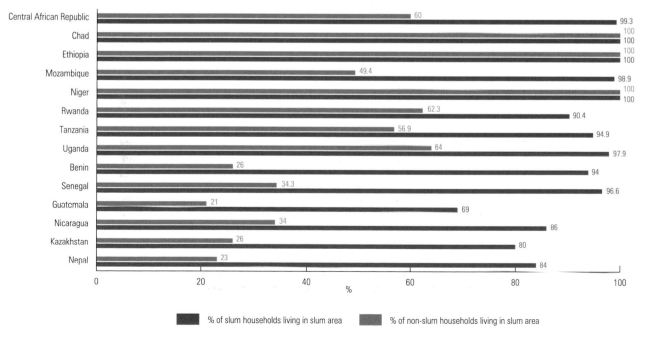

Source: UN-HABITAT, Global Urban Observatory, 2008

Moreover, urban infrastructure focused on upgrading slums should incorporate economic development and employment programmes to enable families to afford public services for their dwellings. Efforts must also ensure that durable, properly sized housing is affordable and accessible to poor families so that they can also afford health care, education and other needs.

Type 2: Countries in which slum areas are highly visible and concentrated settlements in capital and large cities: The isolated underclass

The second category of countries are those where the prevalence of slums is dramatically high in small cities and towns compared with the capital and other large cities. In these countries, there is a clear distinction between slum areas and non-slum areas, particularly in the capital and large cities, while small cities and towns are dominated by slum areas. For example, in the capital and large cities of Benin, 94 per cent of slum households live in slum areas, while 74 per cent of non-slum households live in non-slum areas. Only 26 per cent of non-slum households co-reside with slum households in slum settlements, while only 6 per cent of slum households live in non-slum settlements. Côte d'Ivoire has the same prevalence of slum households as Benin, at 65 per cent, but in the large cities of Côte D'Ivoire, a significant proportion of non-slum households live in slum areas (44 per cent), while 12 per cent of slum households live in non-slum areas. In fact, 73 per cent of households, slum or not, live in non-slum areas. In Guinea and Madagascar, where the urbanization process is led by small cities and towns, large proportions of non-slum households live in slum areas. Rwanda and Uganda offer a different scenario, in which the majority of non-slum households live in non-slum areas.

Also in this second group are cities in the Latin American countries of Guatemala, Nicaragua and Peru. In Guatemala, there is a net distinction between slum areas and non-slum areas in the capital and large cities, with non-slum areas hosting primarily non-slum households, and slum areas hosting primarily slum households: only 31 per cent of the residents of non-slum areas are slum households, and only 21 per cent of the residents of slum areas are non-slum households. In Nicaragua, 34 per cent of the residents of slum areas are non-slum households, while 14 per cent of the residents of non-slum areas are slum households. In Peru, the percentages are 14 per cent and 29 per cent, respectively.

This category also includes cities in the Asian countries of Kazakhstan, Nepal and Pakistan. In Kazakhstan, 26 per cent of non-slum households live in slum areas, while 20 per cent of slum households live in non-slum areas. In Nepal, the proportions are 23 per cent and 16 per cent, respectively. In Pakistan, a large proportion of non-slum households live in non-slum areas, with the vast majority of slum households, 90 per cent, living in slum areas.

Type 3: Countries with generally low or moderate slum prevalence: Poverty at the margins

The third group of countries includes those with low or moderate slum prevalence in capital and other large cities, as well as in small cities and towns. In these countries, a large proportion of slum households live in non-slum areas, while almost all non-slum households reside in non-slum areas. In the UN-HABITAT definition, a slum area is a place in which half or more households experience at least one shelter deprivation; the countries in this third category tend to have few slum areas, or slum areas with very small proportions of non-slum households. For example, Ghana has a slum prevalence of 47 per cent, and 31 per cent of its slum households live in slum areas. Overall, slum areas in Ghana host 45 per cent of all urban households. In South Africa, only 5 per cent of non-slum households reside in slum areas, while 30 per cent of slum households reside in non-slum areas. Slum areas in South Africa are home to a smaller percentage of the country's households, 25 per cent, than the overall percentage of slum households, 31 per cent.

A similar situation exists in Brazil, where 13 per cent of non-slum households live in slum areas, and 34 per cent of slum households reside in non-slum areas. Here also, the proportion of households living in slum areas is lower than the total proportion of slum households in the country. In Colombia, only 3 per cent of slum households live in slum areas, while the majority of slum households (60 per cent) live in non-slum areas. Slum areas in Colombia are home to only 10 per cent of the country's slum households – significantly less than the 19 per cent of slum households. In the Dominican Republic, 3 per cent of non-slum households live in slum areas, while 82 per cent of slum households live in non-slum areas. Slum areas are home to only 6 per cent of households there, a third of the proportion of slum households in the country (20 per cent). India offers a different picture, with 31 per cent of non-slum households living in slum areas, while 40 per cent of slum households reside in non-slum areas. Overall, 45 per cent of households live in slum areas, a level similar to the proportion of slum households in the country (49 per cent). In Indonesia, 25 per cent of non-slum households live in slum areas, while 26 per cent of slum households live in non-slum areas. The proportion of households living in slum areas (50 per cent) is similar to the proportion of slum households in the country. In Armenia, 15 per cent of non-slum households live in slum areas, while 21 per cent of slum households live in non-slum areas. Slum areas are home to 39 per cent of the households, a level identical to the proportion of slum households. In Turkey, 16 per cent of non-slum households live in slum areas, while 43 per cent of slum households live in non-slum areas.

In cities of countries with moderate overall prevalence of slums, slum households tend to cluster together, as do

> In cities of countries with moderate overall prevalence of slums, slum households tend to cluster together, as do non-slum households

▲
Bogota night lights.
©rm/Shutterstock

Summary

non-slum households. These cities have adequate urban infrastructure in many places, supporting those residents who can afford housing costs that include access to improved water and sanitation, and durable housing units with sufficient living area. In such places, the urban infrastructure is not yet sufficient to satisfy the needs of all families and provide universal access to adequate shelter. Families must make tradeoffs regarding their access to different amenities in their search for affordable housing; many opt for slum housing that lacks essential services because it is all they can afford or because it is closer to a workplace. This situation is prevalent in several countries in sub-Saharan Africa (Benin, Côte d'Ivoire, Kenya, Malawi, Mali, Senegal, Zambia, and Gabon); Latin America and the Caribbean (Bolivia, Guatemala, Haiti, Nicaragua, and Peru); and Asia (India, Indonesia, Nepal, Viet Nam, and Armenia). A significant number of slum households in these countries also live in non-slum areas, indicating that entrenched poverty is a major factor in the persistence of moderate slum prevalence.

Clearly, not all poor urban households are clustered in underserviced slum areas; they can be located anywhere in cities and still lack one or more elements of adequate shelter. The lack of basic services in cities has various social and economic dimensions that are related to the physical structure of the environments in which people live as well as to the socio-economic conditions of families. Conversely, not all those who live in slums are poor – many people who have risen out of income poverty choose to continue living in slums for various reasons, ranging from the lack of affordable housing in better parts of the city to proximity to family, work and social networks. No single generalization fits slum neighbourhoods; they are as diverse as cities themselves. However, it is clear that expanding urban infrastructure to underserviced or informal settlements is essential for improving the lives of slum dwellers.

The capital and large cities of the second group are becoming more and more spatially divided, with high- and middle-income households living in better-serviced parts of the city, and poor households living in spatially and socially segregated zones in inadequate housing, with few or no basic services. Although the presence of slums does not directly denote levels of urban poverty, their prevalence in a city is an indicator of urban inequality.

Ghana and South Africa offer another type of city, in which most slum households are individual dwellings in different neighbourhoods; some also exist within serviced, middle- and high-income areas. In these countries, non-slum areas are dominant, with slum areas concentrating a small proportion of households. Where housing is more integrated, shelter deprivations are less pronounced than in countries with slum cities – densely inhabited areas in which most households experience multiple shelter deprivations.

Cities in Egypt, Morocco, Colombia, and the Dominican Republic have urban settings in which slum areas, as defined here, host only a small proportion of households. Households classified as slum households are instead located in non-slum areas where the majority of residents enjoy basic shelter services. In most cases, households have access to improved water and improved sanitation; other shelter deprivations are linked to household poverty, which impacts the ability to afford durable housing and sufficient living area. For these families, increased economic opportunities could play a significant role in improving their living conditions.

▲
Agadir, Morocco
©**Socrates/Shutterstock**

Years of Sanctions and Conflict Take Their Toll on Iraq's Cities

Ancient Mesopotamia, or modern-day Iraq, is the birthplace of many ancient cities and civilizations. It was here that the ancient kingdom of Sumer developed more than 7,000 years ago and where the alphabet and arithmetic were invented. The ancient cities of Iraq were centres of political power locally and across borders, sometimes encompassing most of the Middle East, stretching to the Mediterranean Sea.

Today, the country, once self-sufficient in agriculture and possessing a well-educated and skilled population and huge oil wealth, has gone from being one of the most promising countries in the Middle East to one whose human development indicators are among the lowest in the region. Several years of UN sanctions and the more recent war and internal conflicts have left several cities with significant infrastructure and housing challenges. The sanctions period in the 1990s led to a general decline in infrastructure and services in cities, notably power stations, sewage plants and water works. Maternal mortality rates have increased from 117 per 100,000 live births in 1991 to 294 per 100,000 live births in 1999 as the number of hospitals declined from 234 in 1987 to 212 in 2000. Secondary school enrolment fell from 47 per cent to 38 per cent in the same period.

Nearly 70 per cent of Iraq's 29 million people live in cities, with some 5.6 million people living in the capital city of Baghdad. Urban neighbourhoods in Iraq vary from old-style traditional residential areas to serviced sub-divisions with detached houses to squatter settlements. Military action since 2003 has led to damage of dwellings in major cities, although some cities, such as Najaf, have been more deeply affected than others. The Iraq Living Conditions Survey 2004 found that while nearly 10 per cent of homes in Najaf were damaged due to military action, the proportion was much lower in cities such as Baghdad and Mosul, where slightly more than 5 per cent of dwellings were damaged. However, in almost all cases, households were left to their own devices when it came to repairing damaged houses.

Sanctions in the 1990s, poor governance, mismanagement and conflict have led to a general deterioration of living conditions in cities. Poor quality housing and slums are found in decaying historic inner-city areas and in public buildings and spaces that have been claimed by squatters. UN-HABITAT estimates indicate that 53 per cent of Iraq's urban population currently lives in slum conditions, with overcrowding becoming more prevalent. Iraq's cities also face major infrastructure challenges: urban residents view the lack of

▲
Street in Baghdad
©UN-HABITAT

sewers as the most pressing infrastructure problem, followed by lack of electricity and unpaved streets. Urban households experience inadequate access to water and sanitation, disrupted solid waste management services and frequent flooding, all of which are potential health hazards. Almost half of all urban households in Iraq experience problems with water supply at least once a week, with Baghdad being among the worst affected cities. In 2003, Care International reported that 60 per cent of Iraq's water treatment and sewage plants were not functioning. In Basra, for instance, only 11 per cent of the city's area has sewer connections. Almost all households in urban Iraq are connected to the electricity network, but major power cuts remain a perennial problem. In 2006, for example, Baghdad and Najaf experienced power cuts approximately 120 hours per week, while Mosul has power less than 10 per cent of the time.

Despite an upturn in economic indicators that show a doubling of gross domestic product (GDP) from $15 billion in 2003 to $32.3 billion in 2005, Iraqis remain reliant on social assistance, rations and subsidies. The pre-2003 political regime used urban social goods and opportunities as a way of bestowing or withholding patronage, resulting in exclusion of a large proportion of the urban population from the benefits of urban life. An estimated 35 per cent of Baghdad's working population still lives in poverty. Some households are particularly

vulnerable to poverty, including those headed by women or youth.

Iraq's future remains uncertain. A recent survey shows that the country's urban population is deeply concerned with the security situation, which has worsened in the last five years. Perceived or real levels of vulnerability to violence and murder were greater in 2006 than they were in 2002. In 2004, some 90 per cent of households in Baghdad and Mosul heard shooting in their neighbourhoods several times a week. This has created a general sense of fear, prompting parents to constantly worry about whether their children will reach home safely after school. In 2006, Iraq's cities were considered among the most dangerous in the world, with Baghdad being the most unsafe. Internal conflict and sectarian violence since the 2003 war have resulted in several thousand deaths; in July 2006, for instance, 6,000 people were killed in Baghdad alone.

Extremely high levels of violence within Iraq's cities have greatly impacted migration patterns and increased household sizes as people move from one city to the other seeking refuge. It is estimated that as many as 4 million Iraqis have fled the country and more than 1 million are internally displaced. Violent internal conflict has shifted focus from urgent development priorities and has threatened to make the task of rehabilitation and reconstruction long and protracted.

Sources: Republic of Iraq/UN-HABITAT, 2007 and UN-HABITAT Global Urban Observatory, 2008, and other sources.

Helping to locate slums using Earth Observation and Geoinformation Technologies

Satellite image of dense slum settlements bordering green spaces and high-income residential areas in Nairobi.
©Digital Globe, Google Earth, 2008

Civilian Earth Observation and geoinformation technologies can provide complementary information to field surveys that aim to characterize and identify slums. Satellite-based remote sensing provides synoptic overviews over settlements and cities and thus an opportunity to locate slum areas. This can prove to be useful when improving census and field surveys. The satellite images can also provide a description and identification of the physical structure of housing and housing patterns, which may be indicators for slum conditions. These Earth Observation-based measures need always to be confirmed with field information.

Earth Observation can contribute to measuring the durable housing criterion – one of the indicators used to define slum households. The durable housing criterion states that houses should be built in a non-hazardous location, have a permanent structure and be adequate enough to pro-

tect its inhabitants from the extremes of climatic conditions such as rain, heat, cold and humidity. EO contributes to identifying hazardous areas (e.g. unstable slopes, flood plains, industrial zones or railroads) and to characterizing roofing materials (e.g. corrugated iron, plastic sheeting). Earth Observation also provides information on the road network (planned-haphazard, paved-unpaved), building types (number of floors, size) and built-up density (open spaces).

The image shows indicators that could be used to characterize slum and non-slum areas. Slums are often recognized through satellite imagery as they often show dwellings of a smaller size than non-slum dwellings. The estimation of the average size of built-up structures – measured as the diameter of the building surface, or as the surface of the roofs visible in the remotely sensed data – can be quantified through an image decomposition based

on morphological transformations with increasing size, the so-called derivative of the morphological profile (DMP). Satellite images of settlement patterns in Nairobi, Kenya, clearly show a highly dense slum settlement within a wealthy less dense neighbourhood (see image above).

The presence of vegetation in the case of Nairobi can often be associated with the quality of the settlement or neighbourhood. Slums have little vegetation, while more wealthy residential areas show evident presence of green areas. The presence of vegetation can be calculated using a vegetation index, e.g. the normalized difference vegetation index (NDVI). Often only a combination of indicators is needed to differentiate slum and non-slum areas.

Some countries are also using "poverty maps" to identify low-income neighbourhoods, as the maps of three cities in Kenya show. (Fig. 2.5.3)

Source: Joint Research Commission of the European Union, 2008.

FIGURE 2.5.3: **POVERTY INCIDENCE IN NAIROBI, MOMBASA AND KISUMU, 1999**

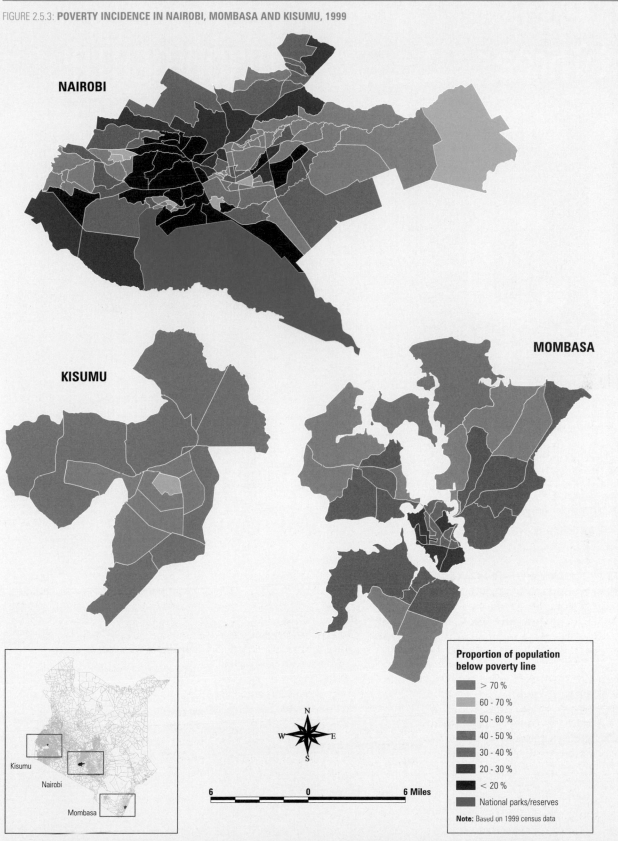

Proportion of population below poverty line

> 70 %
60 - 70 %
50 - 60 %
40 - 50 %
30 - 40 %
20 - 30 %
< 20 %
National parks/reserves

Note: Based on 1999 census data

Poverty maps like the ones of the three Kenyan cities above can be useful in identifying where slums are likely to be concentrated: The maps show that while the capital city Nairobi exhibits both low and high levels of poverty, poverty in the lakeside city of Kisumu tends to be generalized with large proportions of the city's population living below the poverty line. The coastal town of Mombasa, on the other hand, has a relatively prosperous inner core surrounded by areas experiencing high levels of poverty.
Source: Government of Kenya, Central Bureau of Statistics, 2003.

Part Three

03

ENVIRONMENTAL HARMONY

Like any other organic system, cities consume, metabolize and transform energy, water and materials into goods and waste. Part 3 presents an analysis of energy consumption at the city and household levels, which clearly shows that consumption patterns vary widely between developed and developing regions and between low- and high-income households. Although cities consume a disproportionate share of the world's energy, and are responsible for a large share of climate-changing greenhouse gas emissions, Part 3 clearly shows that it is not the level of urbanization in a country or the size of a city that determine the quantity of greenhouse gas emissions per capita; rather, the level of emissions is determined by other factors, such as consumption patterns, lifestyles, income levels, urban form and structure and national and local environmental policies.

Part 3 also presents detailed information on how climate change will impact coastal urban settlements that may be adversely affected by climate change and rising sea levels. Using various examples, this Part also shows how cities present a real opportunity to minimize environmental impacts by improving energy efficiency, minimizing urban sprawl, promoting the use of energy-efficient public transport and improving disaster preparedness.

San Diego city from across the bay on Coronado Island.
©Dane Wirtzfeld/iStockphoto

3.1
Urban Environmental Risks and Burdens

Cairo's rooftops.
©**Sandra vom Stein/iStockphoto**

By 2030, 60 per cent of the world's population will live in urban areas. From a sustainable development perspective, the welfare of future generations depends on how well present generations tackle the environmental burdens associated with urban living. Environmental harmony – between rural and urban areas, and within cities – is a growing concern among urban planners, policymakers and environmentalists.

Cities, when not properly planned, governed or managed, can easily threaten the quality of the air, the availability of water, the capacity of waste processing and recycling systems, and many other qualities of the urban environment that contribute to human well-being.

Low-income groups, particularly those living in slums or deprived neighbourhoods, are particularly vulnerable to the environmental and health risks associated with poor air quality, lack of safe water and poor sanitation. Cities in developing countries tend to struggle most with localized, immediate and health-threatening environmental issues belonging to the "brown" agenda, such as lack of safe water, inadequate sanitation and poor waste management, while cities in high-income industrialized countries are dealing more with the "green agenda", including non-point source pollution and consumption-related burdens, including greenhouse gas emissions that have a global and intergenerational impact.

At the global level, urban environmental burdens are

associated with energy consumption patterns and land use changes that can lead to a rise in greenhouse gas (GHG) emissions – the leading cause of climate change. The global environmental burden of urban activity is often measured through aggregate indicators such as ecological footprints. Although cities and urban-based activities are usually blamed for the increase in GHG emissions globally, UN-HABITAT analyses show that the contribution of cities to GHG emissions is more related to consumption patterns and gross domestic product (GDP) per capita than it is to levels of urbanization.

Environmental burdens in cities of the developing world

Urban environmental burdens may be analyzed at two levels – at the urban and the household level.

At the urban level, the most visible urban environmental burdens are those associated with the environmental and ecological degradation that occurs in and around urban areas as a result of the concentration of production and consumption activities, including industry and motorized transport. Examples include air pollution, urban ground and surface water extraction and contamination, urban waste dumping, the expansion of built-up areas and its effect on natural areas, agriculture, and biodiversity. At the household level, environmental burdens are expressed as environmental hazards in and around people's homes and workplaces that result from poor living conditions (e.g. inadequate access to water and sanitation, indoor air pollution, neighbourhood waste accumulation, pest infestation, and the like). These burdens are particularly acute and dramatic where persistent poverty and precarious conditions have been geographically or socially concentrated. Lack of access to adequate sanitation, in particular, is associated with a variety of health and environmental risks. Currently more than a quarter of the developing world's urban population lacks adequate sanitation. The problem of inadequate sanitation in urban areas is particularly acute in sub-Saharan Africa, Southern Asia and Eastern Asia, where 45 per cent, 33 per cent and 31 per cent of the urban population do not have access to a proper toilet, respectively. Poor hygiene and lack of sanitation account for 1.6 million deaths a year globally.

Air pollution

Air pollution has led to an increase in the incidence of disease and ill health in several developing countries; in many of these countries, lower respiratory disease linked to air pollution is a leading cause of premature death. Middle-income, newly industrializing countries are also facing new challenges associated with the exploding growth in motorized transport and industrialization, such as increase in water and air pollutants. Cities in China and India, for instance, which are experiencing exceptionally high economic growth rates of more than 9 per cent per year, have extremely high levels of air pollution compared to the global average.

The World Health Organization (WHO) estimates that more than 1 billion people in Asia alone are exposed to outdoor air pollutant levels that exceed WHO guidelines, leading to the premature death of half a million people annually. Concentrations of airborne pollutants in many large metropolitan areas in Latin America and the Caribbean also surpass recommended limits. Transport is a major source of direct and indirect air pollution in many Latin American cities. Since polluted air can aggravate existing health conditions and cause increased sensitivity in healthy people, interventions to improve air quality have positive health impacts for all. WHO's Global Burden of Disease project attributes 58,000 annual premature deaths to urban air pollution, which also accounts for 507,000 years of life lost (disability adjusted) in

FIGURE 3.1.1: **AIR QUALITY IN MEGA CITIES**

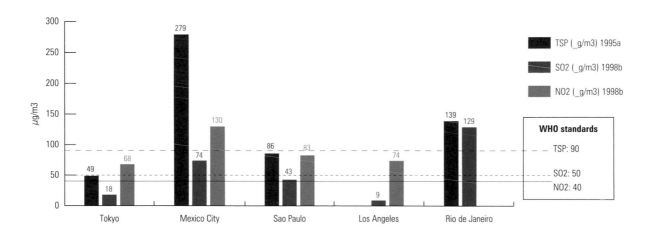

Source: UN-HABITAT, Global Urban Observatory, 2008. Data is from Molina and Molina (2002:5)
Note: Data is for the most recent year between 1990 and 1998. Most is for 1995.
(TSP: Total Suspended Particles, SO2: Sulfur Dioxide, NO2: Nitrogen Dioxide)

Bangkok's strategy to tackle air pollution

As a consequence of population increase, city development and a growing number of motor vehicles on its roads, Bangkok, the capital of Thailand, has experienced serious air pollution problems over the past several decades. Measures recently adopted by the Thai government, however, have helped the growing city manage its air quality, putting Bangkok on the path to cleaner air and better quality of life for its residents.

Transport is the greatest source of air pollutants in Bangkok. Street-level concentrations of air pollutants along the city's major roads can reach hazardous levels, owing to increased numbers of high emission motor vehicles coupled with long distances traveled and extreme traffic congestion. The number of motor vehicles registered in Bangkok soared from 600,000 in 1980 to 4,163,000 at the end of 1999 – a seven-fold increase. Between 1999 and 2007, vehicle registrations continued to rise. By the end of 2007, there were 5,614,294 vehicles choking Bangkok's inadequate street and roadway networks, comprising 3,208,462 passenger cars; 2,261,545 motorcycles; 110,571 trucks; and 33,716 buses.

Results of ambient air quality monitoring indicate that the air pollutants of concern in Bangkok are particulate matter (PM), ozone (O_3), carbon monoxide (CO), sulfur dioxide (SO_2), and nitrogen dioxide (NO_2). The ambient air quality in the city and in general background and roadside areas is shown in Figure 1. This illustrates that PM (PM_{10} and total suspended particles) is the pollutant of greatest concern, and the pollution near roads is more serious than elsewhere in the city.

The Royal Thai Government has adopted a number of measures to mitigate Bangkok's air pollution problems, focusing on maintaining a good quality of life for the general public. The government's ultimate goal is to bring emissions and ambient air quality in line with the National Air Quality Standards or better. One important milestone was the elimination of lead from gasoline in 1996. Now, the ambient air lead concentration in Bangkok is near zero.

Since the 1990s, the government has facilitated ongoing collaboration among the municipality of Bangkok, various sectors impacting air pollution, and the public, resulting in the adoption of air pollution

Bangkok's Skytrain.
©iStockphoto

control strategies for transport-related sources, such as improving fuel quality; enforcing emission standards for new and in-use vehicles; implementing an inspection and maintenance program; reducing vehicle kilometers traveled; and performing roadside inspection, traffic management and gasoline vapor recovery. Air pollution control strategies for stationary sources have also evolved, including requiring environmental impact assessments, enforcing emission standards and fuel oil standards, and implementing monitoring requirements.

To provide transport alternatives and decrease the number of vehicles on the roads, Bangkok developed a new public transport system, featuring a subway line and an aboveground Skytrain, in 2004. The mass-rapid-transit system has helped improve air quality somewhat, but the limited area covered by the system does little to alleviate traffic and curb the city's overall pollution. Bangkok is now working to expand the distance reachable by Skytrain, which will help ensure good air quality even while the population increases.

Thailand has succeeded in mitigating air pollution in Bangkok, but the government continues to conduct research to make use of new knowledge and keep up with rapidly advancing technology. Thailand is disseminating and sharing its experiences in air pollution control with other countries in Asia.

ANNUAL AVERAGE OF PM_{10} IN BANGKOK DURING 1992 - 2005

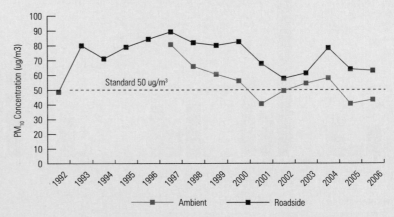

Sources: Thailand Department of Land Transport, 2008, with contributions from Pollution Control Department of Thailand and Clean Air Initiative for Asian Cities Centre.

Ougadougou's Green Brigade

As the capital of one of the poorest countries in the world, Ouagadougou faces great challenges with poverty and environmental degradation. Many of the poorest residents of Burkina Faso's largest city have turned to the city's dwindling green spaces for income by illegally cutting trees to sell firewood. Most of these poor city residents are unemployed females who are the sole providers for their families.

In the early 1990s, Ouagadougou's mayor held a series of meetings with women involved in these environmentally harmful practices to convince them to stop the degradation of the city's green spaces in return for employment. As a result, using his own personal funds, the mayor initiated the "Green Brigade" to combat the city's overwhelming rate of female poverty, to improve city sanita-

tion, and to mitigate environmental damage to the city's green spaces. The Green Brigade would employ women to clean streets and public spaces as an alternative to illegal use of city green space.

Despite the obvious benefits of the programme, women were reluctant to participate or support the initiative because of the cleaning industry's negative cultural stigma. In order to bring value and respect to the occupation, the initiative coupled its employment efforts with educational campaigns on the importance of the industry. Today, the initiative has grown to employ more than 1,700 women.

The programme enhanced its effect on welfare, long-term poverty and sustainability by providing workers with a money-saving scheme and basic

health care for all women employees. More importantly, these jobs brought income and welfare to the city's most vulnerable populations: women and children.

As a result, the city's green spaces and trees are more protected, waste is disposed of in an appropriate manner, and overall hygiene of city residents has improved. The success of the Green Brigade has spread, with more cities in Burkina Faso, as well as cities in Mali, Benin, and Guinea replicating the initiative to address issues of poverty, sanitation, and unsustainable methods of income generation. In 2006, Ouagadougou's Green brigade was awarded the Dubai International Award for Best Practices in Improving the Living Environment for "providing regular employment to needy women while promoting cleanliness".

Source: www.bestpractices.org

Latin America and the Caribbean. Indoor air pollution, on the other hand, is responsible for 26,000 premature deaths and 773,000 years of life lost in the region. WHO also reports that in the year 2000, 54,000 premature deaths in the region resulted from water, sanitation and hygiene factors, and 2,045,000 years of life were lost (disability adjusted)[1].

Studies indicate that the monetary costs of environment-related health problems can reach several percentage points

of gross domestic product (GDP). In 2004, the cost of the damage caused by particulate emissions in Latin America and the Caribbean was 0.5 per cent of the regional gross income[2]. A World Bank survey of Mumbai, Shanghai, Manila, Bangkok, Krakow, and Santiago also found that health impacts of air pollution accounted for two-thirds of the social costs of these cities in 1993[3].

Many developing countries are establishing legislative and policy frameworks to address air pollution at the national and city levels. Most Asian countries, for example, are phasing out lead fuel, and some cities, such as Bangkok, Beijing, Jakarta, Manila, New Delhi, and Singapore, have already made concerted efforts to reduce levels of air pollutants[4].

Indoor air pollution

It is estimated that indoor air pollution is responsible for between 2.7 and 2.8 million deaths annually[5]. UN-HABITAT analyses also show that indoor air pollution is a leading cause of respiratory illnesses among women and children living in Asian and African slums, as they are most likely to be exposed to poorly ventilated cooking areas[6].

Yet indoor air pollution is rarely discussed outside of public health circles, probably because its health consequences are not immediate and are difficult to trace. Thus, indoor air pollution remains a quiet and neglected killer, with lack of global awareness being one of the primary obstacles to the widespread implementation of existing, proven interventions.

Solid fuel (biomass fuels and coal) used for cooking is a leading cause of indoor air pollution, especially in urban slums. The incomplete combustion of solid fuels releases pollutants such as particulate matter (PM), carbon monoxide

FIGURE 3.1.2: **PROPORTION OF CHILDREN IN URBAN AREAS IN SELECTED AFRICAN COUNTRIES WITH ACUTE RESPIRATORY INFECTIONS BY TYPE OF FUEL USED FOR COOKING**

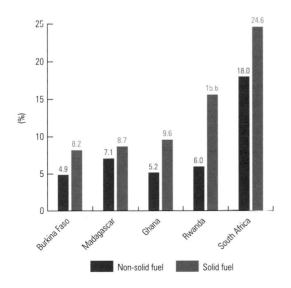

Source: UN-HABITAT, Global Urban Observatory, 2008

(CO), sulphur dioxide (SO2), nitrogen dioxide (NO2) and other organic compounds into the atmosphere, leading to respiratory illnesses. The use of solid fuel has been associated with respiratory infections in children and accounts for a significant proportion of infant deaths in developing countries. Biomass fuels, such as animal dung, crop residues and wood, produce the highest levels of these pollutants thus posing the greatest danger to respiratory health, followed by other solid fuels, such as coal and charcoal. Liquid fuels, such as kerosene and Liquid Petroleum Gas (LPG), are relatively less polluting with electricity being the safest energy source, which places at the top of what is known as "the energy ladder"[7]. Combustion of wood, for instance, emits 50 times more indoor air pollution than gas from a stove[8]. Thus policies to accelerate the transition from biomass fuels to liquid fuels or electricity should be a priority in developing countries. Unfortunately, poor households in many developing countries cannot afford to make this transition; yet the associated cost of this transition would lower poor households' expenditure on fuel in the long run and would have enormous health benefits and reduce global environmental risks.

Use of solid fuels is particularly prevalent in African cities. In the cities of Burkina Faso, Congo, Ghana, Ethiopia,

Rwanda, South Africa and Zambia, the prevalence of acute respiratory infections (ARI) among children under the age of five years is higher in households using solid fuels, such as dung, wood, charcoal, than in households where other sources of energy are used[9]. In the cities of Burkina Faso, including the capital Ouagadougou, the prevalence of acute respiratory infections among children under the age of five is almost two times higher in households using solid fuel for cooking than in those that use non-solid fuels. In the urban areas of Congo, the prevalence of ARI is two times higher in households using dung for cooking than in those using wood or charcoal for cooking. Ethiopia's urban households display the largest variation in the prevalence of ARI in children under the age of five– with nearly 30 per cent prevalence when dung is used for cooking against 8.3 per cent prevalence when charcoal is used and 4.8 per cent prevalence when kerosene is used[10].

Inadequate waste management

Inadequate solid waste management is becoming a health hazard in many cities. Although the amount of waste produced in low-income cities is smaller than that produced by high-income cities, waste management is a growing concern, as the consequences of inadequate collection and disposal impact the ecosystems of cities, contribute to the degradation of the urban environment and pose a health hazard to urban populations.

Cities in developing countries suffer more from the consequences of inadequate urban solid waste collection than cities in the developed world. In Freetown, Sierra Leone, for example, only 35 to 55 per cent of the urban solid waste is collected; uncollected waste is illegally dumped in open spaces, water bodies, and storm-drainage channels, buried, burnt or deposited along the streets or roadsides[11]. In Cairo, Egypt, only one-third of waste is collected and processed by the municipality and the formal sector.[12] In Benin, less than 50 per cent of urban households benefit from collection of household wastes either through a public or private system.[13]

In general, waste generated in cities of the developing world consists mostly of organic material, such as ashes from fuel wood and charcoal, as well as food. In cities such as Freetown, Kigali and Accra, more than 80 per cent of the waste is organic material, compared to 30 per cent or less in cities such as Bologna, Goteborg, Milan, and New York. Although the recycling and reuse of solid waste are common practices in cities of the developing world, these practices are often carried out by the informal sector under hazardous conditions. Furthermore, recycling and reuse of waste remains confined to the informal or private sectors in many cities and has not been seriously adopted as a national policy in many countries.

Poor solid waste management can lead to a range of excreta- and vector-related diseases. Poor drainage, for instance, can lead to leptospirosis (Weil's disease), which is spread through rodent urine and poor drainage in construction. Improperly managed solid waste can clog storm drains, cause flooding and provide breeding and feeding grounds for mosquitoes, flies, and rodents. Collectively, these can cause diarrhoea,

▲
A young girl carries a baby on her back while searching through rubbish for metal scraps to sell in Kroo Bay, Freetown, Sierra Leone: Approximately half of the solid waste in the city remains uncollected.
©Tugela Ridley/IRIN

The informal recycling economy of Asian cities

Garbage dump at Stung Meanchey, Phnom Penh, Cambodia.
©Maciej Dakowicz

Waste recycling in developing countries relies largely on the informal recovery of materials by scavengers or waste pickers. Estimates for cities in Asia and the Pacific reveal that up to 2 per cent of the population survives by recovering materials from waste to sell for reuse or recycling or for its own consumption. In some cities, waste scavengers constitute large communities: approximately 15,000 squatters make their living by sifting through the Smoky Mountain municipal rubbish dump in the Philippines. Similarly, it is estimated that Bangalore has between 20,000 and 30,000 scavengers who make a living from rubbish, while there are between 15,000 and 20,000 waste pickers in Jakarta. Some of these scavenger communities have high levels of organization and have created their own cooperatives.

The presence of sizeable communities making their living from waste has favoured the development of enterprises that form an extensive waste recycling network that has developed without government assistance and without the formation of commercial monopolies. For example, the waste scavengers of Hanoi operate at no cost to the city's municipal authority and provide both financial benefits to the society in the form of avoided costs (such as landfill space, collection

and transport costs, energy, employment generation, and protection of public health) as well as ecological benefits in the form of resource conservation and environmental protection. The recycled materials from waste work their way from the "waste economy" back into the productive economy through an elaborate system of buyers. It is estimated that some 1,500 families make their living by buying and selling waste materials; as a result, a trade network has emerged with clients from Hanoi and the surrounding provinces in Viet Nam regularly visiting individual junk dealers to buy and pre-order specific types of recycled materials. The majority of dumpsite scavengers are women and children, who live in overcrowded, poorly ventilated temporary huts, often on the peripheries of the waste dump. The scavengers seldom have access to public or private latrines, are malnourished and suffer from a range of illnesses, including worm infections, scabies, respiratory tract infections, abdominal pain, fever, and other unspecified diseases.

A similar situation is found in the shantytown of Dharavi in Mumbai, which has been dubbed "India's largest recycling centre". With more than 700,000 people crammed into 175 hectares, Dharavi is the biggest slum in Asia. But Dharavi

can also be defined as a well-organized industrial district with distinct layers of workers dealing with the recycling of waste: scavengers, pickers, waste sorters, specialized waste sorters, and recyclers. Washing and recycling activities are carried out inside the dumps, in unhealthy conditions, using recycled devices. Plastic chopping and smelting operations are also carried out inside the slum district, with serious consequences in terms of disease and pollution.

The economy of Dharavi defies official statistics, as it is self-sustaining and devoid of government bureaucracy. Waste recycling has become an industry in itself and has helped to provide employment to hundreds of people working in some 400 recycling units. It is estimated that Dharavi has as many as 15,000 "factories" where recycled material is converted to products, such as pots and toys. However, all these activities are carried out without any environmental and health protection measures. The price of Dharavi's economy, therefore, is paid in human deaths, diseases and environmental pollution. Moreover, the future of the waste economy is uncertain as plans are underway to resettle the residents to pave way for Mumbai's multibillion-dollar urban redevelopment plan to turn the city into a world-class financial centre by 2015.

Sources: M. Portanuova (2004), La città della spazzatura, Diario, 13 February.
The Economist (2007), "A flourishing slum", 22 December.

Does the urban environment affect emotional well-being?

There is increasing research interest in the correlations between the built environment, geographical location and psychological well-being in cities. The World Health Organization (WHO) Commission on Social Determinants of Health has established that urbanization in and of itself is a determinant of health, and that the urban setting is a lens that magnifies or diminishes a range of social determinants of mental health.

Increasing urbanization is often associated with declining community relationships, social isolation, greater stresses of urban life, concentration of poverty (and subsequent stigmatization), breakdown of family structures, and overcrowding. This could explain why, in almost all countries (with the exception of India, China and Sri Lanka) higher suicide rates are reported in urban areas than in rural areas. Research also indicates that living in a more urbanized environment increases the risk of suicide among women but reduces the risk among men.

Poverty, housing and the living environment

Although the higher incidence of mental disorders in urban areas could be because urban residents are more likely than rural residents to seek health services, studies have found that many psychosocial disorders in urban areas are associated with poor quality housing and living environments. Among the urban poor, lack of financial resources and high costs of living, harsh living conditions and physical exhaustion from lack of transport (especially when living far from the workplace) all contribute to sustained and chronic stress that predispose individuals and families to mental health problems. Overcrowding, noise and air pollution, poverty and dependence on a cash economy, high levels of violence and reduced social support in cities also weaken and devastate both individuals and the social supports that could serve as buffers against mental health problems.

Data from a cross-sectional survey carried out in socio-economically contrasting sub-districts in São Paulo, Brazil, shows that even after key socio-economic variables are controlled, the area of residence has a statistically significant effect on mental health. In Dhaka, a comparison of mental health status between slum and non-slum adolescents shows lower self-reported quality of life and higher "conduct problems" among males living in slum areas. Recent studies have also shown that living in socio-economically deprived neighbourhoods is associated with higher incidences

of depression and higher levels of child problem behaviour than in wealthier areas. A study conducted in 59 New York City neighbourhoods in 2002 found that people living in neighbourhoods characterized by dilapidated or poorly maintained built environments were 36 to 64 per cent more likely to report lifetime depression than respondents living in better-serviced neighbourhoods. This could be explained by the prevalence of daily stressors, such as noise pollution, lack of green spaces, violence and crime, in deprived urban neighbourhoods and the social stigma attached to living in such a place.

Lack of public spaces, sports clubs and other venues for leisure activities can also contribute to youth boredom and idleness, which are directly

> Overcrowding, noise, air pollution, and lack of green spaces and communal meeting places such as parks, are associated with increased stress levels among city residents

linked to substance use and high crime rates, which in turn contribute to mental illnesses. Many studies conducted in Europe and North America have suggested that the type of housing – single-family detached house versus multi-family high-rise dwelling – also impacts mental health, especially among low-income people. In general, people living in high-rise apartments suffer more from psychological disorders than those who live in low-rise housing or in detached houses, although cultural factors play an important role in reducing stress levels. Highly-dense high-rises in Indian and Egyptian cities, for instance, do not appear to have a significant impact on levels of well-being. For low-income residents, living in high-rise apartments is linked with social isolation and lack of access to amenities that aid well-being. Women staying at home with their children are particularly vulnerable; several studies have shown that women in high-rise housing report more loneliness and less social contact with their neighbours

than those in other housing types, owing in part to distance from communal meeting places, such outdoor gardens, play areas, porches, terraces, and patios. At the same time, increasing suburbanization, and the decline in community life and longer commute times associated with it, is also being blamed for increased stress among women and men, regardless of the presence of outdoor amenities and single-family homes in suburban and peri-urban areas.

Overcrowding, or lack of adequate living space, is a key contributor to mental disorders. A 2007 WHO study conducted in overcrowded refugee camps in the Occupied Palestinian Territories reported that high levels of depression and frustration have increased the demand for mental and other health services in the camps. The camps located in the Gaza strip, for instance, have the highest population densities in the world, which are reflected in overcrowded schools and households. Physical congestion and lack of privacy have also put a strain on relationships and increased the risk of infection among camp residents. Stigmatization and fear of violence or eviction have compounded the emotional strain of families living in camps.

Poor-quality housing and living environments not only impact the people who live in them, but also have other consequences, such as rising levels of crime, suicide and violence, which impact all city residents. Mental health promotion thus requires multi-sectoral and multi-layered action, involving government sectors and non-governmental and community-based organizations, and urban planning processes that are more responsive to the psychological needs of residents. New York City, for instance, has in the last decade maintained a lower rate of suicide than the United States as whole by implementing integrated and effective public health practices and developing an extensive knowledge base for services intervention, which involves advanced tracking and surveillance, emergency response, multi-layered public health and social services, gun control, and social norms for community interventions.

In low-income countries, where psychological services are not widely accessible or affordable, health service providers and government agencies need to become more aware of the underlying causes of psychological illnesses, such as poor-quality housing and overcrowding, so that interventions are designed to respond to these causes.

References:
WHO, 2007; WHO Centre for Health Development, 2007; Evans, Wells & Moch, 2003;
Vijayakumar, 2004; New York City Department of Health and Mental Hygiene, (n.d).; Qin, 2005; Galea, et al. (n.d.); Blue, 2000; Izutsu, et al., 2006.

parasitic infections, and injuries. Pools of standing water and flooding can lead to increased incidence of malaria and other mosquito-borne diseases, especially during the rainy season, placing workers and local residents at risk. Public facilities often fall into disrepair for lack of maintenance, setting the stage for accidents and poor waste management. Poor waste collection also increases risks of flooding. Garbage in drains seriously affects a city's storm water management capacity.

In the absence of regular collection of household solid wastes, organic waste fills up public spaces, backyards, lanes, pathways, and vacant lots, where it attracts disease-carrying insects and pests and clog overflowing drainage channels. Associated health problems include high incidence of cholera, diarrhoea and dysentery, especially among children. In Benin, for example, a 2001 Demographic and Health Survey showed that the prevalence of diarrhoea among children under the age of five years was 18.5 per cent in urban households where the garbage is dumped in the yard against 7 per cent in urban households where the garbage is collected. Uncollected household waste is also associated with the spread of respiratory infections. In Benin, the prevalence of ARI is 17.1 per cent among children living in households that dump waste within the compound against 13.6 per cent among children living in

households with regular collection of garbage. In Ethiopia the prevalence of ARI is six times higher among children living in households where the waste is uncollected than among children living in households that benefit from regular waste collection. A 2003 survey in Kenya showed that one out of every four children living in households where garbage is dumped within the yard suffered from diarrhoea compared to less than one in ten children living in households where solid waste is regularly collected.

Lack of drainage, especially in areas of communal water supply, breeds mosquitoes and flies, which can also be a nuisance and spread disease. Water lines flow next to storm drains, which become open sewers (with time, water lines can sag directly into storm drains from neighbourhood activity and illegal connections). Poor management of waste water can increase the spread of malaria in many ways. Mosquito-related diseases, especially malaria and dengue, can spread by extending breeding areas in water that has accumulated in disposed construction materials and holes dug for sand and gravel. Pollution of local water from improper disposal of excreta and domestic waste at work camps can also lead to vector-related diseases, particularly malaria, filariasis, and, sometimes, schistosomiasis.

FIGURE 3.1.3: **WASTE PRODUCTION (KG/YEAR) PER CAPITA IN SELECTED CITIES**

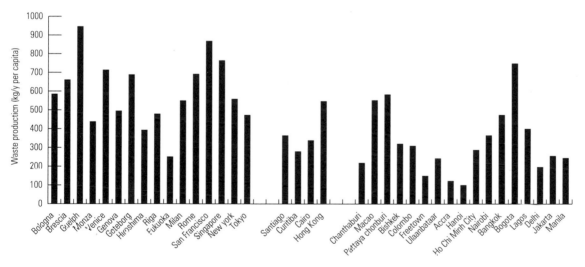

Source: UN-HABITAT Global Urban Observatory 2008
Note: Data derived from various sources, 2000-2007

END NOTES

1   The disability adjusted figure, or DALY, is a summary indicator that combines the impact of illness, disability and mortality on a given population's health.
2   World Bank, 2004a.
3   Lvovsky, et al., 2000.
4   UNEP, 2007b.
5   Bruce, Rogelio & Albalak 2000.
6   UN-HABITAT 2006a
7   Climbing the energy ladder means not only using cleaner fuels, but using fuels that are less costly in the long run. The transition from costly and

polluting fuels to cleaner, more efficient and cheaper fuels thus has long-term social and economic benefits.
8   Ibid.
9   UN-HABITAT Global Urban Observatory 2006, computed from Demographic and Health Surveys, various years.
10 Ibid.
11 Sood, 2004.
12 Palczynski, 2002.
13 UN-HABITAT UrbanInfo database, 2006 version

3.2
Cities and
Climate Change

The earth's surface temperature has increased by between 0.74 and 1.8 degrees Centigrade since 1906. At least part of the global rise in temperature, we now know, is a result of human activity. The global atmospheric concentration of carbon dioxide – one of the greenhouse gases most directly responsible for the greenhouse effect and global warming – has risen by 35 per cent since the year 1750; more than 70 per cent of this rise can be attributed to the burning and consumption of fossil fuels – oil, gas and coal.[1]

In the last few decades, global warming has been exceptionally rapid in comparison to the changes in climate over the past two millennia. The Intergovernmental Panel on Climate Change (IPCC) notes that the rate of global temperature increase in the last 50 years has been twice that of the last 100 years. IPCC estimates that the earth's temperature will rise by between 1.8

and 4 degrees Centigrade over the course of the 21st century, if current levels of greenhouse gas emissions are not curbed.[2] Global warming will have severe impacts on the planet, including increased flood risk and reduced water supply; declining crop yields, especially in Africa; increase in vector-borne diseases, such as malaria and dengue fever; displacement of hundreds of millions of people from coastal cities and small islands; and significant changes in marine ecosystems.

Carbon dioxide (CO_2) comprises 77 per cent of global greenhouse gas (GHG) emissions, with fossil fuel consumption accounting for the bulk (nearly 60 per cent) of these emissions, while deforestation and land use conversion from natural to farmed or built areas account for the rest. Globally, agriculture is responsible for 13.5 per cent of other greenhouse gas emissions, mostly methane and nitrous oxide (N_2O) from agricultural soils, livestock and manure.[3]

It is estimated that the Earth's temperature will rise by between 1.8 and 4°C over the course of the 21st century.
©Clint Hild/iStockphoto

"Heat island" effect

Temperature distribution in urban areas is affected by the urban radiation balance. Solar radiation on urban surfaces is absorbed and transformed into heat. Walls, roofs and paved surfaces store heat and emit long-wave radiation to the sky, taking much longer to cool off than gardens, forests and fields. Areas with dense vegetation stay cooler because the sun's heat causes water held by soil and leaves to evaporate, and shading provided by plants keeps the ground cool. Because urban surfaces trap more heat than plants, urban areas have higher temperatures than surrounding rural areas. This phenomenon is known as the "heat island" effect.

High temperatures in urban areas have a direct effect on the energy consumed by cooling appliances such as air conditioners. In large cities in the United States, the peak electricity load increases 3 to 5 per cent for a 1 °C increase in temperature. This is significant, considering that the average afternoon summer temperature in U.S. cities has increased from 1.1 to 2.2 °C in the last 40 years. It can be assumed that 3 to 8 per cent of the current urban electricity demand is used to compensate for the heat island effect alone. Hot air given off by air conditioning units also contributes to the urban temperature rise. A modelling study in Tokyo found that the waste heat emission from air conditioners is responsible for 1 °C warming in the summer. A similar study in Houston found that air conditioners account for a temperature increase of 0.5 °C during the day and 2.5 °C at night.

Rows of air conditioners on a building in Tokyo
©**Holger Mette/iStockphoto**

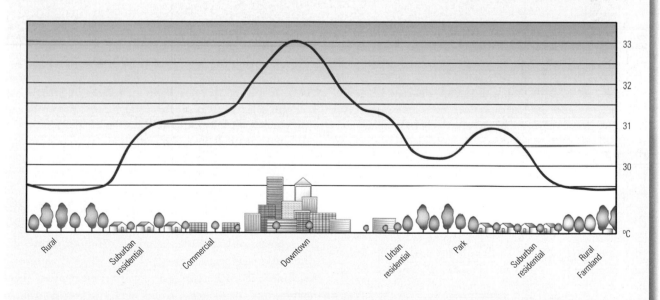

Source: F. Butera (2008), "Towards the renewable built environment", in: Urban Energy Transition, Elsevier.

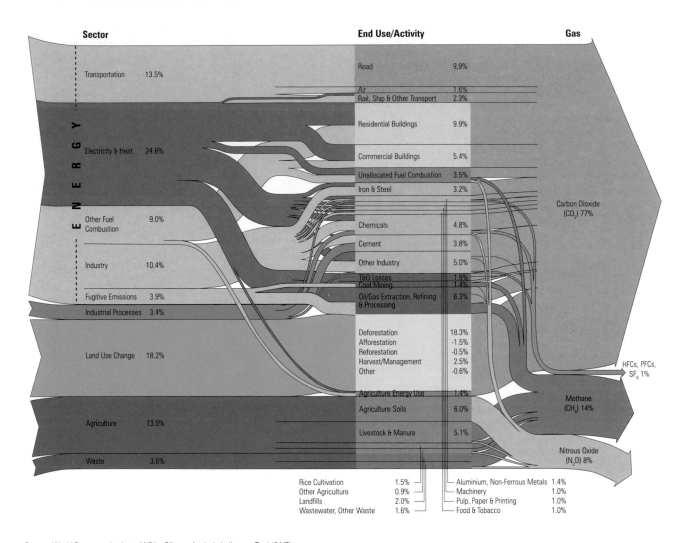

Source: World Resources Institute (WRI) - Climate Analysis Indicators Tool (CAIT)
http://cait.wri.org/

While cities are not the only generators of greenhouse gas emissions, there is no doubt that built-up areas consume more energy, and therefore produce more emissions than undeveloped areas. Energy for heating and lighting residential and commercial buildings generates nearly a quarter of greenhouse gas emissions globally, while transport contributes 13.5 per cent, of which 10 per cent is attributed to road transport (Figure 3.2.1).

In the EU-15,[4] mainly comprising countries in Western Europe, buildings account for approximately one-third of the total energy-related CO_2 emissions; on average, between 1980 and 1990, CO_2 emissions from buildings in the region have increased by 1.7 per cent per annum.[5] In 2002, homes generated the majority (77 per cent) of greenhouse gases emitted by buildings in the region, while the remaining 23 per cent originated from non-residential or commercial buildings,[6] the latter concentrated in cities. Because disaggregated data is not available, it is it not clear what proportion of the overall emissions is generated in urban areas, although since most buildings and transport networks are located in cities, urban areas are most likely responsible for a large proportion of these emissions. However, as the following chapters will show, emission levels are linked much more closely to consumption patterns and levels of income than to levels of urbanization or the size of built-up areas.

Energy for electricity, heating, transport, industry and other uses combined generates more than 60 per cent of greenhouse gases worldwide. Land use change, in the development of large-scale agriculture or infrastructure, has also had a significant impact on levels of CO_2 emissions. Machinery and materials used to convert greenfields – land not previously developed – to built or farmed areas contribute almost as much to worldwide greenhouse gas emissions as residential and commercial buildings, which are the most prominent global source of GHG emissions.

Emissions at the city level

It is no coincidence that global climate change has become a leading international development issue precisely at the same time and virtually at the same rate as the world is becoming urbanized. Cities are key players in the carbon emissions and climate change arenas because most human and economic activities are concentrated in urban areas. Cities generate a large share of most nations' gross domestic product (GDP), which typically translates into high levels of energy consumption for industrial processes compared to non-urban areas. Built-up areas in cities also consume a large amount of the world's energy, which contributes to global warming. Urban areas also influence patterns of energy and land use in the surrounding and more distant areas that affect the livelihoods and quality of life of people who live outside city boundaries.[7] At the same time, however, an increasing number of cities are becoming centres of innovation in alternative energy, developing resources that may reduce our dependence on fossil fuels and make our societies more sustainable.

Rich cities tend to produce more CO_2 emissions than poor cities. Increased incomes lead to changes in lifestyles that tend to increase consumption and energy dependence. North American cities, especially expanding cities in which residents are heavily dependent on private cars as the main mode of transport, typically produce exceptionally high levels of emissions. In the case of the United States, heavy dependence on motorized transport and urban sprawl have emerged as factors contributing to that country's high rate of urban emissions. For example, San Diego in the United States produces more emissions per capita than Tokyo, partly because residents of the latter are less dependant on private motorized transport. In Europe, emissions are lower, even though GDP per capita is similar to that of North America. This difference could be explained by the existence of environmentally friendly policies that promote the use of clean energy, lower electricity consumption, compact urban forms as well as the more prevalent use of public transport in European cities.

Urban sprawl and expansion, combined with widespread use of motorized transport, are significant contributors to levels of emissions in North American cities. Between 1970 and 1990, the total area of the 100 largest urban areas in the United States increased by 82 per cent. Population growth accounted for only half of the increase in land area, indicating that, in many cities around the country, people are living farther from the city centre and spending more time commuting. One study found that the number of miles driven by the average United States resident has increased by 25 per cent in the last 10 years; the amount of time Americans spend in traffic, though, has increased by 236 per cent. Time and fuel lost in heavy auto traffic is worth roughly US$78 billion to the American economy.[8]

Intra-city income inequalities also have a carbon- and climate-relevant dimension. The wealthy generally consume more than the poor and produce more solid waste (a source of methane) than the poor. However, because there is no global database on CO_2 emissions at the city level, it is difficult to correlate affluence and emissions. Furthermore, across high-income cities for which there is more information, CO_2 emissions per capita vary considerably. However, when explaining cities' energy use and greenhouse gas emissions, we need to bear in mind not only the size of a country's economy, its transport and household consumption patterns, but other factors as well, namely:

a) the sectoral and total carbon intensity of the city as measured by tonnes of CO_2 per unit of US$, determined by the fuels and technologies used;

b) the total and sectoral energy intensity as measured by the energy input/ economy output, determined by the fuels and technologies used;

c) the form and structure of the city, whether it is compact (dense) or scattered (urban sprawl), and its transport mode; and

d) the management structures of the city.

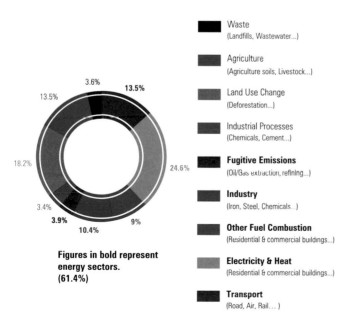

FIGURE 3.2.2: **GLOBAL GREENHOUSE GAS EMISSIONS IN 2000, BY SOURCE**

3.6%   **13.5%**
13.5%

18.2%   24.6%

3.4%
3.9%   9%
10.4%

**Figures in bold represent energy sectors.
(61.4%)**

Waste
(Landfills, Wastewater...)

Agriculture
(Agriculture soils, Livestock...)

Land Use Change
(Deforestation...)

Industrial Processes
(Chemicals, Cement...)

Fugitive Emissions
(Oil/Gas extraction, refining...)

Industry
(Iron, Steel, Chemicals...)

Other Fuel Combustion
(Residential & commercial buildings...)

Electricity & Heat
(Residential & commercial buildings...)

Transport
(Road, Air, Rail...)

Source: World Resources Institute.
Notes: All data is for 2000. All calculations are based on CO_2 equivalents, using 100-year global warming potentials from the IPCC (1996), based on a total global estimate of 41,755 $MtCO_2$ equivalent. Land use change includes both emissions and absorptions.

Emissions at the global and regional level

At the global level, 25 countries with the most greenhouse gas emissions account for approximately 83 per cent of global emissions; in the year 2000, they collectively represented 70 per cent of the global population and 87 per cent of global gross domestic product (GDP)[9]. The United States, China, the European Union, Russia, and India together contribute approximately 61 per cent of global emissions. In the developing world, Eastern Asia was the biggest emitter of CO_2 emissions (5.6 billion metric tonnes) in 2004 nearly three times the emissions produced by Southern Asia (2 billion tonnes) and four times the emissions produced by Latin America and the Caribbean (1.4 billion tonnes). Northern and sub-Saharan Africa produce the least amount of CO_2 emissions, 0.5 billion tonnes and 0.7 billion tonnes respectively.

While Latin American cities generally produce low CO_2 emissions, individual countries in the region, such as Brazil, are among the top 20 emittors of CO_2 globally. In 2000, Latin America was responsible for 12 per cent of global CO_2 emissions, with land use change and deforestation accounting for nearly half of these emissions. The level of greenhouse gas emissions in Brazil is relatively high (337 million metric tonnes in 2004), largely resulting from deforestation in the Amazon basin. Regional methane emissions from anthropogenic sources (mainly livestock farming and the production and consumption of fossil fuels) represent 9.3 per cent of the world total. Brazil, Mexico, Venezuela, Argentina, Colombia, and Peru are responsible for more than 80 per cent of greenhouse gas emissions in Latin America and the Caribbean.[10] Large cities in the region, as well as many medium-sized cities, also emit greenhouse gases, mainly generated by motorized transport and industrial production.

On a global scale, a relationship is evident among emissions, population and GDP rankings, reflecting the importance of population and economic growth as emission drivers. For instance, in the year 2000, 8.7 per cent of the world's population was located in Latin American and Caribbean countries, which emitted 5.8 per cent of global CO_2 emissions, and had the following average GDP per capita: US $637 (low-income nations), US $1,799 (lower middle-income nations) and US $4,795 (upper middle-income nations). In contrast, North America had a GDP per capita of US $28,910 and 5.2 per cent of the global population, but contributed 13.7 per cent of the global emissions in 2000, more than twice that of Latin America and the Caribbean. In contrast, an individual in sub-Sahara Africa accounts for less than a tenth of the CO_2 produced by an average person in the developed world.

In newly industrializing countries, the combined impact of population growth, urbanization, motorization and increased energy use act as drivers of emissions. These factors are particularly significant in countries such as China and India. In 2007, China surpassed the United States as the leading emitter of greenhouse gases; the increase has been attributed mainly to increased coal consumption, industrial processes and changing lifestyles.[11] China's emissions are significantly larger than those of India, even though both countries have roughly similar economic growth rates and population sizes.

Evidence suggests that if current trends continue, climate change may eventually damage national and urban

FIGURE 3.2.3: **RELATIONSHIP BETWEEN URBAN DENSITY AND CO_2 EMISSIONS**

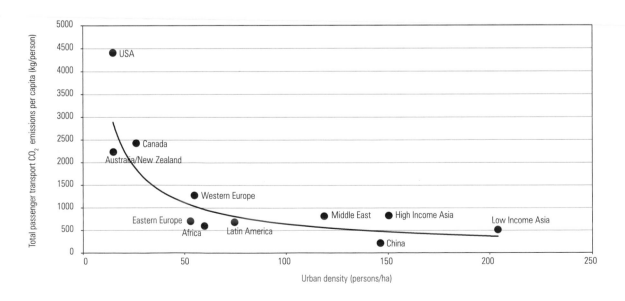

Source: Adapted from Kenworthy 2003

Remains of burnt trees in the Amazon: Deforestation is a significant contributor to global CO_2 emissions.
©iStockphoto

FIGURE 3.2.4: **PER CAPITA CO$_2$ EMISSIONS IN SELECTED CITIES**

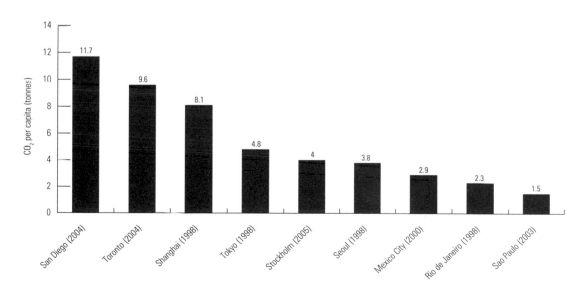

Source: UN-HABITAT Global Urban Observatory 2008
Note: Data from various sources, 1998-2005

economies. Economic losses will emanate from declining agricultural production and increased heat waves, extreme weather, droughts, flooding, biodiversity loss, disease, and soil erosion. It is estimated that abrupt and large-scale climate change could lead to an average loss of 5 to10 per cent in global GDP, with poor countries suffering costs in excess of 10 per cent of GDP. This scenario has been described by former World Bank economist Nicholas Stern as "the greatest and widest ranging market failure ever seen."[12]

A report commissioned by the U.K.[13] in 2006 concluded that tackling climate change is a pro-growth strategy in the long term, as it reduces the risk of disrupting social and economic activities on a massive scale. Efforts to mitigate climate change effects should not, however, hinder productivity or reduce the quality of urban life. The challenge is to find ways to reduce emissions and vulnerability in an environment of equity, prosperity and harmony.

Urban responses to climate change

Many countries and cities have managed to urbanize without placing a huge environmental burden on the world's resources, thereby mitigating climate change. The challenge for cities is to implement policies that encourage lower energy consumption and emissions and to reduce vulnerability of urban populations.

World Bank estimates indicate that in urban metropolitan areas, the transport sector accounts for a third or more of total greenhouse gas emissions. The growing energy needs that countries face in the transport sector, especially in urban transport in developing countries, present major challenges in terms of energy security and the environmental externalities associated with emissions. The growth of secondary cities and urban sprawl contribute to the pressure on existing urban transport networks. A moderate increase in per capita vehicle ownership could lead to a long commute time, changes in land use, and more transport-related air pollution. The trend toward increased motorization, in all its forms, leads to longer travel times for surface public transport (buses)—which in turn induces more auto and taxi use—and to poor traffic safety, the economic inefficiency of increased fuel use, and degradation of the urban quality of life.

Promotion of non-motorized public transport options, is therefore, key to reducing emissions in cities. Reducing consumption of electricity and shifting to cleaner sources of energy would also go a long way in reducing emissions. Several cities have already put in place energy-efficient policies and practices, for example, in 1989, Toronto became the first city to adopt a greenhouse gas reduction target. Since the adoption of the Kyoto Protocol in 1997, several other cities have joined forces to address global warming and reduce emissions, as highlighted below:[14]

TABLE 3.2.1: **GHG EMISSIONS ON A REGIONAL SCALE**

Greenhouse Gas Emissions Diagnostic for OECD and Latin American

	Population (million)	GDP (2000$b)	CO$_2$ emissions (Mt CO$_2$)	Electricity consumption (kWh per capita)	CO$_2$ emissions per capita (t CO$_2$ per capita)
OECD	1,154	26,792	12,794	8,044	11.08
Latin America	432	1,443	850	1,601	1.97
World	6,268	33,391	24,983	2,429	3.99

Source: International Energy Agency (IEA), 2005, cited in Simms and Reid, 2006.

FIGURE 3.2.5: **CARBON EMISSIONS IN USA, EUROPEAN UNION, CHINA AND INDIA, 2005 AND 2030**

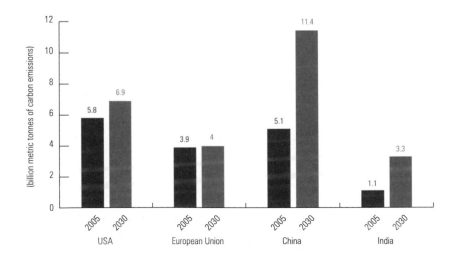

Urbanization levels

	2005	2030
USA	80.8%	87.0%
Europe	72.2%	78.3%
China	40.42%	60.3%
India	28.7%	40.7%

Source: Carbon emissions: International Energy Agency 2007
Urbanization rate: UN Population Division, World Urbanization Prospects 2005

Solar panel installation in Barcelona, Spain
©Snezana Negovanovic/iStockphoto

- The city of Calgary, Canada, is achieving significant electricity savings and reducing greenhouse gas emissions with the EnviroSmart Retrofit Project. Most of Calgary's residential streetlights are being changed to more energy-efficient flathead lenses. Streetlight wattage is being reduced from 200W to 100W on residential local roads and from 250W to 150W on collector roads.

- On 5 November 1999, Vienna City Council adopted the city's Climate Protection Programme (KLIP) as a framework for its Eco-Business plan. The plan was introduced to help enterprises operate and generate profits through eco-friendly practices that benefit both the enterprises and the environment. The initiative is a partnership among the city administration, interest groups, private companies, and management consultants. It promotes environmental protection strategies, efficient use of resources, sustainable development, information exchange, and effective relationships between the city administration and the private sector. To date, 527 enterprises have participated in the Eco-Business plan, implementing more than 9,000 environmental projects. These enterprises have been able to generate savings totalling approximately 30 million Euros. The city has also seen reductions in, solid waste output, by 109,300 tonnes; toxic solid wastes, by 1,325 tonnes; and carbon dioxide emissions,

by 42,765 tonnes. Energy savings total 138.7 million Kwh, and 1,325,000 cubic meters of drinking water has been saved. The Eco-Business plan is now being implemented in Chennai, India, and Athens, Greece.

- The city of Johannesburg, South Africa, is guided by an integrated Environmental Management Policy, the goal of which is to improve the quality of the urban environment. Mitigation measures in place are retrofitting of council buildings, energy savings in water pump installations, and methane gas recovery.

- The Spanish city of Barcelona has addressed the energy-efficiency issue through the Barnamil Campaign, the goal of which is to install solar panels for heating domestic hot water in urban residential areas. Since 2006, Barcelona has made solar panel installation mandatory for all new and renovated buildings to supply at least 60 per cent of the energy needed to heat water.

- In 1997, the municipality of Guangzhou in southern China initiated a five-year Action Programme for improving the living environment to maintain and enhance Guangzhou's attractiveness both as a place to live and do business. The strategic urban plan of Guangzhou provided the overall framework for implementation and resulted in substantial improvements in traffic management, urban greening, sanitation, pollution control, and conservation of natural resources and cultural heritage. The action plan is been replicated in other cities in China, such as Hangzhou, Nanjing, Jinan, Xiamen, Changsha and Chengdu.

- In the U.K., the Leicester Environment Partnership has developed a Climate Change Strategy for the city to stimulate public debate, raise awareness and initiate a plan of action to minimize impacts and effects of climate change. The Climate Change Strategy builds on the 1994 Leicester Energy Strategy and puts in place an integrated approach to the mitigation of climate change across the city. Its objectives are: assessing the city's contributions to climate change; forecasting change in the next 80 years; reviewing progress on targets contained within 1994 Leicester Energy Strategy; identifying how to reduce greenhouse gas emissions; providing a framework for an action programme; and setting up a monitoring framework to assess progress towards targets.

- In the U.S.A., more than 710 cities have joined forces to undertake local actions to meet or beat the Kyoto Protocol target (i.e. 7 per cent reduction in emissions from 1990 levels by 2012) through actions ranging from anti-sprawl land-use policies to urban forest restoration projects. U.S. cities are also partnering with businesses to meet their environmental goals. More than 50 private firms are taking part in the ClimateWise Program, in which cities offer free assessments of a firm's energy, water, solid waste, transport, and recycling, then offer guidance on becoming more energy efficient. The city of Chicago also awards grants for rooftop gardens that help to improve air quality, conserve energy and reduce storm water runoff. And Seattle recently began a programme in which businesses assess and cut greenhouse gas emissions and encourage their workers, customers and suppliers to do the same. Participating cities are encouraged to work with the global ICLEI Local Governments for Sustainability's Cities for Climate Protection Programme to assist them in tracking progress. To support all these efforts, an umbrella body called the World Mayors and Local Governments Climate Protection Agreement was officially launched at the United Nations Climate Change Conference in Bali, Indonesia, in December 2007.

TABLE 3.2.2: **ADAPTATION STRATEGIES**

Sector	Adaptation option/strategy	Policy
Water supply/water hazards	Water storage and conservation techniques; incentives for water conservation; water reuse; water recycling; desalination; increase water use efficiency; public education; flood risk map; public participation flood adaptation and mitigation programs; greater investment in water supply systems; controlled use of urban and rural groundwater.	Urban water policies and integrated water resources management; water-related hazards management; integrating climate change into public policy; policy to control groundwater extraction.
Infrastructure/ settlement (including cities in the coastal zones)	Cleaning drainage system and replacement of primary sewer system; encourage infiltration and increasing depression and street detention storage; re-designing structures; relocation; seawalls and storm surge barriers; dune reinforcement; land acquisition and creation of wetlands as buffer zone against sea level rise and flooding; protection of existing natural barriers; maintaining defensible space around each building/neighborhood.	Design standards and codes; regulations; integrate climate change considerations into design; land use policies; insurance; financial incentives; public education regarding risk of living in hazard prone areas.
Human health	Heat-related public health action plans; emergency medical services; access to public 'cooling centers'; improved climate sensitive disease surveillance and control; access to safe water and improved sanitation; greater ingovernmental coordination and cross-boundary coordination.	Public health policies that recognize climate risk; strengthen health services; intergovernmental, regional and international cooperation; greater investment in health services.
Urban transport	Environmentally friendly transport system; energy efficient cars; car pooling; efficient public transportation system; new design standards and planning for urban roads, rail, etc., to cope with warming and drainage; fuel substitution.	Integrating climate change considerations into urban transport policy; investment in research and development; incentives for energy efficient car industry.
Energy	Strengthening of overhead transmission and distribution lines; underground cabling for utilities; increasing energy efficiency; emphasis on renewable resources.	Sustainable urban energy policies; regulations; fiscal and financial incentives to encourage use of green energy and building; incorporate climate change in design standards and codes.

Source: Extract from Mirza 2007.

Poverty reduction as an adaptation strategy

The Stern Review on the Economics of Climate Change (2006), commissioned by the Government of the United Kingdom, is unusual among discussions on climate change in its explicit recognition that climate change adaptation in low- and middle-income countries has to reduce the vulnerability of the urban poor. If cities and countries had been more successful in the last five decades in reducing poverty, upgrading slums and providing infrastructure and services to low-income settlements, adaptation costs would be much lower. The deficiencies in infrastructure, housing and services in slums and informal settlements means that the cost of adaptation includes not only putting in place the necessary infrastructure but improving the durability of housing and expanding the scale of public service provision. The report notes key areas of action that could help reduce vulnerability to the effects of climate change: improving food security and overcoming the structural causes of famine; building robust education and health systems; better urban planning that includes provision of services and infrastructure to the most vulnerable groups; and gender equality.

Source: Satterthwaite et al., 2007

▲
Nanjing, China.
©City of Nanjing

NOTES

1 Intergovernmental Panel on Climate Change, 2007.
2 UNEP, 2007b.
3 Data drawn from the World Resources Institute's Climate Analysis Indicators Tool, online database version 3.0.
4 Eu-15 comprise the following 15 European countries: Austria, Belgium, Denmark, Finland, France, Germany, Greece, Ireland, Italy, Luxemburg, Netherlands, Portugal, Spain, Sweden, and the U.K.
5 Constantinos et al., 2007.
6 Petersdorff, et al., 2004.
7 Hardoy, Mitlin & Satterthwaite, 2004.
8 Knaap, 2008.
9 Baumert, Herzog & Pershing, 2005.
10 UNEP Regional Office for Latin America and the Caribbean and SEMARNET (Secretaria de Medio Ambiente y Recursis Naturales), 2006.
11 Netherlands Environmental Assessment Agency, 2007.
12 Stern, 2006.
13 Stern, 2006.
14 City examples from UN-HABITAT Best Practices database, www.bestpractices.org and other sources.

3.3
Cities at Risk from Rising Sea Levels

▲
Raised slum dwellings built near the banks of the River Buriganga, Dhaka, Bangladesh. Cities in river deltas are particularly vulnerable to flooding.
©Manoocher Deghati/IRIN

In the 20th century, sea levels rose by an estimated 17 centimetres, and conservative global mean projections for sea level rise between 1990 and 2080 range from 22 centimetres to 34 centimetres.[1] Oceans, which have been absorbing 80 per cent of the temperature increase attributable to global warming, are expanding as ice sheets in the North and South poles melt. These events have led to a rise in sea levels and increased flooding in coastal cities.

The projected rise in sea levels could result in catastrophic flooding of coastal cities. Thirteen of the world's 20 megacities are situated along coastlines. Coastal cities that serve as ports are a vital component of the global economy. In fact, the importance of port cities in international trade has grown significantly, particularly in developing countries, as the volume of sea trade has more than doubled in the last 30 years. Port cities have, therefore, not only grown in terms of population, but in terms of asset value, as well.[2]

A recent study by the Organisation for Economic Cooperation and Development (OECD)[3] found that the populations of Mumbai, Guangzhou, Shanghai, Miami, Ho Chi Minh City, Kolkata, New York City, Osaka-Kobe, Alexandria, and New Orleans will be most exposed to surge-induced flooding in the event of sea level rise. By 2070, urban populations in cities in river deltas, which already experience high risk of flooding, such as Dhaka, Kolkata, Rangoon, and Hai Phong, will join the group of most exposed populations.

The same study found that the value of economic assets, including buildings and infrastructure, that might be lost in the event of severe flooding could amount to as much as US $3,000 billion (in 2005 dollars). Port cities whose assets are most exposed to rising sea levels are located mainly in three countries – the United States, Japan and the Netherlands – and include New York City, Tokyo and Amsterdam. By 2070, port cities in Bangladesh, China, Thailand, Viet Nam, and India will have joined the ranks of cities whose assets are most exposed. Any rise in sea levels is therefore potentially catastrophic for millions of urban dwellers and the global economy. Given the heavy concentration of people and assets in port cities, the failure to develop effective adaptation strategies risks creating not just local, but international, consequences.

Cities and urban populations at risk

The low elevation coastal zone – the continuous area along coastlines that is less than 10 metres above sea level – represents 2 per cent of the world's land area but contains 10 per cent of its total population and 13 per cent of its urban population.[4] Seventeen per cent of the total urban population in Asia lives in the low elevation coastal zone, while in South-Eastern Asia,

more than one-third of the urban population lives in these extremely vulnerable zone. In Northern Africa, 18 per cent of the urban population lives in the low elevation coastal zone, while in sub-Saharan Africa, the figure is 9 per cent of the total urban population. And in the island states of Oceania, more than 20 per cent of the urban population inhabits the low elevation coastal zone.

Coastal towns are by far the most developed of Africa's urban areas and, by implication, the concentration of residential, industrial, commercial, agricultural, educational and military facilities in coastal zones is high. Nearly 60 per cent of Africa's total population living in low elevation coastal zones is urban, representing 11.5 per cent of the region's total urban population. Major coastal African cities that could be severely be affected by the impact of rising sea levels include Abidjan, Accra, Alexandria, Algiers, Cape Town, Casablanca, Dakar, Dar es Salaam, Djibouti, Durban, Freetown, Lagos, Libreville, Lome, Luanda, Maputo, Mombasa, Port Louis, and Tunis.

Although the proportion and number of urban dwellers in coastal African cities is relatively smaller than in Asian cities, African cities will be among those most adversely affected by sea level rises, as they are poorly equipped to cope with its impacts. Many cities in Africa and other less-developed regions do not have the infrastructure to withstand extreme weather conditions. Lack of adequate drainage, embankments and preparedness could, therefore, lead to devastating consequences in coastal African cities.

Because the urban poor tend to live in hazardous locations, such as flood plains, and in poor quality housing, they are also most at risk of the health and property damages that accompany flooding. As Figure 3.3.9 illustrates, in Dhaka, slum settlements are already most vulnerable during cyclones and heavy rainfall. Climate change and rising sea levels would make these slum settlements more vulnerable to flooding, but they would also affect the city's non-slum areas.

There are 3,351 cities in the low elevation coastal zones around the world. Of these cities, 64 per cent are in

FIGURE 3.3.1: **URBAN DENSITY (PERSONS PER SQ KM) BY ECOSYSTEM, 1995**

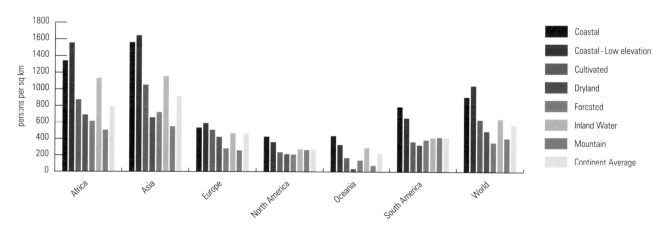

Data reported in Figure 6, in Balk et al, 2008, "Urbanization and ecosystems: Current patterns and Future Implications"

developing regions; Asia alone accounts for more than half of the most vulnerable cities, followed by Latin America and the Caribbean (27 per cent) and Africa (15 per cent). In the developed world, 1,186 cities are at risk. Two-thirds of these cities are in Europe; almost one-fifth of all cities in North America are in low elevation coastal zones. However, Japan, with less than 10 per cent of its cities in low elevation zones, has an urban population of 27 million inhabitants at risk, more than the urban population at risk in North America, Australia and New Zealand combined.

Low elevation coastal zones host both rural and urban populations, but urban populations comprise the majority of those living at the edge of the world's coastlines. In the industrialized, developed world, up to 86 per cent of the populations living in low elevation coastal zones are urban dwellers. In Latin America and the Caribbean, nearly three-quarters of the population in coastal zones are urban inhabitants. Even in the least-urbanized regions of Asia and sub-Saharan Africa, the low elevation coastal zones have larger urban populations than rural populations (55 per cent and 67 per cent, respectively).

Urbanization levels in low elevation coastal zones are higher than in other types of ecosystems around the world. Globally, nearly 60 per cent of the people living in low elevation coastal zones live in cities, compared with 44 per cent in dryland ecosystems and 47 per cent in cultivated areas. In sub-Saharan Africa, more than two-thirds of the population living in low elevation coastal zones is urban; in contrast, only 30 per cent of the population living in cultivated areas is urban, and dryland ecosystems are the least urbanized, with only one-quarter of their populations living in cities.

Urban low elevation coastal zones also are more densely developed than urban inland zones. Global average density along coastlines is 1,100 inhabitants per square kilometre, compared to 500 inhabitants per square kilometre in dryland ecosystems and 700 inhabitants per square kilometre in cultivated areas. Densities in urban low elevation coastal zones are highest in the developing world, where an average of 1,500 inhabitants occupy every square kilometre. Some regions have denser urban low elevation coastal zones than others. In Southern Asia, for instance, densities in these zones average 2,600 inhabitants per square kilometre, which are comparable to densities in sub-Saharan Africa (2,500 inhabitants per square kilometre). In fact, the densities of urban populations in Southern Asia and sub-Saharan Africa are more than twice those of urban populations in dryland ecosystems and cultivated areas. In the developed world, on the other hand, the average density in low elevation coastal zones is 600 inhabitants per square kilometre, which is much lower than both the global and the developing-world average. This reflects a general condition of low urban densities in countries of North America and Europe. The exception is Japan, where the average density in urban low elevation coastal zones is the same as that of the developing world – 1,500 inhabitants per square kilometre – which is higher than the global average.

TABLE 3.3.1: **URBAN POPULATION AT RISK FROM SEA LEVEL RISE**

Region	Urban population (000s)	LECZ Population (000s)	Urban population in LECZ (000s)	% of LECZ urban to total urban	% of urban in LECZ
Africa Total	282,143	55,633	32,390	11.5%	58.2%
Northern Africa	88,427	30,723	15,545	17.6%	50.6%
Sub-Saharan Africa	193,716	24,911	16,845	8.7%	67.6%
Asia total	1,430,917	449,845	235,258	16.4%	52.3%
Eastern Asia	709,199	159,969	109,434	15.4%	68.4%
Southern Asia	415,209	140,964	56,023	13.5%	39.7%
South-Eastern Asia	169,099	137,245	61,201	36.2%	44.6%
Western Asia	102,655	11,472	8,482	8.3%	73.9%
CIS Asia	34,756	194	119	0.3%	61.0%
LAC	319,629	33,578	24,648	7.7%	73.4%
Oceania	2,017	852	442	21.9%	51.9%
Developing Total	**2,034,706**	**539,908**	**292,738**	**14.4%**	**54.2%**
Europe (inc. CIS Europe)	500,943	50,200	39,709	7.9%	79.1%
N.America	255,745	24,217	21,489	8.4%	88.7%
Japan	101,936	29,347	27,521	27.0%	93.8%
Australia & New Zealand	18,002	2,846	2,421	13.5%	85.1%
Developed Total	**876,627**	**106,611**	**91,140**	**10.4%**	**85.5%**
World total	**2,911,333**	**646,519**	**383,878**	**13.2%**	**59.4%**

Source: Coastal Analysis Data Set utilizing GRUMP beta population and land area grids (CIESIN, 2005), Low Elevation Coastal Zone created from SRTM elevation grid (CIESIN, 2006)
LECZ = Low Elevation Coastal Zone
LECZ: land area that is contiguous with the coast and 10 meters or less in elevation.

The Thames Flood Barrier, London's first line of defence against floods.
©**Adrian Dracup/iStockphoto**

TABLE 3.3.2: **URBAN DENSITY BY ECOSYSTEM**

Region	Density in urban LECZ (000s/km²)	Density in urban Dryland (000s/km²)	Density in urban cultivated land (000s/km²)
Africa Total	1.7	0.8	1.0
Northern Africa	1.3	0.8	1.2
Sub-Saharan Africa	2.5	0.8	0.9
LAC	0.6	0.4	0.4
Asia total	1.9	0.7	1.2
Eastern Asia	2.1	1.2	1.5
Southern Asia	2.6	0.9	1.1
South-Eastern Asia	1.7	1.0	1.2
Western Asia	0.5	0.4	0.7
CIS Asia	0.7	0.3	0.4
Oceania	0.4	0.9	0.3
Developing Total	**1.5**	**0.7**	**1.0**
Europe (inc. CIS Europe)	0.6	0.4	0.5
N.America	0.4	0.2	0.2
Japan	1.5	NA	0.8
Australia & New Zealand	0.3	0.0	0.2
Developed Total	**0.6**	**0.3**	**0.4**
World total	**1.1**	**0.5**	**0.7**

Source: Data Set utilizing GRUMP beta population and land area grids Source: (CIESIN, 2005) (All grids 1km resolution) constructed by Deborah Balk and colleagues at the City University of New York (CUNY) and Columbia University.
LECZ = Low Elevation Coastal Zone

Countries with the highest proportion of their urban population living in the low elevation coastal zone include Suriname, Guyana, the Bahamas, the Netherlands, Bahrain, Viet Nam, Liberia, Senegal, and Djibouti, while those with the largest numbers of people living in the zone include China, India, Japan, Indonesia, the United States, Bangladesh, Viet Nam, Thailand, Egypt, and the Netherlands.[5]

The share of the urban population living in low elevation coastal zones vis-à-vis the total population living in low elevation coastal zones is highest in the developed world. For instance, 89 per cent of all people living in low elevation coastal zones in North America live in cities. However, in terms of numbers, Asia (excluding Japan) has the largest number of city dwellers at risk of flooding in the low elevation coastal zone, with more than 235 million people (15 per cent of the total urban population) living there. Japan alone has more than 27 million people at risk of the consequences of sea level rise in the event of global warming.[6] Heavily populated delta regions that contain large cities such as Dhaka, Shanghai and Bangkok are also particularly vulnerable to sea level rises. However, it is important to note that not all countries and cities are equally vulnerable to flooding in the event of a rise in sea levels, as some cities have better flood protection mechanisms than others. Nonetheless, in the event of large-scale flooding, it is difficult to predict which cities will remain safe.

In most Caribbean island states, 50 per cent of the population resides within 2 kilometres of the coast; these populations will be directly affected by sea level rise and other climate impacts on coastal zones.[7] Increased sea temperatures are already contributing to coral destruction around the islands. Climate change will affect the physical and biological characteristics of coastal areas, modifying their ecosystem

structure and functioning, including loss of biodiversity, fisheries, and shorelines; and increased vulnerability of coastal mangroves and wetlands to storm surges, increased salinity and ecosystem change. The sub-region's mountainous areas are also at risk of serious impacts associated with climate change. Among other expected changes, mountainous areas will experience losses in many of the environmental goods and services they provide, especially water supply to urban areas, basin regulation, and associated hydropower potential. Caribbean cities, too, are extremely vulnerable to disasters borne of both natural and human activity, with negative microeconomic and macroeconomic consequences at the local, regional and national levels. Urbanization patterns, especially in low-income areas, further heighten urban vulnerability. The Economic Commission for Latin America and the Caribbean estimates that in the 2004 hurricane season alone, the total economic impact of natural disasters in the region amounted to US $7,559 million.

A warmer climate will generally increase the exposure of developing-world populations to tropical diseases and respiratory irritants. In Latin America, a large proportion of the population lives in mountain ranges, including large urban areas situated above 2,000 metres, normally not exposed to tropical diseases such as dengue and malaria. Increased temperatures will affect the prevalence of vector-borne tropical diseases in higher altitudes. Diarrhoeal diseases also may increase as a result of more frequent and severe floods and drought. An increase in the frequency and severity of extreme weather events will result in more frequent humanitarian emergencies, particularly affecting populations in high-risk areas such as coastal zones, river valleys and cities. Climate change is also expected to lead to an increase in rodent-borne

---

FIGURE 3.3.2: **URBAN DENSITY BY ECOSYSTEM**

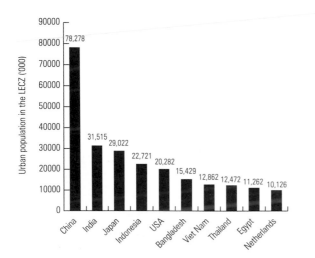

Source: McGranahan, Balk and Anderson (2008), A summary of the risks of climate change and urban settlement in low elevation coastal zones. In The New Global Frontier: Cities, Poverty and Environment in the 21st Century, G. Martine, G. McGranahan, M. Montgomery and R. Fernandez-Castilla (eds). Earthscan: London. Based on data generated for McGranahan, Balk and Anderson (2007)
LECZ = Low Elevation Coastal Zone

FIGURE 3.3.3: **COUNTRIES WITH THE LARGEST URBAN POPULATION IN THE LOW ELEVATION COASTAL ZONE**

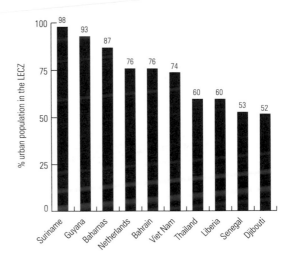

Source: McGranahan, Balk and Anderson (2008), A summary of the risks of climate change and urban settlement in low elevation coastal zones. In The New Global Frontier: Cities, Poverty and Environment in the 21st Century, G. Martine, G. McGranahan, M. Montgomery and R. Fernandez-Castilla (eds). Earthscan: London. Based on data generated for McGranahan, Balk and Anderson (2007)
* Countries with an urban population of fewer than 100,000 were excluded from this list.

Sheffield floods, June 2007.
©**Andy Green/iStockphoto**

diseases: warmer climates and changing habitats have allowed rodents to move into new territories.

Many countries in Latin America and the Caribbean are at increased risk of natural disasters resulting from climate change. The region is subject to extreme climatic events and natural phenomena that take place in frequently recurring cycles – namely, earthquakes, tropical storms, hurricanes, floods, droughts, and volcanic eruptions. As these events become more and more frequent, the region's increasingly fragile ecological and social systems will be put to the test.

Actions in urban areas have a major influence on whether the risks arising from the direct and indirect effects of climate change can be reduced. Well-planned and well-governed urban areas can greatly reduce risks – while unplanned and poorly governed cities can greatly increase them.

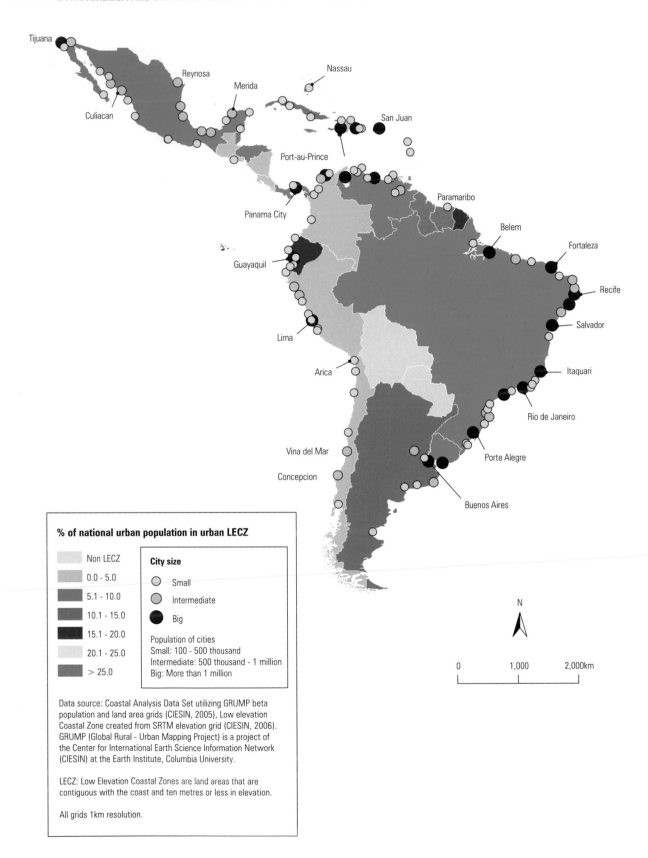

% of national urban population in urban LECZ

Non LECZ
0.0 - 5.0
5.1 - 10.0
10.1 - 15.0
15.1 - 20.0
20.1 - 25.0
> 25.0

City size

○ Small
◐ Intermediate
● Big

Population of cities
Small: 100 - 500 thousand
Intermediate: 500 thousand - 1 million
Big: More than 1 million

Data source: Coastal Analysis Data Set utilizing GRUMP beta population and land area grids (CIESIN, 2005), Low elevation Coastal Zone created from SRTM elevation grid (CIESIN, 2006). GRUMP (Global Rural - Urban Mapping Project) is a project of the Center for International Earth Science Information Network (CIESIN) at the Earth Institute, Columbia University.

LECZ: Low Elevation Coastal Zones are land areas that are contiguous with the coast and ten metres or less in elevation.

All grids 1km resolution.

N
0   1,000   2,000km

Source: UN-HABITAT Global Urban Observatory 2008

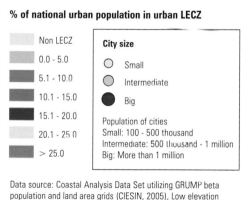

Izmir
Jerusalem
Jeddah
Aden
Karachi
Chittagong
Kolkata
Bangkok
Chennai
Colombo
Ha Noi
Taipei
Ho Chi Minh City
Kuala Lumpur
Singapore
Jakarta
Sapporo
Seoul
Tokyo

% of national urban population in urban LECZ

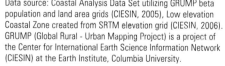

Non LECZ
0.0 - 5.0
5.1 - 10.0
10.1 - 15.0
15.1 - 20.0
20.1 - 25.0
> 25.0

City size

Small
Intermediate
Big

Population of cities
Small: 100 - 500 thousand
Intermediate: 500 thousand - 1 million
Big: More than 1 million

Data source: Coastal Analysis Data Set utilizing GRUMP beta
population and land area grids (CIESIN, 2005), Low elevation
Coastal Zone created from SRTM elevation grid (CIESIN, 2006).
GRUMP (Global Rural - Urban Mapping Project) is a project of
the Center for International Earth Science Information Network
(CIESIN) at the Earth Institute, Columbia University.

LECZ: Low Elevation Coastal Zones are land areas that are
contiguous with the coast and ten metres or less in elevation.

All grids 1km resolution.

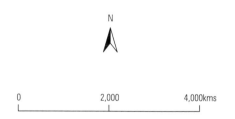

N

0   2,000   4,000kms

Source: UN-HABITAT Global Urban Observatory 2008

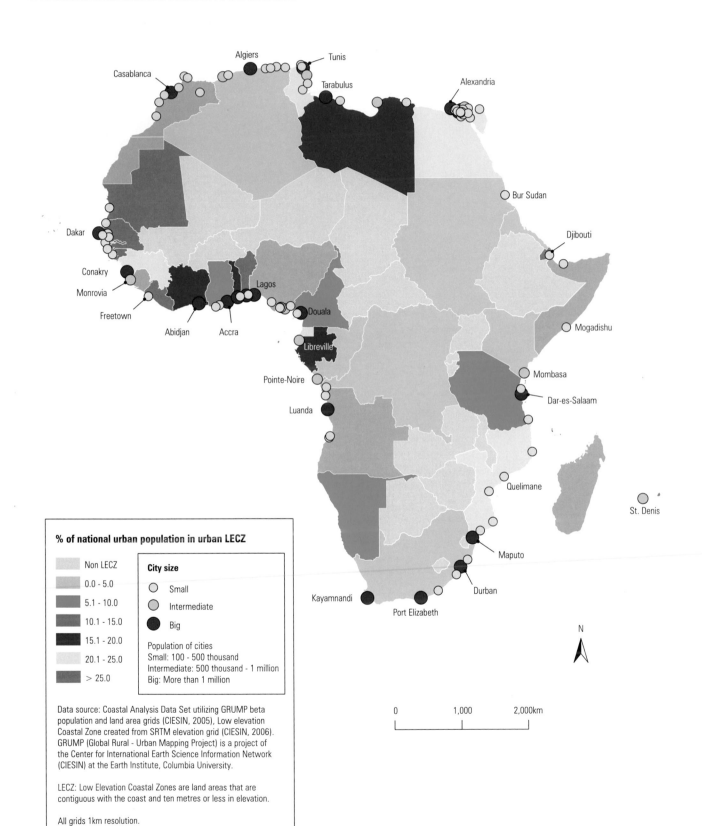

% of national urban population in urban LECZ

	Non LECZ
	0.0 - 5.0
	5.1 - 10.0
	10.1 - 15.0
	15.1 - 20.0
	20.1 - 25.0
	> 25.0

City size

○ Small
◐ Intermediate
● Big

Population of cities
Small: 100 - 500 thousand
Intermediate: 500 thousand - 1 million
Big: More than 1 million

Data source: Coastal Analysis Data Set utilizing GRUMP beta population and land area grids (CIESIN, 2005), Low elevation Coastal Zone created from SRTM elevation grid (CIESIN, 2006). GRUMP (Global Rural - Urban Mapping Project) is a project of the Center for International Earth Science Information Network (CIESIN) at the Earth Institute, Columbia University.

LECZ: Low Elevation Coastal Zones are land areas that are contiguous with the coast and ten metres or less in elevation.

All grids 1km resolution.

0   1,000   2,000km

N

Source: UN-HABITAT Global Urban Observatory 2008

FIGURE 3.3.7: **POPULATION DISTRIBUTION, URBAN PLACES, AND LOW ELEVATION COASTAL ZONES IN NORTH AFRICA**

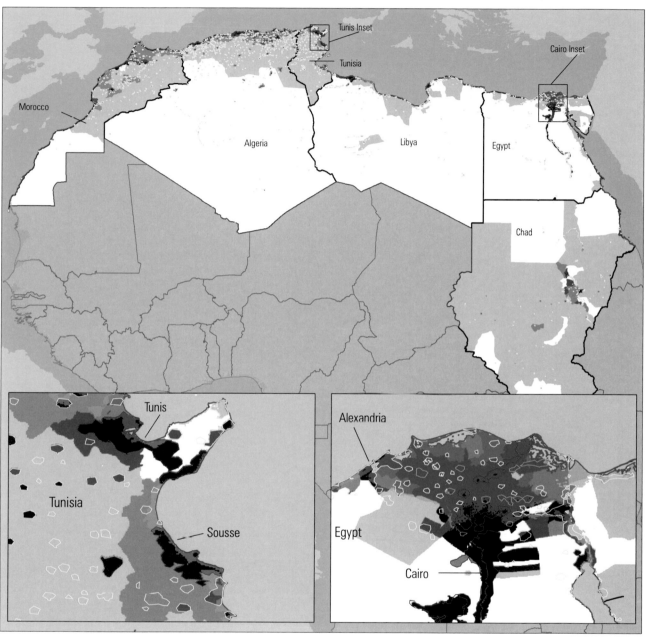

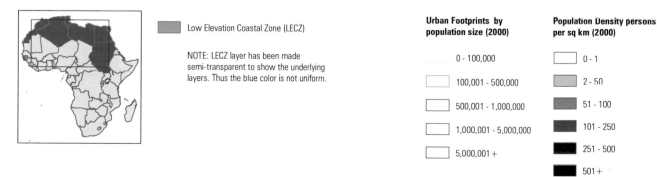

Urban Footprints by population size (2000)

- 0 - 100,000
- 100,001 - 500,000
- 500,001 - 1,000,000
- 1,000,001 - 5,000,000
- 5,000,001 +

Population Density persons per sq km (2000)

- 0 - 1
- 2 - 50
- 51 - 100
- 101 - 250
- 251 - 500
- 501 +

Low Elevation Coastal Zone (LECZ)

NOTE: LECZ layer has been made semi-transparent to show the underlying layers. Thus the blue color is not uniform.

Data Source: GRUMP 1KM population surface (BETA), 1KM urban extent mask (BETA), 2007 Available at http://sedac.ciesin.columbia.edu/gpw/Map produce by D. Balk and colleagues, Baruch College, and CIESIN, Columbia University. GRUMP (Global Rural - Urban Mapping Project) is a project of the Center for International Earth Science Information Network (CIESIN) at the Earth Institute, Columbia University.

CITIES AT RISK FROM RISING SEA LEVELS

FIGURE 3.3.8: **PROPORTION OF POPULATION AND LAND AT RISK DUE TO SEA LEVEL RISE IN AFRICA**

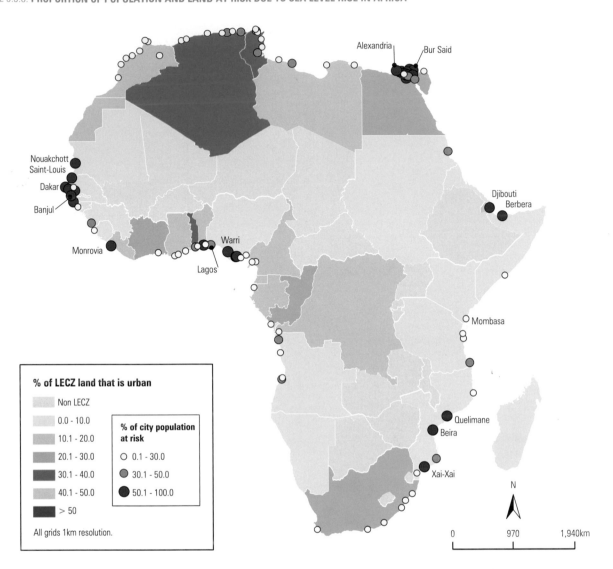

% of LECZ land that is urban

- Non LECZ
- 0.0 - 10.0
- 10.1 - 20.0
- 20.1 - 30.0
- 30.1 - 40.0
- 40.1 - 50.0
- > 50

% of city population at risk
- ○ 0.1 - 30.0
- ◉ 30.1 - 50.0
- ● 50.1 - 100.0

All grids 1km resolution.

0   970   1,940km

Country Name	City Name	Population (%) at risk in Low Elevation Coastal Zone	Land (%) at risk in Low Elevation Coastal Zone	City Size
Egypt	AlMatariyah	100.0	100.0	Small
Egypt	Damanhur	100.0	100.0	Small
Egypt	Dikirnis	100.0	100.0	Small
Egypt	Disuq	100.0	100.0	Small
Egypt	Kafr ashShaykh	100.0	100.0	Small
Senegal	Saint-Louis	100.0	100.0	Small
Egypt	Dumyat	99.6	99.7	Intermediate
Egypt	Diyarb Najm	98.7	98.7	Small
Mauritania	Nouakchott	98.6	98.2	Small
Mozambique	Quelimane	97.9	97.9	Small
Egypt	Abu Kabir	97.7	97.8	Small
Egypt	Bur Said	97.2	94.1	Small
Egypt	Kafr azZayyat	96.4	96.6	Small
Nigeria	Bugama	95.6	95.5	Small
Benin	Cotonou	94.7	85.4	Big
Egypt	AlMahallah alKubr	93.4	94.2	Big
Nigeria	Warri	90.8	92.0	Small

30-50% of population and land are at risk in 15 cities while 10-30% are at risk in 36 cities

Country Name	City Name	Population (%) at risk in Low Elevation Coastal Zone	Land (%) at risk in Low Elevation Coastal Zone	City Size
Egypt	Tanta	88.	89.0	Intermediate
Egypt	Mit Ghamr	85.3	84.2	Small
Nigeria	Abonnema	85.2	86.5	Small
Egypt	Alexandria	85.1	68.8	Big
Senegal	Kaolack	82.6	80.6	Small
Egypt	AzZaqaziq	80.9	81.0	Intermediate
Liberia	Monrovia	80.6	83.1	Small
Senegal	Ziguinchor	75.4	75.3	Small
Mozambique	Beira	65.3	65.3	Small
Nigeria	Port Harcourt	64.4	61.9	Intermediate
Senegal	Dakar	61.6	47.6	Big
Mozambique	Xai-Xai	59.6	59.1	Small
Senegal	Mbour	56.9	57.0	Small
Gambia, The	Banjul	56.1	44.0	Small
Djibouti	Djibouti	55.7	55.5	Small
Somalia	Berbera	53.6	53.2	Small
Egypt	Ismailia	50.2	52.0	Small

30-50% of population and land are at risk in 15 cities while 10-30% are at risk in 36 cities

Data source: Coastal Analysis Data Set utilizing GRUMP beta population and land area grids (CIESIN, 2005);
Low Elevation Coastal Zone created from STRM elevation grid (CIESIN, 2006).
GRUMP (Global Rural - Urban Mapping Project) is a project of the Center for International Earth Science Information Network (CIESIN) at the Earth Institute, Columbia University.

African cities at risk

Alexandria, Egypt
©iStockphoto

ALEXANDRIA (Egypt): An assessment of the vulnerability of the most important economic and historic centre along the Mediterranean coast (the cities of Alexandria, Rosetta and Port Said) suggests that, with a sea-level rise of 50 cm, more than 2 million people would have to abandon their homes, 214,000 jobs would be lost, and the cost in lost property value and tourism income would be over US $35 billion, which does not include the immeasurable loss of world famous historic, cultural and archaeological sites.

LAGOS (Nigeria): Lagos, with a total population of nearly 10 million inhabitants, lacks adequate infrastructure to cope with flooding. "Normal" rainfall brings flooding to many areas of the city, largely as a result of inadequacies in sewers, drains and wastewater management. Any increase in the intensity of storms and storm surges is likely to increase such problems, as much of the land in and around Lagos is less than 2 meters above sea level. Many low-income settlements are built in areas at high risk of flooding (many on stilts), largely because safer sites are too expensive.

Source: Satterthwaite, et al., 2007.

BANJUL (Gambia): Most of Banjul is less than 1 metre above sea level. Flooding is common after heavy rains in the city in settlements established on reclaimed land in dried-up valleys, and in settlements close to mangrove swamps and wetlands. Problems with flooding are likely to intensify under a warmer climate with an increase in the strength and frequency of tropical storms.

ABIDJAN (Côte d'Ivoire): Although some important areas of Abidjan lie on a plateau and may escape the direct effects of sea-level rise, major economic centres, including the nation's largest port and much of the international airport, are on land less than 1 meter above sea level. A sea-level rise in Abidjan is likely to inundate 562 square kilometers along the coastline of the Abidjan region, as lowland marshes and lagoons dominate the coastal zone. Average retreat will vary from 36 to 62 meters.

MOMBASA (Kenya): Mombasa is Kenya's second-largest city, with a population of more than 800,000 and is the largest sea port in East Africa, serving many countries in the region. An estimated 17 per cent of Mombasa's area (4,600 hectares) could be submerged by a sea-level rise of 0.3 meters, with a larger area rendered uninhabitable or unusable for agriculture because of waterlogging and salt stress. Sandy beaches, historic and cultural monuments, and several hotels, industries and port facilities would also be negatively affected. Mombasa already has a history of disasters related to climate extremes, including floods that have caused serious damage and loss of life nearly every year.

BAMENDA (Cameroon): Approximately 20 per cent of Bamenda's 250,000 residents live on floodplains and roughly 7 per cent live in informal settlements on steep slopes. Land clearance for settlement and for quarrying and sand mining, along with other land-use changes caused by urban expansion, have further created serious problems of soil erosion. Soil that is washed down the hills blocks drainage channels and changes peak water flows. Degradation of the land has exacerbated problems with floods.

Dhaka's extreme vulnerability to climate change

A woman working at a tannery in Dhaka, Bangladesh.
©**Manoocher Deghati/IRIN**

Take one of the most unplanned urban centres in the world, wedge it between four flood-prone rivers in the most densely packed nation in Asia, then squeeze it between the Himalaya mountain range and a body of water that not only generates violent cyclones and the occasional tsunami, but also creeps further inland every year, washing away farmland, tainting drinking water, submerging fertile deltas, and displacing villagers as it approaches – and there you have it: Dhaka, the capital of Bangladesh and one of the world's largest megacities.

Add the expected impact of climate change to this cauldron and it's a recipe for disaster. Experts believe that the melting of glaciers and snow in the Himalayas, along with increasing rainfall attributable to climate change, will lead to more flooding in Bangladesh in general, especially in cities located near the coast and in the delta region, including Dhaka. Dhaka may also experience increased temperatures from rising levels of vehicle exhaust emissions, increased industrial activity and increased use of air conditioning.

Researchers studying the impact of climate change on Dhaka predict that the city will be affected in two major ways: flooding and drainage congestion, and heat stress. The elevation in Dhaka ranges between 2 and 13 metres above sea level, which means that even a slight rise in sea level is likely to engulf large parts of the city. Moreover, high urban growth rates and high urban densities have already made Dhaka more susceptible to human-induced environmental disasters. With an urban growth rate of more than 4 per cent annually, Dhaka, which already hosts more than 13 million people, is one of the fastest growing cities in Southern Asia, and is projected to accommodate more than 20 million by 2025. The sheer number of people living in the city means that the negative consequences of climate change are likely to be felt by a large number of people, especially the urban poor who live in flood-prone and water-logged areas.

A recent mapping and census of slums conducted by the Centre for Urban Studies in Dhaka shows that nearly 60 per cent of the slums in the city have poor or no drainage and are prone to frequent flooding. The problems associated with flooding are compounded by poor quality housing and overcrowding. The survey found that more than one-third of Dhaka's population lived in housing where almost all the structures were too weak to withstand large-scale environmental disasters. Although Bangladesh has among the highest population densities in the world (at 2,600 persons per square mile), the population density in slums is roughly 200 times greater – an astounding figure, considering that nearly all slums are dominated by single-storey structures. Approximately 80 per cent of the slum population in Dhaka lives in dense slum clusters of between 500 and 1,500 persons per acre. Overcrowding is extremely prevalent; more than 90 per cent of slum dwellers share a single room with three or more people.

Floods in dense, poorly serviced settlements can lead to other hazards, which have a significant impact on the health of urban poor residents. Floodwaters in slums can mix with raw sewage and breed water-borne diseases, such as diarrhoea, typhoid and scabies. Water supplies also become contaminated during floods, as pipes in slum areas are likely to be damaged or to leak.

Experts generally agree that apart from taking active steps to reduce the possibility of global climate change itself, cities can take steps to prevent the harmful aspects of natural disasters by improving planning, putting in effective infrastructure and establishing disaster preparedness. Plans for flood protection are already underway in greater Dhaka; the government, as result of frequent flooding in the 1980s, has already completed construction of embankments, concrete reinforced walls and pumping stations in the most dense part of the city. Technical solutions are possible, but these solutions must also take into consideration unresolved development problems, such as the city's growing slum population, which has doubled in the last decade, and which shows no signs of abating.

Sources: OCHA/IRIN & UN-HABITAT, 2007; Rabbani, 2007; Centre for Urban Studies, National Institute of Population Research and Training & Measure Evaluation, 2006.

FIGURE 3.3.9: **FLOOD-PRONE SLUM AND NON-SLUM SETTLEMENTS IN DHAKA**

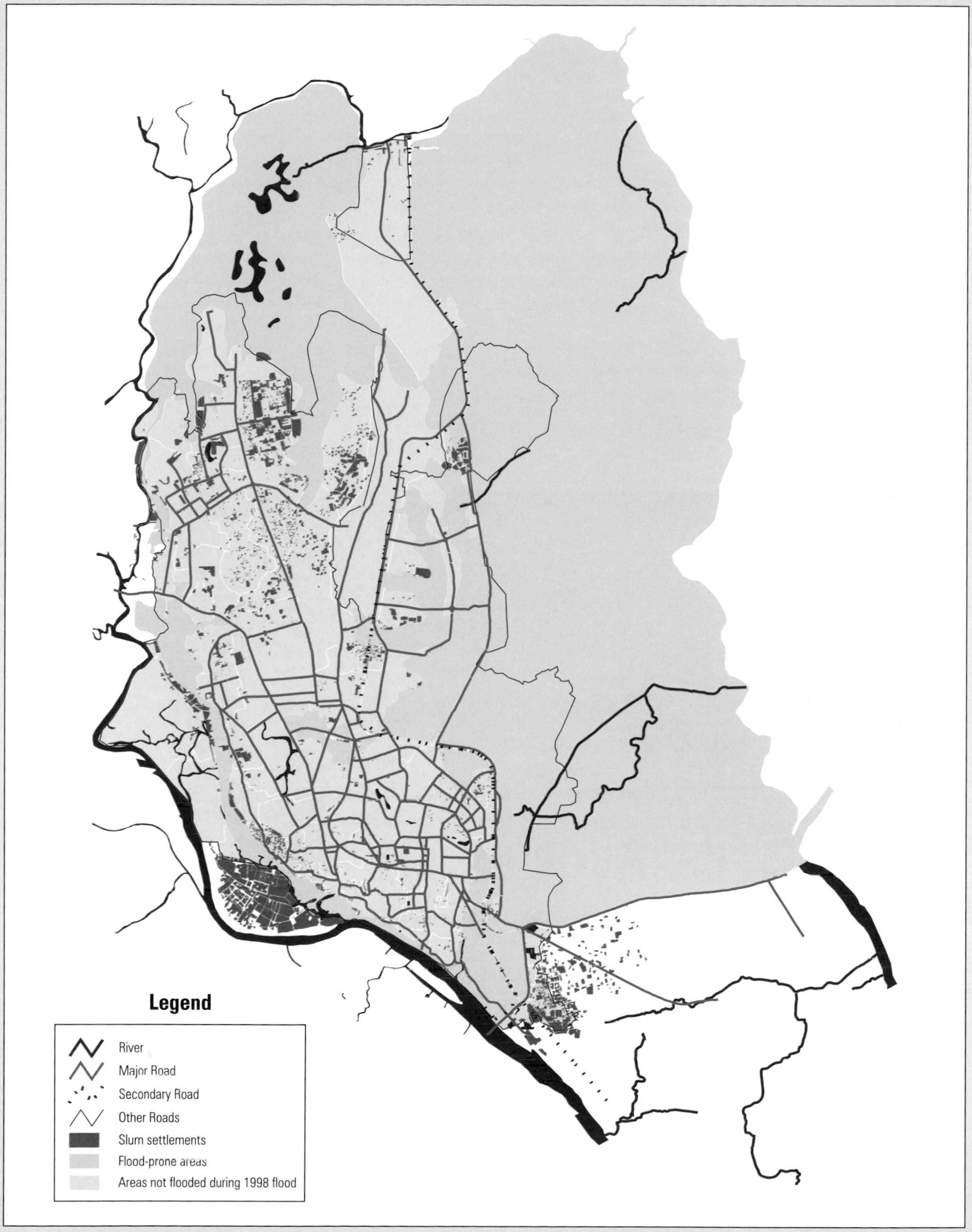

Legend

- River
- Major Road
- Secondary Road
- Other Roads
- Slum settlements
- Flood-prone areas
- Areas not flooded during 1998 flood

Sources: Centre for Urban Studies (Slum Map), Bangladesh, 2005 and Bangladesh Centre for Advance Studies (Flood Map), 1998.
Map adapted by UN-HABITAT Global Urban Observatory, 2008

Cuba: A culture of safety

Most local and national governments are ill-equipped to manage and adapt to environmental hazards, including climate variability and climate change. This is a developmental issue, and it makes large sections of urban populations vulnerable to any increase in the frequency or intensity of storms, to increased risk of disease or constraints on water supplies, and to increases in food prices, to which wealthier, better governed cities are typically quick to adapt. A shift from disaster response to disaster preparedness and disaster risk reduction, which would have significant relevance for urban resilience to climate change, has not yet occurred in most city and national level policies.

Cuba is a hurricane-prone island in the Caribbean. When Hurricane Wilma struck in October 2005, this small island managed to evacuate 640,000 people from its path, with just one fatality. The sea charged one kilometer inland and flooded the capital, Havana, yet no one died or was injured. This was not a one-time response, but built upon many years of experience in dealing with hurricanes. In the seven years between 1996 and 2002, six major hurricanes hit Cuba, yet a total of just 16 people died. In each case, hundreds of thousands of people – sometimes 700,000 to 800,000 at a time – were successfully evacuated, often within 48 hours.

The Cuban population has developed a culture of safety. Many ordinary people see themselves as actors with important roles to play in disaster preparation and response. Education and training, a culture of mobilization and social organization, and a government priority to protect human life in emergencies promote this vision. At the heart of Cuba's system is a clear political commitment, at every level of government, to safeguard human life. This allows for a centralized decision-making process alongside a decentralized implementation process equally necessary for effective emergency preparedness and response. The system has been tried and tested so many times that high levels of mutual trust and confidence exist between communities and politicians at every level of the system.

Tangible assets supporting disaster preparedness include: a strong, well-organized civil defense, an efficient early warning system, well-equipped rescue teams, and emergency stockpiles and other resources. Intangible assets are effective local leadership, community mobilization, solidarity among a population that is "disaster aware" and educated about what actions to take, and local participation in evacuation planning.

Source: Simms & Reid, 2006.

Havana, Cuba: The city has developed a culture of safety in the face of frequent hurricanes.
© **John Woodworth/iStockphoto**

Dhaka, Bangladesh
©**Manoocher Deghati/IRIN**

NOTES

1. Nicholss, 2004. The Intergovernmental Panel on Climate Change projects a worst case scenario of 1 metre sea-level rise by 2100.
2. Organisation for Economic Cooperation and Development (OECD), 2007.
3. OECD, 2007. The analysis focused on the exposure of population and assets to a 1 in 100 year surge-induced flood event (assuming no defences) rather than "risk" from coastal flooding.

4. McGranahan, Balk & Anderson, 2007.
5. McGranahan, et al., 2007.
6. Coastal Analysis Data Set utilizing GRUMP (Global Rural and Urban Mapping Program) beta population and land area grids (CIESIN 2005). Data as of October 2007
7. Vergara, 2005.

3.4
Energy Consumption in Cities

The urban metabolism

Energy consumption is the largest contributor to carbon dioxide (CO_2) emissions, the leading cause of climate change. It is important to understand which sectors consume the most energy to take appropriate remedial actions for emissions reduction. It is helpful to view cities as organic systems that have their own metabolism.[1] The metabolism of a city involves physical inputs – energy, water and materials – that are consumed and transformed, by means of technological and biological systems, into wastes and goods, or the city's outputs. Like any thermodynamic system, urban energy consumption can either be efficient or inefficient. An environmentally successful and energy efficient – or sustainable – city should ideally combine economic growth with social equity and minimum waste production (including greenhouse gas emissions).

To meet minimum waste standards, cities must fulfil two prerequisites: minimization of fossil fuel use and material inputs; and maximization of recycling and reuse of energy, water and materials. The need for sustainable, or harmonious, urban development further requires cities to function with a circular, rather than a linear, metabolism. But first understanding how cities came to develop high-impact, linear metabolism systems is essential for knowing how to find effective means to make the shift to sustainable, circular metabolic systems.

The contribution of cities to global warming derives basically from combustion processes – from the production of energy. But energy also plays a vital role in sustaining the metabolism of cities. Agriculture, which sustains both rural and urban populations, for instance, also contributes to greenhouse gas emissions. Land use change (for urban development or for cultivation), and agriculture combined account for more than 30 per cent of global greenhouse gas emissions (Fig. 3.4.1).

FIGURE 3.4.1: **LINEAR AND CIRCULAR URBAN METABOLISM**

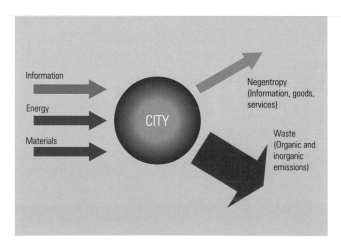

Today's city

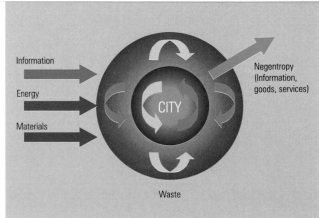

Sustainable city

Source: Figure courtesy of F. Butera

Power lines against a stormy, cloudy sky
©iStockphoto

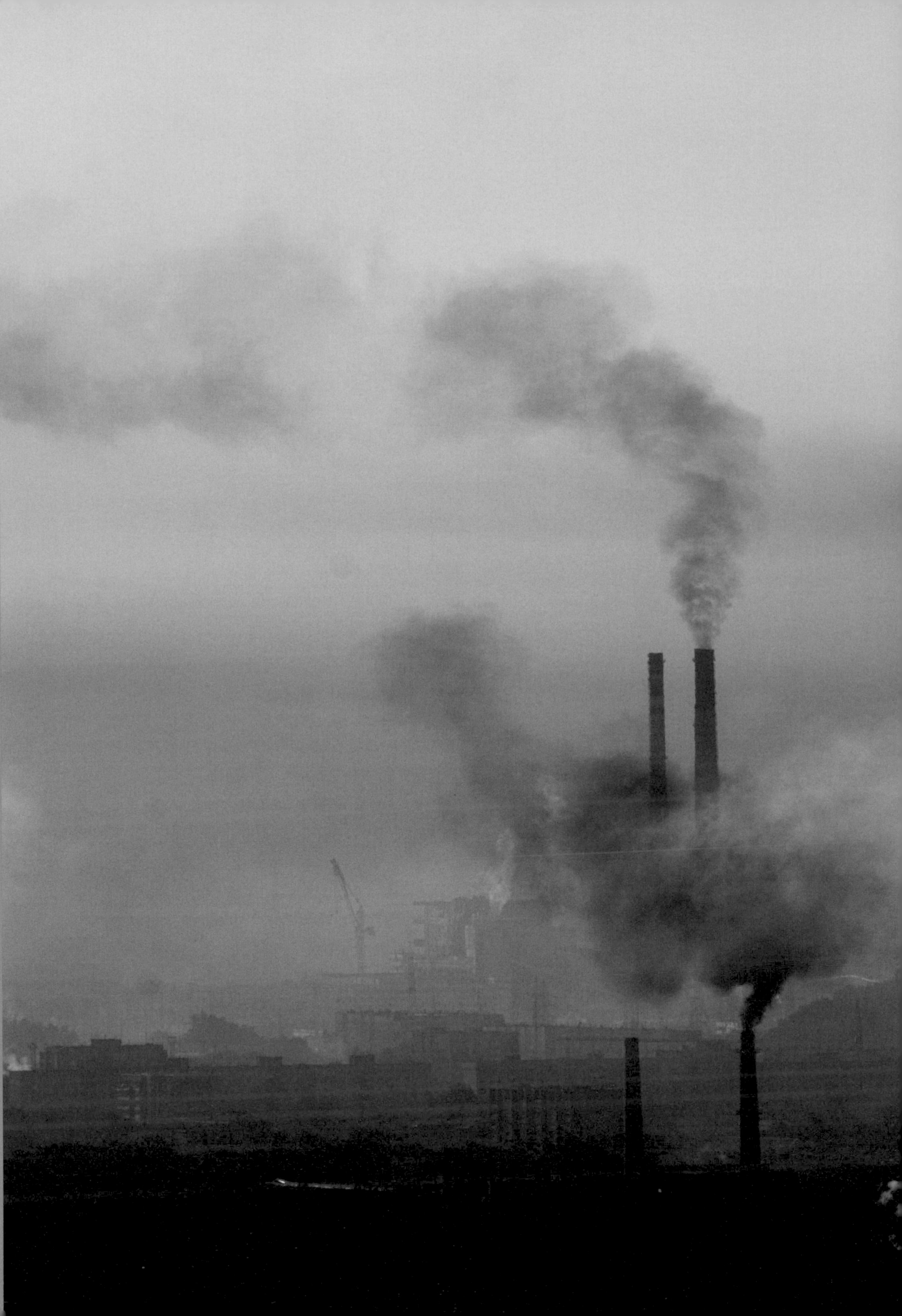

World 1990

5.1%
5.9%
8.5%
19.3%
4%
5.7%
19.8%
36.8%

Total Final Consumption
5,566,234 (1000 metric toe a)

World 2001

5.1%
7.8%
2.5%
5.5%
27.5%
19.7%
31.9%

Total Final Consumption
7,585,443 (1000 metric toe a)

+36%

Europe 1990

4.8%
8.8%
2.7%
23.8%
4.3%
20.7%
34.9%

Total Final Consumption
1,198,340 (1000 metric toe a)

Europe 2001

4%
9%
3%
6%
27%
19%
32%

Total Final Consumption
1,858,697 (1000 metric toe a)

+55%

North America 1990

5.8%
12.3%
16.3%
1.2%
8.2%
27.2%
29%

Total Final Consumption
1,468,100 (1000 metric toe a)

North America 2001

4.3%
12.5%
16.5%
1.2%
7.2%
27.2%
31.1%

Total Final Consumption
1,725,599 (1000 metric toe a)

+18%

Central America & the Caribbean 1990

2.6% 3.3%
3.2%
3.3%
20.4%
27.5%
39.7%

Total Final Consumption
125,054 (1000 metric toe a)

Central America & the Caribbean 2001

2.7% 3.6% 2%
3.6%
22.1%
31.3%
34.7%

Total Final Consumption
138,513 (1000 metric toe a)

+11%

South America 1990

4.5% 2.8%
4.4%
19.5%
3.4%
27.6%
37.8%

Total Final Consumption
222,271 (1000 metric toe a)

South America 2001

5.1% 3.4%
4.3%
16.5%
3.8%
28%
38.9%

Total Final Consumption
304,536 (1000 metric toe a)

+37%

■ Residential

■ Industry

■ Road Transport

■ Other Transport

■ Agriculture

■ Commercial and Public Services

■ Other

TECHNICAL NOTES:

Residential includes all energy used for activities by households except for transport.

Industry includes a combination of all industrial sub-sectors, such as mining and quarrying, iron and steel, and construction. Energy used for transport by industry is not included here, but is reported under transportation.

Road Transport includes all fuels used in road vehicles, including military, as well as agricultural and industrial highway use. The sector excludes motor gasoline used in stationary engines and diesel oil used in tractors.

All other transport refers to all fuel used for non-road transport except fuel used for international marine bunkers and ocean, coastal, and inland fishing. It includes transport in the industry sector and covers railways, air, internal navigation (including small craft and coastal shipping not included under marine bunkers), fuels used for transport of minerals by pipeline and non-specified transport.

Agriculture includes all activities defined as agriculture, hunting, and forestry. The sector therefore includes energy consumed by ocean, coastal and inland fishing in addition to the energy consumed by traction, power, and heating.

Commercial & Public Services includes, for example, wholesale and retail trade; the operation of hotels and restaurants; post and telecommunications; real estate, renting and business activities; the collection, purification and distribution of water; maintenance and repair of motor vehicles and motorcycles; financial intermediation, except insurance and pension funding; computers and related activities; sewage and refuse disposal; public administration and defence; education; and other community, health, social and personal service activities.

Non-energy Uses and "**other**" includes the use of petroleum products such as white spirit, paraffin waxes, lubricants, bitumen and other products. It is assumed that these products are used exclusively for non-energy purposes. This category also includes the non-energy use of coal (excluding peat) and fuel inputs for the production of ammonia and methanol. All fuel use not elsewhere specified is included here.

Source: Prepared by International Energy Agency, reported in World Resources Institute, Earthtrends, www.earthtrends.wri.org

FIGURE 3.4.3: **ENERGY CONSUMPTION IN SELECTED CITIES IN HIGH-INCOME, INDUSTRIALIZED ECONOMIES**

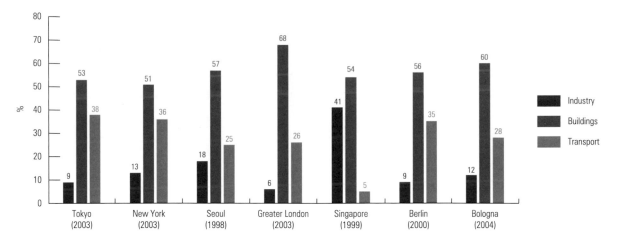

Source: UN-HABITAT Global Urban Observatory 2008
Note: Data from various sources, 1999-2004

FIGURE 3.4.4: **ENERGY CONSUMPTION IN SELECTED CITIES IN MIDDLE-INCOME COUNTRIES**

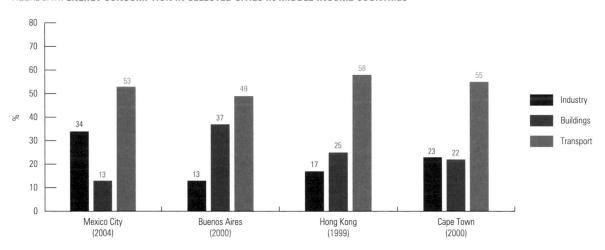

Source: UN-HABITAT Global Urban Observatory 2008
Note: Data from various sources 1999-2004

FIGURE 3.4.5: **ENERGY CONSUMPTION IN SELECTED ASIAN CITIES**

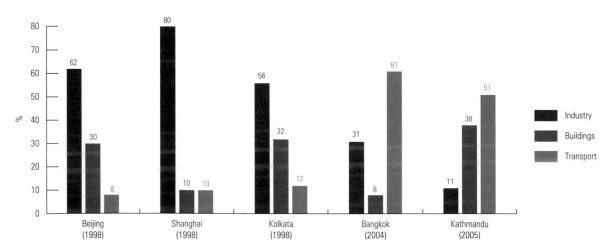

Source: UN-HABITAT Global Urban Observatory 2008
Note: Data from various sources, 1998-2005

Energy consumption by sector

In the early phase of industrialization, European cities looked like the cities of today's emerging economies, with heavy industries running on coal, producing high levels of urban air pollution and emissions. The amount of energy used to produce one unit of gross domestic product (GDP) was very high, due mainly to the high energy consumption of the industrial and construction sectors. In developed, industrialized cities, energy is consumed primarily through the maintenance and operation of built-up infrastructure, rather than on industry.

In the wealthier cities in the industrialized world, most energy is used to heat and light residential and commercial buildings; transport and industry follow as the second and third greatest consumers of energy. As Figure 3.4.3 shows, residential and commercial buildings account for more than half of the energy consumed in cities such as London, Bologna and Tokyo, while the transport sector consumes between 25 and 38 per cent of energy, with the exception of Singapore, which has successfully made urban mobility more energy efficient. Industry consumes less than 10 per cent of energy in cities such as Berlin and Tokyo because economic activities in there have moved away from industry to services.

Transport is the highest consumer of energy in cities such as Mexico City, Hong Kong and Cape Town, followed by residential and commercial buildings and industry (see Figure 3.4.4). Cities in the developing world show different energy end-use distribution according to their size and their stage of economic development. In megacities such as Beijing, Shanghai and Kolkata, industries consume more than 50 per cent of total energy uses, reflecting the fast growth of Chinese and Indian economies, while in large cities of countries whose economies are growing at a slower pace, the transport sector consumes more than half of the total energy used. Some industries in Chinese cities are voracious consumers of energy. Shanghai's industrial sector, for instance, consumes as much as 80 per cent of energy, compared to 10 per cent consumed by transport.

▲
Tokyo skyline at dusk: Residential and commercial buildings account for more than half of the energy consumed in Tokyo.
©iStockphoto

Ecological footprint

The ecological footprint is a measure of how much productive land and water an individual, a city, a country, or the whole global population require to produce all the resources they consume and to absorb all the waste they generate, using the prevailing technology.[2] The total ecological footprint of a given place or people is the sum of cropland, forest, grazing land, fishing ground, built-up land, and carbon and nuclear energy footprints required to sustain them and to absorb their outputs.[3] The world ecological footprint is measured in hectares (1 ha = 10,000 m²) of biologically productive space with world-average productivity.

Today, humanity's ecological footprint is 2.2 ha per person – over 21 per cent greater than the earth's biocapacity (1.8 ha), or its capability to regenerate the resources used. In other words, it now takes more than one year and two months for planet Earth to regenerate what we, its inhabitants, use in a single year.

Middle- and low-income countries, on average, do not contribute to the global over-consumption of resources, but exceptions include China and India, whose ecological footprints are twice their biocapacity. There are exceptions in the high-income countries too, such as New Zealand and Canada, whose ecological footprints are less than half their biocapacity.

The total ecological footprint can be subdivided into specific categories of consumption and waste production. The **carbon footprint** is calculated as the area of forest that would be required to absorb CO_2 emissions from fossil fuel combustion, excluding the proportion absorbed by the oceans. The **biomass fuel footprint** is calculated as the area of forest needed to grow wood and other forest products used as fuel. The hydropower footprint is the area occupied by hydroelectric dams and reservoirs. The **energy footprint** – of both carbon-based and nuclear-generated energy sources – accounts for more than half of the total world ecological footprint. At the city scale, the energy footprint is even more dominant.

Ecological footprints of cities are usually higher than those of their countries, but there are exceptions. For instance, as shown in Figure 3.4.9, the ecological footprints of Berlin and Wellington are smaller than those of Germany and New Zealand, respectively. In general, richer cities have larger footprints than poorer cities. The figure highlights the width of the gap in natural resource use between high-income North American cities and poor cities of developing countries, but also between cities in the United States and in the rest of the world, including Canada. This shows that the same quality of life can be achieved with very different environmental impacts.

FIGURE 3.4.6: **ECOLOGICAL FOOTPRINT OF COUNTRIES BY INCOME (2003)***

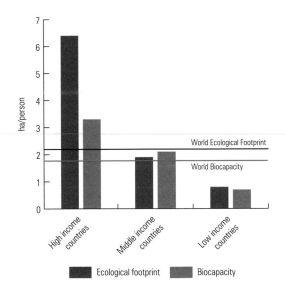

*High-Income Countries: Australia, Austria, Belgium & Luxembourg, Canada, Cyprus, Denmark, Finland, France, Germany, Greece, Ireland, Israel, Italy, Japan, Korea Republic, Kuwait, Malta, Netherlands, New Zealand, Norway, Portugal, Saudi Arabia, Slovenia, Spain, Sweden, Switzerland, United Arab Emirates, United Kingdom, United States of America.

Middle-Income Countries: Albania, Algeria, Angola, Argentina, Armenia, Azerbaijan, Belarus, Bolivia, Bosnia Herzegovina, Botswana, Brazil, Bulgaria, Chile, China, Colombia, Costa Rica, Croatia, Cuba, Czech Republic, Dominican Republic, Ecuador, Egypt, El Salvador, Estonia, Gabon, Georgia, Guatemala, Honduras, Hungary, Indonesia, Iran, Iraq, Jamaica, Jordan, Kazakhstan, Latvia, Lebanon, Libya, Lithuania, Macedonia, Malaysia, Mauritius, Mexico, Morocco, Namibia, Panama, Paraguay, Peru, Philippines, Poland, Romania, Russia (and USSR in 1975), Serbia and Montenegro, Slovakia, South Africa, Sri Lanka, Swaziland, Syria, Thailand, Trinidad and Tobago, Tunisia, Turkey, Turkmenistan, Ukraine, Uruguay, Venezuela.

Low-Income Countries: Afghanistan, Bangladesh, Benin, Burkina Faso, Burundi, Cambodia, Cameroon, Central African Rep, Chad, Congo, Congo Dem Rep, Côte d'Ivoire, Eritrea, Ethiopia, Gambia, Ghana, Guinea, Guinea-Bissau, Haiti, India, Kenya, Korea DPRP, Kyrgyzstan, Laos, Lesotho, Liberia, Madagascar, Malawi, Mali, Mauritania, Moldova Republic, Mongolia, Mozambique, Myanmar, Nepal, Nicaragua, Niger, Nigeria, Pakistan, Papua New Guinea, Rwanda, Senegal, Sierra Leone, Somalia, Sudan, Tajikistan, Tanzania, Togo, Uganda, Uzbekistan, Viet Nam, Yemen, Zambia, Zimbabwe

Source: World Wildlife Fund,, ZSL, GFN, Living planet report 2006, http://assets.panda.org/downloads/living_planet_report.pdf

FIGURE 3.4.7: **ECOLOGICAL FOOTPRINT BY COMPONENTS IN SELECTED CITIES**

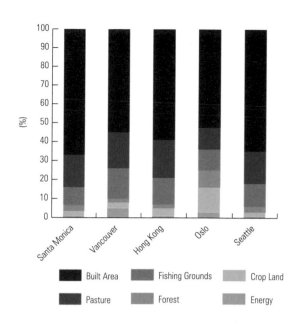

Source: UN-HABITAT Global Urban Observatory 2008
Note: Data from various sources

FIGURE 3.4.8: **ECOLOGICAL FOOTPRINT OF BERLIN FOR THE YEAR 2000**

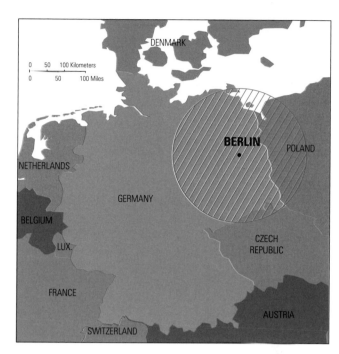

Source: Jens Pacholsky

FIGURE 3.4.9: **ECOLOGICAL FOOTPRINT OF SELECTED CITIES AND OF THE COUNTRIES WHERE THEY ARE LOCATED**

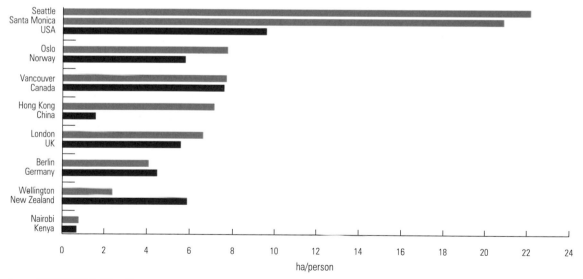

Source: UN-HABITAT Global Urban Observatory 2008
Note: Data from various sources

NOTES

[1] Bettencourt et al., 2007
[2] Wackernagel & Rees, 1996.
[3] Global Footprint Network, 2007

3.5

Urban Energy Consumption at the Household Level

▲
Electricity meters in a city apartment building
©Wendell Franks/iStockphoto

Trends in developed countries

Studies suggest that residential and commercial buildings are responsible for about 30 per cent of the greenhouse gas emissions of countries belonging to the Organization of Economic Cooperation and Development (OECD) countries.[1] Actions aimed at reducing emissions from buildings depend not only on climate, building type and level of economic development, but also on lifestyle, energy sources availability and structure of the local energy system.

Heating of residential and commercial buildings ranks first in the household energy end uses in developed countries, and is one of the main causes of energy-related greenhouse gas emissions. The main obstacle to the reduction of emissions derives from the fact that much of the current urban building stock in Europe was designed and constructed when energy was cheap and global warming was unheard of. Inefficient design and construction, combined with the prevalent use of cement, steel and glass in modern architecture, have led to energy waste in buildings, which rely heavily on energy-intensive heating and cooling systems.

Paradoxically, old buildings – built in the 19th century or before – are less energy-dependent than those built in the 1960s and 1970s. This is because, in the past, buildings were designed to obtain the highest comfort levels with the minimum use of energy technologies, using appropriate building materials suited to the local climate. The result of the modern trend towards using energy-intensive building materials not appropriate for local climates has led to the very high energy consumption figures in developed countries.

In cities of developed countries, the energy consumed by residential buildings is significant, as shown in fig 3.5.1. In London, Seoul, Berlin, and Bologna, for instance, residential buildings consume more than 50 per cent of the total energy used. However, in cities experiencing rapid economic growth, such as those in China, the commercial sector consumes the bulk of energy.

Since energy consumption for both heating and cooling is strongly affected by the quality of building envelopes, building design has a tremendous impact on energy demand. Adopting energy-efficient building regulations – including requirements for insulation, low-impact building materials and flexibility to improve as technologies change – is important for countries to reduce their dependence on scarce resources, however, regulations are seldom fully enforced.

Builders often complain that well-insulated buildings are more costly to build than poorly insulated buildings, but evidence shows that the savings on household energy bills quickly offsets the higher initial cost of construction. Poor insulation also increases the costs of heating, which impacts low-income households most acutely. The European Community Household Panel (ECHP), for instance, recently revealed that 17 per cent of households in the EU-15 declare an inability to adequately heat or insulate their homes.[2] The latest available estimates suggest that in 2004, some 2 million households in the United Kingdom experienced difficulty in keeping their homes warm at an acceptable level of cost.[3] The same applies to Southern Europe, where an alarming 45 per cent of households in Greece, 55 per cent in Spain

and 74 per cent in Portugal[4] are not able to meet reasonable comfort conditions because of their inability to pay for the fuel needed to heat their un-insulated buildings. A study carried out in 2004 in the major Athens, Greece, area found that poor insulation of residential buildings was directly related to heating expenditures: the lower the income of the household, the higher the cost of heating per person and unit of surface.[5]

Adequate building envelope insulation and good-quality buildings do not just lead to lower energy consumption and higher comfort levels, but also to better health of the occupants. In many recent surveys in Eastern Europe, households have complained about insufficient heat from dilapidated district heating systems, which have resulted in increased rates of illness. For example, in Sevastopol, Ukraine, 56 per cent of inhabitants of poor quality housing got sick because indoor temperatures were too low.[6]

Since the early 1980s, however, a growing concern about energy conservation has led central governments and cities to implement new regulations for buildings. In spite of the regulations, the overall impact on energy use has been rather limited, for several reasons, namely:

- The regulations apply only to new buildings or to old buildings that have been completely renovated, and not to old buildings that form a large proportion of the building stock in Europe.

- Living space increases as household incomes rise. The average size per dwelling in the EU-15 countries has increased from 84 square metres in 1985 to 89.5 square metres in 2001, at an average annual rate of 0.4 per cent or 0.3 square metres per annum.[7] The size of U.S. dwellings has grown even more. In California, the floor area of a new single-family home has doubled from approximately 100 square metres in 1972 to 200 square metres today[8]. As the average size of dwellings increases, more energy is used for heating and air conditioning. Moreover, larger houses are being shared by smaller families. The size of families in the developed world is decreasing, with a concomitant increase in the number of dwellings necessary to accommodate one or two occupants. This phenomenon is especially attributable to the increasing number of elderly people. An urban audit of 258 cities in the European Union found that an increasing number of people are living alone and that the average living space per inhabitant varies significantly among cities. City dwellers in Denmark, the Netherlands, Sweden, and Germany, for instance, have more than twice the living space of urban inhabitants in Romania, Latvia and Poland.[9]

For these and other reasons, tighter measures are needed to limit energy consumption both in existing and new buildings. In some places, new buildings are designed to be carbon neutral, as is the case in the U.K., where carbon-neutral building regulations will be enforced by 2016.

FIGURE 3.5.1: **SHARE OF ENERGY CONSUMPTION IN RESIDENTIAL AND COMMERCIAL SECTORS IN SELECTED CITIES IN HIGH-INCOME COUNTRIES**

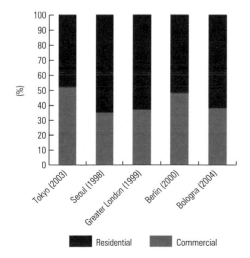

Source: UN-HABITAT, 2008
Note: Data derived from various sources, 1998-2004

Trends in developing countries

In developing countries, population growth, urbanization and economic development are having a huge impact on the construction industry. The most striking example comes from the rapidly growing economy of China, where new buildings are being constructed at the rate of an estimated 1.8 billion square metres per year.[10] China is taking energy conservation seriously by enforcing new building regulations; India, too, has made compliance with its Energy Conservation Building Code, launched in 2007, mandatory.

In the 21st century, the energy requirements for heating buildings in developing countries that experience cold winters will grow sharply – not only because of increases in dwelling size, but also because of the rising comfort threshold of households. This phenomenon has already occurred in developed countries where, at the beginning of the 20th century, even the wealthiest households heated only one room in their dwelling,[11] and the temperature usually did not exceed 18 °C. At the end of 20th century, the same households were heating their whole dwelling, even the unoccupied rooms, and the required comfort threshold rose to more than 20 °C.

Energy policies addressing the residential sector should set as a priority the improvement of the building envelope, especially in dwellings occupied by low-income people. Increases in fuel prices create the most economic problems for low-income residents, and if fuel prices rise precipitously for whole communities, social problems are likely to follow.[12] The fuel or energy ladder implies that change in household income is reflected in the type and cost of fuel used. In general, low-income households tend to use fuels that are more costly and more energy inefficient, such as charcoal and biofuels. Thus, climbing the energy ladder not only improves the quality of life of poor households, but it also makes them less likely to use fuels that are costly and harmful to the environment. Low energy, appropriately designed buildings, therefore, not only contribute to climate change mitigation but also reduce the vulnerability of the poor.

Cities play a crucial role in the implementation of national standards, as they have the capacity to issue building permits and ensure projects meet energy-efficiency code regulations, and they can introduce new energy conservation rules in master plans. City administrations usually overlook, however, such details as the embedded energy in construction materials. Especially in emerging economies, where the construction sector is growing fast, a large amount of energy consumed by the industrial sector goes into the production of cement, steel, aluminum, and glass – materials needed for building construction. Among the global warming mitigation actions cities should consider the use of low embedded-energy construction materials that can be derived by introducing innovations in traditional materials and construction techniques to improve performance and durability.

▶

Construction of a very tall skyscraper in Pudong, China: New buildings in China are being constructed at the rate of an estimated 1.8 billion square meters a year.
©Robert Churchill/iStockphoto

Energy-efficient buildings in Beijing

Since 1991, Beijing has implemented mandatory energy-saving design standards for new housing. Residential buildings that have not been designed according to the energy-efficiency standards are not allowed to start construction. By the end of 2003, a total of 120 million square meters of energy-efficient residential buildings had been built, of which 60 million square meters of residential buildings had met the energy-efficiency design standard, which requires a 50 per cent reduction in energy use over buildings designed before 1991.

Energy-efficient buildings have brought about substantial social benefits. The average room temperature in an energy-efficient residence during the winter has gone up to more than 18 °C. In June 2004, Beijing issued an energy efficiency building standard requiring a 65 per cent reduction in energy use for residential buildings. The city took the new measure because it still lags behind advanced international levels, even with its 50 per cent energy efficiency standard. The difference is not in material, equipment or construction techniques, but in the design standard. In recent years, the area of newly started and resumed construction in Beijing has stayed above 100 million square meters annually. With such large-scale construction, if weaker energy efficiency standards continued to prevail, the result would be heavy energy consumption too difficult and costly to remedy in the future.

To raise the quality of construction and ensure compliance with the energy-efficient design standard, Beijing has compiled a local standard for the "Inspection and Acceptance Criteria for Insulation Projects in Energy Efficient Residential Buildings", the first of its kind in China. The standard lists requirements for material quality, construction technology, quality inspection and management, supervision and inspection and acceptance involved in building energy efficiency and insulation projects. It calls for random on-site inspections to supplement project monitoring.

Source: Xingyue, 2004.

▲
Apartment block in Beijing, China
© Jimmy Wang/iStockphoto

Embedded energy

Energy consumption in buildings occurs in five phases. The first phase corresponds to the manufacturing of building materials and components, termed "embedded energy". The second and third phases correspond to the energy used to transport materials from production plants to building sites and the energy used in the actual construction of the building, which are referred to as "grey energy" and "induced energy", respectively. In the fourth phase, energy is consumed in the running of the building when it is occupied – "operational energy". Finally, energy is consumed in the demolition process of buildings as well as in the recycling of their parts. Concrete, aluminum and steel, for instance, are among the materials with the highest embedded energy content and their production is also responsible for large quantities of CO_2 emissions. Plastic is another energy-intensive material.

In aggregate terms, embedded energy consumption accounts for a significant share of the total energy use of a country; in the case of the United Kingdom, estimates suggest that 10 per cent of the total energy consumption is embedded in building materials. Embedded energy can be reduced by choosing different building materials. Studies show that the total energy consumption in manufacturing of steel beams is two to three times higher and the use of fossil fuels is 6 to 12 times higher than in the manufacturing of glued laminated timber beams. Dutch studies reveal that an increase in wood use could reduce CO_2 emissions by almost 50 per cent.

Source: UNEP, 2007.

Energy used for cooking

While most energy in residential buildings in EU-15 countries is used for heating, an entirely different picture emerges in the dwellings of the lowest-income inhabitants of cities in developing countries, where energy (produced mainly by burning kerosene or charcoal) is primarily used for cooking. In developed countries, energy for cooking ranges from between 4 and 7 per cent of the total household energy consumption, while in a large number of developing countries, cooking comprises the majority of households' energy consumption.

Use of traditional biomass fuels (such as animal dung, crop residues, wood, and charcoal) for cooking and heating is generally declining in non-slum urban areas of developing countries; many slum dwellers, too, are switching to non-biomass forms of energy as soon as they are in a position to afford it. In urban India, for example, the share of biomass fuels in urban areas has declined from 49 per cent in 1983 to 24.4 per cent in 1999, owing to increased availability of other sources of energy (liquid petroleum gas, kerosene and coal).[13]

Many households in African and Asian cities, however, still rely mainly on biomass fuels for cooking. Estimates suggest that in the Kenyan capital of Nairobi, a large proportion of urban households' requirements are met by charcoal; that corresponds to a consumption of approximately 91,250 tonnes annually, which equals the destruction of more than 900,000 tonnes of green wood each year.[14] In Dhaka's slums and squatter settlements, biomass is burned at a rate of 0.25 kg per day per person, resulting in 500 tonnes of fuelwood burned per day.[15]

Demographic and health surveys conducted in several developing countries between 1995 and 2003 show that a large majority of households in sub-Saharan African cities are still primarily dependent on biomass fuels for cooking.[16] In these cities, urban living has not led to change in use of cooking fuels in slum areas, or in non-slum areas. For example, in Benin, 86 per cent of urban households use wood or charcoal for cooking. The use of wood and charcoal is not confined to Benin's slum areas: 74 per cent of non-slum households also use these fuels for cooking, compared with 92 per cent of slum households. In Benin, the energy transition in non-slum areas is mainly

FIGURE 3.5.2: **HOUSEHOLD ENERGY USE PATTERNS IN EU-15, 1997**

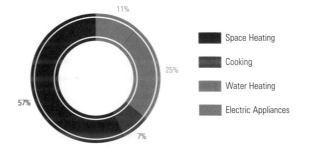

Source: Commission of the European Communities, 2001.

FIGURE 3.5.3: **LOW-INCOME HOUSEHOLD ENERGY USE PATTERNS IN CAPE TOWN, 1996**

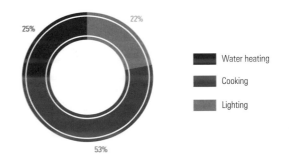

Source: Winkler, et al., 2005.

Nearly a quarter of urban Indian households use traditional biomass fuels for cooking.
©Gilles Delmotte/iStockphoto

from wood to charcoal; use of gas, kerosene and electricity for cooking is not yet an option for many households. Since many households in African cities cannot afford kerosene and liquefied petroleum gas (LPG), the large majority continue to rely on fuel wood and charcoal. However, the use of solid fuels in non-slum areas of African cities cannot be linked to lack of financial resources – a disturbing trend noted in African cities is the continued use of solid fuels even in non-slum areas where households can afford electricity, kerosene and LPG for cooking. This suggests that when people move up the economic ladder, they change fuels for heating and lighting, but not necessarily for cooking.

However, the transition from biomass to other sources of energy for cooking has been observed in other cities of African countries, including Gabon, Kenya and Nigeria. In cities of these three countries, use of gas and kerosene for cooking is

more common than use of solid fuel. In Gabon, 68 per cent of urban households use gas, while in Kenya and Nigeria, use of kerosene for cooking is quite common among urban households (47 per cent and 46 per cent, respectively). It is interesting to note, however, that in Nigeria, which is among the larger producers of petroleum, a large proportion of urban households still rely on wood and charcoal for cooking (49 per cent). Zimbabwe offers a somewhat different picture: use of kerosene is prevalent not just in urban areas but in some rural areas as well.

It is clear that the urban transition in many sub-Saharan African countries has not yet translated into an energy transition, as it has in developed countries and most countries of Latin America, North Africa and Asia. In Egypt and Morocco, for instance, the use of gas for cooking is almost universal. However, some Asian and Latin American cities still have large proportions of urban residents who are dependent on biomass fuels. In Bangladesh, Nepal, Guatemala, and Nicaragua, more than 40 per cent of urban households are still dependent on biomass fuels.

In general, the lower the income of the household, the higher its share of traditional biomass used for cooking.[17,18] The size of the settlement also plays a role. In intermediate and small cities, the share of traditional biomass fuels used for cooking is higher because they are easily available, and it might not be economically viable for households to set up alternative energy sources, such as electricity.

Incomplete combustion processes of biomass fuels contribute to greenhouse gas emissions. As illustrated in Figure 3.5.7, biomass cookstoves release significant levels of carbon dioxide, carbon monoxide, methane, and nitrous oxide, not only polluting the environment, but also putting the people who use them at risk of exposure to dangerous toxins. Biomass stoves are also notoriously inefficient. The energy efficiency of traditional cooking devices is poor: more than 80 per cent of the heat generated while cooking with wood on a traditional fire does not end up "in the pot".

Improving the efficiency of traditional cooking devices, reducing the amount of wood fuel needed, and reducing indoor air pollution have become priorities in the development of improved stoves. Several types of improved stoves have

FIGURE 3.5.4: **SHARE OF ENERGY USED FOR COOKING IN URBAN HOUSEHOLDS IN INDIA, 1999/2000**

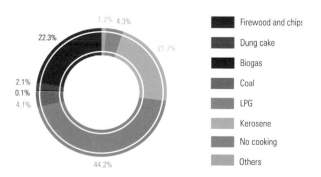

Firewood and chips
Dung cake
Biogas
Coal
LPG
Kerosene
No cooking
Others

Source: Pandey, 2002

FIGURE 3.5.5: **EMISSIONS BY COMMON COOKING FUELS PER MEAL**

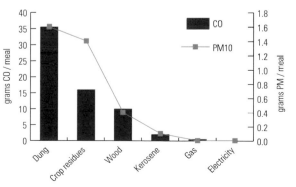

Source: Smith, et al., 2000.

been developed all over the world, in different models to suit varying available materials and skills, types of fuel, food and cooking habits, and other requirements, all aiming to lower costs, improve energy efficiency and reduce or eliminate indoor air pollution.

From the perspective of climate change mitigation, however, improved stoves are not sustainable in the long run. They may continue to play an important interim role in improving the quality of life of the urban poor, but the long-term goal should be to eliminate household use of unprocessed solid fuels. The charcoal fuel cycle is probably the most greenhouse gas-intensive major fuel cycle in the world, even when the wood is harvested renewably, which it often is not.[19] Each meal cooked with charcoal in sub-Saharan Africa has 2 to10 times the global warming effect of cooking the same meal with firewood and 5 to 16 times the effect of cooking the same meal with kerosene or LPG, depending on the gases that are included in the analysis and the degree to which wood is allowed to regenerate.[20] A study carried out for India[21] confirms that LPG and kerosene show the lowest greenhouse gas emission, compared with all the other commonly used

fuels, with exception of biogas, the emissions of which are negligible.

Poverty and lack of basic services in urban areas contribute to the growth of carbon emissions because the urban poor are forced to rely on polluting and unsustainable sources of energy for cooking and lighting. Moving up the economic ladder, therefore, often means moving up the energy ladder, as higher incomes mean people can afford energy-efficient fuels that are less polluting and that produce fewer greenhouse gases. Lack of access to electricity and other energy sources in many countries has forced people to rely on traditional biomass fuels, as in Liberia, where the electricity supply is unreliable in urban areas. Given the abundance of Liberia's forests, fuel wood and charcoal are becoming the principal sources of energy in urban areas; consumption skyrocketed both during and after recent civil conflicts there. The UN Food and Agricultural Organization (FAO) suggests that because of the continuous absence of electricity supply in Liberia's urban sectors and the lack of other alternative sources of household energy supply in most parts of the country, the demand for fuel wood is expected to increase.

FIGURE 3.5.6: **DISTRIBUTION OF URBAN HOUSEHOLDS BY TYPE OF FUEL FOR COOKING IN SELECTED COUNTRIES**

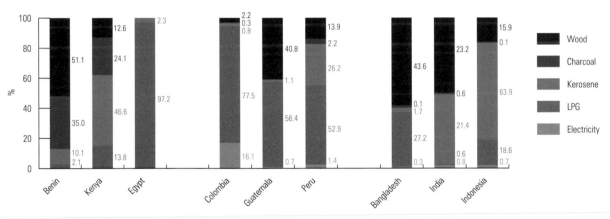

Source: UN-HABITAT, Global Urban Observatory, 2008

FIGURE 3.5.7: **GREENHOUSE GAS EMISSIONS FROM A TYPICAL BIOMASS COOKSTOVE**

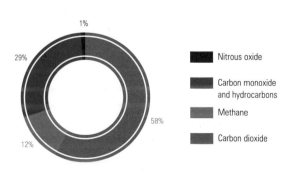

Adapted from Holdren & Smith, 2000

FIGURE 3.5.8: **PROPORTION OF FAMILY INCOME USED FOR ENERGY IN LOW-INCOME HOUSEHOLDS IN SELECTED CITIES AND COUNTRIES**

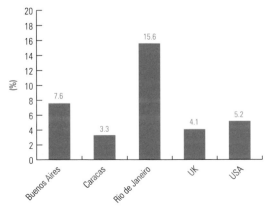

Source: World Energy Council, 2006

▲
Rising incomes have led to increased electricity consumption in Chinese cities.
©**Andrew Wood/iStockphoto**

Electricity consumption

Average electricity consumption in the world's households ranges widely from zero in the lowest-income households of cities in developing countries to more than 16,600 kilowatt hours per year in urban Norwegian dwellings,[22] where electricity is traditionally used for almost everything – from space heating to cooking.

The range of electricity consumption around the world cannot be justified only by income or climate. For instance, while the diffusion and types of appliances in Europe and the United States are quite similar, electricity consumption and consequent CO_2 emissions vary greatly both between the two regions and within them. In San Francisco, the average household electricity consumption is 2.4 times lower than the U.S. average and 2.6 times higher than that of Milan, Italy, or 1.5 times higher than that of London, U.K. In the city of Oxford in England, household electricity consumption is 2.3 times higher than that of the Italian city of Bologna.

In the United States, the difference between national average electricity consumption and consumption in individual cities is mainly explained by the fact that in some cities, other sources of energy are available, such as natural gas. The differences in energy consumption between U.S. and European cities can also be attributed to differences in size and efficiency of appliances and lifestyles. Refrigerators in the U.S., for example, are generally larger than European refrigerators, and not all states impose minimum efficiency requirements on domestic appliances, as does the European Union. Within Europe, the differences in energy consumption are also determined by differences in the cost of electricity among countries. In general, high household electricity consumption is the consequence of low-efficiency appliances. The size of the dwelling, user energy consciousness and the cost of electricity also play important roles.

Air conditioning is increasingly contributing to household electricity consumption, in urban areas of both developed and developing countries. In Shanghai, the rise has been particularly sharp, increasing from 0.2 air conditioners per dwelling in 1994 to 1.6 air conditioners per dwelling in 2004.[23] It is not surprising then, that Shanghai's residential and commercial air conditioning load accounts for 40 per cent of the peak electricity load in the summer.[24] In other Chinese cities, such as Guangdong, Beijing and Chongqing, the average number of air conditioners per dwelling now exceeds 1; in Chongqing,[25] air conditioning accounts for 40 per cent of summer electricity peak load,[26] similar to that of Shanghai.

Electricity consumption in China is also growing with the increasing prevalence of electrical heating systems, especially in cities where electrical heating was not previously available. In Shanghai, a survey of more than 1,000 households showed that the air conditioner is used as a heat pump for an average of 3 hours per day in the winter.[27] Electricity consumption is expected to grow in China as incomes rise and as lifestyles change, especially in urban areas.

Improving efficiency of household appliances is crucial for reducing electricity consumption. In Europe, energy labeling that informs consumers about the energy consumption of appliances is standard practice and compulsory. Similar approaches have been developed in Japan. The United States has been promoting Energy Star, a voluntary labeling programme designed to identify and promote energy-efficient products. In China, minimum energy standards were introduced in 2003 and are being updated.

But while increased energy efficiency can have wide-ranging benefits, the full extent of these benefits is difficult to capture in developing countries, where appliances and technologies with low initial costs might be preferred, where capital for replacing inefficient equipment might not be available, and where regulatory or technical standards might be inadequate.

FIGURE 3.5.9: **ELECTRICITY CONSUMPTION PER HOUSEHOLD (KWH/YEAR) IN SELECTED CITIES AND COUNTRIES**

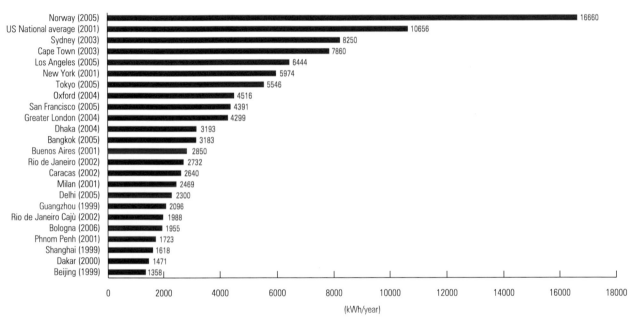

Source: UN-HABITAT Global Urban Observatory 2008
Note: Data from various sources, 1999-2006

FIGURE 3.5.10: **SHARE OF COMMERCIAL AND RESIDENTIAL ELECTRICITY CONSUMPTION IN SELECTED CITIES**

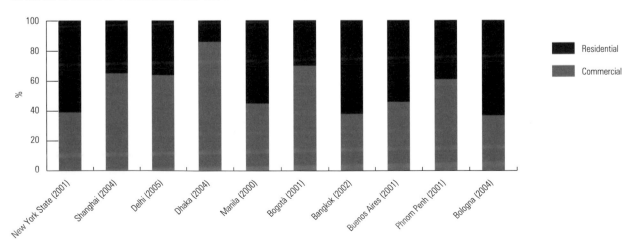

Source: UN-HABITAT Global Urban Observatory 2008
Note: Data from various sources, 2001-2004

Cape Town: Scaling the energy ladder

Cape Town, unlike most African cities, is unique in that its electricity consumption is extremely high, even though 60 per cent of its population comprises low-income households. This is largely explained by the fact that electricity is used in almost all household appliances, including those for cooking and hot water production, even among the low-income share of the population. This derives from a national policy that has been promoting extensive electrification and low-cost electricity for the poor, with the aim – almost fully reached – of eliminating the health hazards associated with the use of biomass and improving residents' quality of life. In Cape Town, the first 50,000 kilowatt hours per month are provided for free to low-income households, but this amount meets only a small part of the households' electricity needs. High- and middle-income households consume nearly three times as much electricity as low-income households, as illustrated in the graph below, with the largest proportion of consumption going towards heating water. In low-income households, on the other hand, a large proportion of electricity is used for cooking.

FIGURE 3.5.11: **HOUSEHOLD ELECTRICITY CONSUMPTION DIFFERENCES IN CAPE TOWN**

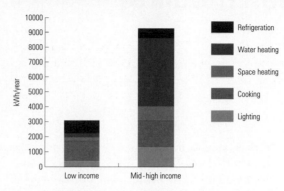

Source: Winkler, et al., 2006.

NOTES

1 UNEP, 2007a.
2 Healy, 2003.
3 U.K. Department for Business, n.d.
4 Balarasa, et al., 2007.
5 Santamouris, et al., 2007.
6 World Bank, n.d.
7 ENERDATA, 2003.
8 Rosenfeld, 2004.
9 European Commission, 2007.
10 Siwei, 2004.
11 Butera, 2004.
12 Lampietti, 2002.
13 Padey, 2002.
14 City of Nairobi Environment Outlook, 2007.

15 UNEP, 2005.
16 UN-HABITAT, 2006b.
17 Modi, et al., 2006.
18 Barnes, et al., 2004.
19 Goldemberg, 2000.
20 Bailis, et al., 2004.
21 United States Environmental Protection Agency, 2000.
22 Statistics Norway, 2004.
23 Long & Bai, 2007 .
24 Shanghai Research Institute of Building Sciences (SRIBS) & Politecnico di Milano (BEST), 2006.
25 Long, et al., 2004.
26 Mingjia, 2004.
27 Long, et al., 2004.

3.6
Urban Mobility

Urban mobility has become a key concern in cities of both developed and developing nations as it impacts the liveability of cities. Motorized urban transport, in particular, has become a hot topic among policymakers, planners and environmentalists who are seeking ways in which to minimize its negative effects, including greenhouse gas emissions, traffic congestion and air pollution.

Motorized urban transport accounts for a large share of energy consumption in cities, ranging from more than half of total energy consumption in cities such as Mexico City, Cape Town and Hong Kong to roughly a quarter of total energy consumption in cities such as London, Seoul and Bologna. Any policy aimed at mitigating the effects of climate change must, therefore, list motorized urban transport among its priorities.

In principle, reducing CO_2 emissions from the transport sector is much easier than cutting those from the building sector. The reason is simple: while new buildings can be constructed to consume low or zero energy, the energy consumption of existing buildings can only be improved to a limited extent, and buildings are made to last several decades or even centuries. Since the average lifespan of a motor vehicle is 15 years, however, any new approach that involves a change in vehicle technology or a shift to different mobility technologies and techniques can be implemented in a relatively short time. In other words, since a significant reduction of CO_2 emissions in the building sector implies the substitution of most of the existing building stock, this option is not feasible. With transport, the complete substitution of the motor vehicle stock is possible within a relatively short time. Transport, therefore, is a key element in our race toward keeping the earth's temperature at an acceptable level.

A study of automobile dependence in a sample of 84 cities around world found that although income levels determine degrees of motorization, wealth alone does not provide a consistent or satisfactory explanation of transport patterns in cities, since there is no significant statistical correlation between per capita private transport energy use and metropolitan GDP per capita.[1] While cities in the United States, Australia and New Zealand lead the world for the number of passenger cars per 1,000 persons, Eastern European cities rank first for number of passenger cars per dollar GDP. Even African cities have a rate of car ownership relative to wealth that is more than twice that of the United States. This could be explained by the large inequalities in income distribution in poorer cities, and the large proportions of low-income people. Western Europe and high-income Asian cities have placed more emphasis on public transport, rather than on individual car ownership, and therefore have lower ratios of car ownership to wealth.

Despite the perception that the private car plays a dominant role in urban mobility everywhere, data shows that this is true only in the United States, Canada, Australia, New Zealand, and the Middle East. Elsewhere, non-motorized and mass transit modes prevail. In Western Europe, for instance, non-motorized transport accounts for 50 per cent of urban trips. The trend in developing countries and Eastern European cities, however, is toward increased use of private cars – a result of economic growth and policies that prioritize the construction of urban freeways and parking spaces. Decisions at the national level to support and promote car factories, as many Asian countries have recently made, also support the impression of an irresistible trend toward the uncontrolled diffusion of private motorization.

The 84-city study also found that urban form strongly influences energy consumption and CO_2 emissions. Urban density and CO_2 emissions have a direct, inverse correlation: in general, the lower the density of a city, the higher its emissions from the transport sector. This suggests that more compact cities are not only more energy-efficient but are also less carbon-intensive. The prevalence of freeways encourages car use, which also impacts carbon emissions. Freeways and parking spaces in city centres reduce traffic congestion, however, removing private vehicles from otherwise crowded city streets. In Tokyo, as well as in other large Japanese cities, passenger vehicle purchasers are required to prove that they have forward contracts for garaging within 5 kilometres of their residence before taking ownership.

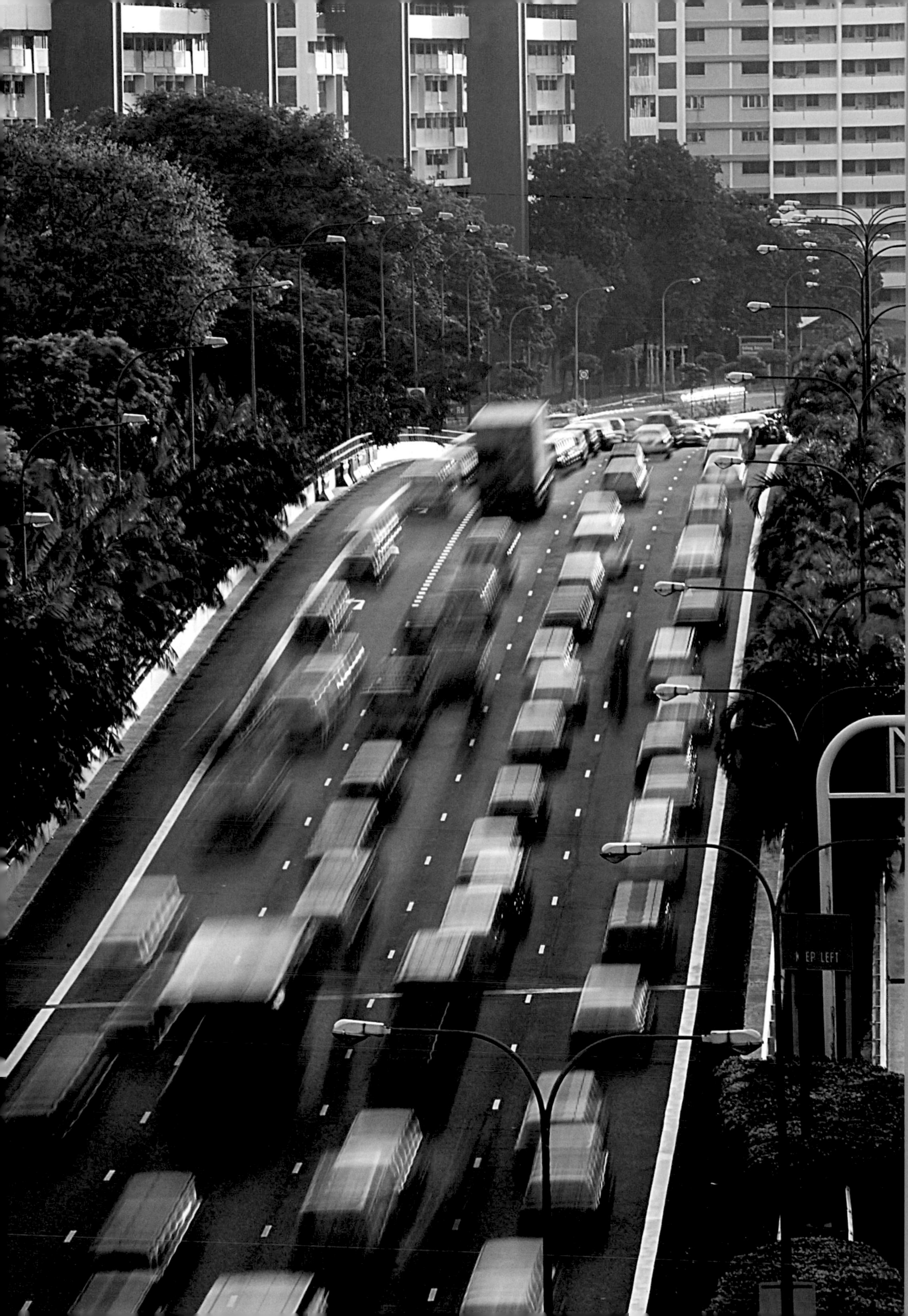
EP LEFT

Private cars are the dominant form of transport in the United States, Australia, New Zealand and the Middle East.
©Elena Elisseeva/iStockphoto

FIGURE. 3.6.1: **SHARE OF MOTORIZED AND NON-MOTORIZED PRIVATE AND PUBLIC TRANSPORT IN SELECTED REGIONS AND COUNTRIES**

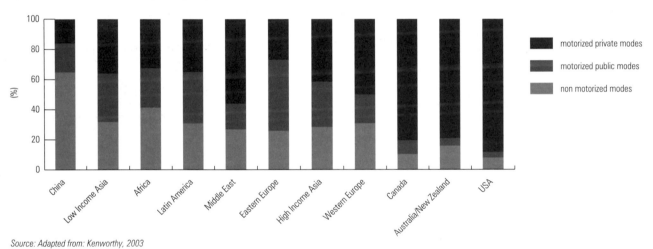

- motorized private modes
- motorized public modes
- non motorized modes

Source: Adapted from: Kenworthy, 2003

FIGURE 3.6.2: **RELATIONSHIP BETWEEN LENGTH OF FREEWAY PER PERSON AND PASSENGER CAR KILOMETRES**

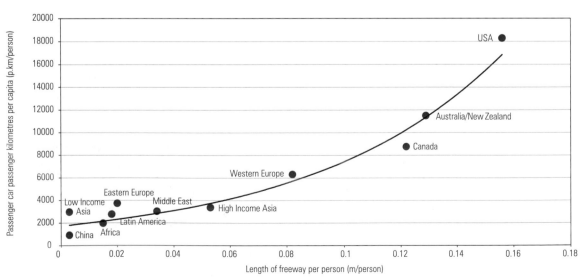

Source: Adapted from: Kenworthy 2003

▲
Morning traffic in Beijing
©**Tor Lindqvist/iStockphoto**

FIGURE 3.6.3: **ENERGY USE BY TRAVEL MODE BY REGION**

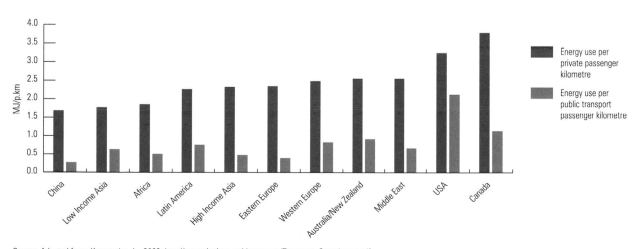

■ Energy use per private passenger kilometre

■ Energy use per public transport passenger kilometre

Source: Adapted from: Kenworthy, J. , 2003; http://cst.uwinnipeg.ca/documents/Transport_Greenhouse.pdf

An analysis of 28 cities[2] shows that while car use tends to be higher in cities of the developed world, a significant number of cities in the developing world, particularly in Asia, have very high car ownership. Bangkok and Dar es Salaam, for instance, have more cars per capita than Tokyo and Mumbai. On the other hand, in Singapore, the number of private vehicles per 1,000 inhabitants is lower than that of many cities in the developing world – a result of the city-state's effective mobility policy.

Taxis in New York City
©**Imre Cikajlo/iStockphoto**

FIGURE 3.6.4: **TOTAL TRANSPORT (PRIVATE AND PUBLIC) CO$_2$ EMISSIONS IN SELECTED REGIONS AND COUNTRIES**

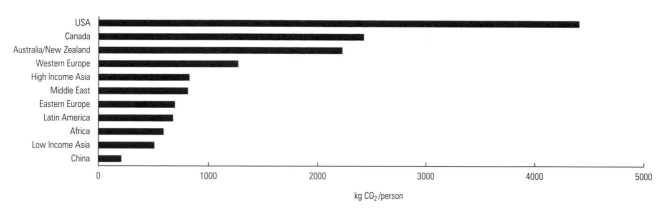

kg CO$_2$/person

Source: Adapted from: Kenworthy, J. , 2003; http://cst.uwinnipeg.ca/documents/Transport_Greenhouse.pdf

FIGURE 3.6.5: **CAR OWNERSHIP IN SELECTED CITIES**

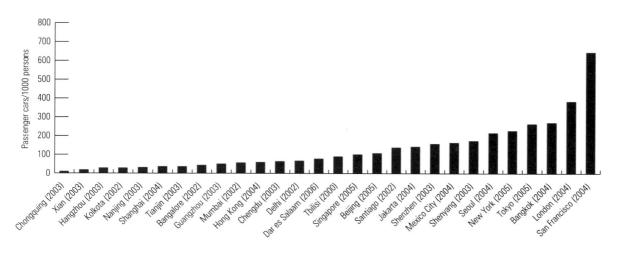

Source: UN-HABITAT Global Urban Observatory 2008
Note: Data derived from various sources, 2000-2004

FIGURE 3.6.6: **PRIVATE CAR OWNERSHIP IN SELECTED LARGE AND MEGACITIES**

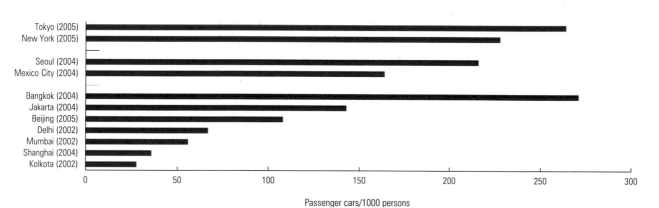

Passenger cars/1000 persons

Source: UN-HABITAT Global Urban Observatory 2008
Note: Data derived from various sources, 2000-2004

FIGURE 3.6.7: **PRIVATE CAR OWNERSHIP IN SELECTED CITIES**

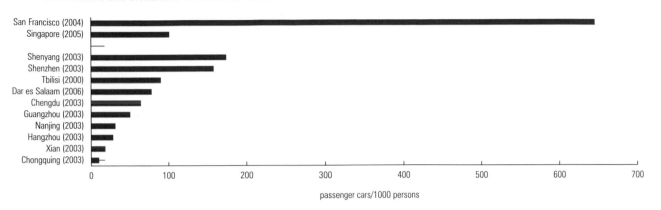

passenger cars/1000 persons

Source: UN-HABITAT Global Urban Observatory 2008
Note: Data derived from various sources, 2000-2004

FIGURE 3.6.8: **TRANSPORT MODE SPLIT IN SELECTED CITIES**

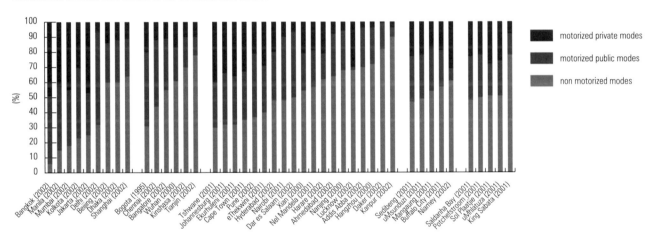

motorized private modes

motorized public modes

non motorized modes

Source: UN-HABITAT Global Urban Observatory 2008
Note: Data derived from various sources, 1995-2002

FIGURE 3.6.9: **TRANSPORT MODE SPLIT IN CITIES IN THE DEVELOPED WORLD**

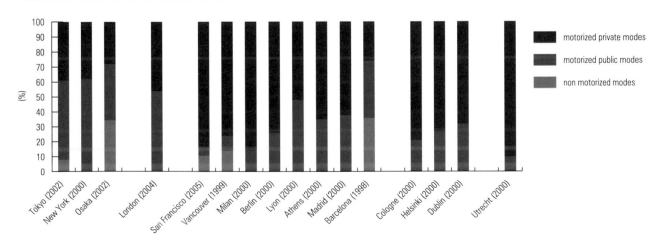

motorized private modes

motorized public modes

non motorized modes

Source: UN-HABITAT Global Urban Observatory 2008
Note: Data derived from various sources, 1998-2005

London buses: A congestion charge introduced in 2003 has significantly reduced traffic in the city centre.
©**Michele Lugaresi/iStockphoto**

In many cities with environmentally conscious policies, mayors are struggling to find a way to clear streets of private passenger vehicles. In London, under Mayor Ken Livingstone, a congestion charge introduced in 2003 has significantly reduced traffic in the city centre. The charge is imposed on cars entering central London between 7 a.m. and 6:30 p.m. As a result, many commuters have switched to public transport, and traffic delays have been reduced by one-third. Under Mayor Jaime Lerner in the 1970s and 1980s, the Brazilian city of Curitiba developed a specially designed bus system using dedicated bus lanes along radial routes from the city centre. The development of the system gave priority to mass transit by developing "trunk lines" running along major roads, with up to three lanes accessible only to buses. And from 1998 to 2000, Bogota, Enrique Peñalosa the Mayor of Bogota led a campaign to promote bicycle use and walking in the city by developing 300 kilometres of bicycle paths and pedestrian-only streets. The Colombian capital has also been experimenting with banning the use of cars at certain times of the day, and the experiment is proving to be popular.

NOTES

[1] Kenworthy, J., Transport Energy Use and Greenhouse Gases in Urban Passenger Transport System: a Study of 84 Global Cities, Third Conference of the Regional Government Network for Sustainable Development, Notre Dame University, Fremantle, Western Australia, September 2003 http://cst.uwinnipeg.ca/documents/Transport_ Greenhouse.pdf.
[2] Analysis by Federico Butera was commissioned by UN-HABITAT for this report.

Part Four

04

PLANNING FOR HARMONIOUS CITIES

Cities are not just brick and mortar; they represent the dreams, aspirations and hopes of societies. In a way, each city has its own "personality", with its strengths and weaknesses, failures and successes. A city's "soul" is exhibited through its cultural heritage, its traditions and its social fabric. Part 4 argues that the management of a city's human, social, cultural and intellectual assets is as important for harmonious urbanization as the management of its infrastructure, its social amenities and its public spaces. It reflects new and innovative approaches to urban planning and development that engage citizens more directly and that are inclusive and pro-poor. The approaches call for enlightened political leadership, clear long-term political commitments, progressive sectoral and institutional reforms, and mobilization of domestic resources to scale up actions and sustain harmonious urban development. The approaches must also respond to the following emerging priorities and concerns: i) *regional or spatial disparities,* ii) *urban inequalities;* iii) *urban environmental risks and burdens, including climate change;* and iv) *metropolitan expansion or the growth of "city-regions".*

▶
Egypt
©Manoocher Deghati

4.1
Inclusive Urban Planning for Harmonious Urban Development

Urban environments, whether growing or shrinking, teeming with youthful energy or accommodating an ageing population, are places of great diversity – diversity that facilitates the development of culture and economic growth, but that also divides populations, often creating entrenched inequalities that stymie efforts to eradicate them.

The pressures of growth, socio-economic inequality and environmental degradation in cities of the developing world present great challenges to good governance and development, but they also present opportunities for new approaches to urban planning and management that advance local assets, focus on social justice and lead to harmonious urban development. Urban planning practices that aim to improve residents' quality of life and engage them in their own well-being are highly context-sensitive, varying from city to city based on political climate, social networks and the goals of cities and people. The essential elements of inclusive urban planning, however, are transferrable. They evolved as a positive response to disengaged, top-down planning practices of the past – *exclusive* urban planning designed to assert the power of the state and the priorities of government over everyday life. Urban planning that focuses exclusively on technical efficiency or ideology and ignores the reality of how people live in cities is not sustainable and can foster exclusion. In order to be effective, urban planning has to place the needs of people at the forefront of practice. On the other hand, lack of effective planning can exacerbate inequalities and promote exclusion in cities. The challenge is to ensure that planning is done with people in mind.

Beyond modernism

Throughout the 20th century, governments attempted to abolish urban inequalities – and the accompanying perceived threats of disease, crime and urban blight – by destroying the environments in which they flourished, razing poor neighbourhoods and relocating their inhabitants, or replacing substandard buildings with tenements and public housing. Grand modernist urban planning schemes to improve cities and reshape societies around common goals and behaviours led to comprehensive planning projects, such as Brasilia, the master-planned capital of Brazil, and Chandigarh, capital of the Indian states of Punjab and Haryana. Both cities were built in the mid-20th century in previously undeveloped areas, planned by European architects commissioned by national governments. Intentionally designed without reference to the surrounding cultures or social norms, the cities featured large-scale buildings and public spaces organized around utopian notions of order, efficiency and progress.[1] Such projects failed to standardize human behaviour, however, and often prompted outright rebellion, as when residents of Chandigarh ignored rules against expanding shopping areas and allow cows to roam the streets.[2]

Approaches to urban planning and development have changed in recent years with the decentralization of government decision-making and the invigoration of democratic processes in most countries around the world. As local governments have taken on more responsibility for the success of their cities, it has become increasingly important to engage citizens directly, planning for the future by learning from the present and past realities of underserved communities. Not only are inclusive practices mandated by funders such as the World Bank and the Cities Alliance, but they have also become law in countries such as South Africa, where the national Reconstruction Development Programme requires power-sharing and equal representation in all development projects.[3] How well urban planning succeeds in solving issues of uneven spatial development, socio-economic integration and environmental degradation by engaging citizens and focusing on local decision-making depends on a variety of factors, however, including political priorities, local capacity and the empowerment of the most vulnerable urban residents.

Rapid urban growth in the developing world is often associated with the ill effects of urbanization: traffic congestion, poor air quality, crime, overcrowding, and slums. High growth rates put pressure on city administrations to deliver infrastructure, housing and poverty alleviation programmes, but the experience of many major cities that are growing rapidly (at a rate of more than 2.5 per cent per year) shows that bottlenecks in infrastructure, telecommunications, basic services and gender equality can be offset with good governance and visionary urban planning. UN-HABITAT recently analyzed trends and conditions in several rapidly

Public park in Kuala Lumpur
©**Madanmohan Rao**

growing cities of the developing world; the following sections discuss the implications of those trends, and the policy environments in which they have developed.[4]

Political commitment to pro-poor development makes a difference

Urban planning is not just a technical issue – it is also highly political. As urban scholar Peter Marcuse asserts, "cities and places are not 'disordered'; the issue at stake is rather establishing who is ordering the city, for what purposes, in the interest of what".[5]

Realizing that urban planning must be supported by political processes, some countries and cities have developed statutes that make resource allocation more equitable and

that ensure urban planning is carried out within the context of larger national frameworks. Urban reforms in Brazil, for example, have been supported by various legislative and political frameworks, including the City Statute of 2001, the National Council of Cities, and the establishment of a Ministry of Cities.[6]

Political commitment by the top municipal or national leadership often plays a critical role in slum improvement or reduction; in fact, countries that have drastically reversed slum growth rates usually do so after the top leadership has made slum reduction or improvement a national priority.[7] An analysis of the annual expenditures of São Paulo, Brazil, between 1975 and 2000 when the metropolitan area was managed by leaders of different political persuasions, found that the infrastructure investments in the more deprived metropolitan regions of São

Cairo
©**Madanmohan Rao**

Paulo increased during periods when city leaders professed a pro-poor agenda.[8] The role of political leadership in and commitment to pro-poor urban planning is also evident in the Brazilian city of Curitiba, which is known internationally as a "best practice" in urban planning, as well as in the Colombian capital of Bogota, where former mayor Enrique Peñalosa sought to make socio-economic equity a cornerstone of the city's development in the late 1990s. Similar patterns have emerged in the Indian city of Hyderabad, where, between 1995 and 2004, the greater metropolitan area adopted an infrastructure-led growth model by launching a globally oriented information technology hub. In some cases, pro-poor investments transcend ideology or narrow political interests. In Turkey, for instance, a commitment to modernization through technology and infrastructure development has been espoused by populist, elitist and military governments since the 1970s, when the leadership in Turkey committed itself to a blanket improvement in rural and urban infrastructure, transport and communication.

Political commitment to a pro-poor urban development agenda can also be observed in other highly centralized societies, such as Egypt, Morocco and Tunisia – countries that have been among the most successful in reducing slum growth rates in recent years.[9] Although the infrastructure of Cairo and other Egyptian settlements has been boosted by channeling huge investments in water, sanitation and housing, one key ingredient is missing – people's participation. Even though the delivery of services happens through consultative processes, it has been carefully crafted through non-governmental organizations (NGOs) affiliated with the central government.[10]

Performance monitoring helps ensure sustainable service delivery

The experience of successful cities illustrates the importance of performance monitoring, either from the bottom up or from the top down, of agencies charged with delivering services. Accountability in municipal implementation of infrastructure development is very strict in countries such as China, Viet Nam and Cambodia. In Viet Nam, for instance, the central government has assigned high priority to piped water distribution in urban areas; implementation is the responsibility of provincial water authorities, and in the large cities, of water enterprises attached to local governments. As a result, despite high rates of urban population growth, coverage rates have expanded remarkably in a short time.[11]

Critical to this relationship is the local authority's ability to exercise performance monitoring, which currently remains the responsibility of the central government in most developing countries. However, many cities, such as Bogota, have adopted bottom-up performance monitoring techniques that are making local authorities more accountable to citizens.

Another strategy for performance monitoring is to enhance citizen participation in planning and decision-making through processes such as participatory budgeting. Among the cities that have adopted participatory budgeting in sectors such as housing, water, sanitation, education, and health, are the Brazilian cities of Porto Alegre and Belo Horizonte. Participatory budgeting is a systematic way of engaging people in discussions at different levels to decide on priorities and budget allocations. Also embraced by this system is results-based monitoring, implemented indirectly by client satisfaction indicators, collected through surveys, or indirectly inferred through rates of participation in budgeting.[12] Cities in Indonesia use surveys, with support from the World Bank, to understand citizens' attitudes towards municipal services.[13] Other cities that rely on citizen participation in monitoring urban performance include Naga City in the Philippines and Bogota in Colombia.[14]

Partnerships between citizens and governments are important for poverty elimination and infrastructure development

Decentralization and participatory governance approaches are becoming more common in various countries, with local authorities and citizens playing a key role in decision-making. Most countries that have followed decentralization policies in recent years have delegated authority to local governments, but they have not necessarily delegated the financial resources and technical capacity to carry out essential improvements. Reciprocal relationships between central and local governments are key to the ability of decentralization programmes to render municipalities effective in infrastructure development and poverty alleviation. Strong links to, and coordination with, national governments and national development targets allow cities to make efficient investments in infrastructure and complement national objectives while realizing local goals.

The virtues of decentralization and participatory approaches are well known, yet problems associated with these approaches include cooptation of the process by certain favoured groups or individuals and exclusion of the poorest residents from participatory processes, resulting in resources being allocated unequally or to the wrong target groups. These problems can be minimized by providing external oversight and evaluation; ensuring that central governments work closely with local authorities to align local and national objectives; and by fostering self-sufficiency among community members and groups, who can organize to provide important information and ongoing support to relevant development efforts, as well as start their own initiatives. Local political structures must be accountable and transparent if participation is to result in empowerment – the ability of communities to sustain development initiatives that improve their lives.[15]

Citizen participation in the governing of cities offers benefits other than sustainability and bottom-up monitoring – it also allows for cost sharing and sustainability. The Asian cities of Jakarta, Delhi and Hyderabad display an abundance of participatory programmes, where non-governmental organisations (NGOs), community-based organizations (CBOs) and municipalities engage in partnerships for poverty elimination schemes, focusing on housing and primary health care for women and children. One example is the Garda Emas programme in Bogor, Jakarta, which helped to halve the number of urban poor families from 33,000 in 1999 to 16,000 in 2003.[16]

NGO-driven initiatives are also common in Delhi. For instance, an NGO called Asha, which is active in 32 slums in the Yamuna River basin, has forged participation with the government and municipalities to upgrade and regularize slums. Its success also lies in an integrated approach, using health care as an entry point.[17] Such integrated programmes have been proven most successful in bringing women on board.

Metropolitan expansion can help alleviate population pressure, but the timing and quality are important

Metropolitan growth can happen spontaneously, or by design. Urban planning helps cities manage growth by design, through preventative or curative strategies; the timing of visioning, forecasting, plan-making, and implementation are all important to the success of city strategies. Using the preventative approach, the city of Curitiba, Brazil, steered its population towards the periphery of the city to decongest the inner core in anticipation of future growth. Cairo, Egypt, on the other hand, built new towns in the desert, as the growth and density of the population concentrated in the city became unmanageable.[18] The Turkish town of Gaziantep, on the Syrian border, envisioned itself as a regional growth centre; it started using controlled expansion at its periphery in the 1970s, before the anticipated in-migration from the eastern part of the country was realized.

Steering growth to wider zones and urban corridors does not always create liveable metropolitan settlements, however, even if interventions are implemented at the right time; the process could, in fact, have negative consequences, with the central city or peripheral towns losing their economic vitality or becoming isolated areas rife with poverty. The desert towns surrounding Cairo, for example, alleviated housing shortages but did little to improve livelihoods or accessibility, as they lack the employment opportunities and public transport facilities that are available in the city centre.[19]

The most crucial element determining functional and equitable metropolitanization is to build the economic and physical infrastructure of settlements simultaneously, while establishing the connectivity of new settlements to the city centre, as well as to other peripheral settlements. Two of the most remarkable examples of this approach include Curitiba and Hyderabad. In Curitiba, land use and transport planning were linked to direct urban growth outward while maintaining accessibility to the city centre.[20] In Hyderabad, metropolitan growth was channeled in the desired direction via the creation of a high-tech periphery known as "Cyberabad". Industry-driven settlement development is also being implemented in Delhi through NOIDA, the New Okhla Industrial Development Authority.

Planning for mixed use, blending residential buildings, commercial and industrial establishments and industrial parks, creates an organic relationship among space, employment opportunities and population. Creating an economic base for a diverse social fabric also helps minimize social segregation.

Inclusive urban planning for social integration: Reducing socio-economic inequalities in cities

Urban planning guides future action.[21] Often, the kind of guidance that planners provide is technical: estimates and forecasts based on statistical data; projections of a city's future development patterns. But planning happens in communities, with people, too, where decisions about actions for desired futures are made. Planning is value laden and context-sensitive; what works in one place may not in another. Local history, culture and ecology are among the most significant considerations shaping urban planning today. These specificities confirm that there are no recipes for

urban harmony or social integration, and that the replication of formulas is not a sustainable solution. While globalization has made it easier than ever for planners to exchange ideas and practices from places around the world, they work within local confines. Not unlike politics, planning is always local.

The planning process can, in itself, help achieve urban harmony and mitigate segregation of the rich and poor. Rather than a reactive and repetitive procedure that focuses only on land use changes, planning as a discipline can stimulate social cohesion by articulating a strategic vision that depicts a common future for a community. Participatory processes, in diverse forms and capacities, can generate a sense of belonging that is not only fertile soil for harmony but also a tool for increasing the chances of the plan being widely accepted and properly implemented. If participatory processes are to be successful, however, they must allow for authentic engagement of all affected by the proposed plan. In diverse urban neighbourhoods with entrenched inequalities, authentic participation – wherein residents have real power in the process, as equal partners or controlling interests – is often difficult for residents to achieve. More often than not, marginalized residents find themselves in tokenistic relationships with decision-makers: they are informed, consulted or even placated, but not powerfully engaged.[22]

Inauthentic or ineffective participation has happened particularly in places where rising urban land values and

▲
A trader in South Africa
©**Madanmohan Rao**

economic growth goals have prioritized relocating informal settlements or poor neighbourhoods in favour of private development. In the Philippines, for example, residents of informal settlements in the centrally located National Government Centre area in Metro Manila lost their formerly powerful voice of resistance against eviction as increasing land values and decreasing state supports put excessive pressures on available land.[23] In Johannesburg, where collaborative, externally funded city development strategies have attempted to address both economic growth and pro-poor development goals, powerful bureaucratic processes have managed to reorient local priorities after perfunctory participatory activities have ended; citizens in one process had no lasting, authentic place in decision-making, but their interests were instead represented by city leaders for the remainder of the planning process.[24] To reduce socio-economic inequalities, planning processes must overcome social and political barriers to sharing decision-making power with those most critically affected.

Creating harmony out of injustice, building equity anew

Some cities have successfully enabled collaboration among community activists, environmental groups, NGOs, and private sector entrepreneurs and developers to create a new landscape for the pursuit of urban planning. The case of Lima, Peru, is illustrative of informal practices that have been conducive to social and spatial integration. Progressive urban legislation passed in 1961 legalized a large number of the informal neighbourhoods that developed in Lima's periphery. During the severe 1980s economic downturn, the informal economy replaced the withdrawing state to supply production, commerce and welfare, including health and food supply services. In the 1990s, this informal structure allowed low-income residents to access services such as public transportation and information communications technology connectivity. Today, there are visible signs of the gradual integration of the former informal areas into mainstream urban dynamics, to the extent that local researchers even talk about a new middle class emerging in these areas. Shopping centres have been built in the oldest and most consolidated parts of the informal districts to meet the demands of these "new consumers".[25]

Cato Manor, in the South African city of Durban, was a similarly peripheral settlement in the early 1900s, but its development trajectory went in a very different direction. Initially cultivated as farmland by Durban's first mayor, Cato Manor gradually became settled by Indian market gardeners, then Africans who built or rented shacks on the land. In 1932, Cato Manor was incorporated into the Durban municipality, making the shack settlements illegal under the *apartheid* government's rules, but the authorities turned a blind eye and people continued to settle in the area. By the mid-1940s, Cato Manor "had become home to a vibrant, mixed-race community displaying racial harmony and mutual understanding".[26] Durban's rapid urban growth increased the pressure on Cato Manor, which soon became engulfed by the

metropolitan region. The community received no recognition or social amenities from the *apartheid* government, but it continued to grow; by 1960, it was a sprawling, mixed-race, informal settlement of more than 120,000 people – home to the poor of the city.

In the early 1960s, the government conducted forced removals in pursuance of its separate development policy. Indians and Africans were moved to separate, peripheral new dormitory townships, far from employment opportunities, public transit, shopping areas and other amenities Cato Manor residents had enjoyed by virtue of living in the city. No urban planning vision supplanted the Cato Manor community, other than an ideological agenda; the 2,000 hectare site sat largely vacant for the next 25 years.

After the collapse of the *apartheid* government in the early 1990s, the redevelopment of Cato Manor emerged as a priority, and the Cato Manor Development Association formed to facilitate and drive the reconstruction of the site. The approach to reconstruction was based on the concept of integrated development, a fairly innovative approach when the project began in 1993.[27] Now tried and tested, the lessons from Cato Manor's redevelopment form the basis of a number of new urban reconstruction initiatives in South Africa. The provision of housing and sustainable urban infrastructure were key elements of the reconstruction initiative, but the planning concept also included an array of parallel and supportive programmes involving the provision of social facilities, including schools, libraries, parks, sports fields, playgrounds, and a community health centre; social and economic development projects; skills development programmes; institutional and community development; and communications tools, including a community newspaper, radio station and web site. A fully participatory planning and development process helped ensure broad-based consensus, and a focus on integrated urban planning created a compact, mixed-use and mixed-income neighbourhood connected to the surrounding urban amenities. The project received recognition as a UN-HABITAT best practice and has been hailed internationally as an example of successful area-based development.

Regional cooperation aids urban harmony

Municipalities compete to attract investment and human capital for economic development. Competition can lead to imbalanced growth, and the success of one municipality could mean stagnation for its neighbours if planning is not coordinated, making partnerships among municipalities especially critical. Inter-municipal planning processes must overcome bureaucratic and political barriers if a region is to create social, economic and environmental harmony.

In the Netherlands, the municipal governments of Wageningen, Ede, Rhenen and Veenendaal, with a combined population of 217,000, realized that spatial issues increasingly exceeded their own municipal boundaries; they decided to join forces to prepare a regional plan. In 2002, the four municipalities formed WERV, a network for inter-municipal cooperation, which was originally focused on spatial and landscape development around a central green area known as the Binnenveld. The scope of WERV later expanded to cover social affairs, culture, housing, mobility and economics. The region expects strong pressures for urban growth, especially in areas adjacent to main arteries and nodes, but developing a concerted spatial policy for four municipalities in two provinces is not without administrative and political complexity. Continued dialogue has enabled WERV to move forward since its inception. In six years, WERV has been able to put together an economic action plan, integrated housing schemes and two structure scenarios of spatial development for the years 2015 and 2030, which have been accepted by the four local authorities and are used as a framework for decision-making at the municipal level.

The need for inter-municipal coordination is not new. Metropolitan Montevideo, Uruguay, has struggled with intra-city inequalities for more than 50 years. Montevideo, with 1.8 million inhabitants, concentrates two-thirds of Uruguay's population and accounts for 80 per cent of the country's GDP. Uruguay is administratively divided in 19 *Intendencias*, or departments, which are charged with their own land use and urban regulation. The Montevideo metropolitan area covers three departments: Montevideo, Canelones and San José. Montevideo's first master plan was prepared in 1930. Its modernist ideals, like those of Brasilia and Chandigarh, emphasized monumental structures; its main outcome was the construction of a waterfront promenade and the city's main parks. The second master plan, prepared in 1945, introduced concepts such as functional zoning and greenbelts. Within the framework of the 1945 plan, the Montevideo department decided to protect rural areas by halting the release of land for urban use. However, no provisions were made to accept urban growth, such as the increase of density in the existing urban fabric. The scarcity of land triggered a price increase in Montevideo and rampant speculation in the bordering departments of Canelones and San José, which attracted low-income people who could not afford Montevideo prices.

Canelones and San José expanded along connecting axes with very modest housing and virtually no infrastructure. At the same time, Montevideo's middle-class population moved away from downtown areas to modern apartment buildings or detached houses along the east coast, where public investments in infrastructure accommodated the influx. Physical improvements in wealthier areas of Montevideo created a strong divide between it and the outer metropolitan region, which began to function as a "dormitory city" populated by low-income families. The physical and social segregation among the departments worsened during the years of military rule in Uruguay, 1965 to 1972, when inequalities deepened, informal settlements expanded and violence and crime rates soared. The old city centre was so neglected that today, more than 60,000 buildings are vacant or occupied informally by very poor families.

The absence of cross-departmental instruments and the lack of empowerment in Montevideo have hindered harmonious development. In 1998, the Montevideo departmental government approved the Montevideo Urban Plan (POT). The plan includes general guidelines for city development and proposes specific local plans, however, the main problem – lack of regional cooperation – remains unresolved. The POT considers the Montevideo department and not its greater metropolitan area, where the poor live and where the lack of infrastructure is most notable. The POT is undergoing revision as the city continues to demand further structural coordination. In 2005, the city took a step towards integration with the creation, at the national level, of a Metropolitan agency. Its mandate is to coordinate and manage urban policy among the three departmental governments. Lack of empowerment in the region has resulted in the new agency having to focus its efforts on building consensus around specific issues such as transport rather than analysing and proposing policies for the integrated and harmonious development of Montevideo.[28]

The importance of leadership in planning for social integration

Clearly, coordinated policy and action are essential for creating harmonious urban development and reducing socio-economic inequalities in cities. Leadership is another vital prerequisite. In Bogota, Colombia, a series of political leaders from Mayor Jaime Castro, who took office in 1992, to Mayor Enrique Peñalosa, who served from 1998 to 2000, helped establish an emphasis on the public good, each making considerable contributions to socio-economic and cultural harmony in the Colombian capital. During his term, Peñalosa presented his fellow citizens with a vision of urban harmony focused on equity – the cornerstone of a great city. Equity translates into the empowerment of citizens by providing them with meaningful and effective access to employment, housing, education, health services, public places, and transit networks.

Significantly, Peñalosa engaged market mechanisms to make a better Bogota. "With the market economy," Peñalosa said, "we are not going to have income equality. But cities can do much to construct quality of life equality".[29] Reordering the city's public policy priorities, he developed a highly efficient bus rapid transit system, restricted automobile use during peak hours, and initiated a 340-kilometer long bicycle network throughout the city. Seeking to recapture Bogota's public realm, Peñalosa's administration revitalized public spaces, enhanced the pedestrian network and provided for convenient access to natural settings and urban parks, particularly in lower-income areas. Moreover, the city built schools, nurseries, and libraries where most needed: the poorest quarters of Bogota. Peñalosa initiated programme to reform urban land use and advanced programs of micro credit and public-private partnerships for small business and local communities.[30] In his aspiration to turn Bogota into a harmonious and just city, Peñalosa deployed urban planning tools and techniques based on public participation and consensus.[31]

Hong Kong Peak Tram.
©Li Wa/Shutterstock

Bogota main square
©**Dario Diament/Shutterstock**

Urban planning and the environment: Liveability and urban harmony

Bogota is notable not only for its effective leadership and forward-thinking planning decisions, but also for the environmental benefits that have resulted from the city's planning efforts. The development of the pedestrian and bicycle network – which includes the longest continuous pedestrian corridor in the world, the 17-kilometer "Alameda Porvenir" – has facilitated an increase in the percentage of trips in the city made by bicycle, from less than 0.4 per cent to almost 4 per cent.[32] Residents' mode shifting, or switching from higher- to lower-polluting modes of travel, is one reason Bogota's environmental agency cites for reduced levels of ambient air pollution in the city following the development of the comprehensive TransMilenio mass-transit system in 2000. One study found that levels of sulfur dioxide in the air had decreased by 44 per cent one year after the TransMilenio system began operation. Levels of all other monitored air pollutants – particulate matter, nitrogen oxides, carbon monoxide, and ozone – also decreased significantly just one year after the implementation of the improved mass transit system.[33] Bogota's successes illustrate that large developing-country cities with challenging economic and social conditions can make significant improvements in residents'

quality of life through responsible urban planning and visionary leadership.

Equitable urban planning follows naturally from environmental improvement, beginning with bringing every part of a city in line with international standards for improved water, sanitation, housing durability, and sufficient living space. But creating harmonious cities requires much more than eliminating slums – it requires a concerted effort to protect populations from environmental hazards, ensure adequate and affordable service delivery, conserve energy usage by switching to clean fuels from polluting sources such as coal, and reduce cities' environmental footprint and impact on areas beyond their borders. Such environmental quality efforts are an important component of the city development strategies supported by the Cities Alliance, which advocates for the integration of a variety of environmental quality measures directly into city planning processes, rather than leaving them to be added on at the end.[34] Improving the urban environment for all, practicing integrated spatial development and committing to social equity in planning are urban planning goals and strategies that are instrumental to creating harmonious cities around the world.

Planning with women in mind

Increasing evidence points to the fact that women and men experience the city differently: women in many cities face barriers to accessing urban public spaces and housing; they also face institutional barriers that prevent them from decision-making in local government and planning institutions.

Policymakers and urban planners often fail to make gender-sensitive decisions, owing in part to the dearth of research on women's and men's needs and priorities in cities. Lack of gender-sensitive urban planning can result in *de facto* segregated public spaces – spaces that hinder women's safety or make it difficult for them to carry out their multiple roles as caregivers, workers, providers of basic services, and community leaders.

If planning is about creating places and spaces that function well for everyone, then it is imperative that city planners take women's concerns into account. A survey by the Royal Town Planning Institute found that the top concerns of women in the United Kingdom were: personal safety; environmental justice; access and mobility; affordable housing; and public toilets and other local facilities, such as shops, community facilities for children and the elderly, schools, meeting places, parks, leisure facilities, and playgrounds. Low-income women in developing countries have to contend with other issues, such as lack of access to water in poor neighbourhoods, inappropriate or unaffordable transport, insecure tenure, and poor sanitation, all of which severely impact women's health and pose additional burdens on their time.

One way of ensuring that women's concerns are reflected in urban planning is to encourage greater participation by women in local government and planning institutions. In the 1980s, locally elected women within the Council of European Municipalities and Regions (CEMR) felt the need to create a forum to promote the idea of gender equality in elected assemblies. A CEMR survey in 1999 revealed that in 15 countries of the European Union, only one out of five local elected representatives was a woman. Some countries, such as Sweden, had better female representation than others. However, since then, several countries have introduced laws and quotas aimed at making local government institutions and structures more inclusive. Following are some examples:

- A law passed in France in the year 2000 requires that municipalities with populations of more than 3,500 present an equal number of male and female candidates for election.

- Since 1999, the Norwegian Statistics Office has published a gender equality index that al-

▲
Women and children crossing a road in London
© **David Burrows/Shutterstock**

lows for the classification of cities according to six indicators: kindergarten coverage for children; percentage of female municipal council members; education levels of women and men; number of women per 100 men aged 20 to 39; labour force participation of women and men; and incomes of men and women.

- Every year, the Greater London Authority organizes the Capital Woman conference, which is specifically planned to provide the Mayor of London with an opportunity to consult with the women of London and to launch the annual *State of London's Women* report.

- In Italy, gender-based budgeting experiments are underway in the provinces of Modena, Siena and Genoa.

- The City of Montreal established the Women and the City programme in 1990, which has succeeded in making women's safety, particularly on public transport, a high priority. Women, who represent more than 60 per cent of public transport passengers in Montreal, are allowed to get off between two bus stops in order to arrive closer to their destination.

- Finland's Ministry of Social Affairs and Health has founded a databank comprising indicators that monitor gender equality at the local and regional levels. And in the Metropolitan Region of Helsinki, persons travelling with babies on the public transport system can do so for free. The policy has helped encourage mothers, as well as fathers traveling with their children, to use public transport.

- Barcelona has a long-standing commitment to women's equality; it hosts an office that promotes women in decision-making and municipal management and is also the host of the European Union-funded programme and network on women's equality in selected European and Latin American cities.

- The Seoul Metropolitan government supports and implements a range of initiatives that promote gender equality and improve the welfare of women and children.

- The city of San Francisco is implementing the Convention for the Elimination of All Forms of Discrimination against Women at the local level even though the United States is not a signatory to the UN Convention.

- The Philippines has introduced legislation on the Gender and Development (GAD) Budget, which mandates all government agencies and instruments to allocate a minimum of 5 per cent of their total budget to GAD programmes and projects.

- In some cities, such as Mumbai, Mexico City and Tokyo, women-only compartments have been designated on commuter trains to prevent sexual harassment of women by male commuters.

- In Vienna, the Municipal Department of Promotion and Coordination of Women's Issues has developed and tested approaches and standards for city-wide implementation of gender mainstreaming in all areas, including design of public spaces, housing and street lighting.

Sources: Royal Town Planning Institute, 2007; Council of European Municipalities and Regions, 2005. UN-HABITAT Best Practices and Local Leadership Programme, n.d.

Searching for the soul of the city

Cities are not just brick and mortar; they represent the dreams, aspirations and hopes of societies. Each city has its own "personality", its strengths and weaknesses, failures and successes. The city's "soul" is exhibited through its cultural heritage, its social fabric, its intellectual and creative assets, its vibrancy and its distinct identity. Cities that lack "soul" are characterized by a conscious or unconscious desire to obliterate memories and to destroy the "spirit of the place".

A city with soul reflects its own heritage and ethos. It has an urban rhythm that is faithful to its inhabitants, while integrating universal values that make it vibrant and liveable. Such as city is not only sustainable, but as the British sociologist Charles Landry describes it, is a "balance between chaos and order", which is necessary to sustain innovation, creativity and enterprise.

A city may have good infrastructure and amenities but if it is marked by fear or divisiveness, or if its human, social, cultural and intellectual assets are not allowed to flourish, then it begins to decline or perish. Such cities tend to lack cultural and social diversity. These "apartheid cities", where neighbourhoods are physically separated by race or social class, are characterized by lack of social interactions and conviviality as people retreat into their gated communities or dense slums. These cities also tend to have few public spaces where people of all social classes and backgrounds can interact freely.

There are other cities that have good physical infrastructure and amenities, but lack vibrancy and diversity. They are focused primarily on function and utility. These cities are often developed using a blueprint of what a minority elite desires and aspires for, and do not reflect the collective desires or shared legacies of the majority of their inhabitants. The urban design does not take into consideration the local context, history, climate or social fabric of the city. Urban fragmentation and segregation are prevalent in these cities as new real estate developments cater to the needs of only the upwardly mobile minority.

"Cities with soul" are cities whose spirit resides in the collective memories of their people, their (tangible and intangible) cultural heritage and common vision. Their streets and neighbourhoods are heterogeneous and multifunctional; their unique and distinctive nature is an expression of their soul.

But how does one measure a city's soul? One way is to measure its level of "liveability". Surveys that determine a city's "liveability use indicators such as air quality, affordability, public transport and

▲
The Grand Mosque in Djenne in Mali.
©**Daniel Biau**

economic viability to rate cities. The Economist Intelligence Unit, for instance, has consistently rated Canadian and Australian cities, such as Vancouver and Melbourne, as among the most liveable places in the world for their low crime rates, highly developed infrastructure and recreational facilities. The Mercer Quality of Living Survey, on the other hand, rates European cities, such as Zurich, Vienna and Geneva, for offering the best quality of life, using indicators such as political stability, banking services, air pollution levels, public services and climate.

Some researchers have also made a case for rating cities for their ability to attract the "creative classes" – highly educated and well-paid workers in technology, entertainment, journalism, finance, high-end manufacturing and the arts, who share a common ethos valuing creativity, individuality, difference and merit. The Creativity Index, developed by urban researcher Richard Florida, for instance, rates San Francisco, Austin, Boston, San Diego and Seattle highly for being among the most open and diverse large metropolitan areas in the United States – qualities that help these cities to attract intelligent, creative people whose ideas and inventions help fuel the local economy.

These surveys often respond to the needs of a globalizing world, where cities are becoming regional, international or global hubs of commerce and trade or competing to become so. The pressure to demolish old historic buildings and neighbourhoods that do not add value to the needs of a globalizing economy is, therefore, greater than ever. The pressure to change the face – and sometimes the spirit – of cities is becoming more intense in many parts of the world.

Western-style modernity is also threatening the historic environment and some of the cultural assets of cities. The emphasis on new things, clean lines and modern design is intense; older buildings, especially those in need of repair and rehabilitation and those in the inner core or central business districts of cities, are considered to have low economic potential. The problem with this "one size fits all" approach to urban design is that many cities are starting to look alike, which makes them less interesting. As a recent article in Spiegel Online noted, these cities epitomize boredom "with their non-descript architecture, cookie-cutter shopping malls and corporate-franchised culture, they exude a dull vibe that can be found anywhere around the world".

Yet, it is not only development and the demand for "progress" that threaten to erase a great deal of a city's historical and cultural assets. Poverty, neglect, decay and intense overuse cause rapid deterioration of many historic buildings and old neighbourhoods. This phenomenon has been observed, for example, in Mumbai, Havana, Luanda, Cairo, and historic cities such as Ahmadabad and Lamu town. Fortunately, efforts are under way in most of these cities to restore their historical legacy; in Havana, for instance, the Cuban government declared the city's historic centre as a top priority area for conservation in 1993.

In some cities, modernization is often done in the name of tourism. Yet in the process of modernizing a city to attract tourists, the very qualities that make these cities attractive tourist destinations are inadvertently sacrificed. Fortunately, many governments and local authorities are realizing that loss of cultural heritage has huge environmental and economic costs. In 1995, for instance, plans to build a highway near the ancient Giza Pyramids in Egypt were thwarted after the government realized that the highway would have seriously damaged this famous archaeological site.

The challenge facing many cities is how to improve infrastructure, reduce poverty, promote economic growth and create a healthy living environment without destroying the cultural fabric of society. Stone Town in Zanzibar, Tanzania town offers some lessons in this regard. When Tanzania liberalized its economy in the early 1990s, the town was under pressure to become more tourist-friendly and to rehabilitate the old historic Stone Town that incorporates elements from African, Arab and Indian cultures. UNESCO, which declared Zanzibar's Stone Town as a World Heritage Site in 2000, has described the town's rehabilitated narrow winding alleys, unique architecture and bustling bazaars as "an outstanding material manifestation of cultural fusion". Rehabilitation of historic buildings has also increased the town's tourism potential.

The soul of the city is not static; it needs to be nurtured over time, preserved and maintained. The small city of Allegheny in Pennsylvania revived the city's cultural and environmental assets in the 1970s by forming community and neighbourhood organizations that led preservation efforts and created new cultural institutions, with the support of the government and private foundations. The city of Budapest rehabilitated historical districts through social and cultural-led programmes as a way of bringing more social harmony to the city.

Many European cities have used more integrated approaches to urban regeneration programmes, and a large number of cities are placing culture at the heart of regeneration and urban renewal. These cities see their future through a lens that values the present while looking to the past to enhance the urban experience. They have managed to "shed the skin without losing the soul" because they understand that people and the quality of their lives and livelihoods are fundamental assets that need to be nurtured. They also understand that a city's heritage is reflected in its diverse ethnic communities that are in themselves an important economic asset.

New urban renewal programmes utilize revitalization as a way to improve not only the physical, but also the non-physical elements of urban space through creative means that advance the "quality of place" concept or promote what has been termed as "cultural infrastructure". Many urban revitalization programmes recognize the importance of the arts as a means of regenerating communities in order to develop community cohesion and identity, and eventually to foster interconnected identities among different communities. These programmes are often combined with greening initiatives and landscape art to improve the sense of place of urban streets and neighbourhoods.

The preservation of the built heritage through the conservation, renewal or revitalization of historic centres, traditional urban cores and buildings has the potential of providing cities with a distinctive physiognomy that can be marketed to promote economic development and tourism. Studies have also shown that the preservation of the built heritage creates social solidarity and civic pride among inhabitants, thereby promoting social cohesion.

However, as cities are increasingly transformed into heterogeneous, multi-ethnic and multi-cultural societies, the protection and enhancement of the built heritage requires new strategies and thinking on ways of creating distinctive place-identity solutions for better cultural, social and ethnic integration and inclusion. These place-identity solutions can be created by constructing new public spaces that promote social and community interactions as a way to complement (rather than confront) the local built heritage. Cities can provide culturally diverse social groups and individuals with a "spatial membership" and a possibility to integrate their own values, identity and history into the social and physical fabric of cities. These cities accentuate notions of multiculturalism and complexity, overlapping (instead of separating) local layers of identity as a way of being inclusive.

Successful examples of the mix of old and new urban spaces where innovative designs are employed are the Spanish cities of Barcelona, Seville, Bilbao and Valencia that simultaneously express the specificity of the place and the links with the world beyond. These cities not only create new forms of cultural locality, they also promote urban economic development.

Sources: Dammert, & Borja, 2004; Florida, 2002; Landry, 2002; ISOCARP, 2008; Leger, 2008, Moreno, 1993; Langenbach 2007; Friedmann, 2007; Dragicevic, 2007; Spring, 2008, Gospodini, 2002; Di Cicco, 2006; UNESCO World Heritage Centre, Follath & Spörl, 2007; "Economist.com, 2007; Mercer Quality of Living Global City Rankings, 2008.

NOTES

1 Shatkin, 2002.
2 Brolin, 1972.
3 Lyons, Smuts & Stephens, 2001.
4 This chapter draws largely from Bazoglu, 2007, and from a framework document for the World Urban Forum 2008 prepared for UN-HABITAT by the International Society of City and Regional Planners (ISOCARP), based in The Hague, Netherlands.
5 Zunino, 2006.
6 Fernandes, 2007.
7 UN-HABITAT, 2006a.
8 Marques & Bichir, 2003.
9 UN-HABITAT, 2006.
10 Bazoglu, 1998.
11 Peterson & Muzzini, 2006.
12 Bretas, 1996.
13 World Bank, 2005.
14 UN-HABITAT Best Practices and Local Leadership Programme, n.d.
15 Lyons, Smuts & Stephens, 2001.
16 Ibid.
17 Ibid.
18 Bazoglu, 1998.
19 Sutton & Fahmi, 2001.
20 Rabinovich, 1996.
21 Forester, 1999.
22 Arnstein, 1969.
23 Shaktin, 2002.
24 Parnell & Robinson, 2006.
25 Fernández-Maldonado, 2006.
26 Maharaj & Makhathini, 2004.
27 Robinson, 2005.
28 Viana, 2007.
29 Holcim Foundations Forum, 2007.
30 American Planning Association, 2006.
31 Reilly, et al. 2008.
32 Wright & Montezuma, 2004.
33 Ibid.
34 Cities Alliance, 2006.

4.2
Building Bridges:
Social Capital and Urban Harmony

▲
Arab men playing backgammon, Old city, Jerusalem, Israel
©**Salamanderman/Shutterstock**

In recent years, increasing attention has been paid to the question of whether the absence of social networks, or what is known as "social capital", is affecting the quality of life in cities. Indeed, a great paradox of big cities is that proximity and high densities do not necessarily provide for strong social ties and networks. It is the very freedom, privacy and anonymity offered by city life, in fact, that weaken "social capital" – the networks of civic engagement that facilitate cooperation and mutual benefit in society.

Recent studies have shown that residents of large metropolitan areas are significantly less likely than residents of small towns and villages to attend public meetings, to be active in community organizations, to attend religious activities, to sign petitions, to volunteer, to work on community projects or even to visit friends.[1] One study of eight countries in Latin America found that levels of trust and community participation – two dimensions of social capital – tend to be significantly higher in rural areas than in large metropolitan areas, although the poor in some cities exhibit high levels of community participation, but not high levels of trust. The highest levels of social capital in the region were found in the rural areas of Costa Rica and Honduras, while Managua, the capital of Nicaragua, exhibited the lowest levels of trust and community participation.[2] (Fig. 4.2.1)

Diversity and residential mobility have been blamed for the lack of cooperation and social engagement in urban neighbourhoods.[3] When people move frequently, as urban residents often do, or if they do not share a common identity, they are unlikely to cooperate with each other or to be involved in the same social activities.[4] Other factors also inhibit the development of social capital, including crime, which may prevent people from going out and meeting others; political affiliation, where people who support a particular party or politician may have more access to resources than those who do not; and disputes over resource allocation. These factors become more important in cities where inequalities are high and where access to resources of the state are politicized.

Social capital can help reduce vulnerability in urban areas

Scholarly interest in social networks, social cohesion and solidarity is hardly new. Since the 19th century, social scientists have elaborated on the ways in which industrialization and urbanization erode the solidarity and ties among family and community members. In the mid-19th century, for instance, Mark Twain, the American journalist and satirist, described New York City as "a splendid desert – a domed and steepled solitude, where a stranger is lonely in the midst of a million of his race". Karl Marx described the vulnerability of individuals in a modernizing urban world as *alienation*, a concept further elaborated by 20th century urban sociologists in studies of social networks. The value of such networks and social relationships became known as social "capital", elevating the study of social networks from the social into the economic sphere.[5] The central idea behind social capital is that *"networks of social contacts may represent a form of capital resource … with important potential returns on investment".*[6]

Human beings have a variety of assets, which may or may not translate into income, but which nonetheless play an important role in determining levels of poverty and vulnerability within a household or a community. These assets include: human assets (such as skills and good health); natural assets (such as land); physical assets (such as access to infrastructure); financial assets (such as savings and access to credit); and social assets (such as networks of contacts and reciprocal obligations that can be called upon in time of need, as well as political influence over resource allocation).

Social capital is now recognized by the international community[7] as a key asset, among others, that determines the progress of societies and one that promotes social harmony and cohesion. Social assets, which form part of a household's social capital, play an important role in reducing the vulnerability of individuals and communities. While human capital is the aggregate pool of skills and capabilities acquired through education and other forms of investment in people, social capital is the feature of social-life networks, norm and trust that enable a group of people, a community, a city, or a nation to channel their collective energy for a shared objective. In essence, social capital refers to "the glue that holds groups and societies together".[8]

The social capital of a household has much to do with quality of life, and even survival. Links to family-based networks, occupation-based groups of mutual help, rotating savings and credit groups, and other associations – all part of a household's social capital – can be the source of transfers in cash or in kind in the event of an emergency or job loss. For instance, people with little or no income may be protected from material deprivation by a network of friends or relatives who provide material support in times of need or crisis. When these assets are lost or weakened, as they often are when people live in urban settings far from close or extended family networks, individuals and communities are at risk of descending into absolute poverty. One study, for instance, found that migrants who had no social contacts in Kenya's capital city of Nairobi had less access to information about livelihood issues, such as housing and employment, than those migrants who had a more robust network of friends and relatives in the city.[9] In other words, "connected" migrants have a better chance of obtaining employment and housing in cities than those who are "unconnected". Lack of access to housing, basic services or employment, in turn, further impacts poverty levels.

Social capital is also critical as a form of protection against further marginalization. In many slums around the world, for example, social capital manifests itself in the form of

FIGURE 4.2.1. **LEVELS OF TRUST AND COMMUNITY PARTICIPATION BY COUNTRY AND SETTLEMENT TYPE IN LATIN AMERICA**

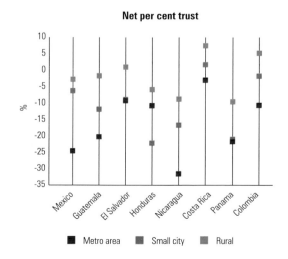

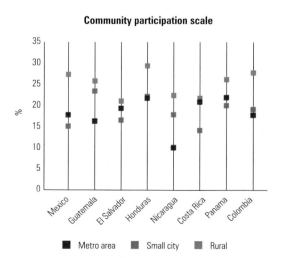

Source: Rosero-Bixby, 2006.

local associations and networks that residents mobilize to resist evictions or to negotiate for better services. The critical difference between successful economies and those that fail, some suggest, is the inherent level of trust. "High-trust" societies, or those that have high levels of social capital, tend to recover from crises much more quickly than those in which individuals and communities distrust each other or do not cooperate.[10] A recent World Health Organization report has also shown that social capital is one of the most important factors for improving the social determinants of health in urban settings.[11]

The spontaneous manifestation of social capital as collective action in communities surfaces powerfully when they are hit by natural disasters or other calamities. When all inhabitants of a community or a city face an emergency, they become an extended network of mutual aid; this form of social capital has been observed as a universal pattern that cuts across regions, nations and time periods. Cognizant of the spontaneous collective reaction of societies to natural or man-made disasters, the UN's Office for the Coordination of Humanitarian Affairs (OCHA), has developed a strategy to use this energy to rescue people until national and international aid arrives.

In view of climate change and the increasing frequency and destructiveness of natural disasters around the world, social capital should not be neglected as a policy instrument in mitigating the potential damage caused by crises. Customary social capital is a survival strategy in cities such as Colombo, Nairobi, and Bangalore, where traditional funeral societies – groups formed to take care of funeral expenses and to mitigate the financial burdens borne by grieving families – and savings groups compound residents' savings and provide a measure of protection against emergencies; in Johannesburg, where membership in religious organizations, informal savings clubs, bulk buying and communal eating arrangements help residents make the most of their resources; and in the slums of Ankara, where reciprocal labour pooling for the preparation of traditional bread and other durable food items ensures that all families have the staples they need.

"Ties that bind also exclude"

Social capital that is manifested in self-help or other community-centred groups may help communities survive, but it may also reinforce structural inequalities in society. Self-help groups that have little or no contact with government agencies may, in fact, be perpetuating their own poverty, because they are unable to tap into public resources that would enable them to achieve sustained development. In many cases where such collective efforts provide the best security for residents, formal institutions have failed to develop and social capital becomes a substitute for the state. This helps explain why many societies that have high levels of social solidarity remain poor.

Studies conducted in Latin America, for instance, show that despite high levels of solidarity among communities, particularly indigenous communities, lack of connections to powerful people outside of the community prevents them from prospering. Even when they manage to attract government services, such communities typically do not develop sufficient productive activities to lift them out of poverty.[12] A 1996 participatory poverty assessment by the World Bank in Kenya, for instance, showed that the more than 30,000 self-help groups in the country remained isolated solidarity groups caught in poverty traps.[13]

Similarly, women's groups may find themselves trapped in enclaves that ensure that they remain outside of power structures dominated by men. Qualitative studies and programme experience have shown that women have a much higher capacity to be engaged in the welfare of their communities, but their participation is mostly informal, local, and cyclical.[14] Formal structures, such as associations and local authorities, which are mostly dominated by men, intimidate women, unless and until they have a critical mass of women represented. Another significant dimension of women's networking resources depends on their life stage. While single, young women just out of primary and secondary schools often prove to be resourceful activists within their neighborhoods, once they marry and have children, their involvement decreases. However, it is also evident that the same women mobilize their networks again when their children are no longer dependent on them.[15] It is for these reasons that policies that do not take into account the gender patterns of social capital are either destined to fail entirely, or to fail to bring women's knowledge and skills to the table as vital community resources.

In other cases, social activities are localized to a particular group, such as workers agitating for higher wages, and are ultimately resolved at the group level, rather than involving counterparts (such as trade union movements) elsewhere. In these cases, the group's negotiating power is restricted by size and level of sophistication, and is less likely to affect policy or to result in broader forms of collective identity or solidarity.[16]

Overuse of the self-help tradition may also encourage governments to abdicate their responsibilities towards poor or under-serviced groups. As governments cease to fulfill their functions, informal networks, militia or guerrilla movements become substitutes for the state, as has happened in many strife-torn countries in Africa and Latin America.[17] In Nairobi, for instance, militia groups operating in low-income neighbourhoods are known to provide all sorts of services to slum residents, including security. The most notorious of these groups, known as the Mungiki, control various sections of low-income estates, both as criminal gangs and as a form of "community policing".[18]

World Bank studies have also shown that practices reliant on social capital can have negative social outcomes, ranging from social exclusion, corruption and inequality to the perpetuation of social stratification. "Social capital can explain much social exclusion because the ties that bind also exclude", writes Deepa Narayan of the World Bank's Poverty Group.[19]

In socially stratified or deeply unequal societies, the invocation of social capital often fosters the maintenance of the status quo. Those who belong to social networks that

An insurance booth in South Africa: Funeral societies and savings groups in low-income settlements can be the source of transfers in cash or kind in case of emergency.
©**Madanmohan Rao**

already have access to resource allocation decisions of the state or the private sector are much more likely to exclude other groups from powerful networks, much as membership in exclusive clubs or associations restricts the benefits of social capital to a particular group of individuals. If social capital is formed around ethnic identities, it may also serve to polarize societies where ethnicity has been politicized, as evident in many conflict-ridden African countries in recent years. In these cases, decisions by powerful groups serve to reinforce exclusion rather than to foster inclusion and equal treatment of others. When powerful groups use their social networks to practise corruption and cronyism, social capital can actually be detrimental to society. In some countries, resource control by powerful social networks prevents economic growth from translating into greater equality.[20] The challenge is to understand how social capital operates under different circumstances so that negative consequences can be minimized.

Using social capital to transform communities

Studies show that social capital can only become a tool of real social transformation and equity when it is used not just to "get by" but to "get ahead". Social capital for the purposes of getting by has a strong bearing on the **survival** of individuals or communities, but social capital formed for the purpose of getting ahead has a bearing on the **development** of communities.

The strengthening of social capital among and across groups for the positive social transformation of societies and promotion of the public good requires a combination of policy responses that include providing access to information and information technology, including residents in participatory planning and governance, and restructuring economic policies to ensure equity. In an ideal scenario, good governance coupled with high levels of cross-cutting ties among social groups lead to positive economic and social outcomes. However, in countries where there is a high degree of exclusion and inequality, excluded groups may organize

Identifying bonds and bridges in slum and non-slum areas of Addis Ababa

▲
Boys play football in one of the suburbs in Addis Ababa, Ethiopia.
©Manoocher Deghati/IRIN

UN-HABITAT conducted its first Urban Inequities Survey (UIS) in Addis Ababa, Ethiopia, in 2004. The survey, carried out in collaboration with Ethiopia's National Statistical Office and the Municipality of Addis Ababa, was administered to 1,500 households with the goal of understanding how, on a socio-economic level, people living in the city's slums and its planned neighbourhoods experience the city differently.

Two areas of Addis Ababa – Bole, a wealthy neighbourhood, and Akaki Kaliti, a slum inhabited by the city's poorest residents – proved particularly relevant to studying contrasts in how residents from different socio-economic backgrounds experience social relationships and build social capital. UIS data from both areas illustrates pat-

terns familiar to social capital researchers: residents of the slum, Akaki Kaliti, attested to the interdependence of neighbours and described more social bonding overall within the community than did residents of the wealthy neighbourhood, Bole. In Bole, however, residents expressed a greater openness to diversity and described more behaviours that bridge social networks rather than rely strictly on members of their own close groups. While 83 per cent of all Addis Ababa residents surveyed belong to *idirs*, community groups that fund funerals and provide aid to families in emergencies, it is the routine habits of daily life – taking care of neighbours' children, gathering information from and visiting friends, trusting and networking with others – that describe the powerful influences of social capital in communities.

The UIS measured bonding social capital with several indicators of neighbourly trust and sociability among friends. More UIS respondents from Akaki Kaliti than from Bole consistently reported that people in their neighbourhood are willing to help them, that neighbours can be counted on if money is urgently needed, and that they can depend on neighbours to take care of their children in emergencies. Residents of Akaki Kaliti also reported that they are more dependent on their neighbours for information about government policies, jobs, education and other opportunities in the city than residents of Bole, who look to their neighbours and friends as the best sources of such information half as often. The survey revealed that sociability, too, differs among respondents from the two communities. More residents of Akaki Kaliti than Bole had met someone at a public place or coffee shop over the previous month, received visitors at home, or paid a visit to someone else's home, though fewer residents of either place were likely to participate in home visits than to meet in a public place.

Bridging social capital – which creates opportunities for members of a group to connect with others who are different, and who may have more resources – is more prevalent in Bole than in Akaki Kaliti, as indicated by UIS data on the groups with whom people in each community network and interact regularly. While respondents from both communities claimed low levels of trust in people from groups not their own, those from the wealthy neighbourhood had met or visited with people of different ethnic, tribal or religious groups twice as often in the previous month as those from the slum. Respondents from Bole were also more likely to vote for political candidates from other ethnic groups or tribes, and more people from Akaki Kaliti claimed that diversity in the community causes problems.

Clearly, residents of the slum rely heavily on neighbours and friends from their own ethnic and tribal communities, interacting in enclaves of similar-ity. Residents of the wealthy neighbourhood are less beholden to close neighbourly ties and have more opportunities and inclination to reach out to those unlike themselves. Helping poor communities like Akaki Kaliti develop bridging social capital through education and outreach may generate more resources and give residents – especially young people – perspectives on what opportunities might be available to them outside of the neighbourhood. Such efforts, however, must also work within the tightly knit, interdependent networks on which poor communities depend, and acknowledge the distrust of people from different groups that exists in many enclaves.

TABLE 1: **INDICATORS OF BONDING SOCIAL CAPITAL - PER CENT OF RESPONSES IN ADDIS ABABA URBAN INEQUITIES SURVEY**

Components and indicators	Addis Ababa Total (%)	Bole (%)	Akaki Kaliti (%)
Trust in neighbours:			
Those who believe that people in his/her neighbourhood are willing to help one if one needs	28	29	42
Those who believe that neighbours/friends could be counted on if urgent money is needed	50	46	52
Those who can count on one or more people who could provide this money	49	46	52
Those who believe they can count on neighbours to take care of their children during emergencies	50	40	52
Neighbours/relatives/friends as sources of vital information: Those who believe that neighbours and friends are the best source of information on …			
Government policies	30	15	44
Jobs, education and other opportunities in the city	38	14	45
Sociability: Over the last month, those who …			
Met someone at a public place/coffee shop, etc.	38	27	46
Received visitors at home	23	16	31
Paid a visit to someone else's home	29	19	39

TABLE 2: **INDICATORS OF BRIDGING SOCIAL CAPITAL - PER CENT OF RESPONSES IN ADDIS ABABA URBAN INEQUITIES SURVEY**

Components and indicators	Addis Ababa Total (%)	Bole (%)	Akaki Kaliti (%)
Trust in diverse social groups: Those who strongly believe that …			
People from same ethnic group could be trusted	13	19	17
People from other religious groups could be trusted	4	10	4
Networking with different groups:			
Those who met or visited people of different ethnic/tribal group in the last month	21	30	14
Those who met or visited people of different religious groups in the last month	15	22	10
Diversity in community causes problems	48	39	46
Those who would vote for candidates of other ethnic group/tribe	68	74	57

Source: UN-HABITAT Urban Inequities Survey: Addis Ababa, 2004.

to challenge the power of the dominant group. If excluded groups manage to build bridges across social groups, they prosper; if they do not manage to transcend social barriers to gain access to public resources, societies become embroiled in conflict, violence or even anarchy.

When used positively, however, social capital can help develop community consciousness and confidence, thereby increasing communities' ability to negotiate with authorities for more or better resources – a strategy known as "linking" social capital. Linking social capital is most critical in the transformation of societies because it enables marginalized or excluded communities to gain access to state resources and to people with power, authority or influence, which can have a positive impact on their development. Linking social capital is especially critical for poor urban communities because it enables them to gain access to formal organizations, including the state, and to negotiate more effectively for resources.[21] Cities are particularly relevant environments for fostering linking social capital, as people have at least physical access,

if not economic and social access, to public institutions and government officials.

Strengthening of social capital has become one of the three pillars of programme interventions in developing countries, along with the strengthening of financial and human capital. Social cohesion – the potential of individuals to engage in the wider social, political, economic, and cultural environment – has also been seen as a key component of democracy, national development and social transformation. Development agencies have become more aware, too, that the presence of strong social networks can have a positive impact on governance institutions, and that knowledge and information can mitigate risk and improve the livelihoods of the poor. Not knowing about their rights, services they could access, plans for their areas or options available for tackling certain problems puts the poor at a disadvantage and increases their vulnerability. Providing access to traditional and new media, therefore, may reduce the vulnerability of populations in many countries.

▲
School children in Durban, South Africa.
©**Rasna Warah**

Indeed, the growing use of information technology in sub-Saharan Africa has proven invaluable for reducing poverty and increasing the number of opportunities available to the urban poor. A study in Nairobi's slums found that many dwellers in the city are using mobile phone technology to operate small businesses, to keep in touch with rural family members, and to obtain information on the availability of housing and other basic services.[22] Access to information about employment opportunities is critical to the survival of poor urban communities. In Rio de Janeiro, for instance, Viva Favela, a donor- and private sector-funded web site, is enabling impoverished urban youth to find jobs. Improving access to information about employment opportunities, health facilities, schools, laws and other resources is a critical tool for developing social capital among the urban poor, as lack of access to such information – rather than discrimination per se – has been identified as one of the reasons why poor communities remain poor. The work of non-governmental organizations with the urban poor on issues of advocacy is important, as are official channels of news and information, such as public radio and other media.

Citizen participation in public affairs is also a form of social capital that can be mobilized to improve the lives of the urban poor. In Brazil, for instance, participatory budgeting has helped to shift the allocation of public resources from rich to more needy communities, while e-governance models that rely on citizen participation have been adopted by various European governments. These approaches have led to social transformation, less inequality and greater transparency.

Community participation in national and local development initiatives is also critical in ensuring that programmes and projects are sustainable. Myriad evaluations of Grameen Bank's micro-credit schemes in Bangladesh, for instance, reveal that the success of the programme resulted not only from the financial, but also the social assets of small groups of women who enforced social control mechanisms to prevent defaults on loan payments.

The power of linking social capital is its capacity to bring about social, economic and political transformation. The unprecedented growth of civil society organizations and people's movements in recent years is a manifestation of the formalization of social capital into organizations or federations that can effectively demand change in policies at the local, national and international levels. As individuals, the urban poor have little power, but collective action through mobilization and organization make their voices heard. The United Nations Development Programme (UNDP)'s experience in South Asia shows that once mobilized, people choose the direction in which they want to move and are better able to address the root causes of their deprivation.[23] Federations of slum dwellers in India, Kenya and South Africa, for instance, have had some success in gaining public recognition as legitimate voices of the urban poor that can negotiate on behalf of slum communities. Community-led efforts are most likely to be successful if they rally around a common goal, and if they are combined with activities that lead to economic empowerment and poverty reduction.

NOTES

1. Putnam, 2000.
2. Rosero-Bixby, 2006.
3. Montgomery, et al., 2003.
4. Some countries, such as Bhutan, are also looking more closely at non-tangible social indicators, such "happiness levels" to formulate development policies. Bhutan 2020, the country's long-term development blueprint, notes that Bhutan's approach to development is firmly rooted in its rich tradition of Mahayana Buddhism that stresses "individual development, sanctity of life, compassion for others, respect for nature, social harmony, and the importance of compromise". The blueprint also cautions that while modernization and urbanization have their benefits, they may erode the values and assets that Bhutan has built over the centuries and may lead to negative consequences, such as high levels of urban poverty and environmental degradation. Bhutan's National Human Development Report 2000, for instance, states that the country considers Gross National Happiness to be far more important than Gross Domestic Product because its focus is on "enriching people's lives, improving their standard of living, and augmenting people's economic, spiritual and emotional well-being". The report further argues that economic indicators do not adequately capture many aspects of Bhutan's largely rural economy, which is non-monetised and fail to reflect the kingdom's vast and diverse natural resources and its rich cultural and religious heritage.
5. Bazoglu, 1992.
6. Policy Research Initiative (PRI), 2005.
7. That the concept of social capital has multiple definitions is both a blessing and a curse. In this text, we formulate a synthesized definition, mostly drawn from the work of Robert Putnam, who defines social capital as "the feature of social life networks, norm and trust", and the definition of Michael Woolcock, as "calling on friends and relatives", marked by a more minimalist approach. See Putnam, 2000 and Woolcock, 2005.
8. Narayan, 1999.
9. Warah, 2005.
10. Fukuyama, 1995.
11. WHO Centre for Health Development, 2008.
12. Narayan, 1999.
13. Narayan, & Nyamwaya, 1996.
14. Bazoglu, 1992.
15. Bazoglu, 1992.
16. This phenomenon has been observed in China, where workers' disputes remain confined to the "cellular" level of the factory, and often remain isolated and directed at local officials rather than at systems and structures. See Lum, 2006.
17. For a detailed analysis of the various scenarios, see Narayan, 1999.
18. Anderson, 2002.
19. Narayan, 1999.
20. Li, Squire, & Zou, 1998.
21. Woolcock, 2000.
22. Warah, 2005.
23. UNDP, 1998.

4.3

Unifying the Divided City

Slum Upgrading Policies and Strategies that Work

Many city leaders and national governments assume that slum growth is a natural consequence of urban growth – that as cities grow economically, and as incomes improve, slums will disappear naturally over time. However, evidence indicates that innovative and inclusive policies and institutions that are tailor-made to local needs have a key role to play in determining whether slums will grow, whether they will be upgraded or whether they will be ignored in national development plans and policies. In this section, we use policy evidence drawn from the experiences of 23 countries analyzed in 2005/6 and another survey of 52 cities in 21 countries conducted by UN-HABITAT and the Cities Alliance more recently to understand the impact of policies on bridging the divided city.

The evidence shows that political will and political support for slum upgrading, slum prevention and urban poverty reduction are critical to the success of any programme aimed at improving the living conditions of the urban poor. Success in managing slum growth is not accidental. It requires strategies, policies and procedures that are clear, concise, and easy to follow. It also requires innovation, both in institutional performance and in the development of inclusive policies. Unfortunately, in many countries and cities of the developing world, slum growth management has experienced limited success, and in others it has failed completely. While it is typically easier to explain failures of policy responses than the reasons for success, this part of the report presents policy evidence on what has worked in efforts to unify the divided city – to reduce disparities between the formal and the informal city and knock down the wall that separates them physically, socially and economically.

Some governments choose to largely ignore the rapidly growing slums in their cities, treating them as "zones of silence" with regard to public knowledge, opinion and discussion about urban poverty,[1] even though, quite often, "invisible" or informal parts of cities are growing faster than the "visible" or formal areas. Many governments confine their actions on slums to symbolic gestures and political slogans while deeming informal settlements "illegal", thereby legitimizing their neglect of slums and making slum clearance and mass evictions legitimate actions in the eyes of the state. All such cases of policy failure in the developing world have a common denominator: a benign neglect of "spontaneous" housing solutions that are considered pathological responses to urban growth.[2]

Failure to address the slum challenge can take several forms; cities may recognize slums but blame their existence or proliferation on a neighbouring municipality, migrants from other countries or other government departments and institutions. In these cases, institutional responses are permeated by a lacklustre tone of quasi-resignation: "*the problem is not really ours, and besides it is too huge to be tackled*".[3] Most governments' responses lie somewhere between action and inaction: they are aware of the slum problem and they plan to pursue institutional strengthening and some level of reforms, but it is difficult to implement actions because insufficient support and funding limit capacity, or because good programmes do not have financial support, or because they lack co-ordination.[4]

When actions are put into practice, they are often linear processes, designed, implemented and monitored as new, separate, stand-alone initiatives – "pilot" projects that develop without continuity carried over from past experiences, and without making use of built-up learning systems. Often, there is inadequate time for experimentation, feedback, debate, and attitudinal change – what innovation is all about. One of the major reasons for the limited success of many strategies is that they lack high-level political support and willingness to take the necessary steps and make the choices to address slums as part of sustainable development policies.

Harnessing the drivers of change

On the other end of the spectrum are national and local governments that are making concerted efforts to reduce slum growth by taking the issue of slums seriously and making a real difference in the lives of urban residents.

▲
Low- and high-income housing in São Paulo.
©**Tuca Vieira**

Strategies that work not only improve the physical living conditions of slum dwellers, but they also preserve non-tangible assets, such as sense of place, sense of belonging and culture of mutual solidarity. Such strategies improve existing slums without disturbing social ties and create conditions to prevent the formation of slums of the future.

Policy evidence drawn from the experiences of 23 countries analyzed by UN-HABITAT in 2005/6[5] and a later one of 52 cities in 21 countries conducted by UN-HABITAT and the Cities Alliance sums up the formula for successful slum upgrading and prevention as follows: a) governments recognize the existence of slums; b) they commit to addressing the issue of slums by taking innovative actions or instituting bold policy reforms; c) they adopt planning measures to meet their commitments; d) they implement effective actions that they check and revise, setting up conditions to learn from experience; and e) they scale up the adopted system to the national level. These governments take the responsibility for improving the lives of slum dwellers squarely on their shoulders by committing, planning and doing, checking, learning, and redoing again at the national level. Policy and

institutional analysis of responses to surveys from the 52 cities in the UN-HABITAT/Cities Alliance study points to six key ingredients that explain the success of any large-scale slum upgrading strategy. When governments harness all or some of the following six elements together, the possibility of success is higher.

1. Awareness and political commitment

Awareness precedes action. Governments that recognize the existence of slums understand the need to do something about them because they are persuaded by the benefits of the intervention. In the early 1990s, the government of Egypt declared the existence of slums in its cities as an emergency situation, which led to the creation of an emergency budget plan for slum upgrading. Since then, the country has reduced its proportion of slum dwellers by more than 22 per cent nationwide. Sri Lanka has for a long time acknowledged the difficult conditions endured by urban residents living in slums, shanties and tenements, and the environmental hazards often present in their poor neighbourhoods. As early as the 1970s, the

▲
Bangkok
©**Madanmohan Rao**

country enacted pro-poor reforms, including free education, health care and housing programmes.[6] In the last 15 years, the country has more than halved the nationwide slum prevalence from 25 per cent in 1990 to 11 per cent in 2005.[7]

Awareness in most countries is related to basic service delivery and public health, particularly improving sanitation and hygiene conditions. Attending to slum conditions has historically been important for urban development in general; in the late 19th century and the early part of 20th century, for example, concerns about the impacts of poor sanitation and overcrowding in slums on the health of non-slum residents led to large low-cost public housing programmes in cities such as London and Paris. The urban poor may live in appalling conditions, but governments often do not intervene until slums threaten the social fabric of society or pose a general health hazard. Disaggregated information on slum and non-slum indicators can provide valuable information on differences in access to health, education and other basic services, which can help prompt governments to take action. In this regard, the establishment of monitoring systems and indicators, as UN-HABITAT has done, to collect information and analyze trends in slum and non-slum areas is critical. Thailand, for example, developed a low-income housing programme in the late 1970s with a strong slum upgrading component following a comprehensive and reliable analysis of the situation of the urban poor conducted by the National Housing Authority. The country has since managed to dramatically reduce the proportion of slum dwellers from nearly 20 per cent in 1990 to less than 1 per cent in 2005.

Awareness also means assessing and forecasting trends and risks. The city of Cape Town has developed an incremental-phase approach to upgrading informal settlements in response to the growing housing backlog and associated slum formation, which the authorities recognize have the potential of undermining social stability, slowing down economic expansion and even deterring future investments. As a response, this South African city has created an informal settlement master plan with clear targets for the future provision of services and areas to be progressively upgraded. This focus on priorities and outcomes permits the city to develop a more coherent system of implementation, linking budget and investment processes.

Electoral and political processes can also raise governments' awareness of slum issues, particularly in countries where the poor form significant voting blocs. Even if in some cases political pronouncements are not backed by actions, the electoral process can contribute to raising the profile of slums and integrating them into the social and economic development agenda. In Costa Rica, for instance, electoral political commitment resulted in the integration of slum upgrading as one of the seven pillars of the national social policy in the mid-1980s, and more recently in the reform of the national financial system of housing that increased by 20 per cent the financial resources of informal settlements, known as *tugurios*.

Raising awareness is often the job of non-governmental organizations (NGOs) and civil society at large. Advocacy organizations champion the positions and rights of slum dwellers and of the poor in general. Some of them act as watchdogs scrutinizing the fulfillment of policies and actions. For instance, the NGO *Réseau Social Watch Bénin* has set itself the task of monitoring the fulfillment of the Millennium Development Goals and the national poverty reduction strategy in Benin. In other cases, the interaction between the government and civil society translates into legislative norms and government-funded programmes for urban poverty reduction. In Mexico, for instance, the central government programme, Re-appropriation of Public Space, has integrated consultations with the target beneficiaries as a mechanism for identifying the specific interventions to be included in the executive plan. Sometimes civil society organizations, such as Shack/Slum Dwellers International perform both an advocacy and executive role.

In all successful cases, awareness-raising and advocacy comprise the first step towards a strategy of action that can lead to high-level political and government commitment and that can influence key institutions to take responsibility for implementation.

2. Institutional Innovation

Policies and institutions that impact harmony in cities can be broadly classified into two main categories: long-term policies and institutional innovations. The first category comprises policies that encapsulate how states perceive urbanization issues, their broad agendas for reform and the institutional and organizational set-up and mandates that will be put in place to achieve the policy goals. While the presence of such policies shows a vision for long-term action in the realm of urban development that could parallel other economic and industrial policy initiatives in the long run, developing countries more often than not lack one or all of the essential components to see them through: organizational competence, sustained finances, adequate physical and institutional infrastructure, and human skills for planning and implementation. More often than not, implementation of long-term policies suffers because the necessary governmental agencies are neither sufficiently coordinated nor independent enough to undertake the associated projects. Managing urbanization also tends to fall to city planning agencies, which are given little or no extra resources to tackle the problems unleashed by economic development.

The potential gaps in implementing a long-term vision are what make the second category of policy initiatives – institutional innovations – extremely important. Institutional innovations serve the needs of local contexts and are effective because they entail the introduction of a new scheme or organizational form that improves policies and institutions, helping them work better for those within them and those who benefit from them. They are innovative because they target the usage of existing resources and capacity to tackle urbanization issues through simple changes in organizational structures for the provision of services, and because they are tailor-made to suit the needs of the local context in the

short term. Institutional innovations may or may not be coordinated with the long-term integrated policy frameworks of countries to tackle urbanization.

What is critical about innovative policies and institutions is that they target the informal institutions that support people in rapidly urbanizing and growing areas, honouring their cultural and social habits and practices and their perceptions. Most institutional innovations have focused on two important areas: facilitating the provision of housing and other services for the poor in urban and peri-urban areas, and improving administrative coordination amongst organizations to promote effective delivery of services using existing resources.

Innovations in institutional and organizational practices that seek to provide services

Findings from the city surveys show that many countries have embarked upon initiatives that attempt to better coordinate policymaking and service delivery, creating a direct relationship between government and civil society initiatives and the improvement of urban residents' lives. The following innovations in institutional and organizational practices have helped ensure better delivery of services and greater security of tenure in cities.

The government of the Philippines grants an exemption in the payment of transfer taxes for landowners who donate property to community associations, seeking to create an incentive for such initiatives. In addition to allowing free transfer of land titles to community groups, the government of the Philippines has also developed mechanisms for the issuance of rights-based security of tenure or interim titling instruments that entitle settlers to use plots of land. As a complementary effort, local housing boards have developed a community mortgage programme and housing microfinance scheme through which the poor can receive mortgages and access to financing for low-cost housing needs. A total of 140,000 families gained security of tenure in 2006 under these schemes.

The Namibian government has developed an upgrading strategy for poor and very poor populations called the Incremental Upgrading and Development Strategy. This strategy provides minimum service levels and gives poor households an option to obtain ownership and upgrade services in a progressive manner. What is novel about this initiative is that it provides solutions for informal settlements across a wide spectrum of income groups, and it provides social, health and education services along with housing and other more typical physical services.

The South African government emphasizes a social housing policy that provides so-called Community Residential Units. Through the policy, the government seeks to convert existing buildings – mainly hostels that once housed single men – into low-rent, family friendly units to provide accommodation for people near their areas of work. Land reform policies also seek to redress loss of land or housing as a result of Group Areas

Apartheid Legislation. The city of Cape Town has adopted an incremental approach to upgrading informal settlements by improving the capacities of the management team and the institutional responses to the provision of affordable land. An interesting aspect of the city's policy towards slum prevention and improvement is its prioritization model, which weighs different demands on the limited resources through a priority rank scoring system. The government of Cape Town has compiled a comprehensive informal settlement-ranking database, which is used to make decisions on how to commit resources for the city's poor. Cape Town's initiatives reflect the local context, where the price of land is more than 10 times greater than in Johannesburg or 14 times greater than in other South African cities such as Durban.

In South Africa's Gauteng province, a Backyard Rental Housing Policy focuses on interventions from an income, tenure and housing perspective. As part of this policy, the rental housing stock is upgraded to improve the living conditions of landlords and tenants, as well as whole communities. The Backyard Rental Policy will eventually regularize the rental market in urban areas of the Gauteng Region. Housing allocation is based on a Housing Demand Database that is compiled for the region and is meant to ensure that sustainable community projects that respond to collective needs are implemented in the region. The policy is a move towards more inclusive housing policy and integrated human settlements.

In Zambia, the government has implemented a cost-sharing policy in an attempt to maintain a continuous process of improvement in peri-urban areas, where it retains 35 per cent of the amount collected from ground rent in informal settlements to invest in the improvement process. The government has also initiated a funding programme, called Squatter Upgrading Bank Accounts, through local authorities, which identify priority settlements for upgrading and facilitate funds.

These are not the only innovative efforts in the developing world that have the chance to turn around existing systems without expending huge amounts of resources. Others include the Nepalese attempt to establish municipal partnership development funds in more than half of the municipalities around the country. In China, more than 120 prefecture-level cities have adopted an innovative policy to fund slum upgrading by allocating a fixed ratio of 10 per cent from land transfers to bolster low-rent security funds; 37 such cities have dedicated the money raised through this strategy to slum upgrading initiatives.

Administrative innovations

UN-HABITAT and the Cities Alliance also found that most administrative innovations in surveyed cities were targeted at improving inter-municipal coordination for urban development, by creating more intermediate levels of government, encouraging greater civil society participation and granting greater autonomy to local administrative authorities within metropolitan areas. For example, the Egyptian government has acknowledged the variegated nature of slums in its cities and hence seeks to develop, approve and promote strategies and tools to deal with each type of slum in the typology created for differentiated policy interventions. South Africa is committed to devising management decision-making tools for upgrading poor informal settlements in a community-involved manner. A dedicated housing section now exists in all of the municipalities in the country to improve access to low-cost housing for the poor. Several countries and cities have also sought to establish administrative mechanisms that ensure greater transparency of operation and equitable distribution of resources. The prioritization model created in Cape Town is a case in point. Some other countries, such as Sri Lanka, are seeking to create organizational innovations that promote common strategy development and priorities in urban services, and that enhance civil society participation and social responsibility.

Several other such innovations go towards institution strengthening, and hence are discussed in the next section. The common thread through all such interventions is that they seek to address the disjuncture in the present organization of services for the urban poor, through important yet context-specific, low-cost organizational reforms.

3. Policy Reforms and Institutional Strengthening

In many countries and cities, priority needs and actions are not translated into policies, or policies are not supported by budgets. Sometimes policies and priorities change when new leadership or new governments take over with new development agendas. Long-term, institutionalized policy reforms and visions are thus needed to ensure that slum upgrading and urban poverty reduction programmes do not suffer setbacks whenever the city leadership or government changes.

Some countries have overcome this obstacle by undertaking progressive pro-poor reforms to improve the tenure status of slum dwellers or to improve their access to basic services and better housing. Successful policy reforms share similar attributes: they target investments with a pro-poor focus supported by clear legislation; they have a long-term vision and they are normally the result of consensus.

The UN-HABITAT and Cities Alliance study of 52 cities identified two types of policy responses to slum upgrading: stand-alone interventions, in which informal settlements are either the main objective of the intervention or are a special component of a broader response; and integrated approaches, in which slum upgrading is part of a broader response within national or regional frameworks of poverty alleviation and national development plans – where slum operations do not appear as specific actions, but rather as a set of interventions that directly or indirectly reduce poverty or improve basic services in slums.

Focused slum upgrading initiatives take different forms in different countries and cities; they can be the result of national

Shacks in Soweto, South Africa
©Steven Allan/iStockphoto

policies on improving slum conditions with full or limited involvement of local authorities and communities, or they can be the result of local initiatives, where local authorities take centre stage in slum upgrading actions. Effective central government responses to slums have taken place in Cuba, Egypt, Jordan, Morocco, and Tunisia, while successful actions resulting from local government initiatives have taken place in several cities in Brazil, Colombia and Mexico.

It is increasingly apparent, however, that coordinated actions of central and local governments are taking place as a result of new forms of national governance based on principles of subsidiarity, institutional coordination and democratic participation. South Africa's Slum Act, for example, has created a new social institutional compact as part of the national policy to eliminate slums. The compact involves different levels of governments and actors: wards, councils and communities propose and approve projects; municipalities define action plans, coordinate implementation and supervise; and provincial authorities set up selection criteria and apply for funding to the central authorities, who allocate resources.

A coordinated approach in the development and implementation of policies among different levels of government is taking place in decentralized governments such as Brazil, India and Mexico, and also in centralized governments, such as Egypt, where the national slum upgrading programme is evolving towards more participatory processes in terms of decision-making and resource allocation. Governors in this country are now establishing management boards for slum areas with representation of civil society and the private sector.

Central and local authorities in some countries are adopting a coordinated approach, as in Nepal, Namibia and Burkina Faso, which are all witnessing rapid political changes. Nepal, for instance, has developed a slum upgrading strategy and investment plan with support from the Cities Alliance that aims to upgrade 100 slums between 2007 and 2010. This initiative has yet to prove that it can scale up to the appropriate level, but innovative governance arrangements have created an *ad hoc* committee for slums with a clear distribution of responsibilities, whereby central authorities formulate policies, rules and regulations, allocate resources, facilitate stakeholder participation, and monitor implementation. Local authorities, in turn, prepare programmes and projects, generate some resources and implement selected projects.

Indirect interventions that have been shown to reduce slum growth include those that address the larger issue of economic growth and development, with or without an explicit reference to slums. Malawi's growth and development strategy, for instance, includes basic services as part of infrastructure development, and the provision of services to slum dwellers is part of the country's overall infrastructure development. In Sri Lanka, the national poverty reduction strategy includes slum interventions, and in Burkina Faso, slum improvement and prevention is an integral part of the country's strategic framework to fight urban poverty. In other cases, interventions are defined based on the spatial delimitation of a physical area such as a deprived neighbourhood or a zone in which inhabitants live in extreme poverty. In Mexico, the Habitat Programme intervenes in well-demarcated informal settlement areas through integrated actions that involve central, provincial and local authorities.

Another trend is also emerging, in which slum dwellers are active partners in slum upgrading projects, rather than just beneficiaries. Policies of entitlement are shifting to policies of co-operation, through which slum dwellers' financial viability, their ability to make down-payments or to actively

▲
Nairobi skyline
©**Kondrachov Vladimir/Shutterstock**

participate in programmes are factors in determining access to government subsidies for new housing or house improvements. This approach has been adopted in Cuba, for instance, where a new focus on community involvement in the planning, preservation and rehabilitation of homes has developed, and where reliance on volunteers and self-help housing rather than on state-led construction is becoming more common.

Policy reforms also take place on the institutional front – particularly changes in modes of operation and practices, and a deeper transformation of the patterns of behaviour within the public sector, including governments' relationships with private and social actors. These reforms comprise, for instance, strengthening municipal decentralization, reinforcing municipal structures, supporting better horizontal and vertical coordination of government agencies, and training civil servants.

The restructuring of institutions can be interpreted as a kind of policy reform, as the strengthening of existing government agencies or the creation of new ones may lead to more effective action on slum and urban poverty issues. Some countries have established ministries that deal mainly with cities; the establishment of the Human Settlements Ministry in Burkina Faso (established in 2005), the Ministry of Social Development and Human Settlements in Costa Rica (established in 2006), and the Ministry of Cities in Brazil (established in 2003) are positive developments, as they enable governments to allocate more resources and budgets to urban issues. In some countries, entire ministries have been established to deal with specific metropolitan areas, such as Kenya's Ministry of Nairobi Metropolitan Development (established in 2008), which focuses on developing the

capital city and its larger metropolitan area. The existence of a dedicated line ministry can help make urban issues more visible in the public eye and ensure their continuity in public policy discussions.

At the city level, the creation of municipal "slum units" shows the commitment of local authorities to devoting special attention to slum upgrading, as with the urban poor affairs office in Iloilo City in the Philippines, the post of settlement improvement officer in the Zambian city of Kaitwe, or the office of community architects in Cuba. When these local units work well, they not only cater to the housing and basic service needs of the urban poor, but they also eliminate duplication and overlapping functions with regard to poor neighborhoods' needs, facilitate policy coordination and enhance the effective monitoring of activities within sectors.

Other countries that perform well in managing slum growth are implementing long-term pro-poor policy reforms. These reforms include the development of legal and regulatory frameworks, as well as policy and institutional environments that foster economic activity and promote social development. In some countries, reforms are integrated into economic and social development plans aimed at further expanding the size of the economy, cutting poverty and creating jobs. In most countries, however, reforms are sectoral solutions in land, housing and finance that are enabling central government bodies, local authorities and urban poor communities to improve people's access to land, housing and basic services.

Some of the major pro-poor reforms are conventional interventions combined with innovative solutions in specific areas. This is the case, for instance, with Sri Lanka's Ceiling and Housing Property Housing Reform, instituted in 1972, complemented in the year 2000 by a financial reform to use municipal funds for slum upgrading in areas where residents do not have tenure rights. This combined solution aims both to prevent the growth of new slums and to upgrade existing ones. A number of other individual states and cities are also drawing on conventional interventions to create innovative solutions. India's use of transferable rights to free up land for low-income housing and slum dwellers, and Namibia's incremental approach to slum improvements as part of the National Development Plan, are good examples of this approach.

In other countries, innovative solutions include a set of pragmatic responses developed by the central government or local authorities. For instance, in the Philippines, a combination of land, finance and housing reforms are taking place simultaneously. More than 60 governmental proclamations have provided secure tenure to approximately 70,000 families as part of the efforts of the Housing and Urban Development Coordinated Council to provide full recognition and acceptance of rights-based secure tenure arrangements. Concurrently, a Community Mortgage Programme has been initiated with funds allocated from the national Social Housing Finance Corporation and local authorities. This innovative scheme is helping people who live in informal settlements to purchase the land they occupy under the concept of communal ownership. From 2004 to 2007, the financing scheme enabled more than 52,000 families to own the land they occupy in more than 450 slum settlements. A housing reform strategy is also tapping investments of the private sector to help in the production of social housing for underprivileged families by allocating a percentage of commercial housing projects to social housing. This balanced housing requirement and other innovative measures have yet to prove their impact on reducing slum growth. However, the reforms are empowering local governments and community associations to respond in a more coordinated manner to informal settlement growth in cities.

In some countries, reforms are more unusual solutions that respond to specific conditions. China's slum upgrading strategy, for example, combines land, administrative, fiscal, economic, and housing reforms as part of the country's efforts to change the agricultural status of "city villages" – or slum areas – to urban areas with a permanent status. This is the case, for instance, in the capital city of Beijing, where Tong County was reclassified and renamed as the Tongzhou District of Beijing, as part of a strategy to integrate the slum into the urban fabric. The process begins when the government changes land uses and acquires community land, then hands it over to developers, who upgrade the "city villages" according to approved urban plans. Social and economic reforms follow. Housing reforms and programmes expand the housing supply, particularly for low-income groups, and improve basic services and existing housing conditions. This process is not exempt from distortions that bring benefits to non-poor urban residents, but it also paves the way to improve the urban living environment in deprived areas.

4. Effective Policy Implementation

"Delivery" is the key word in effective policy implementation, but delivery presupposes the existence of a sound policy that is ready to put into practice. There are, however, serious and often neglected issues about how policies and programmes can be effectively implemented locally and what elements must be in place for implementation to occur. All too frequently, a plethora of initiatives from various agencies exist at the same time, operating in a disconnected manner rather than as a coordinated effort. There are also "too many players and at the same time none", as a senior official from Malawi noted when qualifying government interventions. In many cases, slum upgrading projects aim to improve only one aspect of a settlement, such as housing, without addressing other infrastructure and social needs, such as roads, schools and employment opportunities. A lack of holistic, integrated planning for these settlements ends up negating or duplicating different groups' efforts to improve urban living conditions. In other cases, institutional relations are dysfunctional or disabling rather than productive and empowering; national and local governments do not have clear financial, legal and technical criteria for intervention.

In addition to experiencing organizational hitches, line ministries and local authorities in many developing countries lack technical expertise; thus, "decisions are taken by persons with limited knowledge in the area", as stated by one of the respondents to the 52-city UN-HABITAT/Cities Alliance survey. Effective policy implementation should instead start at the top level of decision-making with processes that are transparent and involve key actors. In such a process, participants first define priorities and set up targets that are realistic, commonly agreed upon and presented as part of a common vision; follow with an implementation strategy that has clear financial and human resources allocated; and conclude by producing the intended results or outcomes. By implementing this three-step process at different levels, some countries and cities are reducing the prevalence of slums and preventing their formation in the first place. In general terms, these countries and cities are implementing policies in a transparent, pro-poor and well-coordinated manner. In Sri Lanka, for instance, the urban development authority at the central government level is in charge of slum upgrading planning and funding, and municipal councils carry out consultations. The projects are normally implemented by private or state-owned enterprises. Community-based organizations participate in city and community development councils, and slum dwellers' organizations receive community contracts from the municipality. This multi-level, multi-organizational and multi-professional response is bringing together not just slum upgrading and prevention agendas, but also the democratic decision-making structure of local and central authorities.

The ability to get things done involves, in most cases, a coordinated response from different levels of government with the active participation of other actors. This is not just a technical issue: effective policy implementation cannot be separated from matters such as transparency, public accountability and public participation.[8] Policy analyses of country performance on slum upgrading and prevention by UN-HABITAT and the Cities Alliance confirms that governments that are doing well in this area are developing coordinated responses in the formulation and implementation of policies with clear responsibilities for central and local governments. Central governments typically take the lead on slum- and poverty-related policies, as they have the power and authority to institute pro-poor reforms and the mandate and ability to allocate resources. This is the case in India, for example, where the central government has allocated a budget of US$12.5 billion to upgrade infrastructure and basic services in 63 cities over a period of seven years through the Jawaharlal Nehru National Urban Renewal Mission project launched in 2005. On the other hand, local authorities often coordinate operational actions to bring together different actors and, in some cases, they develop innovative approaches to slum upgrading and prevention that can be replicated nationwide. The city of Cape Town, for instance, recently developed a model that prioritizes slum upgrading interventions by weighting and ranking them as part of a city scoring system that is linked to budgetary allocations. This model could easily be replicated at a larger scale across the country.

Clearly, effective policy implementation requires well-coordinated responses by national and local authorities. Approaches may be top-down or bottom-up; what matters is the presence of a governance structure that focuses on the link between the two levels of government, where issues such as trust, freedom to act within agreed regulatory frameworks, and complementary efforts form the basis of a successful relationship. It is true that central and local governments can have different political orientations or strategic interests. However, established rules and regulations with clear institutional arrangements and budgets, and agreed-upon conflict resolution mechanisms, can ease tensions, disputes and controversies. In Mexico, for instance, after several discussions about roles, mandates and responsibilities, the central, provincial and local authorities agreed to jointly implement the Habitat Programme for poverty reduction, which has an important slum upgrading component. Various other countries as diverse as Burkina Faso, Namibia, the Philippines, Cambodia, and Brazil are building new houses, improving existing ones and upgrading informal settlements through well-coordinated relationships between central and local authorities.

"Getting things done" also requires the participation of other actors, particularly civil society and the private sector. The UN-HABITAT/Cities Alliance 52-city questionnaire and analysis shows that despite frequent policy discourses about public-private partnerships, the private sector is not a key player in slum upgrading and prevention. This does not mean, however, that the private sector is absent in the lower end of the housing market; on the contrary, informal landlordism is prevalent in many sub-Saharan African countries, including Kenya and Zambia. In some countries, the private sector's involvement actually hinders pro-poor policies, as a questionnaire response from Cambodia suggests: *"Policies are supposed to upgrade the living conditions of urban poor dwellers in Phnom Penh and other cities in Cambodia, but the real implementation provides little benefit to urban poor communities; sometimes it also threatens the poor, as the private sector has gained more and more influence in the government".*

Participation of community members has become an important way to ensure poor residents' needs and interests remain at the forefront of policy and programme implementation. In recent years, local governance and decentralization policies have opened more and more room for direct, broad-based participation of communities both in decision-making and implementation. Participation is described in many forms. One is simply the inclusion of urban residents on special policy committees, boards, or discussions of non-government representatives; residents may also have individual or collective interests as members of the private sector, civil society or associations of the urban poor more broadly. In other cases, however, participation occurs along much more structured lines. This is the case in South Africa, where, through the Integrated Development Planning process, municipalities prepare five-year strategic plans that are reviewed annually in consultation with communities and stakeholders. In the Philippines, too, ward forums and city development councils facilitate participatory processes involving local communities to ensure transparency and more equitable distribution of resources. In other cases, traditional forms of implementation are still effective mechanisms for slum upgrading; for example, the city of San José contributes building materials, while communities provide labour as part of a cooperative plan to improve housing conditions in poor neighborhoods.

In most countries of the developing world, transparency and participation in public decision-making is increasingly supported by the law of the land. Public inquires are often mandatory; they not only facilitate participation, but in some cases they also inform decision-makers who can ensure that all relevant issues are taken into account and weighed accordingly. For instance, the creation of the residential development committees in Zambia is a major institutional change to help people in slums to participate in development activities. Other governments are also making community and neighbourhood associations their official counterparts in local governance, with community groups playing an intermediary role between residents and local authorities. In Kenya, for example, the establishment of the Community Development Fund has ensured greater participation of communities in decisions regarding the use of public funds. However, in many countries, the concerns of poor communities remain sectoral and neighbourhood-oriented, focused on separate issues such as waste disposal, basic service delivery and secure tenure; this sectoral approach leaves decisions regarding the whole of the city to other actors who may or may not attend to the needs of marginalized groups.

Finally, effective policy implementation also means "getting the right people to do the job" –particularly engineers, surveyors, architects, planners, accountants, and project managers – by placing them properly and improving the service culture, capacity and work ethic. The organizational development plan of Cape Town includes such a strategy to facilitate the optimal provision, organization and deployment of its staff so as to enable the city to achieve its goal and objectives. The focus of the transformation plan is shifting the culture and managerial practices of the city to ensure delivery and high-quality performance.

5. Setting up Monitoring and Evaluation Mechanisms

Although the practice of monitoring and evaluating urban policies and programmes is not new, few countries and cities are systematically carrying it out, and when they do, the evaluation process rarely goes beyond the traditional *post facto* approach. Since monitoring and evaluation are not part of the policy cycle, it is difficult for many countries to identify what has worked in previous policies; it is also difficult to improve policy and programme implementation, to learn from the process and even to identify the impact of policies and programmes.

Some countries and cities, however, are showing strong commitment to monitoring and evaluation by creating or revising objectives, outputs and targets and by setting up benchmarks to help them increase the potential for effective policy formulation and implementation. It is therefore not surprising that countries and cities with monitoring and evaluation plans are more successful in the delivery of basic services and housing improvements than those without such plans. For instance, in 2002, the Government of Chile committed to reducing slum prevalence from 10.65 per cent to 3.6 per cent[9]; to do so, it initiated an aggressive programme called Chile Barrio, which has a strong monitoring and evaluation component. Similarly, the government of Thailand has been implementing programmes to construct homes for one million low-income households since 2003 in close collaboration with commercial and public banks that are carefully supervised by government agencies. Recently, Cambodia committed to upgrading 100 slum communities per year in the capital city of Phnom Penh over five years with full involvement of poor communities, both in implementing and monitoring activities. Other countries, such as Brazil and South Africa, are making concerted efforts to develop long-term action plans for slum upgrading and urban poverty reduction by setting clear targets and establishing monitoring systems and institutions to ensure policies are implemented.

Of course, there is no one perfect model for evaluation and monitoring; some countries adopt top-down approaches while others prefer bottom-up approaches. In countries such as Cuba,

▲
Beijing
©Madanmohan Rao

Cambodia, China, and Viet Nam, upward accountability for municipal implementation of housing and infrastructure is strict; in this monitoring system, the state remains the sole authority exercising performance monitoring,[10] whereas in countries such as Brazil, Colombia, Mexico, and South Africa, local governments are in charge of the monitoring process, often including stakeholders' views in the evaluation process. Bottom-up performance monitoring creates more chances to generate and encourage citizen participation in planning and decision-making, as has been the case in Sri Lanka and Indonesia, where client and resident satisfaction indicators are collected through household surveys.

An increasing number of cities are implementing local monitoring systems and indicators to collect information and to analyze trends. The city of Makati in the Philippines, for example, has set up a mechanism to review sectoral accomplishments *vis-à-vis* targets set on a monthly basis. Windhoek, the capital city of Namibia, has recently created a national community land information programme to collect data and information as part of the city's Informal Settlement Upgrading Programme. Quito, Ecuador, also has a system of citizen participation and performance evaluation standards to monitor improvements in slum areas and public spaces. And the South African city of Cape Town has recently established a monitoring system to scrutinize the implementation of the newly created informal settlement master plan.

Few local authorities use external advisory panels of academics or professionals in the private sector as peer review mechanisms that can help them track progress, distill and capture lessons, and signal when a change of direction is necessary. Peer review, however, could facilitate the use of evaluation findings to prepare a further critical stage of policy formulation.

6. Scaling Up Actions

Most developing countries lack the financial, human and institutional resources to support large-scale slum upgrading. The revenue base of most governments is weak, and actors that could provide funding, such as entities in the private sector, typically do not consider the implementation of slum upgrading policies and programmes a priority. Even when governments embark on scaling-up activities, they do not adequately assess the associated pitfalls and setbacks and often embark on these programmes without testing their viability, leading to a high risk of failure. Frequently, governments scale up some programmes too quickly, without having the necessary proof that the new approaches really lead to other positive social or economic benefits and results. In some cases, local or regional policies and actors prevent large-scale initiatives that have some potential of success simply because slum upgrading does not serve their interest. In many countries, slum dwellers are an important voting bloc for politicians, and upgrading activities could potentially disperse voters or make them less accessible.

Successful scale-up operations, therefore, require strong political will on the part of policymakers and other actors. They also require leadership and commitment and the capacity to bring together different people and institutions. For instance, Costa Rica committed to reducing slum prevalence by 50 per cent and is now organizing institutions and groups around the newly created Ministry of Social Development and Human Settlements to develop the necessary capacity to improve the well-being of slum residents.

Once governments have tried and tested pilot or preliminary interventions, they need to document, define and refine successful approaches. Countries that are doing well

▲
City street in Mombasa, Kenya.
©**UN-HABITAT**

are setting up monitoring and evaluation mechanisms than enable them to determine the effectiveness of their approach in any moment of the project cycle. Countries such as Brazil, Mexico, South Africa, and Thailand developed a vision to scale up from the beginning of the project, using a method that has been designed, pre-assessed and tested for large-scale coverage. Other countries decided to expand slum upgrading and prevention operations once they knew that initial results were successful. This is the case, for instance, with Indonesia's Kampong Improvement Programme, which began on a modest scale and grew from covering a few neighbourhoods or a single city to the whole nation.

For the scaling-up process to be sustainable, governments need to support institutional and system development to meet the new requirements of a larger volume of operations. They also need to develop partners' capacity to implement the programme, particularly that of local authorities, whose organizational responses must be strengthened to carry out the work.

Contrary to common perception, scaling up is not always about quantity of operations – quality matters, too. This could mean replicating approaches and methods, and expanding partners and funding sources. Some countries in Latin America and Asia, for instance, are experimenting with public-private partnerships to upgrade slums through land-sharing deals that benefit both slum dwellers and private developers. This often entails building consensus among all those who participate in the programme. Consensus-building becomes critical in countries where interests of various stakeholders are conflicting. South Africa's relative success in managing slum growth is the result of the active participation of various layers of government in addressing slum upgrading at a large scale and preventing slum growth in some cities. For example, in 2003, the Gauteng Department of Housing formed a provincial housing agency, Xhasa ATC, that is closely working with local authorities and the National Department of Housing. Scaling up also entails involving community organizations that can serve as platforms for decision-making

and action at the local level. In Malawi, the Ndirande squatter upgrade that took place in the 1990s and led to the formation of the Community Development Committees has now been replicated in all low- income areas in virtually all cities in the country. In Nepal, the Slum and Community Empowerment and Upgrading Programme that was initiated in Kathmandu has now expanded to other municipalities with the strong involvement of slum communities.

In most cases, success in scaling up is driven by a huge mobilization of domestic resources. National governments and local authorities used multiple funding sources to reach a large-scale programme. The South African Breaking New Ground Initiative is bringing together public, private and social financial efforts to support slum upgrading programmes with significant government subsidies for the very poor. The City of Makati in Metro Manila is implementing economic and social development strategies that are private sector-led with innovative means of delivering basic service to the economically disadvantaged sector of the society. Slum communities are contributing to upgrading through their own savings and by leveraging various sources of local funding; the city of Johannesburg, for instance, has identified priority poor settlements, where neighbourhood upgrading banks are collecting community funds that are combined with other government sources. Donor financing has also played an important role in supporting slum upgrading over the last few decades through investments and loans, but perhaps more importantly, by supporting technological and financial innovation and the implementation of strategic pilot projects. In Costa Rica and Cuba, for instance, external financial support is used to develop the local building materials industry.

Finally, success in scaling up slum upgrading interventions requires multifaceted responses merging different products and tools and targeting different social groups. In Sri Lanka, for instance, government interventions include self-help construction programmes, financial mechanisms to enable slum dwellers to access domestic private capital, social housing policies, and pro-poor budgetary allocations.

NOTES

1 Moreno, 2002b.
2 A quote from the UN-HABITAT/Cities Alliance questionnaire collected in Egypt: *"The results so far are that many slum areas have improved physically but did not take out the stigma of being informal areas and are usually still expanding and increasing in densification. An acceptance of different nature/standard of such areas compared to the formal city is needed on the part of government officials, and at the same time an identity of the locality has to be created/promoted with the local communities"*.
3 Questionnaire responses to the UN-HABITAT/Cities Alliance Survey.
4 Garau, 2008.
5 Findings of this analysis were described in UN-HABITAT's *State of the World's Cities 2006/7*.

6 The Parliamentarian Act on Ceiling and Housing (1970s) followed by the creation of the National Housing Development Authority that promoted the implementation of mass housing programmes such as the One Hundred Thousand Housing Programme and the One Million Housing Programme. UN-HABITAT, 2006b.
7 All slum data in this chapter is based on estimates and projections by UN-HABITAT'S Global Urban Observatory.
8 Hunter & Marks, 2008.
9 Gobierno de Chile, 2004.
10 Bazoglu, 2007.

4.4
Addressing Rural–Urban Disparities for Harmonious Regional Development

At the beginning of the 20th century, as European cities began to spread with the rise of industrialization, British author and intellectual H.G. Wells made a prescient prediction: that soon, modern urbanites would see little distinction between the city and the countryside. "The old antithesis will cease, the boundary lines will altogether disappear," he wrote. "It will become merely a question of more or less populous".[1]

Today, the sprawling urban landscapes of the developed world seem to have confirmed Wells's prediction. Talk of edge cities, post-suburban territories and regional development takes for granted the disappearance of clear rural and urban boundaries in countries whose populations became primarily urban more than 50 years ago.

In developing countries, too, distinctions between rural and urban are becoming blurred as urbanization spreads.

▲
Cairo
©**Madanmohan Rao**

Recognition of rural-urban systems and the interdependencies of populations living and working in both areas have created new prospects for poverty alleviation in the rapidly changing economic, technological and informational environments of many regions in the developing world.[2] Policies and development initiatives, however, largely remain tied to traditional concepts of growth poles and simple urban diffusion models that assume separate rural-agricultural and urban-industrial objectives. Development theorists have viewed rural-urban interactions alternately as parasitic and exploitative or supportive, but planning efforts have remained separate, disconnected from the real networks and flows of people, goods and ideas throughout what can be described as a porous rural-urban *interface*.

Evidence about the flaws of assumptions and planning efforts that adhere to an urban-rural dichotomy is giving rise to a new view that focuses on promoting positive two-way interactions and reciprocal relations between rural and urban areas, focusing on developing networks to improve quality of life and create harmonious regions. Regional growth and development is changing the way people relate to their environments today; addressing disparities and promoting harmonious development requires that policy-making catch up to the reality of the connected and interdependent lives led by rural and urban dwellers around the world.

From rural and urban to "ruralopolis" and "*desakota*": The changing rural-urban interface

The geography of rural and urban space is changing, creating ambiguous landscapes in different regions of the developing world, from suburban and peri-urban environments around fast-growing large cities on one extreme to "ruralopolises" on the other: rural economic and social systems fused with metropolitan spatial arrangements.[3] Research in East and Southeast Asia points to the emergence of high-density rural areas dubbed "*desakotas*" ("city villages"),[4] formed as a result of the expansion and influence of metropolitan economies. These terms refer to a new process of *region-based* – as opposed to city-based – urbanization and can be understood in relation to changing international divisions of labour, international networks and regional spill-over from one mega-urban region to another. The *desakota* constitutes a spatial by-product of high-tech production spilling out of heavily congested cities – particularly Jakarta, Manila and Bangkok – into nearby cheaper but still easily accessible rural areas. In physical terms, the landscape still appears to be predominantly rural with vast areas devoted to cultivation, while a large proportion of household income is derived from non-agricultural activities.

Globalization and its associated forces also seem to be changing the structure of major Latin American cities such as Buenos Aires, Lima, São Paulo, and Mexico City to a polycentric form, where much of the growth is not necessarily within the urban perimeter, but in hot-spots – smaller towns and secondary cities – within the wider metropolitan regions.[5] In this context, "urban archipelagos" are emerging with diffuse boundaries between the urban and the rural.[6]

From an ecological perspective, the changing rural-urban interface can be characterized as a heterogeneous mosaic of "natural," "productive" or "agro-ecosystems" and "urban" ecosystems, affected by material and energy flows demanded by urban and rural systems. This interface is not only distinctive because of its ecological features but also because of its socio-economic heterogeneity and fragmented institutional context. In socio-economic terms, the composition of the rural-urban interface is diverse and subject to rapid changes over time. Small farmers, step-wise migrants, informal settlers, industrial entrepreneurs and urban middle-class commuters may all coexist in the same territory but with different and often competing interests, practices and perceptions. The interface is also characterised by a lack of institutions capable of addressing the links between rural and urban activities.

The box below describes the main characteristics that differentiate poverty in rural and urban areas, and also some of the many ways in which the rural and the urban rely on each other. The table suggests that rural-urban interdependencies among the poor are likely to intensify in the "urban transition".

Urban plus Rural as opposed to Urban versus Rural

A number of trends regarding rural-urban linkages have been observed in the last decade.

1. Urban agriculture is increasingly practised by the poor to supplement declining incomes and to mitigate food and income insecurities.

2. Retrenchment and deepening of urban poverty occasioned by structural adjustment has triggered a process of "return migration", with households returning to their rural homes in order to survive.

3. Urban-to-rural household remittances are declining, while spiralling transport costs reduce the ability of poorer urban households to import food from their rural relatives.

4. In a number of countries, large numbers of temporary agricultural workers employed by commercial farms, especially during the harvest season, are urban-based, giving rise to a diversification of income sources among poor urban households. This, together with urban agriculture, is putting to test traditional definitions of "urban" and "rural", as both their physical and occupational boundaries are becoming increasingly blurred.

5. Technological advances are fuelling the "metropolitanization" of the world economy, further strengthening and creating linkages between rural and urban areas through a web of horizontal and vertical networks among settlements, which are further creating a system of "city regions" in various parts of the world.

Poverty in the rural-urban interface: Is the dichotomy obsolete?

The dynamics of the rural-urban interface have yet to be fully recognized by policymakers and development agencies, which typically refer to rural and urban experiences of poverty as distinct from each other. Addressing disparities across the rural-urban interface and understanding how they influence and interact with each other is critical, but how to do so remains a challenge. On the one hand, discussing and treating rural and urban poverty separately fails to understand the extent to which the livelihoods and assets of many poor (and, indeed, non-poor) draw on resources and opportunities in both rural and urban areas.[7] On the other hand, an understanding of poverty that no longer distinguishes between "rural" and "urban" runs the risk of ignoring the differences between the contexts, which above all imply differences in the level of income needed to avoid poverty, but also differences in "the possibilities for household food production, the price and availability of food and basic services, the cost of housing, the nature of environmental hazards and the influence of government on access to employment, housing and basic services".[8] The risk of facing deprivations and the nature of those deprivations depend in large part on where people live and work.[9]

The interdependencies of populations in rural and urban areas cannot be understood simply in terms of income-level measurements of poverty.[10] First, conventional methods of poverty measurement link income to the cost of food but fail to establish the income needed for non-food items, such as health care, education, housing, water provision, and sanitation. Second, such methods say little about how the poor manage by deploying multi-spatial household strategies and diversified livelihoods and by drawing on rural-urban linkages and flows. Socio-economic relations differ not only in terms of income inequality but also inequality in access to land, credit, information and other resources, and these differences encompass a host of socially created categories, including ethnicity, class and gender.[11] The simple rural-urban dichotomy belies a much more complex reality for people living in the ambiguous environments in between.

A closer look at flows of people and resources across the rural-urban interface reveals the existence of a system in that defies rural and urban distinctions, suggesting a need for better, more regionally focused ways of conceptualizing how populations get their own needs met and create opportunities for improving their lives.

Rural-urban flows

Complex interactions are influencing social and environmental change at the rural-urban interface, including flows of people, money, information, natural resources, and wastes.[12] These flows can start in either rural or urban areas, and, in fact, it is often difficult to identify their source, as processes driven by factors and decisions at different levels might be cumulative and mutually reinforcing, converging on a single process. Migration from rural to peri-urban areas, for example, might be promoted by deteriorating physical environments and restrictive political conditions for agricultural practice. This might be seen as a "rural problem", but decreasing opportunities in rural areas can result from commercialization of crop production driven by city-based demand. In most cases, environmental and social changes in the rural-urban interface are not simply the result of either the movement of rural households into ecologically vulnerable areas or a unidirectional spread of urbanisation into agricultural land.

▲
Open-air vegetable market in Kabul.
©**Rasna Warah**

Flows of people

Rural-urban migration has been the central focus of much of the body of research on rural-urban linkages and interactions. However, recent studies have identified a broad range of people's movements between rural and urban areas, revealing a significant diversity of situations with regard to migration patterns and their justification, including the following.

- *Rural-rural migration:* A synthesis study commissioned by the UK Department for International Development (DFID) Natural Resources System Programme revealed that people facing diminishing access to and control over land and other natural resources do not always step directly from rural- to urban-based livelihoods but rather to other natural-based production systems located in other rural and nearby peri-urban areas.[13]

- *Urban-rural migration:* Several recent studies show that "despite widely held beliefs that flows are always rural-to-urban, migration from the urban to the rural areas is increasing. This type of movement is often associated with economic decline and increasing poverty in urban areas. In sub-Saharan Africa, significant numbers of retrenched urban workers are thought to return to rural 'home' areas, where the cost of living is lower".[14]

- *Circular migration:* Studies of temporary and circular migration in Asia reveal that these patterns are more common and greater in impact than permanent rural-urban migration. A study in Roi-et Province, Thailand, revealed that "much of the interaction of rural households with cities is temporary, comprising often a month or two and not simply on an agricultural slack season basis".[15]

- *Step-wise migration:* In India, poor migrants often settle in rural and peri-urban areas close to the city and commute on a daily basis, as they cannot afford to live in the city. Sharing dwellings and other facilities with other migrants helps them to reduce their costs. They even distribute unemployment within the group, "absorbing the risk of uncertainty".[16]

- *Straddling* is a commonplace practice among Kenyan migrants: keeping one foot in the town and the other in the countryside. In Durham, South Africa, maintaining both an urban and a rural base provides not only a safety net for poor urban dwellers in times of economic hardship but also in times of political violence.[17]

- *Commuting* from rural to peri-urban and urban areas is another commonplace practice. In some respects, commuters take the "best of both worlds", benefiting from the service, marketing and job opportunities offered by urban areas while retaining land and the possibility of growing their own food, and, unlike households with migrants, avoiding labour shortages during the farming seasons. Of course, the possibility of commuting is highly dependent on affordable and regular transport connections.[18]

Clearly, households actively search for ways to diversify their livelihoods and adapt dynamically to different threats and opportunities. Reciprocal links between rural and urban households often persist after migration, such as when urban households take advantage of social connections to get the food they need from rural relatives. A study in Windhoek, Namibia, revealed that, over a one-year period, two-thirds of all households surveyed in the city regularly received food from rural areas, mainly from relatives. The most vulnerable and marginal households in urban areas were typically those with weaker or no links to their relatives in rural areas.[19]

Reciprocal rural-urban links are also made clear in studies that illustrate how rural workers diversify their sources of income to meet needs of both rural and urban populations. Studies have found that the proportion of rural households' income earned from non-farm activities can be as high as 80 to 90 per cent in Southern Africa and 30 to 50 per cent in the rest of sub-Saharan Africa.[20] In Southern Asia and Latin America, this proportion represents around 60 and 40 per cent, respectively, of the total income of rural households.[21] In Nigeria, the growth of urban-type income-generating activities in rural areas is associated not only with increasing suburbanization and industrial activities, but also with people bringing back ideas from cities, as an offshoot of rural-urban migration.[22] Rural household demand for non-agricultural commodities may, in fact, be the single most important factor in the growth of rural towns.[23]

Flows of money

The impact of monetary flows on poverty alleviation differs between rural and urban areas because urban households typically rely more on a cash economy than rural ones. However, considering the significance of remittances from urban migrants for rural household budgets, the poor in rural areas may be negatively affected by unemployment, income reduction or high expenses faced by their urban counterparts. The bulk of migrant remittances appear to be dedicated to supplementing rural households' expenditures on food, consumer goods, health and education,[24] but there is also evidence of the role remittances can play in enhancing investments in local productive activities. In Viet Nam's Red River Delta, for example, "seasonal migration to work in the urban construction sector is an essential source of cash, which in turn is invested in the intensification of agricultural production in migrants' home villages".[25]

Flows of information

Along with media and communication technologies, informal and interpersonal networks act as vehicles of rural-urban communication and exchange, and as conduits for new ideas. Interpersonal networks, especially, constitute a powerful vehicle by which rural and urban dwellers exchange experiences, information and ideas. Such networks might be confined to close webs of family members and friends – often enhanced through migration and commuting – or open to wider groups. In some cases, distant sources of information about livelihood opportunities might be more powerful than local and national sources. A study of rural-urban linkages among a number of villages in Indonesia revealed that recruitment of migrant labourers for work in Malaysia was channelled through migrant networks in Malaysia to specific villages and not from urban centres in Indonesia.[26]

Flows of natural resources, waste and pollution

The rural-urban interface can be defined as a highly dynamic and complex system of land use, constituted by a singular mosaic of ecosystems. The breaking down of supportive reciprocal relations between rural and urban areas tends to aggravate unsustainable patterns of natural resources use and the transference of environmental problems, as when cities draw resources from regions beyond their physical and jurisdictional limits and transfer pollution and wastes to their

hinterlands and beyond. The wealthier the city, the larger the area from which it draws environmental resources – the larger its "ecological footprint" becomes.[27] The expansion of the ecological footprint of a city has important implications for the rural-urban interface, both in terms of increasing pressures on its carrying capacity and in terms of missing opportunities, as when food is imported from distant regions rather than supplied from the city's hinterland.

Land in the rural-urban interface is often under intensive pressure, owing to processes of use conversion and commercialization. These are not only the result of urban sprawl, but also of the loss of farming land in rural areas because of "de-agrarianisation" or even to the abandonment of customary practices of land occupation, as illustrated by several studies in East and West Africa.[28] Other factors include immigration of the poor from rural areas; the urban poor moving towards the outskirts where rents and land prices are lower; the better-off building new houses in less-congested areas; loss of agricultural land because of expansion of the city

▲
Garbage dump in South America
©**Michael Zysman/iStockphoto**

(usually along major transport routes); speculation and land use changes prompted by industrial location policies or by the development of special and large-scale infrastructures. Land use changes might also respond to the relatively "spontaneous" strategies of the poor (both from rural and urban areas) to access land in proximity to diversified livelihood opportunities, to market forces, or to public policies aimed at restraining urban sprawl, dispersing industrial development, or locating special physical infrastructure with high potential environmental impacts away from densely populated areas.[29]

Because of the availability of open space and accessibility from urban areas, the rural-urban interface can become the "backyard" for urban waste disposal, often surpassing the absorptive capacity of receiving areas and imposing severe impacts on the health of ecosystems and human populations. Solid and liquid waste disposal in the rural-urban interface requires specific management approaches, given the combination of different pollutants from multiple sources – domestic, industrial and agricultural. In spite of the fact that many waste treatment facilities are located in the rural-urban interface, capital resources invested in environmental quality monitoring and management facilities are often fewer than in core urban areas.

Planned interventions: Towards harmonious regional development

Recognizing the flows of people, resources and wastes throughout rural-urban systems, and the disparities experienced by people in both rural and urban communities, creates opportunities for planned interventions and policy-making that both enhance the use and state of natural resources and improve the livelihoods and living conditions of poor women, men and children. Interventions are typically associated with one of three main planning perspectives: *rural*, which tends to focus on localised and discrete actions; *urban*, which seeks the transformation of planning systems and their allied institutions; and *regional*, which attempts to act upon rural-urban pressures and flows. The rural and urban perspectives remain most common, but the regional perspective offers the greatest opportunities for understanding the dynamic needs of populations and creating linkages for harmonious development.

The rural perspective: Localized and discrete actions

Initiatives based on a rural perspective aim to improve living conditions and the social infrastructure necessary to increase rural production and to improve the living conditions of the poor through localized actions. The geographical focus here is either on rural areas or peri-urban villages, which often retain land-based livelihoods and fall under the jurisdiction of rural authorities while being increasingly influenced by urban areas, regardless of their proximity. A common shortcoming of this perspective is that it tends to focus on only the immediate and medium-term concerns of specific localities and communities, often neglecting the urban and regional dimension and the long-term perspective required for the sustainable management of resources and services in the rural-urban interface.

The urban perspective: Transformation of planning systems

A number of initiatives at the city level seek to address two sets of issues: the management of the relationship between urban systems and their hinterlands, and the quality of life of urban and peri-urban dwellers.[30] A general evaluation of this approach suggests that projects tend to focus initially on immediate issues of concern traditionally associated with basic infrastructure and sanitary engineering projects, such as piped water supply and sanitation. It takes a long time to build consensus and to move away from the direct interests or concerns of participating stakeholders to more strategic long-term issues affecting the development process as a whole. The main constraint of many initiatives under this perspective is that all too often they operate outside mainstream government decision-making, so results remain marginal to the development process.

The regional perspective: Actions upon rural-urban pressures and flows

The third intervention model characterises programmes that purposely focus on the development of reciprocal links between rural and urban areas. This model is based on a regional planning perspective that acknowledges that current urbanization trends are leading to, and being shaped by, rural-urban linkages. According to the regional perspective, a country's settlement pattern is the source of its planning problems, a reflection of deeper socio-economic difficulties and inequalities, which requires tackling critical socio-economic and political issues rather than localized urban or rural solutions. Interventions that act upon rural-urban pressures and flows think of the territory as a networked model, in which planning and policy initiatives are developed for multi-sectoral, interrelated and complementary activities. They emphasize connectivity of the system and development of infrastructure in both rural and urban areas and between minor centres, rather than concentrating just on linkages with major cities.

The regional perspective emphasizes acting upon the vacuum generated by urban and rural institutions and by sectoral policies that reinforce the rural-urban divide. The approach is strategic rather than comprehensive in that it focuses on key entry points with the potential to reinforce rural-urban links: mobility; agricultural and non-agricultural production; trade and commodities; and natural resources and wastes.

Mobility

Conventional planned interventions on people's mobility and poverty reduction have tended to address rural-urban migration only as a unidirectional flow, mostly perceived as negative. Countries have developed a wide repertoire of policies to curb rural-urban migration, including: outright bans on urban migration in South Africa and strict migration controls in China; forcible return to rural areas in Mozambique; promotion of scattered urbanization through resettlement policies in Ethiopia and the Brazilian Amazon region; creation of new capitals or growth poles in Nigeria, Tanzania and Brazil; and territorial decentralization through the promotion of small and medium-sized towns as in Pakistan and Egypt.[31] In contrast, current research on people's mobility between rural and urban areas suggests that rather than aiming to organize such flows to redress rural-urban demographic and economic imbalances, policymakers need to understand them in their full complexity.

Agricultural and non-agricultural production

Enhancing production and trade between rural and urban areas is a popular option among those concerned with rural-urban linkages to ease disparities. Many interventions have focused on promoting increased trade of tools needed for agriculture production and better flow of consumer goods demanded by rural households.[32] Likewise, linking rural food production and urban consumers can help ensure food security, as can assisting people in the peri-urban context to find sustainable livelihoods.[33] In the same way in which agriculture is being increasingly promoted in urban areas, rural non-agricultural industrialization is starting to be promoted in a number of countries, as well. Examples include the strategy adopted for the promotion of Town and Village Enterprises (TVEs) in China. TVEs expanded rapidly in China in the post-reform period. As a result of the promotion of TVEs between 1978 and 2000, the number of workers in the rural non-farm sector grew by 27 per cent per year, while the rural labour force recorded an annual increase of 2.6 per cent.[34]

Trade and commodities

In economic terms, planned interventions aimed at promoting reciprocal rural-urban linkages tend to distinguish among consumption linkages (demand for final products), production linkages ("backward" or "forward" supply of inputs among producers), and financial linkages (e.g., rents extracted by urban landlords, remittances by migrants, rural savings channelled through urban institutions).[35] Interventions are increasingly emphasising the development of both formal and informal cooperative and contractual systems aimed at improving rural producers' access to urban markets. They aid production and consumption linkages through programmes that support rural agro-industry and income-generating activities, such as the Cooperative Programme for the Development of Rural Agro Industry (PRODAR). PRODAR links a variety of institutions concerned with promoting the potential of rural agro industry in Latin America and the Caribbean, providing support from production to broker.[36] In Ethiopia, "milk groups" – established with the help of the government and the Finnish International Development Association – provide an alternative market and connect smallholders to the formal milk market.[37]

Natural resources and wastes

From an environmental perspective, the rural-urban interface confronts two sets of challenges, and the articulation between them is crucial to the design of strategic interventions that benefit the poor and enhance the reciprocal sustainable development of both rural and urban areas.

The first group of challenges relates to the environmental conditions of the rural-urban interface as a support system for low-income people in developing countries, who face health and life risks and physical hazards related to the occupation of inappropriate sites, lack of access to basic water and sanitation, and poor housing conditions. They also face environmental changes that impact their livelihood strategies, decreasing or increasing their access to different types of capital assets. The second group of challenges is linked to the sustainability of regional patterns of renewable and non-renewable resource extraction and to minimizing transfer of environmental costs from rural and urban systems to the interface between both. The rural-urban interface is subject to many competing interests, often without adequate institutions to strike balances that ameliorate poverty, protect the environment, maximize the productivity of human and natural resources, or draw synergy from urban and rural relationships. Both sets of challenges are interconnected, and the principles and goals laid out in the UNCED Agenda 21 (1992) and the Habitat Agenda (1996) stress the need to address them as such. Environmental degradation in the rural-urban interface cannot be considered in isolation from the processes taking place in a wider region. Environmental problems affecting the quality of life of the poorest communities demand urgent attention, but these issues cannot be disassociated from the long-term problems affecting the sustainability of the natural resource base. This ultimately demands broadening the focus of planned interventions beyond localized environmental problems to a consideration of the sustainability of the urban bioregion.

More sustainable forms of urbanization therefore require a more coherent approach to the rural-urban interface. Successful approaches tend to work through the concept of the urban region, where the comparative advantages of cities and their adjacent peri-urban and rural jurisdictions are combined to promote a more balanced use of natural resources such as land, water and energy, and to support mutually reinforcing social and economic development initiatives. Many approaches are emerging that seek to create sustainable linkages between rural and urban areas.[38] One example is Nakuru, a rapidly growing city in Kenya's Rift Valley, where proposals for future growth through a Localizing Agenda 21 exercise have been closely tied to resources such as water and a national park in the city's hinterland. This initiative combines the use of Strategic Structure Plans with Urban Pacts, creating a process of vision, action and communication.[39]

A new kind of policy for harmonious regional development

There is now a considerable and expanding body of evidence supporting the notion that rural-urban interactions can result in harmonious regional development outcomes. However, unless carefully managed, rural-urban linkages can also increase the vulnerability of the urban and rural poor. The increasing interdependency of urban and rural systems is not only spawning new forms of urbanization but also new rural-urban coping strategies to avoid poverty and to reduce poor communities' vulnerability to socio-economic, environmental and political shocks and stress.[40] Rural-urban interactions therefore demand serious consideration both in terms of the likely impacts of existing policies focused on either urban or rural areas and in terms of future planned interventions that take the dynamics of these interactions into account, seeking to adapt to shifting economic, political, environmental and social conditions and transcending conventional geographic categorizations.

TABLE 4.4.1: **POVERTY AND THE RURAL-URBAN CONTINUUM**

RURAL >>	RURAL-URBAN INTERDEPENDENCIES	<< URBAN
Livelihoods drawn from crop cultivation, livestock, forestry or fishing (i.e. key for livelihood is access to natural capital)	<< **Funding flows** (remittances) from urban migrants for rural development.	**Livelihoods** drawn from labour markets within non-agricultural production or making/selling goods or services
Access to land for housing and building materials not generally a problem	>> **Rural-urban food transfers**, rural support in bringing up urban dwellers' children	**Access to land for housing** very difficult; housing and land markets highly commercialized
More distant from government as regulator and provider of services	<< **Accommodation** and support for family or fellow villagers who come to urban areas to study or seek employment	**More vulnerable to 'bad' governance**
Access to infrastructure and services limited (largely because of distance, low density and limited capacity to pay?)	>> **Cheaper accommodation** for low-income urban workers in nearby rural areas	**Access to infrastructure and services** difficult for low-income groups because of high prices, illegal nature of their homes (for many) and poor governance
Fewer opportunities for earning cash; more for self-provisioning. Greater reliance on favourable weather conditions.	<< **Access to** different branches of **government and public services**	**Greater reliance on cash** for access to food, water, sanitation, employment, garbage disposal, etc.
Access to natural capital as the key asset and basis for livelihood	>> **Access to customary** institutions	**Greater reliance on house as an economic resource** (space for production, access to income-earning opportunities; asset and income-earner for owners – including de facto owners)
	<< Stimulus for more **diversified livelihood** options	
	>> **Rural markets** for urban dwellers who derive an income from selling goods and services	
	<< **Information** about urban opportunities and alternative/ additional income sources to potential migrants and commuters.	
	>> **Seasonal employment** for urban dwellers in agriculture or rural development projects or on collecting or purchasing resources from nearby rural areas	
	>> Support to protect the assets of urban dwellers retaining **land and livestock** in rural areas	
	<< **Urban refuge** for some of the poorest rural dwellers whose livelihoods were destroyed by development projects, wars, oppression or disasters	
	>> **Rural refuge** for poor urban dwellers in times of economic and political hardship	
Urban characteristics in rural locations, including: prosperous tourist areas, mining areas, areas with high value crops and many local multiplier links, rural areas with diverse non-agricultural production and strong links to cities.	Many of these interdependencies tend to intensify in emerging landscapes such as: • Peri-urban (PU) areas • Clusters and networks of villages and small and medium size towns and cities • Ruralopolises • Extended metropolitan regions	Rural characteristics in urban locations (urban agriculture, 'village' enclaves, access to land for housing through non-monetary traditional forms, etc.)

Source: Analysis based on Satterthwaite, 2000.

Achieving Spatially Balanced Human Settlements in Cuba

In the 1950s, Cuba's capital city, Havana, was home to 21 per cent of the population as a whole and 40 per cent of the country's urban population. It also accounted for 70 per cent of the country's industrial activity not related to sugar, 90 per cent of imports, 55 per cent of the construction industry, 61 per cent of hospital beds, 63 per cent of doctors, 80 per cent of university graduates and most of the country's tourism capacity. The concentration of productive activities and services in Havana encouraged migration to the capital, which absorbed more than half of all rural-urban migrants in the country.

Havana's advanced development stood in stark contrast to conditions in the rest of the country. While the western areas around Havana were densely settled and developed with improved infrastructure and communications systems, Cuba's eastern areas were sparsely populated and dedicated to agricultural activities, and people in its mountain communities lived at subsistence levels. The disparities among Cuba's residents prompted the government to institute a new political and administrative structure in 1976 that prioritized decentralization and the development of provincial centres. Since then, Havana's share of employment in the country's industrial and service sectors has diminished as provincial capitals and smaller urban and rural settlements have gained the capacity to absorb the country's growth and provide attractive opportunities for residents. While Havana maintains its political and administrative primacy, the city now plays a less dominant role as a population centre and the migratory pressure on it is negligible.

Owing to the Cuban government's social policies, human settlements in the country have developed over time into a spatially balanced network: 593 urban settlements are home to more than 8.5 million (76 per cent) of Cuba's inhabitants; another 2.7 million people live in some 6,500 rural settlements, and only 835,000 (7 per cent) live outside such structures. Twelve provincial capitals are home to a significant proportion of industrial enterprises and account for a high percentage of employment in the administrative and service sectors. These cities are able to provide top-quality services and act as development centres for their respective regions. Another 142 administrative centres of various sizes cover a territory of about 670 square kilometres and act as intermediate service centres. Smaller urban and rural settlements that have no political or administrative functions have acquired the necessary infrastructure to provide basic ser-

Havana, Cuba
© **Steven Miric/iStockphoto**

vices in the fields of education, health, culture, and sport, and are reasonably well connected to higher-level centres.

Cuba's network of cities, towns, villages, and hamlets of various sizes cover most of the country, enabling significant integration of urban and rural settlements. The diversification of livelihoods is an indicator of the parity urban and rural settlements have reached, and the interdependence of their residents: 46 per cent of agricultural workers live in urban settlements, while 30 per cent of workers based in rural settlements or scattered throughout the countryside are engaged in non-agricultural activities. The country's diverse network of settlements has also enabled the efficient distribution of facilities for the provision of social services, leading to a significant improvement in the quality of life and higher and more consistent levels of health, education, and access to drinking water and sanitation around the country.

Key to Cuba's development of a spatially balanced and harmonious network of human settlements has been the decentralization of economic leadership and the provision of essential infrastructure and services to both provincial centres and rural agricultural communities. At the same time that

the government invested in industrial development programmes and high levels of services in major administrative centres, it also developed the agricultural sector and encouraged the rural population to form compact settlements, so that even the smallest communities could be provided with infrastructure for electricity, drinking water, connecting roads, and basic facilities for education, health, culture, and sport.

As is the case with all practical systems, the Cuban approach has its limitations and drawbacks. Development levels in the eastern provinces are still lower those in the west, indicating a need for more emphasis on local economic development in eastern cities and towns, and more decentralized planning and urban management that encourages sustainable, strategic and participatory approaches. Overall, Cuba's experience shows that, to achieve a more balanced development of human settlements, political will to move the process forward is of primary importance. It is also essential to implement policies with an emphasis on sustainable development, taking into account the economic, social and environmental factors in different areas, the interrelationships between them, and the wants and needs of citizens.

Source: National Statistics Office, Cuba 2005a and 2008b; CIEM 1996; INIE National Economic Research Institute, Cuba, 2005, National Housing Institute, Cuba, 2001.

The European Spatial Development Perspective

European Structural Funds have been instrumental in helping European Union (EU) countries meet their economic and physical development targets, but disparities in development and quality of life persist in the region. Gross domestic product (GDP) per capita of several of the emerging-market countries that have joined the EU since 2004 – including Poland, Latvia, Bulgaria, and Romania – remains less than half the European average. Structural Funds aim to reduce such regional imbalances and promote social and territorial cohesion.

One of the EU's Structural Funds, the European Regional Development Fund (ERDF), is supporting the development of spatial planning and policy-making focused on fostering a harmonious polycentric urban system, enhanced accessibility to infrastructure and knowledge, a new relationship between urban and rural areas, sustainable development, conservation of the environment, and the protection of cultural heritage around the continent. Realizing this new approach to planning and development is the objective of the European Spatial Development Perspective (ESDP), a voluntary, pro-active shared scheme that aims to reframe planning and policy-making ideas throughout Europe. It addresses the functional integration of cities, and cities, regions and rural areas to increase competitiveness and socio-economic cohesion. Through ESDP, the EU aims to promote local, regional and interregional networking, cooperation and exchange of experiences that can help reduce inequality within European regions and cities – an issue of particular importance for the new member countries in which cities are not yet strong engines of growth, innovation and development.

A polycentric urban system – with sustainable and competitive "regional cities" – requires a well-balanced spatial structure at all levels, as well as the acknowledgment of social and cultural differences. The approach is working well in several European city-regions, including the Belfast-Londonderry region in Northern Ireland. Belfast has been hailed as a leader in regional planning with the successful implementation of its Northern Ireland Regional Development Strategy, known as *Shaping Our Future*. The strategy was adopted in 2001 to develop regional planning that recognizes the diversity of Northern Ireland's people and places; achieves a more cohesive society based on equal opportunity, spatial equity, sensitivity to the city's divided community, a more sustainable approach to transport, and an outward-looking perspective; and makes the region more competitive. Since its implementation, *Shaping Our Future* has stimulated strategic planning in Belfast-Londonderry and provided a proactive framework for local communities to work together. Such efforts, with the guidance of the ESDP, illustrate the importance of a spatial perspective for harmonious regional development.

Sources: European Commission, Regional Policy Directorate (2004), Cities and the Lisbon Agenda: Assessing the Performances of Cities, Brussells.
Eurostat (2007). http://europa.eu/abc/keyfigures/qualityoflife/wealthy/index_en.htm.
Albrechts, L., Healey, P. & Kunzmann, K. (2003). "Strategic Spatial Planning and Regional Governance in Europe." Journal of the American Planning Association, 69:2.

NOTES

1. Wells 1902.
2. Douglass 1998.
3. Qadeer 2000.
4. McGee 1991.
5. Gilbert 1993; Aguilar & Ward 2003; Armstrong & McGee 1985; Villa & Rodriguez 1996; Browder et al. 1995.
6. Simon et al. 2006.
7. Satterthwaite 2000.
8. Ibid.
9. Ibid.
10. Jerve 2001; Satterthwaite 2000; SOFA 2002.
11. Douglass 1998.
12. Allen et al., 1999.
13. Mattingly & Gregory 2006.
14. Potts 1995, in Tacoli 1998b.
15. Douglass 1998, referring to a study by Lightfoot, et al. 1983.
16. Oxford Policy Management 2004.
17. Tostensen 2004.
18. Satterthwaite 2000.
19. Frayne 2005.
20. Ellis 1998.
21. Reardon et al. 2001, cited in Tacoli 2006.
22. Oxford Policy Management 2004c.
23. Gibb 1986; Grandstaff 1990; Douglass 1998.
24. Regmi & Tisdell, 2002.
25. Hoang et al. 2005.
26. Douglass 1998.
27. Rees 1992.
28. Lupala 2001; Bah et al. 2003.
29. Dávila 2006.
30. Allen and You 2004.
31. Lynch 2005.
32. Hodder 2000.
33. Frayne 2005.
34. Fleisher & Yang 2004.
35. ODI 2002.
36. Weber et al. 1997.
37. Chowdhury 2005.
38. For a detailed review of initiatives undertaken by different international agencies to improve aspects of environmental planning of the rural-urban interface and PUI see Budds and Minaya (1999), downloadable from www.ucl.ac.uk/dpu/pui/output2.htm.
39. Mwangi 2001.
40. Frayne 2005.

4.5
Metropolitan Governance: Governing in a City of Cities

▲
Hong Kong
©Xing Zhang

Around the world, urban populations are spreading out beyond their old city limits, rendering traditional municipal boundaries, and, by extension, traditional governing structures and institutions, outdated. This global urbanization trend has led to expansion not just in terms of population settlement and spatial sprawl, but also, and perhaps more importantly, in terms of urban residents' social and economic spheres of influence. As the distinguished urban planner John Friedmann has noted, "we can no longer treat cities apart from the regions surrounding them".[1]

The functional areas of cities transcend their physical boundaries. Cities have extensive labour markets, real estate markets, service markets, and financial and business markets that spread over the jurisdictional territories of several municipalities and, in some cases, over more than one state or provincial boundary, or even across international borders.

Increasingly, the practical and economic reach of cities and the growth of city-regions demands more integrated planning, service delivery and policy decisions than multiple but individually bounded cities can provide. Governing in a "city of cities" has therefore become much more complex than governing in a lone municipality, since a decision taken in one city affects the whole region in which the city is located. The development of complex inter-connected urban areas introduces new challenges of governance, particularly metropolitan governance.

Metropolitan governance arrangements affect the levels of harmony and disharmony in cities. Spatial, economic, social, and environmental harmony all depend on effective metropolitan governance, in which city leaders cooperate rather than compete to manage crime, poverty, social inequalities, transport system delivery, infrastructure development, and other issues. Concerns related to increasingly divided urban societies, together with inequalities and poverty that stretch across large metropolitan areas, point to the need for balanced urban development policies embedded in metropolitan planning and governance frameworks. Cities of different sizes often struggle with issues of metropolitan governance and inter-city harmony, with some experiencing demographic or economic decline and others facing rapid growth and development. Effective metropolitan governance offers potential for urban development that manages such inequalities and creates harmonious regions.

The challenges associated with building effective metropolitan governance arrangements are increasingly complex and integrated. They include:

- the absence of institutional consensus about the delimitations of a unique territory, making the possibility of joint action and convergence on interventions difficult;
- different visions and technical and political positions of authorities in the metropolitan area, with each city authority needing to respond to the requirements of the part of the city it governs[2];
- legal restrictions of municipalities on the formulation and implementation of plans and programmes beyond their politico-administrative jurisdictions;
- specialized functions of different municipalities with asymmetrical fiscal systems and notable differences between rich and poor municipalities;
- the existence of politically fragmented institutions for governing metropolitan areas, in the context of important challenges regarding uneven decentralization processes, heightened challenges of metropolitan transportation, deficiencies in critical infrastructure, and the growing need to expand the coverage of social services, address environmental problems, and compete with other cities at a national, continental, and often, a global scale.

The challenges of equitable development among different groups in metropolitan areas also point to the need for major improvements in the provision of public services such as health, decent shelter, education, water and sanitation. Urban poverty has been increasing, and in many cities, spreading outwards, making the peripheries of some metropolitan areas the poorest and most heavily under-serviced settlements.

These complex issues are highly integrated; their resolution is dependent upon the capacity of area-wide governing institutions to work together in systems relevant to each specific place. Deficient intergovernmental relations, inadequate popular local representation processes, weak sub-national institutions and poor financing mechanisms to support sub-national government systems pose critical questions for policymakers and leaders in all levels of government, as well as for researchers, planners and international agencies.

Empirical evidence shows[3] that urban areas around the world continue to relentlessly expand both in terms of density and horizontal space,[4] many growing and spreading over different administrative boundaries. There is a need to govern these large areas in a coherent fashion. The importance of recognizing the challenges of metropolitan governance stems from the fact that the world's cites are critical sites for economic production, agglomeration and proximity; for social and cultural development and interaction; for innovation and creativity; and are an essential staging ground for connecting local societies and economies to external networks and the global economy.[5]

From clearly delineated areas to inter-municipal territories

Traditional urban land market theory characterizes cities as having one city centre or central business district, well-defined limits of residential and industrial growth, and a clearly delineated area of commercial influence in a defined larger region, often the surrounding rural hinterland. The reality of cities today, however, is much more complex. Around the world, many once-independent cities have grown into vast metropolitan areas with more than one business centre, diffuse boundaries often defined not so much by local geography as by global reach, extended commercial areas of influence, and highly diversified economies.

For example, the metropolitan area of Mexico City, home to more than 19 million people, extends over the territories of two states and the Federal District, and includes as many as 58 municipalities. The economy of Buenos Aires covers the territories of the city of Buenos Aires, with 3 million people, and the 32 municipalities of the province of Buenos Aires, home to 9 million people. Similarly, in Africa, Metropolitan Johannesburg, with a population of 7.2 million people, encompasses Ekurhuleni (made up of the East Rand), the West Rand District Municipality and the City of Johannesburg, which hosts 3.4 million people.[6] Abidjan, with a population of 3.8 million, has expanded to encompass 196 local government units that include municipalities and surrounding rural areas.[7] In Asia, the Metropolitan Manila Area in the Philippines is composed of 10 cities and seven municipalities, with a total population of approximately 11 million, while Cebu City comprises seven cities and six municipalities, with a total population of nearly 2 million people. The Tokyo metropolitan region, with a population of 35 million, contains 365 municipal areas.[8] In North America, Metropolitan Minneapolis-Saint Paul, with a population of some 3 million people, includes 188 cities and townships.[9] Portland, Oregon, with approximately 1.8 million inhabitants, covers three counties and 24 local governments.[10]

Conceptualizing these vast, and often diffuse, urban territories and their spread across existing municipal boundaries and broader jurisdictions is a difficult task. This conceptual challenge reflects a movement in local governance reform that is in a continuous state of flux, experiment and reformulation. The fact that no internationally agreed-upon definition of a metropolitan area exists adds to the complicated task of understanding how these "cities of cities" function around the world. Most comparative statistics on cities and metropolitan areas are based on data with some limitations in terms of reliability and comparability, owing to varying definitions of what comprises an urban or metropolitan area in different countries. And because metropolitan areas are rarely legally defined entities, there may be a number of different possible boundaries for a commonly understood extended urban area, such as, for example, New York City and the New York Metropolitan Area, or the City of Toronto and the Greater Toronto Area. Different designations result in different population and sizes estimates.

Modes of metropolitan governance

Despite the fact that metropolitan areas appear in almost all regions of the world, their governance systems differ dramatically, varying on two major criteria: the *degree and level of centralization or control over urban functions* in the metropolitan area or region; and *the degree of formality* in the relationships among the various units in the metropolitan area.

Level and degree of centralization and control

According to a comprehensive study by the National Research Council of the United States in 2003, which examined the metropolitan issue for developing countries, there are four major categories, or models, of metropolitan governance systems. The first, and least structured, is the **fragmented** model. This model is characterized by a number of autonomous or semi-autonomous local government units, each with jurisdiction over particular functions or a specific local territory. Coordination among the individual municipalities or agencies within this structure is usually voluntary and is often sporadic. The most prominent examples of this model, for both larger and smaller metropolitan areas, come from the United States.

A second, related approach is the **mixed** model. In this model, many semi-autonomous local municipalities and governmental organizations work together as a metropolitan area, with some functions falling under the aegis of regional, provincial or national government agencies, while other functions remain the responsibility of local governments. The mixed model presumes a certain level of regionalization of the metropolitan structure, with municipalities and other authorities taking on different levels of regional governance according to the administrative structure of the state.[11] The participation of municipalities depends quite often on the willingness of higher levels of government to build consensus among them; it also depends upon their relative weight in terms of demographic, economic and political power. In this model, what is known as the "principle of mutual consideration" integrates the interests of different localities as part of the general metropolitan vision and, simultaneously, the metropolitan vision integrates each municipality into the city. Examples of mixed models are the Moroccan cities of Casablanca and Rabat, the North American cities of Los Angeles and Miami, the county of Stockholm and the province of Milan.

In the mixed model, governments often coordinate spatial and functional operations by establishing specific mechanisms or institutions throughout the metropolitan area for the delivery of services and *ad hoc* functions.[12] In Bangkok, for example, one can describe three "rings" of metropolitan governance. In the first ring, the core city of Bangkok with an estimated population of 5.7 million, there is a Bangkok Metropolitan Administration; in the second ring is the Bangkok Metropolitan Region (BMR), which had a total population of 11.5 million people in 2000. Outside the BMR is an expanding third ring, the Extended Bangkok Region, with an approximate population of 17.5 million. The two outer rings are made up of a number of provinces and hundreds of local governments. Many of the most important individual functions, in all three rings, are carried out by state enterprises, national governments, and local authorities. Alternatively, many functions in the fields of health, education, and infrastructure provision are carried out under contract by private service agencies.[13]

In China, the central government guides overall urban development, but metropolitan governance and management take on different operational forms in different cities, with variations in the levels of involvement and cooperation between the central, provincial and municipal governments. Intergovernmental relations vary across cities. Beijing, for example, is directly under the leadership of the Chinese central government, whereas Guangzhou and Harbin are under the leadership of Guangdong and Heilongjiang provinces, respectively. Decision-making powers regarding transport infrastructure construction in all three cities rest with the municipality in cooperation with higher-level government departments of transport, and private construction companies – enterprises appointed by the municipalities – implement the projects. Many cities operate as fairly autonomous municipalities as a result of a shift in governance structures in the recent years, which have evolved from highly centralized systems to decentralized ones.[14]

In some cases, mixed models involve international trans-boundary cooperation systems such as the Oresund Committee, which coordinates strategic projects between the metropolitan area of Copenhagen in Denmark and the urban area of Malmo in Sweden; or the Trans-Boundary Permanent Inter-Municipal Conference in the Lille Agglomeration, involving both France and Belgium.

A third logical form of metropolitan governance is the **centralized** model. In this model, the functions and governance of a large metropolitan area are under the control of the central government and its specialized state agencies. Examples of this model are Ho Chi Minh City, Viet Nam, and Havana, Cuba. Ho Chi Minh City, which had a population of just over 5 million in 2005,[15] is divided into 22 inner and outer districts, each of which has its own People's Committee and Planning Development Sub-Committee. Members of these committees are normally members of the Viet Nam Communist Party. Most major functions (including urban planning) are under the control of the national government.[16] Havana is another example. Since 1975, Greater Havana

Residential and commercial buildings in Singapore
©Modanmohan Rao

has been governed as a city province with 15 municipalities, including such centres as Old Havana, Central Havana, and the Plaza de la Revolución. In 2005, the Greater Havana region had an estimated population of 2.1 million.[17] While a recent account of Havana's governance stresses that locally elected municipal delegates have some formal deliberative powers, most important and contentious issues are referred to higher levels of government for decision.[18] Hong Kong and the city-state of Singapore also operate with centralized models. Until recently, urban problems in Greater Santiago, Chile, were solved by sectoral policies implemented by the different ministries of the central government with a rather limited participation of the local communities.

The fourth type of metropolitan governance is known as the **comprehensive** model. In this model, local authorities have considerable functional power and autonomy over aspects of the whole metropolitan area. Versions of this model are the Metro Area of Helsinki, governed by a Metropolitan Council composed of five municipalities; the Metro Region of Copenhagen; and the Metropolitan District of Quito. In Helsinki, the Metropolitan Council has extensive jurisdiction over various sectors such as transport, land use, environment

and economic development, funded by the state through its Sectoral Development Fund and fiscal revenues obtained at the metropolitan level.

Similar versions of the comprehensive model have operated in Abidjan, Côte d'Ivoire, since 1980, and since November 2000, five major South African cities have seen the municipalities in their metropolitan areas amalgamated into what are locally called "unicities".[19] In the case of Cape Town, for example, the Cape Town Metropolitan Municipality has gained unique powers over a wide range of services, such as land-use management, water and waste water, electricity and gas reticulation, transport, policing, and environmental health. With a staff of 21,297 and a budget (including both recurrent and capital elements) of approximately US$2.21 billion, it is one of the most sophisticated municipal governments in Africa.[20]

In terms of historical development, however, Abidjan is in many ways the leader in African metropolitan governance. In 1980, the government of Côte d'Ivoire created a two-tier political and administrative structure for the metropolitan area of Abidjan. At the lowest level were ten communes, with elected mayors and councils who had responsibility for such local functions as the administration of markets, allocation of plots for public purposes, maintenance of clinics and primary schools, and the operation of social centres. The major functions of the upper-tier government were waste disposal and management; sanitation, traffic regulation, road and park maintenance; and town planning. The mayor of the upper-tier metropolitan council was chosen by his communal colleagues. Major utilities such as water and electricity were managed by private, licensed companies. While this system worked reasonably well for more than 20 years, it was replaced in 2001 by the "District of Abidjan", consisting of the original ten communes (with their own governance systems) supplemented by three large sub-prefectures on the outskirts of the city. Beginning in 2002, the new District of Abidjan was reconfigured administratively under a governor, who, in turn, is appointed to a five-year term by the president of the republic. The governor represents the winning party in the communal elections and is assisted by a district council of 51, whose members are two-thirds elected at large and one-third selected by the communes. The same distribution of functions between the district and the communes is the same as it was between the old "City of Abidjan" and the communes before 2001.[21]

Degree of formality in governance structure and processes

A second, and arguably more common, way of characterizing metropolitan functions is by their degree of formality. In principle, there are two possibilities: either **formal structures** of metropolitan governance (which can be one- or two-tiered, and can be based on formal cooperative structures that bring together many municipalities and agencies); or **informal structures** of cooperation among agencies and municipalities. Various scholars have argued that some formal structure of metropolitan governance needs to be drawn up both to rationalize provision of public services (such as transport, policing, and waste disposal) over large areas, and to prevent inequities of resource distribution among different contiguous areas.[22] In large cities with extensive impoverished neighbourhoods, whether contiguous or scattered, the poor may find better collective representation in a formal, metropolitan-level structure than in isolated local government units. Depending on how representation and governance are structured, there should, in principle, be little difference as to whether metropolitan governance is more or less successful in small or large cities. Ultimately, as cities grow, they must respond to the functional challenges of adequate financial

Trafalgar Square, London
©**Rasna Warah**

empowerment, a broad operational mandate across sectors, the necessity to achieve a degree of civic engagement for the whole city, and the need to incorporate built-in systems of monitoring and feedback. To the extent they meet these challenges, distributional inequities can be mitigated, even as development takes place.

There are both "strong" and "weak" examples of the formal model. In strong versions of the model, central authorities have strong leadership and clear lines of authority; in weak versions, central authority is limited and there are often unclear lines of authority connecting the participating councils or local government units. "Strong" examples are the former Greater London Council, abolished in 1986; the present Comunidad Autonomy de Madrid; and the Metropolitan District of Quito. Other examples are the French Urban Communes of Lille, Bordeaux and Strasbourg; the Glasgow Clyde Valley Joint Committee; and the Stadsregio of Rotterdam, a public entity of voluntary status that is composed of 40 members elected by each municipality and the Regional Council and chaired by the mayor of Rotterdam.[23] "Weak" examples are the Verband Regio Stuttgart, the present Greater London Authority, the Metropolitan District of Portland,[24] and the Regional Authority of Bologna. In the developing world, the formal models of the five South African unicities comprise "strong" examples, as does the new District of Abidjan. Other strong formal metropolitan governance structures in the developing world are operating in the major Chinese cities of Shanghai, Beijing, Tianjin and Chongqing, which have been designated as provinces by the central government. More "weak" examples of formal structures include the metropolitan governments of Bangkok, Manila and Munich.

Some formal structures are represented by specific associations created for planning and urban management purposes at the metropolitan level. These associations are specialized bodies with consultative powers, such as the *Agence d'Urbanisme* in France, the Planning Association of German Cities, the Metropolitan Junta in Portugal, and the Urban Planning and Environmental Protection agency of Greece[25] The main obstacles of these specialized agencies are limited financing mechanisms, the capacity of negotiation with other agents and administrations and the difficulties of maintaining cooperation among different municipalities, particularly in rapidly changing and uncertain political and social environments.

Examples of **informal** metropolitan governance structures are much more numerous, for several reasons. The first reason has to do with regional and cultural factors. There are approximately 361 metropolitan areas in the United States, for example; practically none function under a single multi-purpose governance structure, but rather, they work together according to various degrees and forms of cooperative arrangements. The second reason has to do with politics. As metropolitan areas grow in size and economic importance, higher levels of government may be wary of creating alternative power structures by institutionalizing municipal governance for large numbers of people. Third, many

differences and conflicts of interest exist among the many municipal governments and other local government agencies that make up a single metropolitan area. These differences are complicated by growth and competition and the fluidity of economic and social change. Finding the correct way of representing such diverse and sometimes transitory interests in a single structural "package" is difficult and often takes a number of attempts and revisions. Finally, many arguments have been made against formalization of governance relationships within large metropolitan areas. Letting different areas settle their own issues by voluntary means may give an optimal outcome on many fronts, particularly in relation to where people should wish to live, where businesses locate, and how and in what form they pay taxes for common services. The economic basis of this argument was originally proposed by Charles Tiebout in his seminal article written in 1956.[26] The most well-known examples of informal metropolitan governance structures in Latin America include Santiago in Chile, São Paulo in Brazil, Montevideo in Uruguay, Mexico City and Guadalajara in Mexico, but there are many others as well.

Governing for harmony in a city of cities

While recognizing that generalized recommendations and prescriptions are often inappropriate, that models are usually never directly transferable, and that the peculiarities of each case must be attended to, common challenges and characteristics for success in the governance of metropolitan areas begin to emerge from different cases and recent literature, and current research on the so-called "state of the art", that can help to inform a policy dialogue on metropolitan governance.

Threshold requirements for good practice

How locally elected representatives and citizens democratically control the process of policy formulation and management functions of metropolitan governance is critical to determining their success and longevity. Inadequate popular local representation processes in metropolitan-level institutions creates tensions, particularly where stakeholders are excluded or accountability is called into question. If institutions lack legitimacy they are often short-lived.

Effective leadership is critical for overcoming fragmentation and building consensus across metropolitan areas. Strong leadership can overcome individualism and competition across political "turf" and build recognition that more metropolitan-wide collective action is empowering at both a national and an international level. In the case of Cape Town,[27] for example, strong collegial leadership and coalition-building are seen as critical to managing a complex set of relationships embedded in the fractured and highly contested ethnic and political dynamics within the Cape Town local, metropolitan and supra-metropolitan area. In Cape Town, there is currently an executive mayor, supported by an advisory mayoral committee. Members of the larger council, of which the committee is a part, are elected every five years by a combination of ward elections and proportional representation. Elaborate attention to the processes of democratic local election gives legitimacy and visibility to the leadership of this single-tier metropolitan council that represents more than 3.5 million people who constitute 64 per cent of the total population of the Western Cape province and 78 per cent of the province's economy.

The ability to build consensus and coordinate actions among municipalities facilitates investments in infrastructure and amenities that make the metropolis more productive as a whole and more competitive internationally. Strong leadership in the affairs of metropolitan governance means not only building consensus, but also aggregating fragmented interests in a way that builds legitimacy and accountability to stakeholders in the process. When governance institutions are fragmented or are *ad hoc* creations, corrupt practices can gain strength. Where fragmentation exists, accountability practices are weakened, and individuals and networks can be more easily empowered and gain control over a policy sector.

Efficient financing is a core requirement for metropolitan governance. Deficient financing tools at the local level have often hampered metropolitan governance, and the redistribution of responsibilities among different levels of government has not always been sustained by a corresponding allocation of resources, empowerment or financing tools that would make it possible to raise the necessary funds. If such weaknesses are common at the level of individual municipalities, then the problems of raising finances to support broader metropolitan areas are compounded. Devolution of revenue-raising capacity by central and provincial or state governments to local

governments does not necessarily improve the financial powers for effective metropolitan governance. Indeed, municipal sub-units in metropolitan areas might gain power at the expense of the existing metropolitan governance structures. For example, the Metropolitan Manila Development Authority (MMDA) actually became more dependent on central government grants following passage of the Local Government Code in 1991, which gave local government units within the broader metropolitan area the authority to collect a range of taxes. As a result, the MMDA lost a share of the local government units' regular income and its share in real property tax and other local tax revenues.[28]

Highly fragmented governance arrangements in many metropolitan areas make efficient financing for area-wide service provision a difficult and ongoing challenge. Recent literature [29] suggests that this is true regardless of the metropolitan governance models in place. In general, municipalities are reluctant to transfer financial resources to metropolitan-level structures, and cooperative arrangements often break down in the absence of solid legal frameworks and constitutional support for revenue sharing with the metropolitan "tier" of governance. As a result, metropolitan authorities often lack adequate resources for governing and face difficulties in raising new resources.

Without a clear, permanent and sufficient financial mechanism, it is difficult for metropolitan areas to generate territorial solidarity through which to redress social and economic inequalities for more harmonious development. Some metropolitan areas have developed sustainable financial mechanisms to support policies and programming, including

▲
Amman, Jordan
© **Simon Podgorsek/iStockphoto**

Lille, France, where the Funds of Solidarity and Economic Development redistribute revenue collected through local taxes; Berlin and Munich, Germany, where regional and state financial transfers fund metropolitan needs; the metropolitan areas of Helsinki, Finland, and Stockholm, Sweden, which have supportive local revenue tax systems; and Copenhagen, Denmark, which has a financial system funded through transport services.[30]

Effective citizen participation in decision-making and in the allocation of resources across a multiplicity of metropolitan agencies is essential, but it can also be challenging to make the mechanisms of participation accessible, easily understood and representative, as required by the principles of transparency and democracy. In the case of Amman, Jordan[31] a "Comprehensive Development Plan" is currently underway to address urban development to the year 2025. The first phase of the plan concerns the expansion of the city to link different socially distributed sites and territories around Amman under one administrative body; the goal of the plan is to better reflect the actual metropolitan area of the city, which has reached a vast 1,860 square kilometres. The city held public hearings and brainstorming sessions in 2007 during the preparation of the 2025 plan, but the targeted participants were not representative of the whole community. Moreover, the process implemented an informative participatory approach as opposed to an interactive one. Effective citizen participation is crucial for Amman's successful growth, particularly as the metropolis' expansion is driven by an influx of refugees. Palestinian refugees first flooded into Jordan as a result of the Arab and Israeli wars of 1948 and 1967, then came refugees of the Lebanese Civil War in the 1970s, followed by Kuwaitis and others forced from their homes by the Gulf War in the 1980s. As a result of the Gulf Crisis of 1990, Amman has further absorbed a new wave of return migrants of Jordanian and Palestinian workers from Iraq and Kuwait, and most recently, as a result of the recent Iraq Crisis. UNHCR estimates that 700,000 Iraqis have moved to Amman since 2003. In addition, various socio-economic and geopolitical transformations in the region have made Amman a magnet for major real estate development projects with expensive high-rise buildings affecting the urban form of the city. In this context, effective citizen participation in strategic planning exercises is fundamental to the success of the Greater Amman Municipality.

The Challenges of Metropolitan Governance

Jurisdictional coordination is one of the most pressing challenges common to cities worldwide. This challenge takes two forms: vertical, multi-level jurisdictional coordination of services across multiple levels of government; and horizontal, inter-jurisdictional coordination of services across the metropolitan area. Where the former challenge exists, inter-governmental relations involved in the governance of cities are often in flux, with extensive and complex decentralization processes in motion in many countries worldwide. Multiple tiers of government and various levels of state agencies are involved in the affairs of urban governance, often at the expense

of municipal-level actors. Where the latter challenge exists, governing institutions are often fragmented, uncoordinated and in many cases *ad hoc*, owing to multiple jurisdictional and electoral boundaries that span the territories of vast metropolitan areas.

The case of Mumbai,[32] India, illustrates the challenges of jurisdictional coordination in a complicated metropolitan environment. The Municipal Corporation of Greater Mumbai (MCGM) governs more than 12 million people[33] within a complex institutional structure of two wider metropolitan areas: an area defined as the Mumbai Urban Agglomeration, with 16.4 million people covering three districts of Maharashtra, including five municipal corporations and three municipal councils; and an even wider area, the Mumbai Metropolitan Region (MMR), covering 4,355 square kilometres and including seven municipal corporations, 13 municipal councils, parts of neighbouring districts and more than 900 villages. The MCGM holds elections every five years, in which 227 councillors are directly elected from its wards, and the mayor and deputy mayor of the corporation are elected from amongst the councillors.

The Municipal Corporation of Greater Mumbai, however, is just one entity responsible for planning, development and provision of infrastructure in greater Mumbai. Other key agencies responsible for governance in Greater Mumbai include the Mumbai Metropolitan Region Development Authority (MMRDA). The MMRDA is responsible for the planning and development of the entire metropolitan region in a multi-municipal jurisdiction (7 municipal corporations, 13 municipal councils, parts of neighbouring districts and more than 900 villages). The MMRDA also brings together central and state governments to jointly fund urban development. Although the MMRDA Act specifically prohibits it from undertaking any work that falls under the obligatory or discretionary functions of the MCGM, the Act also gives it overriding power to direct any urban local authority. The result: the MMRDA and MCGM are often in conflict over jurisdictional responsibilities in infrastructure and service development matters. The MMRDA, for example, has been responsible for implementation of the Mumbai Urban Development Project, the Mumbai Urban Transport Project and the Mumbai Urban Infrastructure Project.

This overlapping jurisdictional authority between the Greater Mumbai Metropolitan Corporation and the broader Metropolitan Regional Development Authority is complicated even more by the interplay of three other key agencies also responsible for governance and infrastructure in Mumbai: the Maharashtra Housing and Area Development Authority, the Slum Rehabilitation Authority and the Maharashtra State Road Development Corporation. Each of these agencies performs key functions within the territory governed by the GMMC, and each has different legal status and operates under a complex system of authority. For example, the Maharashtra Housing and Area Development Authority is a nominated body that operates through nine regional boards, three of which directly relate with Mumbai: the Housing and Area Development Board, the Mumbai Buildings Repair and Reconstruction Board and the Mumbai Slum Improvement Board. On the other hand, the Slum Rehabilitation Authority has a different legal status and operates under a different system of authority. It has the status of a corporate entity, with the chief minister of Maharashtra as chairperson. It also has been declared a planning authority, so can function as a local authority for the slum areas under its jurisdiction.

To address metropolitan governance in Mumbai at this juncture requires a re-engineering of metropolitan governance processes, particularly with respect to reducing the multiplicity of agencies and improving jurisdictional coordination, as well as reforming accountability and transparency, improving interaction with citizens and developing appropriate information systems.

This complexity of jurisdictional responsibilities is further compounded in the case of Delhi, India, by the fact that it is the national capital. Metropolitan governance for the city region falls under the National Capital Territory of Delhi (NCTD), consisting of nine urban districts and 27 subdivisions. There are no fewer than 98 urban bodies, local agencies, boards, and authorities serving the city's population of some 14 million people. The three major local authorities include the Delhi Municipal Corporation, the New Delhi Municipal Corporation and the Delhi Cantonment. In addition, the national government of India (in particular the central Ministries of Urban Development, Surface Transport, Environment, Home Affairs, and Defence), together with the state government of the National Capital Territories of Delhi, all exercise significant control over metropolitan governance in Delhi.

The most critical challenge of metropolitan governance confronting the government of National Capital Territory of Delhi (GNCTD) is the continued control by the central government of its administration and affairs. Major decisions for preparing and implementing the city's master plan are still taken by the Delhi Development Authority, a body corporate of the national Ministry of Urban Development. Frequent conflicts in governance arise as a result of this multiplicity of agencies of the central, state and local governments. Jurisdictional overlap, poor coordination, and lack of clarity over responsibilities for land-use planning, development, maintenance, and enforcement has resulted in ineffective and uncoordinated decision-making and actions in this rapidly growing metropolitan area of Delhi.

National and provincial or state governments, while part of the problem in cities such as Delhi, remain essential not only for empowering municipalities to enter into more effective metropolitan governing arrangements, but also for lending legitimacy to the political process and reinforcing metropolitan governance in the long term. In many countries where centralist attitudes towards local government are the norm, metropolitan governance arrangements are inhibited. National assemblies, senates, and other national governing institutions are also frequently in the hands of rural interests, while urban interests are often under-represented. This can result from national representation and electoral systems, or constitutional limitations to address urban

▲
Egypt
©**Madanmohan Rao**

questions. Decentralization aims to remedy this imbalance by systematically transferring functions and resources from central to local governments, thereby improving the provision of services and infrastructure to increase competitiveness and promote local economic growth.

Decentralization efforts can be hampered, however, when higher-level authorities meet these large metropolitan areas on the ground. The institutional structures for metropolitan governance and the institutions for planning and service delivery across urban territories are often fragmented. Governance of these broad territories is by discrete and often numerous municipal governments behaving independently and commonly lacking effective coordinating mechanisms for governing metropolitan areas. Decentralization of responsibilities and powers is therefore often delegated to the municipal structures already in place, even though they are not necessarily serving the metropolitan requirements well.

Effective metropolitan policies and strategies tend to reinforce coordination across different cities that make up the metropolitan area. Coordination is fundamental not only for administering basic needs in areas such as land, transport, environment, and related fiscal and funding solutions, but also for addressing issues of poverty and social exclusion through innovative mechanisms of inter-territorial solidarity.

Land-use planning for spatial harmony is a key criterion of effective metropolitan governance. Both territorial and spatial strategies can be put to use for reducing social disparities. To that end, important functions of metropolitan institutions include land-use planning in peri-urban areas and urban hinterlands, transport development and related infrastructure planning at urban and regional levels. Spatial strategies differ depending on the growth patterns of metropolitan areas, some of which are rapidly gaining population, and others of which are growing slowly or not at all. Of those that are growing, some are consuming more land rapidly, and others are becoming increasingly dense.

Managing transport in large metropolitan areas is especially essential for the advancement of the urban economy and for giving residents access to jobs and services throughout the city region. However, transport investments and services are often implemented, financed, managed, and regulated by different governing institutions and levels of government. Coordination of these processes relies on complex intergovernmental policy networks and organizational management.

Social and economic harmony in cities

Metropolitan government arrangements can be instruments for addressing social cohesion by promoting economic opportunity, infrastructure investment, access to affordable transportation services, and investments in social housing across large metropolitan areas, thus crossing not just political divides but socio-economic ones.

However, institutional fragmentation of metropolitan areas is closely related to the escalating problem of social segregation and disharmony in the world's cities. The Kolkata Metropolitan Area (KMA) in India, for example, is projected to host more than 20 million people in 2025, compared to the present population of more than 15 million. The KMA consists of three municipal corporations, 38 other municipalities, 77 non-municipal census towns, 16 outgrowths, and 445 rural areas, covering about 1,850 square kilometres. Kolkata faces serious deficiencies in urban infrastructure and services, and also faces spatial inequalities spread across the KMA. The high incidence of poverty and inherent spatial inequality poses great challenges to overcoming the lack of coordination across agencies concerned with the provision of housing and services in the metropolitan area.

In the Metropolitan Region of Belo Horizonte, Brazil,[34] which consists of 34 municipalities and has a population of nearly 5 million people, serious inequalities exist between developed and less developed parts of the urban region. Concern about the vast disparities in the area prompted the government of the state of Minas Gerais (the current effective senior government level of the urban region) to partner with the Cities Alliance to conduct research and develop plans for the alleviation of poverty in 16 municipalities in the north zone of the region.[35] Indeed, one of the major reasons for the recent establishment of the metropolitan region was to develop policies and programmes that could reduce inequalities in the region. To provide a basis for this approach, the state government of Minas Gerais has, since 2006, been working on legislation to create a number of major metropolitan agencies to deal with public functions of common interest, such as inter-municipal transportation, the road system, basic sanitation, land use, exploitation of water resources, preservation of the environment, housing, health, and socio-economic development. The formal structures have been reinforced by a number of initiatives by both civil society and the city council of Belo Horizonte.

Clearly, metropolitan governance can help address social and economic imbalances within cities. Creating harmony in a "city of cities" requires a "shared vicinity"[36] that is expressed through political will, financial participation and willingness to create redistribution mechanisms to redress social and economic imbalances produced by the development process and regional and global factors.

Harmony between the built and the natural environment

Managing metropolitan environmental resources such as natural watersheds that spread throughout the jurisdictional territories of several local governments also focuses attention

▲
Street market in Bangalore, India
©**Madanmohan Rao**

on the need to coordinate and overcome the problems of fragmentation in local political institutions. Commonly shared natural resources such as rivers and lakes that span multiple jurisdictions also require new forms of governance to support and protect them.

Urban metropolitan areas demand and consume vast amounts of energy, water and other material resources, and as a result continuously transform and place pressure on the physical environment. Cities are both victims and perpetrators of climate change. They generate the lion's share of solid waste, electricity demand, transport-related emissions, and demand for heating and cooling. On the other hand, cities

and local governments are well positioned to set the standards for healthy, safe, pollution-free environments and to take a leadership role in addressing the challenges related to hazard management as countries adapt to climate change.[37]

Planning for environmental harmony is dependent upon metropolitan governance institutions that effectively span multiple jurisdictions. The challenge for metropolitan institutions to effectively protect, manage and plan for physical environments that span multiple jurisdictions and build environmental harmony across broad metropolitan territories is a core challenge for metropolitan governance worldwide.

NOTES

1. Friedmann, 2007.
2. Borja, 2004.
3. Research in this area includes the studies of McGee & Robinson, 1995; *Environment and Urbanization*, 2000; Myers & Dietz, 2002; National Research Council, 2003; Rojas et al., 2005; Laquian, 2005; *Public Administration and Development*, 2005).
4. Angel, Sheppard & Civco, 2005.
5. McCarney, 2005.
6. Cameron, 2005.
7. Stren, 2007.
8. Sorensen, 2001, p. 22.
9. Hamilton, 1999.
10. Data for urban agglomerations from UN Population Division's *World Urbanization Prospects 2007*.
11. Borja, 2004.
12. This mode of operation is quite usual in the cases of dissolution of metropolitan governments such as London and Barcelona. It is also found in some Australian cities such as Bristol, Perth and Sidney, where the coordination is done by the state governments.
13. Webster, 2004.
14. The case material on China is drawn from *Study on Metropolitan Governance in China*, 2008, an unpublished survey prepared by Suocheng Dong as background case work for UN-HABITAT as part of an exercise on metropolitan governance.
15. UN Department of Economic and Social Affairs, 2006.
16. Ha & Wong, 1999.
17. UN Department of Economic and Social Affairs, 2006.
18. Scarpaci, 2002, p. 191.
19. Cameron, 2005.
20. Schmidt & Kaplen, 2008.
21. Stren, 2007.
22. Jones, 1942, and later, Sharpe, 1995.
23. The mechanism of coordination of the Stadsregio in Rotterdam varies according to the objectives of the cooperation.

24. Lefèvre, 2007.
25. Borja, 2004, p. 48.
26. Tiebout, 1956.
27. The case material on Cape Town used in this chapter is drawn from background case work prepared for UN-HABITAT by D. Schmidt and A. Kaplan.
28. Laquian, 2002.
29. Klink, 2007; Lefèvre, 2007; National Research Council, 2003; Slack, 2007; Stren, 2007.
30. Borja, 2004.
31. The case material on Jordan used in this chapter is drawn from "Policy Analysis for Metropolitan Governance in the City of Amman" (March 2008), an unpublished survey prepared by Maram Rawil and Yasser Rajjal as background case work for UN-HABITAT as part of an exercise on metropolitan governance.
32. The case material on India used in this chapter is drawn from a survey. "Metropolitan Governance in India: Case Studies of Mumbai, Delhi and Kolkata" (2008), an unpublished document prepared by Vinod Tewari as background case work for UN-HABITAT as part of an exercise on metropolitan governance.
33. Population statistics for Mumbai and Delhi, India, are derived from the 2001 census. In 2007, the UN Population Division, however, estimated the population of Mumbai to be 18.9 million, making it the fifth largest urban agglomeration in the world, after Tokyo, Mexico City, New York-Newark and São Paulo.
34. The case material on Brazil used in this chapter is drawn from "Metropolitan Governance Survey" (March 2008), an unpublished document prepared as background casework for UN-HABITAT as part of an exercise on metropolitan governance.
35. This material is from "Questionnaire on Metropolitan Governance: RMBH" by Observatorio das Metropoles of Minas Gerais (2008), p.7.
36. Borja, 2004
37. World Bank, 2007b.

City population by country, 2000-2025

Country	City	Population estimates and projections (thousands)			
		2000	**2010**	**2020**	**2025**
AFRICA					
Algeria	El Djazaïr (Algiers)	2,754	3,574	4,235	4,499
Algeria	Wahran (Oran)	706	852	1,030	1,105
Angola	Huambo	578	1,035	1,567	1,824
Angola	Luanda	2,591	4,775	7,153	8,236
Benin	Cotonou	642	841	1,196	1,411
Burkina Faso	Ouagadougou	828	1,324	2,111	2,632
Cameroon	Douala	1,432	2,108	2,721	2,996
Cameroon	Yaoundé	1,192	1,787	2,312	2,549
Chad	N'Djaména	711	1,127	1,753	2,172
Congo	Brazzaville	986	1,505	1,938	2,150
Côte D'ivoire	Abidjan	3,032	4,175	5,432	6,031
Dem. Republic Of The Congo	Kananga	557	879	1,383	1,698
Dem. Republic Of The Congo	Kinshasa	5,485	9,052	13,875	16,762
Dem. Republic Of The Congo	Lubumbashi	1,004	1,544	2,406	2,943
Dem. Republic Of The Congo	Mbuji-Mayi	932	1,489	2,330	2,851
Egypt	Al-Iskandariyah (Alexandria)	3,600	4,421	5,210	5,652
Egypt	Al-Qahirah (Cairo)	10,534	12,503	14,451	15,561
Ethiopia	Addis Ababa	2,493	3,453	5,083	6,156
Ghana	Accra	1,674	2,332	3,041	3,382
Ghana	Kumasi	1,187	1,826	2,393	2,667
Guinea	Conakry	1,219	1,645	2,393	2,856
Kenya	Mombasa	686	985	1,453	1,763
Kenya	Nairobi	2,233	3,363	4,881	5,871
Liberia	Monrovia	836	1,185	1,753	2,083
Libyan Arab Jamahiriya	Banghazi	945	1,271	1,505	1,590
Libyan Arab Jamahiriya	Tarabulus (Tripoli)	1,877	2,322	2,713	2,855
Madagascar	Antananarivo	1,361	1,877	2,642	3,118
Mali	Bamako	1,110	1,708	2,633	3,214
Morocco	Dar-el-Beida (Casablanca)	3,043	3,267	3,716	3,949
Morocco	Fès	870	1,060	1,243	1,332
Morocco	Marrakech	755	923	1,085	1,163
Morocco	Rabat	1,507	1,793	2,083	2,222
Mozambique	Maputo	1,096	1,621	2,235	2,560
Niger	Niamey	680	1,027	1,580	2,028
Nigeria	Abuja	832	1,994	2,971	3,358
Nigeria	Benin City	975	1,302	1,755	1,991
Nigeria	Ibadan	2,236	2,835	3,752	4,234
Nigeria	Ilorin	653	835	1,123	1,277
Nigeria	Kaduna	1,220	1,560	2,083	2,360
Nigeria	Kano	2,658	3,393	4,487	5,056
Nigeria	Lagos	7,233	10,572	14,134	15,796
Nigeria	Maiduguri	758	969	1,301	1,479
Nigeria	Ogbomosho	798	1,031	1,386	1,575
Nigeria	Port Harcourt	863	1,104	1,479	1,680
Nigeria	Zaria	752	963	1,293	1,470
Rwanda	Kigali	497	947	1,413	1,715
Senegal	Dakar	2,029	2,856	3,726	4,225
Sierra Leone	Freetown	688	894	1,200	1,406
Somalia	Muqdisho (Mogadishu)	1,201	1,500	2,142	2,529
South Africa	Cape Town	2,715	3,357	3,627	3,744
South Africa	Durban	2,370	2,839	3,070	3,173
South Africa	Ekurhuleni (East Rand)	2,326	3,157	3,427	3,539

Country	City	Population estimates and projections (thousands)			
		2000	2010	2020	2025
South Africa	Johannesburg	2,732	3,618	3,916	4,041
South Africa	Port Elizabeth	958	1,053	1,150	1,197
South Africa	Pretoria	1,084	1,409	1,544	1,604
South Africa	Vereeniging	897	1,127	1,236	1,286
Sudan	Al-Khartum (Khartoum)	3,949	5,185	7,017	7,937
Togo	Lomé	1,023	1,669	2,410	2,791
Uganda	Kampala	1,097	1,597	2,506	3,198
United Republic Of Tanzania	Dar es Salaam	2,116	3,319	4,804	5,688
Zambia	Lusaka	1,073	1,421	1,797	2,047
Zimbabwe	Harare	1,379	1,663	2,037	2,247
ASIA					
Afghanistan	Kabul	1,963	3,768	5,836	7,175
Armenia	Yerevan	1,111	1,102	1,102	1,102
Azerbaijan	Baku	1,806	1,931	2,097	2,187
Bangladesh	Chittagong	3,308	5,012	6,688	7,639
Bangladesh	Dhaka	10,285	14,796	19,422	22,015
Bangladesh	Khulna	1,285	1,699	2,294	2,640
Bangladesh	Rajshahi	678	887	1,208	1,396
Belgium	Antwerpen	912	920	920	920
Belgium	Bruxelles-Brussel	1,733	1,744	1,744	1,744
Cambodia	Phnum Pénh (Phnom Penh)	1,160	1,651	2,457	2,911
China	Anshan, Liaoning	1,552	1,703	2,029	2,167
China	Anshun	763	896	1,085	1,164
China	Anyang	763	948	1,156	1,240
China	Baoding	890	1,206	1,482	1,586
China	Baotou	1,655	2,209	2,691	2,869
China	Beijing	9,782	11,741	13,807	14,545
China	Bengbu	805	944	1,142	1,225
China	Benxi	979	1,046	1,249	1,339
China	Changchun	2,730	3,400	4,082	4,338
China	Changde	1,341	1,543	1,852	1,979
China	Changsha, Hunan	2,091	2,832	3,443	3,663
China	Changzhou, Jiangsu	1,068	1,445	1,772	1,894
China	Chengdu	3,919	4,266	5,014	5,320
China	Chifeng	1,148	1,348	1,625	1,739
China	Chongqing	6,037	6,690	7,823	8,275
China	Dalian	2,858	3,335	3,971	4,221
China	Dandong	776	921	1,117	1,198
China	Daqing	1,366	1,842	2,252	2,404
China	Datong, Shanxi	1,518	2,038	2,488	2,653
China	Dongguan, Guangdong	3,770	4,850	5,808	6,157
China	Foshan	754	1,027	1,265	1,356
China	Fushun, Liaoning	1,433	1,516	1,800	1,924
China	Fuxin	631	839	1,036	1,112
China	Fuyang	609	840	1,038	1,114
China	Fuzhou, Fujian	2,096	2,834	3,445	3,666
China	Guangzhou, Guangdong	7,388	9,447	11,218	11,835
China	Guilin	795	1,075	1,323	1,418
China	Guiyang	2,929	3,980	4,818	5,114
China	Haerbin	3,444	3,753	4,421	4,696
China	Handan	1,321	1,775	2,171	2,318
China	Hangzhou	2,411	3,269	3,967	4,217
China	Hefei	1,637	2,214	2,700	2,878
China	Hengyang	873	1,087	1,324	1,418
China	Heze	1,277	1,388	1,655	1,771
China	Huai'an	1,198	1,315	1,571	1,681
China	Huaibei	733	995	1,227	1,315
China	Huainan	1,353	1,515	1,812	1,937
China	Hohhot	1,389	1,878	2,295	2,449
China	Huzhou	1,141	1,288	1,545	1,654
China	Jiamusi	853	1,099	1,345	1,441
China	Jiaozuo	742	915	1,115	1,196

Country	City	Population estimates and projections (thousands)			
		2000	**2010**	**2020**	**2025**
China	Jiaxing	877	1,047	1,268	1,359
China	Jilin	1,928	2,606	3,171	3,376
China	Jinan, Shandong	2,625	2,914	3,453	3,674
China	Jining, Shandong	1,044	1,260	1,525	1,632
China	Jinxi, Liaoning	1,908	2,658	3,248	3,457
China	Jinzhou	858	1,009	1,221	1,309
China	Jixi, Heilongjiang	908	1,006	1,208	1,295
China	Kaifeng	793	918	1,110	1,191
China	Kaohsiung	1,469	1,595	1,899	2,029
China	Kunming	2,594	3,095	3,694	3,928
China	Langfang	711	861	1,048	1,124
China	Lanzhou	2,071	2,785	3,387	3,604
China	Leshan	1,118	1,197	1,427	1,528
China	Lianyungang	682	865	1,060	1,137
China	Liaoyang	725	835	1,009	1,083
China	Linfen	719	891	1,087	1,167
China	Linyi, Shandong	1,932	2,177	2,594	2,765
China	Liuan	1,553	1,771	2,120	2,263
China	Liupanshui	989	1,329	1,632	1,745
China	Liuzhou	1,201	1,629	1,995	2,131
China	Luoyang	1,481	1,830	2,212	2,361
China	Luzhou	1,208	1,673	2,047	2,187
China	Mianyang, Sichuan	1,152	1,509	1,842	1,969
China	Mudanjiang	1,004	1,355	1,662	1,778
China	Nanchang	1,822	2,585	3,168	3,373
China	Nanchong	1,712	2,364	2,881	3,070
China	Nanjing, Jiangsu	3,477	3,813	4,492	4,771
China	Nanning	1,743	2,357	2,873	3,061
China	Nantong	759	1,031	1,269	1,360
China	Nanyang, Henan	1,512	2,115	2,581	2,752
China	Neijiang	1,388	1,525	1,819	1,944
China	Ningbo	1,551	2,092	2,553	2,723
China	Pingdingshan, Henan	904	854	1,006	1,080
China	Pingxiang, Jiangxi	775	1,047	1,289	1,381
China	Qingdao	2,698	2,977	3,521	3,746
China	Qinhuangdao	805	1,092	1,344	1,440
China	Qiqihaer	1,535	1,712	2,043	2,182
China	Quanzhou	1,158	1,592	1,950	2,083
China	Shanghai	13,243	15,789	18,466	19,412
China	Shangqiu	1,349	1,907	2,331	2,487
China	Shantou	1,255	1,756	2,158	2,304
China	Shaoxing	617	846	1,045	1,121
China	Shenyang	4,599	4,952	5,808	6,156
China	Shenzhen	6,069	8,114	9,654	10,196
China	Shijiazhuang	1,947	2,628	3,198	3,405
China	Suining, Sichuan	1,352	1,481	1,766	1,888
China	Suzhou, Anhui	1,509	2,137	2,607	2,780
China	Suzhou, Jiangsu	1,326	1,795	2,195	2,343
China	Taian, Shandong	1,534	1,696	2,022	2,160
China	Taichung	930	1,151	1,400	1,499
China	Tainan	725	791	951	1,021
China	Taipei	2,640	2,651	3,104	3,305
China	Taiyuan, Shanxi	2,521	3,104	3,725	3,962
China	Tangshan, Hebei	1,703	1,977	2,367	2,526
China	Tianjin	6,722	7,468	8,745	9,243
China	Tianmen	1,609	1,777	2,118	2,261
China	Tianshui	1,143	1,279	1,533	1,640
China	Tongliao	790	935	1,133	1,215
China	Ürümqi (Wulumqi)	1,730	2,340	2,851	3,038
China	Weifang	1,372	1,646	1,985	2,120
China	Wenzhou	1,845	2,556	3,111	3,313
China	Wuhan	6,662	7,542	8,837	9,339

Country	City	Population estimates and projections (thousands)			
		2000	2010	2020	2025
China	Wuhu, Anhui	692	868	1,061	1,138
China	Wuxi, Jiangsu	1,410	1,903	2,326	2,481
China	Xiamen	1,977	2,739	3,331	3,545
China	Xi'an, Shaanxi	3,725	4,178	4,931	5,233
China	Xiangfan, Hubei	855	1,164	1,431	1,533
China	Xiantao	1,470	1,618	1,930	2,062
China	Xianyang, Shaanxi	946	1,212	1,480	1,584
China	Xingyi, Guizhou	715	868	1,056	1,133
China	Xining	849	1,142	1,404	1,504
China	Xinxiang	770	968	1,182	1,268
China	Xinyang	1,195	1,677	2,052	2,192
China	Xinyu	772	981	1,199	1,285
China	Xuanzhou	823	899	1,079	1,158
China	Xuzhou	1,648	2,284	2,792	2,975
China	Yancheng, Jiangsu	677	914	1,127	1,209
China	Yantai	1,684	2,301	2,805	2,989
China	Yibin	805	954	1,157	1,240
China	Yichang	704	953	1,174	1,259
China	Yichun, Heilongjiang	816	785	928	997
China	Yichun, Jiangxi	917	1,025	1,231	1,320
China	Yinchuan	795	1,079	1,328	1,423
China	Yingkou	694	847	1,032	1,107
China	Yiyang, Hunan	1,223	1,425	1,714	1,833
China	Yongzhou	976	1,032	1,231	1,320
China	Yuci	660	921	1,141	1,224
China	Yueyang	918	821	961	1,032
China	Yulin, Guangxi	909	1,227	1,507	1,613
China	Zaozhuang	1,990	2,242	2,670	2,846
China	Zhangjiakou	897	1,120	1,364	1,461
China	Zhanjiang	1,340	1,709	2,076	2,216
China	Zhaotong	724	855	1,038	1,113
China	Zhengzhou	2,472	2,738	3,243	3,452
China	Zhenjiang, Jiangsu	688	930	1,147	1,230
China	Zhuhai	809	1,114	1,371	1,468
China	Zhuzhou	868	1,176	1,445	1,548
China	Zibo	2,806	3,209	3,812	4,053
China	Zigong	1,049	1,149	1,375	1,473
China	Zunyi	679	924	1,140	1,223
China, Hong Kong Sar	Hong Kong	6,662	7,419	8,040	8,305
Dem. People's Rep. Of Korea	Hamhung	732	788	851	882
Dem. People's Rep. Of Korea	N'ampo	1,020	1,148	1,232	1,274
Dem. People's Rep. Of Korea	P'yongyang	3,117	3,346	3,537	3,630
Georgia	Tbilisi	1,100	1,108	1,114	1,114
India	Agra	1,293	1,705	2,118	2,364
India	Ahmadabad	4,427	5,726	6,989	7,735
India	Aligarh	653	864	1,083	1,215
India	Allahabad	1,035	1,279	1,592	1,781
India	Amritsar	990	1,299	1,619	1,811
India	Asansol	1,065	1,425	1,776	1,985
India	Aurangabad	868	1,200	1,499	1,678
India	Bangalore	5,567	7,229	8,795	9,719
India	Bareilly	722	869	1,087	1,219
India	Bhiwandi	603	860	1,081	1,212
India	Bhopal	1,426	1,845	2,288	2,553
India	Bhubaneswar	637	913	1,147	1,286
India	Kolkata (Calcutta)	13,058	15,577	18,707	20,560
India	Chandigarh	791	1,051	1,314	1,472
India	Jammu	588	859	1,079	1,211
India	Chennai (Madras)	6,353	7,559	9,170	10,129
India	Coimbatore	1,420	1,810	2,243	2,503
India	Delhi	12,441	17,015	20,484	22,498
India	Dhanbad	1,046	1,330	1,656	1,852

Country	City	Population estimates and projections (thousands)			
		2000	**2010**	**2020**	**2025**
India	Durg-Bhilainagar	905	1,174	1,465	1,640
India	Faridabad	1,018	1,512	1,887	2,109
India	Ghaziabad	928	1,464	1,830	2,046
India	Guwahati (Gauhati)	797	1,054	1,318	1,477
India	Gwalior	855	1,040	1,298	1,455
India	Hubli-Dharwad	776	948	1,184	1,327
India	Hyderabad	5,445	6,761	8,224	9,092
India	Indore	1,597	2,176	2,696	3,005
India	Jabalpur	1,100	1,369	1,703	1,904
India	Jaipur	2,259	3,136	3,867	4,298
India	Jalandhar	694	918	1,150	1,290
India	Jamshedpur	1,081	1,389	1,729	1,933
India	Jodhpur	842	1,062	1,327	1,486
India	Kanpur	2,641	3,369	4,141	4,601
India	Kochi (Cochin)	1,340	1,612	1,999	2,232
India	Kota	692	885	1,108	1,243
India	Kozhikode (Calicut)	875	1,008	1,257	1,409
India	Lucknow	2,221	2,877	3,546	3,944
India	Ludhiana	1,368	1,762	2,186	2,440
India	Madurai	1,187	1,367	1,697	1,897
India	Meerut	1,143	1,496	1,862	2,080
India	Moradabad	626	847	1,062	1,192
India	Mumbai (Bombay)	16,086	20,072	24,051	26,385
India	Mysore	776	943	1,179	1,322
India	Nagpur	2,089	2,611	3,219	3,583
India	Nashik	1,117	1,590	1,981	2,213
India	Patna	1,658	2,325	2,879	3,207
India	Pune (Poona)	3,655	5,010	6,135	6,797
India	Raipur	680	944	1,184	1,327
India	Rajkot	974	1,359	1,696	1,896
India	Ranchi	844	1,120	1,400	1,567
India	Salem	736	933	1,168	1,309
India	Solapur	853	1,135	1,417	1,587
India	Srinagar	954	1,218	1,518	1,699
India	Surat	2,699	4,174	5,142	5,703
India	Thiruvananthapuram	885	1,008	1,256	1,408
India	Tiruchirappalli	837	1,011	1,262	1,414
India	Vadodara	1,465	1,875	2,324	2,592
India	Varanasi (Benares)	1,199	1,434	1,781	1,991
India	Vijayawada	999	1,209	1,505	1,684
India	Visakhapatnam	1,309	1,628	2,020	2,256
Indonesia	Bandar Lampung	743	937	1,172	1,260
Indonesia	Bandung	2,138	2,568	3,156	3,370
Indonesia	Bogor	751	1,003	1,257	1,351
Indonesia	Jakarta	8,390	9,703	11,689	12,363
Indonesia	Malang	757	857	1,065	1,146
Indonesia	Medan	1,912	2,264	2,786	2,977
Indonesia	Padang	716	931	1,166	1,254
Indonesia	Palembang	1,459	1,903	2,361	2,526
Indonesia	Semarang	1,427	1,462	1,792	1,921
Indonesia	Surabaya	2,611	3,035	3,715	3,962
Indonesia	Pekan Baru	588	891	1,128	1,213
Indonesia	Ujung Pandang	1,051	1,374	1,713	1,837
Iran (Islamic Republic Of)	Ahvaz	867	1,056	1,252	1,326
Iran (Islamic Republic Of)	Esfahan	1,382	1,743	2,071	2,185
Iran (Islamic Republic Of)	Karaj	1,087	1,585	1,952	2,061
Iran (Islamic Republic Of)	Kermanshah	729	837	981	1,041
Iran (Islamic Republic Of)	Mashhad	2,073	2,654	3,151	3,315
Iran (Islamic Republic Of)	Qom	841	1,035	1,230	1,302
Iran (Islamic Republic Of)	Shiraz	1,115	1,300	1,521	1,608
Iran (Islamic Republic Of)	Tabriz	1,264	1,484	1,736	1,834
Iran (Islamic Republic Of)	Tehran	7,128	8,221	9,404	9,814

Country	City	Population estimates and projections (thousands)			
		2000	2010	2020	2025
Iraq	Al-Basrah (Basra)	759	923	1,143	1,270
Iraq	Al-Mawsil (Mosul)	1,056	1,447	1,891	2,097
Iraq	Baghdad	5,200	5,891	7,345	8,060
Iraq	Irbil (Erbil)	757	1,009	1,305	1,450
Israel	Hefa (Haifa)	888	1,043	1,159	1,210
Israel	Tel Aviv-Yafo (Tel Aviv-Jaffa)	2,752	3,256	3,600	3,726
Japan	Fukuoka-Kitakyushu	2,716	2,816	2,834	2,834
Japan	Hiroshima	2,044	2,045	2,046	2,046
Japan	Kyoto	1,806	1,804	1,804	1,804
Japan	Nagoya	3,122	3,267	3,295	3,295
Japan	Osaka-Kobe	11,165	11,337	11,368	11,368
Japan	Sapporo	2,508	2,556	2,565	2,565
Japan	Sendai	2,184	2,272	2,288	2,288
Japan	Tokyo	34,450	36,094	36,399	36,400
Jordan	Amman	1,007	1,106	1,268	1,359
Kazakhstan	Almaty	1,142	1,240	1,355	1,404
Kuwait	Al Kuwayt (Kuwait City)	1,499	2,305	2,790	2,956
Kyrgyzstan	Bishkek	770	869	1,011	1,096
Lebanon	Bayrut (Beirut)	1,487	1,941	2,119	2,173
Malaysia	Johore Bharu	630	999	1,294	1,382
Malaysia	Klang	631	1,128	1,503	1,603
Malaysia	Kuala Lumpur	1,306	1,519	1,820	1,938
Mongolia	Ulaanbaatar	763	919	1,044	1,112
Myanmar	Mandalay	810	1,034	1,308	1,446
Myanmar	Nay Pyi Taw	—	1,024	1,321	1,461
Myanmar	Yangon	3,553	4,348	5,361	5,869
Nepal	Kathmandu	644	1,029	1,578	1,907
Pakistan	Faisalabad	2,140	2,833	3,755	4,283
Pakistan	Gujranwala	1,224	1,643	2,195	2,513
Pakistan	Hyderabad	1,221	1,581	2,112	2,420
Pakistan	Islamabad	594	851	1,148	1,320
Pakistan	Karachi	10,019	13,052	16,922	19,095
Pakistan	Lahore	5,448	7,092	9,275	10,512
Pakistan	Multan	1,263	1,650	2,203	2,523
Pakistan	Peshawar	1,066	1,415	1,893	2,170
Pakistan	Quetta	614	836	1,128	1,298
Pakistan	Rawalpindi	1,519	2,015	2,683	3,067
Philippines	Cebu	721	862	1,062	1,153
Philippines	Davao	1,152	1,523	1,910	2,065
Philippines	Manila	9,958	11,662	13,892	14,808
Philippines	Zamboanga	605	856	1,098	1,192
Republic Of Korea	Goyang	744	960	1,012	1,012
Republic Of Korea	Bucheon	763	907	948	948
Republic Of Korea	Incheon	2,464	2,580	2,607	2,607
Republic Of Korea	Gwangju	1,346	1,474	1,507	1,507
Republic Of Korea	Busan	3,673	3,421	3,383	3,383
Republic Of Korea	Seongnam	911	954	971	971
Republic Of Korea	Seoul	9,917	9,762	9,738	9,738
Republic Of Korea	Suweon	932	1,130	1,178	1,179
Republic Of Korea	Daegu	2,478	2,455	2,458	2,458
Republic Of Korea	Daejon	1,362	1,507	1,544	1,544
Republic Of Korea	Ulsan	1,011	1,080	1,102	1,102
Saudi Arabia	Al-Madinah (Medina)	795	1,105	1,364	1,474
Saudi Arabia	Ar-Riyadh (Riyadh)	3,567	4,856	5,866	6,275
Saudi Arabia	Ad-Dammam	639	903	1,119	1,212
Saudi Arabia	Jiddah	2,509	3,239	3,906	4,190
Saudi Arabia	Makkah (Mecca)	1,168	1,486	1,806	1,948
Singapore	Singapore	4,017	4,592	4,965	5,104
Syrian Arab Republic	Dimashq (Damascus)	2,044	2,675	3,293	3,605
Syrian Arab Republic	Halab (Aleppo)	2,222	2,968	3,649	3,993
Syrian Arab Republic	Hims (Homs)	809	1,095	1,365	1,504
Thailand	Krung Thep (Bangkok)	6,332	6,918	7,807	8,332

Country	City	Population estimates and projections (thousands)			
		2000	2010	2020	2025
Turkey	Adana	1,123	1,362	1,557	1,635
Turkey	Ankara	3,179	3,908	4,403	4,589
Turkey	Antalya	595	839	969	1,021
Turkey	Bursa	1,180	1,589	1,817	1,906
Turkey	Gaziantep	844	1,109	1,274	1,340
Turkey	Istanbul	8,744	10,530	11,695	12,102
Turkey	Izmir	2,216	2,724	3,085	3,223
Turkey	Konya	734	978	1,126	1,185
United Arab Emirates	Dubayy (Dubai)	938	1,516	1,894	2,077
Uzbekistan	Tashkent	2,135	2,247	2,636	2,892
Viet Nam	Hai Phòng	1,704	2,129	2,752	3,096
Viet Nam	Hà Noi	3,752	4,723	6,036	6,754
Viet Nam	Thành Pho Ho Chí Minh (Ho Chi Minh City)	4,621	5,723	7,293	8,149
Yemen	Al-Hudaydah	457	951	1,528	1,854
Yemen	Sana'a'	1,365	2,345	3,636	4,382
Yemen	Ta'izz	465	902	1,437	1,743
EUROPE					
Austria	Wien (Vienna)	2,158	2,385	2,476	2,496
Belarus	Minsk	1,700	1,846	1,883	1,883
Bulgaria	Sofia	1,128	1,212	1,236	1,236
Czech Republic	Praha (Prague)	1,172	1,160	1,159	1,159
Denmark	København (Copenhagen)	1,077	1,087	1,095	1,096
Finland	Helsinki	1,019	1,139	1,195	1,220
France	Bordeaux	763	817	853	869
France	Lille	1,007	1,059	1,102	1,120
France	Lyon	1,362	1,443	1,495	1,516
France	Marseille-Aix-en-Provence	1,357	1,418	1,469	1,490
France	Nice-Cannes	894	941	980	997
France	Paris	9,692	9,958	10,031	10,036
France	Toulouse	778	863	900	916
Germany	Berlin	3,384	3,423	3,436	3,436
Germany	Hamburg	1,710	1,777	1,792	1,792
Germany	Köln (Cologne)	963	1,037	1,061	1,061
Germany	München (Munich)	1,202	1,300	1,318	1,318
Greece	Athínai (Athens)	3,179	3,256	3,300	3,326
Greece	Thessaloniki	797	837	865	880
Hungary	Budapest	1,787	1,664	1,655	1,655
Ireland	Dublin	989	1,098	1,257	1,332
Italy	Milano (Milan)	2,985	2,940	2,938	2,938
Italy	Napoli (Naples)	2,232	2,253	2,254	2,254
Italy	Palermo	855	865	869	871
Italy	Roma (Rome)	3,385	3,333	3,330	3,330
Italy	Torino (Turin)	1,694	1,647	1,645	1,645
Netherlands	Amsterdam	1,005	1,044	1,078	1,089
Netherlands	Rotterdam	991	1,014	1,046	1,057
Norway	Oslo	774	858	909	936
Poland	Kraków (Cracow)	756	755	755	755
Poland	Lódz	799	745	735	735
Poland	Warszawa (Warsaw)	1,666	1,724	1,736	1,736
Portugal	Lisboa (Lisbon)	2,672	2,890	3,058	3,086
Portugal	Porto	1,254	1,380	1,476	1,497
Romania	Bucuresti (Bucharest)	1,949	1,947	1,949	1,949
Russian Federation	Chelyabinsk	1,082	1,088	1,085	1,085
Russian Federation	Yekaterinburg	1,303	1,319	1,324	1,324
Russian Federation	Kazan	1,096	1,119	1,122	1,122
Russian Federation	Krasnoyarsk	911	930	935	935
Russian Federation	Moskva (Moscow)	10,016	10,495	10,526	10,526
Russian Federation	Nizhniy Novgorod	1,331	1,269	1,262	1,262
Russian Federation	Novosibirsk	1,426	1,376	1,366	1,366
Russian Federation	Omsk	1,136	1,129	1,125	1,125
Russian Federation	Perm	1,014	1,003	1,007	1,007
Russian Federation	Rostov-na-Donu (Rostov-on-Don)	1,061	1,047	1,044	1,044

Country	City	Population estimates and projections (thousands)			
		2000	2010	2020	2025
Russian Federation	Samara	1,173	1,126	1,119	1,119
Russian Federation	Sankt Peterburg (Saint Petersburg)	4,729	4,508	4,477	4,476
Russian Federation	Saratov	878	831	822	822
Russian Federation	Ufa	1,049	1,000	987	986
Russian Federation	Volgograd	1,010	973	965	965
Russian Federation	Voronezh	854	840	838	838
Serbia	Beograd (Belgrade)	1,127	1,096	1,132	1,163
Spain	Barcelona	4,560	5,057	5,182	5,183
Spain	Madrid	5,045	5,764	5,934	5,935
Spain	Valencia	795	816	841	847
Sweden	Stockholm	1,206	1,285	1,326	1,343
Switzerland	Zürich (Zurich)	1,078	1,119	1,150	1,172
Ukraine	Dnipropetrovs'k	1,077	1,045	1,042	1,042
Ukraine	Donets'k	1,026	978	972	972
Ukraine	Kharkiv	1,484	1,457	1,455	1,455
Ukraine	Kyiv (Kiev)	2,606	2,748	2,772	2,772
Ukraine	Odesa	1,037	977	970	970
Ukraine	Zaporizhzhya	822	778	772	772
United Kingdom	Birmingham	2,285	2,291	2,315	2,323
United Kingdom	Glasgow	1,171	1,164	1,187	1,197
United Kingdom	Liverpool	818	815	836	845
United Kingdom	London	8,225	8,607	8,618	8,618
United Kingdom	Manchester	2,243	2,235	2,258	2,267
United Kingdom	Newcastle upon Tyne	880	887	908	918
United Kingdom	West Yorkshire	1,495	1,539	1,565	1,575

LATIN AMERICA AND THE CARIBBEAN

Country	City	2000	2010	2020	2025
Argentina	Buenos Aires	11,847	13,089	13,653	13,768
Argentina	Córdoba	1,348	1,494	1,606	1,645
Argentina	Mendoza	838	918	993	1,020
Argentina	Rosario	1,152	1,233	1,326	1,360
Argentina	San Miguel de Tucumán	722	832	902	928
Bolivia	La Paz	1,390	1,692	2,027	2,178
Bolivia	Santa Cruz	1,054	1,551	1,876	2,016
Brazil	Baixada Santista	1,468	1,810	2,031	2,095
Brazil	Belém	1,748	2,335	2,639	2,717
Brazil	Belo Horizonte	4,659	5,941	6,597	6,748
Brazil	Brasília	2,746	3,938	4,463	4,578
Brazil	Campinas	2,264	3,003	3,380	3,474
Brazil	Campo Grande	654	830	943	978
Brazil	Cuiabá	686	857	972	1,008
Brazil	Curitiba	2,494	3,320	3,735	3,836
Brazil	Florianópolis	734	1,142	1,328	1,374
Brazil	Fortaleza	2,875	3,599	4,011	4,117
Brazil	Goiânia	1,608	2,189	2,482	2,556
Brazil	Grande São Luís	876	1,106	1,252	1,296
Brazil	Grande Vitória	1,398	1,829	2,067	2,132
Brazil	João Pessoa	827	1,012	1,142	1,183
Brazil	Maceió	952	1,281	1,460	1,510
Brazil	Manaus	1,392	1,898	2,156	2,223
Brazil	Natal	910	1,161	1,316	1,362
Brazil	Norte/Nordeste Catarinense	815	1,059	1,205	1,247
Brazil	Pôrto Alegre	3,505	4,096	4,517	4,633
Brazil	Recife	3,230	3,831	4,236	4,347
Brazil	Rio de Janeiro	10,803	12,171	13,179	13,413
Brazil	Salvador	2,968	3,695	4,114	4,222
Brazil	São Paulo	17,099	19,582	21,124	21,428
Brazil	Teresina	789	958	1,082	1,121
Chile	Santiago	5,275	5,879	6,224	6,310
Chile	Valparaíso	803	880	956	982
Colombia	Barranquilla	1,531	1,907	2,157	2,251
Colombia	Bucaramanga	855	1,073	1,223	1,282
Colombia	Cali	1,950	2,378	2,675	2,786

Country	City	Population estimates and projections (thousands)			
		2000	2010	2020	2025
Colombia	Cartagena	737	948	1,086	1,139
Colombia	Medellín	2,724	3,524	3,975	4,129
Colombia	Bogotá	6,356	8,320	9,299	9,600
Costa Rica	San José	1,032	1,374	1,627	1,737
Cuba	La Habana (Havana)	2,187	2,159	2,150	2,150
Dominican Republic	Santo Domingo	1,854	2,298	2,722	2,885
Ecuador	Guayaquil	2,077	2,690	3,154	3,328
Ecuador	Quito	1,357	1,846	2,189	2,316
El Salvador	San Salvador	1,233	1,520	1,776	1,902
Guatemala	Ciudad de Guatemala (Guatemala City)	908	1,104	1,481	1,690
Haiti	Port-au-Prince	1,653	2,209	3,012	3,346
Honduras	Tegucigalpa	793	1,022	1,317	1,472
Mexico	Aguascalientes	734	927	1,050	1,089
Mexico	Chihuahua	683	841	949	985
Mexico	Ciudad de México (Mexico City)	18,022	19,485	20,695	21,009
Mexico	Ciudad Juárez	1,225	1,396	1,544	1,597
Mexico	Culiacán	749	837	928	964
Mexico	Guadalajara	3,703	4,408	4,847	4,973
Mexico	León de los Aldamas	1,290	1,573	1,758	1,817
Mexico	Mérida	848	1,017	1,139	1,180
Mexico	Mexicali	770	935	1,051	1,090
Mexico	Monterrey	3,266	3,901	4,298	4,413
Mexico	Puebla	1,907	2,318	2,578	2,657
Mexico	Querétaro	795	1,032	1,172	1,215
Mexico	Saltillo	643	802	907	942
Mexico	San Luis Potosí	858	1,050	1,181	1,223
Mexico	Tijuana	1,287	1,666	1,881	1,943
Mexico	Toluca de Lerdo	1,417	1,584	1,743	1,802
Mexico	Torreón	1,014	1,201	1,339	1,387
Nicaragua	Managua	887	944	1,104	1,193
Panama	Ciudad de Panamá (Panama City)	1,072	1,379	1,653	1,759
Paraguay	Asunción	1,507	2,030	2,506	2,715
Peru	Arequipa	705	862	984	1,038
Peru	Lima	7,116	8,375	9,251	9,600
Puerto Rico	San Juan	2,237	2,758	2,803	2,803
Uruguay	Montevideo	1,561	1,504	1,515	1,520
Venezuela (Bolivarian Rep. Of)	Barquisimeto	947	1,184	1,356	1,420
Venezuela (Bolivarian Rep. Of)	Caracas	2,864	3,098	3,482	3,619
Venezuela (Bolivarian Rep. Of)	Maracaibo	1,725	2,200	2,501	2,606
Venezuela (Bolivarian Rep. Of)	Maracay	899	1,060	1,214	1,271
Venezuela (Bolivarian Rep. Of)	Valencia	1,370	1,900	2,172	2,266
NORTH AMERICA					
Canada	Calgary	953	1,182	1,304	1,345
Canada	Edmonton	924	1,112	1,217	1,256
Canada	Montréal	3,471	3,781	4,014	4,108
Canada	Ottawa-Gatineau	1,079	1,182	1,274	1,315
Canada	Toronto	4,607	5,447	5,827	5,946
Canada	Vancouver	1,959	2,219	2,380	2,444
United States Of America	Atlanta	3,542	4,695	5,035	5,151
United States Of America	Austin	913	1,216	1,329	1,372
United States Of America	Baltimore	2,083	2,322	2,508	2,578
United States Of America	Boston	4,049	4,597	4,919	5,032
United States Of America	Bridgeport-Stamford	894	1,056	1,154	1,193
United States Of America	Buffalo	977	1,046	1,142	1,180
United States Of America	Charlotte	769	1,044	1,144	1,183
United States Of America	Chicago	8,333	9,211	9,756	9,932
United States Of America	Cincinnati	1,508	1,687	1,831	1,886
United States Of America	Cleveland	1,789	1,944	2,104	2,165
United States Of America	Columbus, Ohio	1,138	1,314	1,431	1,477
United States Of America	Dallas-Fort Worth	4,172	4,955	5,300	5,419
United States Of America	Dayton	706	800	878	909
United States Of America	Denver-Aurora	1,998	2,396	2,590	2,661

Country	City	Population estimates and projections (thousands)			
		2000	2010	2020	2025
United States Of America	Detroit	3,909	4,203	4,499	4,606
United States Of America	El Paso	678	780	856	886
United States Of America	Hartford	853	942	1,031	1,066
United States Of America	Honolulu	720	813	891	923
United States Of America	Houston	3,849	4,609	4,936	5,049
United States Of America	Indianapolis	1,228	1,491	1,623	1,673
United States Of America	Jacksonville, Florida	886	1,023	1,119	1,157
United States Of America	Kansas City	1,365	1,514	1,645	1,696
United States Of America	Las Vegas	1,335	1,917	2,085	2,146
United States Of America	Los Angeles-Long Beach-Santa Ana	11,814	12,773	13,461	13,672
United States Of America	Louisville	866	980	1,071	1,108
United States Of America	Memphis	976	1,118	1,221	1,262
United States Of America	Miami	4,946	5,755	6,141	6,272
United States Of America	Milwaukee	1,311	1,429	1,553	1,602
United States Of America	Minneapolis-St Paul	2,397	2,695	2,905	2,983
United States Of America	Nashville-Davidson	755	912	999	1,034
United States Of America	New Orleans	1,009	982	1,002	1,037
United States Of America	New York-Newark	17,846	19,441	20,370	20,628
United States Of America	Oklahoma City	748	813	891	922
United States Of America	Orlando	1,165	1,401	1,526	1,574
United States Of America	Philadelphia	5,160	5,630	6,003	6,133
United States Of America	Phoenix-Mesa	2,934	3,687	3,964	4,062
United States Of America	Pittsburgh	1,755	1,889	2,044	2,105
United States Of America	Portland	1,595	1,946	2,110	2,172
United States Of America	Providence	1,178	1,318	1,435	1,481
United States Of America	Richmond	822	944	1,033	1,069
United States Of America	Riverside-San Bernardino	1,516	1,808	1,962	2,021
United States Of America	Rochester	696	781	856	887
United States Of America	Sacramento	1,402	1,662	1,805	1,860
United States Of America	Salt Lake City	890	998	1,091	1,128
United States Of America	San Antonio	1,333	1,522	1,655	1,706
United States Of America	San Diego	2,683	3,002	3,231	3,315
United States Of America	San Francisco-Oakland	3,236	3,544	3,803	3,898
United States Of America	San Jose	1,543	1,720	1,865	1,921
United States Of America	Seattle	2,727	3,174	3,415	3,503
United States Of America	St Louis	2,081	2,260	2,441	2,510
United States Of America	Tampa-St Petersburg	2,072	2,389	2,581	2,652
United States Of America	Tucson	724	854	936	969
United States Of America	Virginia Beach	1,397	1,535	1,667	1,719
United States Of America	Washington, DC	3,949	4,464	4,778	4,009
OCEANIA					
Australia	Adelaide	1,102	1,167	1,258	1,300
Australia	Brisbane	1,603	1,970	2,170	2,233
Australia	Melbourne	3,433	3,851	4,137	4,238
Australia	Perth	1,373	1,598	1,746	1,800
Australia	Sydney	4,078	4,427	4,716	4,826
New Zealand	Auckland	1,063	1,321	1,441	1,475

SOURCE: United Nations Department of Economic and Social Affairs/Population Division, World Urbanization Prospects: The 2007 Revision

Slum population - 2005

Country	Slum population in urban areas (thousands)	Slum population as percentage of urban population (%)	Country	Slum population in urban areas (thousands)	Slum population as percentage of urban population (%)
Afghanistan	4,629		Jordan	719	15.8
Angola	4,678	86.5	Kenya	3,897	54.8
Anguilla	4	36.7	Lao People's Democratic Republic	969	79.3
Antigua and Barbuda	1	4.8	Lebanon	1,757	53.1
Argentina	9,343	26.2	Lesotho	118	35.1
Bangladesh	25,184	70.8	Madagascar	4,022	80.6
Belize	61	47.3	Malawi	1,468	66.4
Benin	2,427	71.8	Mali	2,715	65.9
Bhutan	49		Martinique	6	1.6
Bolivia	2,972	50.4	Mexico	11,686	14.4
Brazil	45,509	29.0	Mongolia	869	57.9
Burkina Faso	1,438	59.5	Morocco	2,422	13.1
Burundi	485	64.3	Mozambique	5,430	79.5
Cambodia	2,309	78.9	Myanmar	7,062	45.6
Cameroon	4,224	47.4	Namibia	242	33.9
Central African Republic	1,446	94.1	Nepal	2,595	60.7
Chad	2,247	91.3	Nicaragua	1,473	45.5
Chile	1,270	9.0	Niger	1,938	82.6
China	174,745	32.9	Nigeria	41,664	65.8
Colombia	5,920	17.9	Oman	1,461	
Comoros	204	68.9	Pakistan	26,613	47.5
Congo	1,285	53.4	Panama	430	23.0
Costa Rica	290	10.9	Paraguay	634	17.6
Côte d'Ivoire	4,589	56.2	Peru	7,329	36.1
Democratic Republic of the Congo	14,115	76.4	Philippines	22,768	43.7
Dominican Republic	1,043	17.6	Rwanda	1,251	71.6
Ecuador	1,808	21.5	Saint Lucia	6	11.9
Egypt	5,405	17.1	Saudi Arabia	4,070	18.0
El Salvador	1,166	28.9	Senegal	1,846	38.1
Equatorial Guinea	130	66.3	Sierra Leone	2,180	97.0
Ethiopia	10,118	81.8	Somalia	2,838	73.5
French Guiana	15	10.5	South Africa	8,077	28.7
Gabon	447	38.7	Sri Lanka	345	
Gambia	371	45.4	Sudan	13,914	94.2
Ghana	4,805	45.4	Suriname	13	3.9
Grenada	2	6.0	Syrian Arab Republic	982	10.5
Guadeloupe	24	5.4	Thailand	2,061	26.0
Guatemala	2,550	42.9	Togo	1,529	62.1
Guinea	1,418	45.7	Trinidad and Tobago	247	24.7
Guinea-Bissau	390	83.1	Turkey	7,635	15.5
Guyana	72	33.7	Uganda	2,420	66.7
Haiti	2,316	70.1	United Republic of Tanzania	6,157	66.4
Honduras	1,169	34.9	Venezuela (Bolivarian Republic of)	7,521	32.0
India	110,225	34.8	Viet Nam	9,192	41.3
Indonesia	28,159	26.3	Yemen		67.2
Iran (Islamic Republic of)	14,581	30.3	Zambia	2,336	57.2
Iraq	9,692	52.8	Zimbabwe	835	17.9
Jamaica	852	60.5			

Source: UN-HABITAT UrbanInfo database 2006

Bibliography

A

ADB, DFID & World Bank. (2006, March). *Asia 2015: Promoting growth, ending poverty.* Proceedings of the Asia 2015 conference, London, U.K.

Addison, T., & Cornia, A.G. (2001, September). *Income distribution policies for faster poverty reduction.* (Discussion Paper No. 2001/93). Helsinki: United Nations University World Institute for Development Economics Research.

Agostini, C. & Brown, P. (2007, March). *Spatial inequality in Chile.* Social Science Research Network. Retrieved 10 July, 2008, from http://ssrn.com/abstract=972771.

Aguilar, A. G. & Ward, P. (2003). Globalization, regional development and mega-city expansion in Latin America: Analyzing Mexico City's peri-urban hinterland. *Cities,* 20(1), 3-21.

Akita, T., Lukman, R.A. (1999). Spatial patterns of expenditure inequalities in Indonesia. *Bulletin of Indonesian Economic Studies,* 35(2), 67-90.

Akita, T., Lukman, R.A., & Yamada, Y. (1999). Inequalities in the distribution of household expenditures in Indonesia: A Theil decomposition analysis. *The Developing Economies,* 37(2), 197–221.

Alam, M. & Rabbani, M.D.G. (2007). Vulnerabilities and responses to climate change for Dhaka. *Environment and Urbanization,* 19(1), 81-97.

Alesina, A., & Di Tella, R. (2001, April). *Inequality and happiness: Are Europeans and Americans different?* (NBER Working Paper No. 8198). Cambridge, MA: National Bureau of Economic Research.

Allen, A., da Silva, N., & Corubolo, E. (1999). Environmental problems and opportunities of the peri-urban interface and their impact upon the poor. Report prepared for the research project, *Strategic environmental planning and management for the peri-urban interface,* Development Planning Unit, London. Retrieved 10 July, 2008, from http://www.ucl.ac.uk/dpu/pui/research/previous/epm/allen.htm.

Allen, A. & You, N. (2002). *Sustainable Urbanisation: Bridging the Green and Brown Agendas,* Development Planning Unit in collaboration with DFID and UN-Habitat, London.

Altimir, O. (2002, December). Income distribution in Argentina 1974-2001. In *Revista de la CEPAL No. 78* (pp. 55-85). Santiago, Chile: Economic Commission for Latin America and the Caribbean.

American Planning Association. (2006). *About Enrique Peñalosa.* Accessed 26 December, 2007, from http://www.planning.org/lenfant/aboutpenalosa.htm.

Anandram, S. (2004, October). *The next wave: Opportunities along the U.S.-India technology corridor.* Paper presented at the India IT Forum, Singapore.

Anderson, D.M. (2002). Vigilantes, violence and the politics of public order in Kenya. *African Affairs,* 101, 531-555.

Angel, S., Sheppard, S.C., & Civco, D.L. (2005). *The dynamics of global urban expansion.* Washington, D.C.: The World Bank.

Antipolis, S. (2002, Novembre). Indicators for sustainable development in the Mediterranean coastal regions: National report of Libya. *Plan Bleu pour l'environnement et le développement en Méditerranée Régional Activité Centre UNEP,* Portoroz, Slovenia.

Armstrong, W. & McGee, T.G. (1985). *Theatres of accumulation: Studies in Latin American and Asian urbanization.* London: Methuen.

Arnstein, S.R. (1969). A ladder of citizen participation. *Journal of the American Institute of Planners.* 35, 216-224.

Asian Urban Center of Kobe. (1987, August). *Report of the Asian conference on population and development in medium-sized cities.* Kobe, Japan: United Nations Population Fund, the City of Kobe and Nihon University Population Research Institute.

Associated Press. (2008, 27 February). UN report predicts half world's people will live in cities by year's end. New York, New York: Author.

Asomani-Boateng, R. & Haight, M. (n.d.). *Reusing organic solid waste in urban farming in African cities: a challenge for urban planners.* Retrieved 1 May, 2008, from http://www.idrc.ca/fr/ev-33948-201-1-DO TOPIC.html.

Australian Bureau of Statistics. (1996). Population growth, capital city growth and development.

Australian Social Trends, 4102. Retrieved 20 July, 2008, from http://www.abs.gov.au.

Australian Bureau of Statistics. (2003). *Australian social trends, 2003.* Retrieved 10 July, 2008, from http://www.abs.gov.au.

B

Bacolod City. (2007). *Most competitive mid-sized city.* Retrieved 20 July, 2008, from http://www.bacolodcity.gov.ph/bacolod city.htm.

Bah, M., Cisse, S., Diyamett, B., Diallo, G., Lerise, F., Okali, D., Okpara, E., Olawoye, J., & Tacoli, C. (2003). Changing rural-urban linkages in Mali, Nigeria and Tanzania. *Environment and Urbanization,* 15(1), 13-23.

Bailis, R., Pennise, D., Ezzati, M., Kammen, D.M., & Kituyi, E. (2004). *Impacts of greenhouse gas and particulate emissions from woodfuel production and end-use in sub-Saharan Africa.* University of California, Berkeley: Renewable and Appropriate Energy Laboratory. Retrieved 1 November, 2007, from http://rael.berkeley.edu/old-site/OA5.1.pdf.

Balaras, C.A., Gaglia, A.G., Georgopoulou, E., Mirasgedis, S., Sarafidis, Y., & Lalas, D.P. (2007). European residential buildings and empirical assessment of the Hellenic building stock, energy consumption, emissions and potential energy savings. *Building and Environment,* 42(3), 1298-1314.

Balk, D., McGranahan, G., & Anderson, B. (2008). Urbanization and ecosystems: Current patterns and future implications. In: G. Martine, G. McGranahan, & M. Montgomery (Eds.), *The new global frontier: Cities, poverty and environment in the 21st century.* London: Earthscan.

Barnes, D.F., Krutilla, K., & Hyde. W. (2004) *The urban household energy transition: Energy, poverty, and the environment in the developing world.* Washington, D.C.: Energy Sector Management Assistance Program. Retrieved 1 May, 2008, from http://www.esmap.org/filez/pubs/8162007122407 UrbanEnergyTransition.pdf.

Baumert, K., Herzog, T., & Pershing, J. (2005). *Navigating the numbers: Greenhouse gas data and international climate policy.* Washington, D.C.: World Resources Institute.

Bazoglu, N. (1992). *The Antalya gecekondu project: Progress, challenges and prospects.*

(Evaluation report for UNICEF's Ankara Office). Ankara: UNICEF.

Bazoglu, N. (1998, January), *Ein Helwan and Al Nahda: Assessment of the urban community development project in Cairo metropolitan area.* (Evaluation report for UNICEF's Cairo Office and the Regional Office for the Middle East and North Africa). Amman: UNICEF.

Bazoglu, N. (2007, July). *Cities in transition: Demographics and the development of cities.* Paper presented at the Innovations for an Urban World Global Urban Summit, Bellagio, Italy.

BBC News. (n.d.). *Special reports: Africa's economy.* Retrieved 20 July, 2008, from http://news.bbc.co.uk/2/shared/spl/hi/africa/05/africa_economy/html/poverty.stm.

Beauchemin, C. & Bocquier, P. (2004). Migration and urbanization in Francophone West Africa: An overview of the recent empirical evidence. Urban Studies, 41(11), 2245-2272.

Benn, H. (2005, September 8). *Connecting people and places.* Speech delivered at the Development Studies Association, Milton Keynes, United Kingdom. Retrieved 8 January, 2008, from http://www.dfid.gov.uk/News/files/Speeches/dsa-connect-pandp.asp.

Bettencourt, L.M.A., Lobo, J., Helbing, D., Kühnert, C., & West, G.B. (2007). Growth, innovation, scaling, and the pace of life in cities. *Proceedings of the National Academy of Sciences of the United States of America*, 104(17), 7301-7306.

Bhagat, R. (2005, March). *Urban growth by city and town size in India.* Paper presented to the annual meeting of Population Association of America, Philadelphia, PA.

Biau, D. (2007). Chinese cities, Indian cities: A telling contrast. *Economic and Political Weekly.* 42(33), 3369-3372.

Birdsall, N., Levine, R., & Ibrahim, A. (2005). *Toward universal primary education: Investments, incentives, and institutions.* London: Earthscan.

Blair, T. (2006, March). Tony Blair's speech to Asia 2015 conference. Retrieved 20 July, 2008, from http://www.asia2015conference.org

Blue, T. (2000). Individual and contextual effects on mental health status in São Paulo, Brazil. *Brazilian Journal of Psychiatry*, 22(3), 116-123.

Borja, J. (2004). *Informe sobre la Gobernabilidad de las Áreas Metropolitanas en el Mundo Actual.* Desafio Metropolitano, Asamblea Legislativa del Distrito Federal, UNAM, México.

Borooah, V. K., Gustafsson, B., & Li, S. (2006). China and India: Income inequality and poverty north and south of the Himalayas. *Journal of Asian Economics*, 17(5), 797-817.

Botswana, Central Statistics Office, 2007.

Bretas, P.R.P. (1996), Participative budgeting in Belo Horizonte: Democratization and citizenship. *Environment and Urbanization*, 8(6), 213-222.

Brolin, B.C. (1972). Chandigarh was planned by experts but something has gone wrong. *Smithsonian*, 3(3), 56-63.

Browder, J., Bohland, J.R., & Scarpadi, J.L. (1995) Patterns of development on the metropolitan fringe — Urban fringe expansion in Bangkok, Jakarta and Santiago. *Journal of the American Planning Association*, 61(3), 310-327.

Building and Social Housing Foundation. (2008). World Habitat Awards 2008.

Butera, F.M. (2004). *Dalla caverna alla casa ecologica — Storia del comfort e dell'energia.* Milano: Edizioni Ambiente.

C

Cameron, R. (2005). Metropolitan restructuring (and more restructuring) in South Africa. *Public Administration and Development*, 25(4), 329-339.

Census of India. (1991). Recent trends in urbanization and rural-urban migration in India: Some explanations and projections. *Urban India*, 15(1), 1-17.

Center for International Earth Science Information Network. (2005). *Coastal Analysis Data Set utilizing GRUMP (Global Rural and Urban Mapping Program) beta population and land area grids.* Retrieved 1 October, 2007, from http://beta.sedac.ciesin.columbia.edu/gpw/.

Centre for Urban Studies, MEASURE Evaluation & National Institute of Population Research and Training. (2006, May). *Slums of urban Bangladesh: Mapping and census, 2005.* Dhaka: Centre for Urban Studies. Retrieved 1 May, 2008, from http://www.cpc.unc.edu/measure/publications/pdf/tr-06-35.pdf.

Centro de Investigaciones de la Economía Mundial (CIEM — World Economy Research Centre). (1996). *Study of human development in Cuba.* Havana: Caguayos S.A.

China Urban Statistical Yearbook, 1991

Chowdhury, S., Negassa, A., & Torrero, M. (2005). *Market institutions: Enhancing the value of rural-urban links.* (FCND Discussion Paper 195). Washington, D.C.: International Food Policy Research Institute.

Cities Alliance. (2006). *Guide to city development strategies: Improving urban performance.* Washington, D.C.: Author.

City Council of Nairobi. (2007). *Environment Outlook.* Nairobi: Author.

Clements, B. (1997). The real plan: Poverty and income distribution in Brazil. *Finance & Development*, 34(3), 44-46. Retrieved 10 July, 2008, from http://www.worldbank.org/fandd/english/pdfs/0997/0180997.pdf.

Cloes, D.V. (2008). Income distribution trends in Brazil and China: Evaluating absolute and relative economic growth. *Quarterly Review of Economics and Finance*, 48(2), 359-369.

Coastal Portal. (2007). *Coastal cities.* Retrieved 10 July, 2008, from http://www.encora.eu/coastalwiki/Coastal_Cities.

Cogneau, D., et al. (2007). *Inequality and Intergenerational Mobility Africa",* July 2007

Cogneau, D., Bossuroy, T., De Vreyer, P., Guénard, C., Hiller, V., Leite, P., Mesplé-Somps, S., Pasquier-Doumer, L., & Torelli, C. (2006). *Inequalities and equity in Africa.* (Working Paper DT/2006-11). Paris: DIAL. Retrieved 10 July, 2008, from http://www.dial.prd.fr/dial_publications/PDF/Doc_travail/2006-11_english.pdf.

Cohen, B. (2004). Urban growth in developing countries: A review of current trends and a caution regarding existing forecasts. *World Development*, 32(1), 23-51.

Commission of the European Communities. (2001, November). *Proposal for a directive of the European Parliament and of the Council on the energy performance of buildings.* Retrieved 4 April, 2008, from http://ec.europa.eu/energy/library/en_bat_en.pdf.

Cornia, G.A. (2005, October). *Policy reform and income distribution.* (DESA Working Paper No. 3). New York: UN/DESA.

Council of European Municipalities and Regions. European Commission — DG Employment and Social Affairs. (2005). *The town for equality: A methodology and good practices for equal opportunities between men and women.*

Creative City Network of Canada. (2005). *Making the case for culture: Urban renewal and revitalization.* Retrieved 20 July, 2008, fromhttp://www.creativecity.ca/resources/making-the-case/urban-renewal-1.html.

D

Dai, E. (2005, June). *Income inequality in urban China: A case study of Beijing.* (Working Paper Series Vol. 2005-04). Kitakyushu, Japan: The

International Centre for the Study of East Asian Development.

Dammert, L. & Borja, J. (2004). *La ciudad conquistada*. EURE (Santiago), 30(90), 124-126.

Dansereau, S. & Zamponi, M. (2005). Zimbabwe: The political economy of decline. Nordiska Afrikaninstitutet, Sweden.

Davao City. (2007). *Achievements and recognition*. Retrieved 20 July, 2008, from http://www.davaocity.gov.ph/about/awards.htm.

Dávila, J. (2006). Falling between stools? Policies, strategies and the peri-urban interface. In D. McGregor, D. Simon, & D. Thompson (Eds.), *The peri-urban interface: Approaches to sustainable natural and human resource use* (pp. 44-56). London: Earthscan.

Delken, E. (2007). Happiness in shrinking cities in Germany. *Journal of Happiness Studies*, 9(2), 213-218.

Demurger, S., Fournier, M., & Li, S. (2006). Urban income inequality in China revisited (1988–2002). *Economics Letters*, 93(3), 354-59.

Di Cicco, P.G. (2006, March). *The soul of the city*. Speech delivered to the mayor of Tampa and civic leaders at the University Club, Tampa, FL. Retrieved 20 July, 2008, from http://www.toronto.ca/culture/pdf/poet/2006/2006TheSoulofaCity.pdf.

Douglass, M. (1998). A regional network strategy for reciprocal rural-urban linkages: An agenda for policy research with reference to Indonesia. *Third World Planning Review*, 20(1), 1-33.

Dragicevic, S.M. (2007). Culture as a resource of city development. In N. Svob-Dokic (Ed.), *The creative city: Crossing visions and new realities in the region*. Zagreb: Culturelink Joint Publications Series No. 11, Institute for International Relations.

E

Eberstadt, N. (1998, 1 September). Asia tomorrow: Gray and male. *National Interest*.

ECLAC. (2002). *Preliminary overview of the economies of Latin America and the Caribbean*. New York: United Nations.

ECLAC, UNFPA & PAHO. (1999, September). Unpublished material from the Latin American and Caribbean symposium on older persons, Santiago, Chile.

Economic Commission for Latin America and the Caribbean (ECLAC). (2000, October). *From rapid urbanization to the consolidation of human settlements in Latin America and the Caribbean: A territorial perspective*. (Working paper LC/G.2116).

Santiago, Chile: Author. Retrieved 20 July, 2008, from http://www.eclac.cl/publicaciones/xml/1/5071/G-2116-i.pdf.

Economist.com. (2007, 22 August). *Where the grass is greener*. Retrieved 20 July, 2008, from http://www.economist.com/markets/rankings/displaystory.cfm?story_id=8908454.

Ellis, F. (1998). Household strategies and rural livelihoods diversification. *Journal of Development Studies*, 35(1), 1-35.

ENERDATA. (2003). *Energy efficiency in the European Union 1990–2001*. SAVE-Odyssee project on energy efficiency indicators, Enerdata SA in collaboration with the Fraunhofer Institute Systems & Innovation Research.

European Commission. (2007). *Eurostat regional yearbook 2007*. Luxembourg: Author.

European Community Directorate General for Regional Policy. (2007, May). *State of European cities report*. (Study contracted by the European Commission). Retrieved 10 July, 2008, from http://ec.europa.eu/regional_policy/sources/docgener/studies/pdf/urban/stateofcities_2007.pdf.

Evans, G.W., Wells, N.M., & Moch, A. (2003). Housing and mental health: A review of the evidence and a methodological and conceptual critique. *Journal of Social Issues*, 59(3), 475-500.

F

Fernandes, E. (2007). Implementing the urban reform agenda in Brazil. *Environment and Urbanization*, 19(177), 177-189.

Fernández-Maldonado, A.M. (2007, June). *Fifty years of barriadas in Lima: Revisiting Turner and De Soto*. Paper presented at the ENHR 2007 International Conference on Sustainable Urban Areas, Rotterdam, the Netherlands.

Fleisher, B. M. & Yang, D. T. (2004). China's labor markets. *China Economic Review*, 14(4), 426-433.

Florida, R. (2002). *The rise of the creative class: And how it's transforming work, leisure, community and everyday life*. Jackson, TN: Basic Books.

Follath, E. & Spörl, G. (2007, 28 August). An inside look at Europe's coolest cities. *Spiegel Online International*. Retrieved 20 July, 2008, from http://www.spiegel.de/international/europe/0,1518,502297,00.html.

Forester, J. (1999). *The deliberative practitioner*. Cambridge, MA: MIT Press.

Frayne, B. (2005). Survival of the poorest: Migration and food security in Namibia. In

L.J.A. Mougeot (Ed.), AGROPOLIS: *The social, political, and environmental dimensions of urban agriculture*. London: Earthscan/IDRC. Retrieved 20 August, 2007, from:http://www.idrc.ca/es/ev-85401-201-1-DO_TOPIC.html.

Friedmann, J. (2007). *The wealth of cities: Towards an assets-based development of newly urbanizing regions*. Paper delivered at the UN-HABITAT Lecture Award Series, No. 1, Nairobi, Kenya.

G

Galea, S., Ahern, J., Rudenstine, S., Wallace, Z. & Vlahov, D. (2005). Urban built environment and depression: A multilevel analysis. *Journal of Epidemiology and Community Health*, 59, 822-827.

Gallup, J.L., Sachs, J., & Mellinger, A.D. (1998, April). *Geography and economic growth*. Paper prepared for the Annual Bank Conference on Development Economics (ABCDE), World Bank, Washington, D.C.

Garau, P. (2008, March). *Policy analysis and recommendations*. Paper commissioned by UN-HABITAT for the *State of the World's Cities Report 2008/9*.

Gaurav, D. & Ravallion, M. (2002). Is India's economic growth leaving the poor behind? *Journal of Economic Perspectives*, 16(3), 89-108.

Gehl Sampath, P. (2007). Intellectual property and innovation in least developed countries: Pharmaceuticals, agro-processing and textiles and RMG in Bangladesh. (Background Paper No. 9 for the UNCTAD LDC Report of 2007). Geneva: UNCTAD.

Gibb, A.A. (1986). Research for regional and national self employment programmes. In R. E. Nelson (Ed.), *Entrepreneurship and self employment training* (pp. 91-109). Manila: Asian Development Bank and ILO.

Gilbert, A. (1993). Third world cities: The changing national settlement system. *Urban Studies*, 30(4/5), 721-740.

Global Footprint Network. (n.d.). *Humanity footprint 1961-2003*. Retrieved 1September, 2007, from http://www.footprintnetwork.org/gfn_sub.php?content=global_footprint.

Gobierno de Chile. (2004, Diciembre). *Informe sobre las metas del Milenio – Meta 11*. Informe a Hábitat, Ministerio de Vivienda y Urbanismo.

Goldemberg, J. (2000). Rural energy in developing countries. In J. Goldemberg (Ed.), *World energy assessment: Energy and the challenge of sustainability*. Nairobi: United Nations Development Programme.

Gospodini, A. (2002, March). *European cities and place-identity*. Department of Planning and Regional Development, School of Engineering, University of Thessaly Discussion Paper Series, 8(2), 19-36.

Government of China. (n.d.). *The 11th five-year plan*. Retrieved 20 July, 2008, from http://english. gov.cn/special/115y_index.htm.

Government of India (2002). *National human development report 2001*. Delhi: Government of India, Planning Commission.

Government of Kenya. (2007). *Kenya integrated household budget survey 2005/6*. Nairobi: Central Bureau of Statistics and Ministry of Planning and National Development.

Graham, C. & Felton, A. (2006). Inequality and happiness: Insights from Latin America. *Journal of Economic Inequality*, 4(1), 1569-1721.

Grandstaff, S.W. (1989). The role of demand in provincial industry. *TDRI Quarterly Review*, 4(4), 8-10, 23.]

Greener, R., Jefferis, K., & Siphambe, H. (2000, July). *The impacts of HIV/Aids on poverty and inequality in Botswana*. Paper presented at the International Conference on AIDS, Botswana.

Grimm, M. (2001, September). *A decomposition of inequality and poverty changes in the context of macroeconomic adjustment: A microstimulation study for Cote d'Ivoire*. (UN University WIDER, Discussion Paper 2001/91). Retrieved 10 July, 2008, from http://www.unu.edu/hq/library/Collection/PDF_files/WIDER/WIDERdp2001.91.pdf.

Gustafsson, B. & Nivorzhkina, L. (2005). How and why transition made income inequality increase in urban Russia: A local study. *Journal of Comparative Economics*, 33, 772-787.

Gwebu, T.D. (2004, July). *Patterns and trends of urbanization in Botswana: Policy implications for sustainability*. Paper prepared for City Futures: An international conference on globalism and urban change. Retrieved 20 July, 2008, from http://www.uic.edu/cuppa/cityfutures/program.html#papers.

H

Ha, H. & Wong, T.C. (1999). Economic reforms and the new master plan of Ho Chi Minh City, Viet Nam: Implementation issues and policy recommendations. *Geojournal* 49, 301-309.

Hamilton, D. (1999). *Governing metropolitan areas*. New York: Garland Publishing.

Hardoy, J., Mitlin, D., & Satterthwaite, D. (2004) *Environmental problems in an urbanizing world*. London: Earthscan.

Hartless, R. (2003). *Application of energy performance regulations to existing buildings*. (Final report of the Task B4, ENPER TEBUC Project, SAVE 4.1031/C/00-018). Watford, U.K.: Building Research Establishment.

Harvey, D. (1989). From managerialism to entrepreneurialism: The transformation in urban governance in late capitalism. *Geografiska Annaler. Series B, Human Geography*, 71(1), 3-17.

Healy, J.D. (2003). Housing conditions, energy efficiency, affordability and satisfaction with housing: A pan-European analysis. *Housing Studies*, 18(3), 409–424.

Heisz, A. (2005). *Ten things to know about Canadian metropolitan areas: A synthesis of Statistics Canada's trends and conditions in census metropolitan areas series*. (Catalogue no. 89-613-MIE – No.009). Ottawa: Statistics Canada.

Henderson, J.V. & Wang, H.G. (2006, September). *Urbanization and city growth: The role of institutions*. (Working Paper, Brown University Department of Economics). Providence, RI: Brown University. Retrieved 20 July, 2008, from http://www.econ.brown.edu.

Hoang, X., Dang, N., & Tacoli, C. (2005). *Livelihood diversification and rural-urban linkages in Viet Nam's Red River Delta*. (Rural-Urban Working Paper No. 11). London: IIED.

Hodder, R. (2000). *Development Geography*. London: Routledge.

Holcim Forum for Sustainable Construction. (2007, April). *Enrique Peñalosa*. Accessed 26 December, 2007, from http://www.holcimfoundation.org/T431/EnriquePealosa.htm.

Holdren, J. P. & Smith, K. R. (2000). Energy, the environment, and health. In J. Goldemberg (Ed.), *World energy assessment: Energy and the challenge of sustainability*. Nairobi: United Nations Development Programme.

Hossain, M.A. & Karunathne, N.D. (2002). *Export response to the reduction of anti-export bias: Empirics from Bangladesh*. (Discussion Paper No. 303, The University of Queensland School of Economics). Brisbane: The University of Queensland, Brisbane.

Hu, X.W. & Yeung, Y.M. (1992). *China's coastal cities: Catalysts for modernization*. Honolulu: University of Hawaii Press.

Hunter, D. & Marks, L. (2008). *Decision-making processes for effective policy implementation*. London: National Institute for Health and Clinical Excellence. Retrieved 10 July, 2008,http://www.nice.org.uk/niceMedia/pdf/SemRef_Decision_Hunter.pdf.

I

IMF Staff. (2003, July). Africa: Recent economic developments and IMF activities. Retrieved 1 November, 2007, from http://www.imf.org/external/np/exr/ib/2003/072403.htm.

INIE National Economic Research Institute, Cuba. (2005, July). *Millennium Development Goals: Cuba second report*. Havana: Mercie Group-ENPESES, CUJAE.

Innovations for an urban world: A global urban summit, Bellagio, Italy, July 2007.

Institute of Applied Economic Research (IPEA). (2007). *Atlas do desenvolvimento urbano no Brazil*. Brasilia: Author.

Inter-American Development Bank. (2000). *Facing up to inequality in Latin America: Economic and Social Progress in Latin America – 1998-1999 Report*. Washington, D.C.: Author.

Intergovernmental Panel on Climate Change. (2000). IPCC Special Report on Emissions Scenarios. Nairobi: Author. Retrieved 1 May, 2008, from http://www.grida.no/climate/ipcc/emission/.

International Institute for Environment and Development. (2000). Poverty reduction and urban governance (special issue). *Environment and Urbanization*, 12(1), 1-250.

International Labour Organization. (2006, October 27). *New ILO study says youth unemployment rising, with hundreds of millions more working but living in poverty*. Retrieved 8 June, 2008, from http://www.cinterfor.org.uy/public/english/region/ampro/cinterfor/news/unemploy.htm.

ISOCARP. (2008, January). *Planning for harmony*. Draft contribution to the UN-HABITAT Framework Document for the World Urban Forum 2008.

Izutsu, T., Tsutsumi, A., Islam, A.M., Kato, S., Wakai, S., & Kurita, H. (2006). Mental health, quality of life, and nutritional status of adolescents in Dhaka, Bangladesh: Comparison between an urban slum and non-slum area. *Social Science and Medicine*, 63(6), 1477-1488.

J

James, R., Arndt, C., & Simler, K.R. (2005, December). *Has economic growth in Mozambique been pro-poor?* (FCND Discussion Paper 202). Washington, D.C.: International Food Policy Research Institute. Retrieved 10 July, 2008, from http://www.ifpri.org/divs/fcnd/dp/papers/fcndp202.pdf.

Jargowsky, P. (1997). *Poverty and place: Ghettos, barrios, and the American city*. New York: Russell Sage Foundation.

Jeffery, C., Jeffery, P., & Jeffery, R. (2008). *Degrees without freedom? Education, masculinities, and unemployment in North India*. Palo Alto, CA: Stanford University Press.

Jerve, A.M. (2001). Rural-urban linkages and poverty analysis. In A. Grinspun (Ed.), *Choices for the poor: Lessons from national poverty strategies* (pp. 89-120). Bergen & New York: CMI/UNDP.

Jiménez, V. (2005). World economic growth fastest in nearly three decades. Washington, D.C.: Earth Policy Institute. Retrieved 20 July, 2008, from http://www.earth-policy.org/Indicators/Econ/2005.htm.

Jones, V. (1942). *Metropolitan government*. Chicago: University of Chicago Press.

K

Kanbur, R. (2000). Income distribution and development. In A.B. Atkinson & F. Bourguignon (Eds.), *Handbook of income distribution*. Amsterdam: North Holland.

Kanbur, R. & Venables, A. (2005, September). *Spatial inequalities and development: Overview of UNU-WIDER Project*. (Working Paper 2005-23). Ithaca, New York: Department of Applied Economics and Management, Cornell University. Retrieved 20 July, 2008, from http://www.aem.cornell.edu/research/researchpdf/wp0523.pdf.

Kanbur, R., Venables ,A.J., & Wan, G. (Eds.). (2006). *Spatial disparities in human development: Perspectives from Asia*. Tokyo: United Nations University Press.

Kasarda, J.D. & Crenshaw, E.M. (1991). Third world urbanization: Dimensions, theories, and determinants. *Annual Review of Sociology*, 17, 467-501.

Kayizzi-Mugerwa, S. (2001, December). *Globalization, growth and income inequality: A review of the African experience*. (OECD Working Paper No. 186). Paris: OECD. Retrieved 10 July, 2008, from http://www.oecd.org/dataoecd/9/58/2731373.pdf.

Kennedy, L. (2007). Regional industrial policies driving peri-urban dynamics in Hyderabad, India. Cities, 24(2), 95-109.

Kenworthy, J.R. (2003, September). *Transport energy use and greenhouse gases in urban passenger transport systems: A study of 84 global cities*. Paper presented at the Third Conference of the Regional Government Network for Sustainable Development, Notre Dame University, Fremantle, Western Australia. Retrieved 1 May, 2008, from http://cst.uwinnipeg.ca/documents/Transport_Greenhouse.pdf.

Kijima, Y. (2006). Why did wage inequality increase? Evidence from urban India 1983–99.

Journal of Development Economics, 81(1), 97-117.

Klink, J. (2007). Recent perspectives on metropolitan organization, functions and governance. In E. Rojas, J. Cuadrado-Roura, & J.M.F. Guell (Eds.), *Governing the metropolis*. Washington, D.C.: Inter-American Development Bank.

Knaap, G. (2008, February). Causes and consequences of urban sprawl. National Center for Smart Growth, University of Maryland. Power Point presentation accessed in February 2008.

Kofoworola, O.F. (2007). Recovery and recycling practices in municipal solid waste management in Lagos, Nigeria. *Waste Management*, 27(9), 1139-1143.

L

Lampietti, J.A. & Meyer, A.S. (2002). *Coping with the cold: Heating strategies for Eastern Europe and Central Asia's urban poor*. (World Bank Technical Paper No. 529). Washington, D.C.: World Bank.

Landry, C. (2002). *The creative city: A toolkit for urban innovators*. London: Earthscan.

Lang, S. (2004, November). Prospect on energy efficiency design standards for buildings. *Proceedings of the International Mayors Forum on Sustainable Urban Energy Development, Kunming, Yunnan Province, China*. Retrieved 19 May, 2008, from http://www.gobrt.org/China_Conference-12-2004-MF_BriefingBook_EN.pdf.

Langenbach, R. (1982, May/June). India in conflict: Urban renewal moves east. *Preservation: The magazine of the National Trust for Historic Preservation*, 46-51. Retrieved 20 July, 2008, from http://www.conservationtech.com.

Laquian, A.A. (2002). Metro Manila: People's participation and social inclusion in a city of villages. In B.A. Ruble, R. Stren, J. S. Tulchin, & D H. Varat (Eds.), *Urban governance around the world*. Washington, D.C.: Woodrow Wilson International Center for Scholars.

Laquian, A. A. (2005). *Beyond metropolis: The planning and governance of Asia's megaurban regions*. Washington, D.C.: Woodrow Wilson Center Press and Baltimore, MD: The Johns Hopkins University Press.

Lee, C. (2005). *Development of free economic zones and labor standards: A case study in Korea*. (International Programs Visiting Fellow Working Papers, Cornell University). Ithaca: ILR School, Cornell University. Retrieved 20 July, 2008, from http://digitalcommons.ilr.cornell.edu/intlvf/20/.

Lefèvre, C. (2007). Democratic governability of metropolitan areas: International experiences and

lessons for Latin American cities. In E. Rojas, J. Cuadrado-Roura, & J.M.F. Guell (Eds.), *Governing the metropolis*. Washington, D.C.: Inter-American Development Bank.

Leger, B. (2008, 26 April). Gay life: The street with soul. Retrieved 20 July, 2008, from http://www.thestar.com/columnists/article/417121.

Li, H., Squire, L., & Zou, H. (1998). Explaining international and intertemporal variations in income inequality. *The Economic Journal*, 108(446), 26-43.

Lim, B.S. (2005, November). Tourism & leisure cities: Driving force for balanced development. *Korea Policy Review*, 26-29. Retrieved 1 November, 2007, from *http://www.mct.go.kr/korea/handata/tour/Tourism & Leisure Cities - Driving Force fo Balanced Development.pdf*.

López-Moreno, E. (1993). *Barrios, colonias y fraccionamientos*. (City Words, Working Paper 2). Paris: UNESCO, MOST, CNRS.

López-Moreno, E. (2002a). *From structural adjustment programmes to poverty reduction strategies*. Nairobi: UN-HABITAT.

López-Moreno, E. (2002b). *Slums of the world: The face of urban poverty in the new millennium*. Nairobi: UN-HABITAT.

Lum, T. (2006, May). *Social unrest in China*. Congressional Research Service Report for Congress. Washington, D.C.: The Library of Congress. Retrieved 10 July, 2008, from http://handle.dtic.mil/100.2/ADA462706.

Lupala, A. (2001). *Urban land management in the peri-urban areas: The case of Dar es Salaam*. Unpublished Ph.D. dissertation, University of Dortmund.

Lupton, R. & Power, A. (2004, July). *The growth and decline of cities*. (Case-Brookings Census Briefs No. 1). London: London School of Economics. Retrieved 20 July, 2008, from http://sticerd.lse.ac.uk/dps/case/cbcb/census1.pdf.

Lvovsky, K., Hughes, G., Maddison, D., Ostro, B. & Pearce, D. (2000, October). *Environmental costs of fossil fuels: A rapid assessment method with application to six cities*. (Working Paper No. 78). Washington, D.C.: World Bank Environment Department.

Lynch, K. (2005). *Rural-urban interaction in the developing world*. London: Routledge.

Lyons, M., Smuts, C., & Stephens, A. (2001). Participation, empowerment and sustainability: (How) do the links work? *Urban Studies*, 38(8), 1233-1251.

M

Maharaj, B. & Makhathini, M. (2004). Historical and political context: Cato Manor, 1845-2002. In P. Robinson, J. McCarthy, & C. Forster (Eds.), *Urban reconstruction in the developing world: Learning through an international best practice* (pp. 27-28). Portsmouth, NH: Heinemann.

Marques, E.C. and Bichir, R.M. (2003). Public policies, political cleavages and urban space: State, infrastructure policies in São Paulo. *International Journal of Urban and Regional Research*, 27(4), 811-827.

Martine, G. (2001, January). *The sustainable use of space: Advancing the population/environment agenda*. Retrieved 20 July, 2008, from http://www.populationenvironmentresearch.org/papers/Martine_paper.pdf.

Martinez-Fernandez, C. & Wu, C.T. (2007, February). Shrinking cities and Australian cases. Proceedings of the conference, *Shrinking cities: Problems, patterns and strategies of urban transformation in a global context*, Berkeley, CA.

Martinez-Fernandez, M.C. & Wu, C.T. (2007). Urban Development in a Different Reality, Berlin 2006.

Mattingly, M. & Gregory, P. (2006, March). *The peri-urban interface: Intervening to improve livelihoods*. (NRSP Brief, DFID). Retrieved 9 August, 2007, from http://www.ucl.ac.uk/dpu/pui/research/previous/synthesis/index.html.

McCarney, P.L. (2005). Global cities, local knowledge creation: Mapping a new policy terrain on the relationship between universities and cities. In G. Jones, P. McCarney, & M. Skolnick (Eds.), *Improving knowledge, strengthening nations: The role of higher education in global perspective*. Toronto: University of Toronto Press.

McGee, T. G. (1991). The emergence of the desakota regions in Asia: Expanding a hypothesis. In N. Ginsburg, B. Poppel, & T. G. McGee (Eds.), *The extended metropolis* (pp. 3-25). Honolulu: University of Hawaii Press.

McGee, T.G. & Robinson, I.M. (Eds.). (1995). *The mega-urban regions of Southeast Asia*. Vancouver: University of British Columbia Press.

McGranahan, G., Balk, D., & Anderson, B. (2007). The rising tide: Assessing the risks of climate change and human settlements in low-elevation coastal zomes. *Environment and Urbanization*, 19(1), 17-37.

Meng, X., Gregory, R. & Wang, Y. (2005). Poverty, inequality and growth in urban China, 1986-2000. *Journal of Comparative Economics*, 33(4), 710-729.

Mercer. (2008, 10 June). *Mercer's 2008 Quality of Living survey highlights*. Retrieved 20 July, 2008, from http://www.mercer.com/qualityofliving?siteLanguage=100.

Messias, E. (2003). Income inequalities, literacy rate and life expectancy in Brazil. *American Journal of Public Health*, 93(8), 1294-1296.

Mingione, E. & Haddock, S.V. (2008). *European urban inequity*. Unpublished paper commissioned by UN-HABITAT for the *State of the World's Cities Report 2008/9*.

Ministry of Planning, Government of Angola. (2008). *Inquérito sobre o Bem Estar da População*. Unpublished document

Mirza, M. (2007, September). *Urban issues, concerns and responses to climate change in the cities of the Americas: What are in the IPCC AR4?* Paper presented to The Response of Urban Areas to Climate Change Seminar, Hunter College, New York, USA.

Modi, V., McDade, S., Lallement, D., & Saghir, J. (2006). *Energy and the Millennium Development Goals*. New York: Energy Sector Management Assistance Programme, United Nations Development Programme, UN Millennium Project, and World Bank.

Molina, M., & Molina, L. (Eds.). (2002). *Air quality in the Mexico megacity: An integrated assessment*. Dordrecht, Netherlands: Kluwer Academic.

Montgomery, M., Stren, R., Barney, C., & Holly, R. (2003). *Cities transformed: Demographic change and its implications in the developing world*. Washington, D.C.: National Academies Press.

Municipality of Shanghai. (n.d.). *Shanghai Municipality*. Retrieved 10 April, 2008, from www.demographia.com.

Mwangi, S.W. (2001). Local Agenda 21 experiences in Nakuru: Processes, issues and lessons. (Working Series papers on Urban environmental Action Plans and Local Agenda 21, Working Paper 10). London: IIED.

Myers, D.J. & Dietz, H.A. (Eds.). (2002). *Capital city politics in Latin America: Democratization and empowerment*. Boulder, CO: Lynne Rienner.

N

Narayan, D. (1999, July). *Bonds and bridges: Social capital and poverty*. Washington, D.C.: The World Bank. Retrieved 10 July, 2008, from http://info.worldbank.org/etools/docs/library/9747/narayan.pdf.

Narayan, D. & Nyamwaya, D. (1996). *Learning from the poor: A participatory poverty assessment in Kenya*. (Environment Department Papers, Paper No. 034). Washington, D.C.: The World Bank.

National Bureau of Statistics of China. (2002-2006). *China statistical yearbook 2002-2006*. Beijing: Author.

National Housing Institute, Cuba. (2001, May). *Cuba's national report to Istanbul+5*. Havana: Author.

National Research Council. (2003). *Cities transformed: Demographic change and its implications in the developing world*. Washington, D.C.: National Academies Press.

National Statistics Office, Cuba. (2000). *Cuban population yearbook*. Havana: Author.

National Statistics Office, Cuba. (2005a). *Cuban statistical yearbook*. Havana: Author.

National Statistics Office, Cuba. (2005b). *Population and housing census*. Havana: Author.

National Statistics Office, Cuba. (2006). *Cuban social and economic outlook*. Havana: Author.

National Statistics Office South Korea. (2005). *Internal migration in 2005*. Seoul: Author.

Netherlands Environmental Assessment Agency. (2007, June 19). *China now no. 1 in CO_2 emissions; USA in second position*. Press release. Retrieved 5 December, 2007, from http://www.mnp.nl.

New York City Department of Health and Mental Hygiene (n.d.). *Suicide prevention and public health in New York City*. Retrieved 12 March, 2008, from http://www.omh.state.ny.us.

Nicholss, R.J. (2004). Coastal flooding and wetland loss in the 21st century: Changes under the SRES climate and socioeconomic scenarios. *Global Environmental Change*, 14(1), 69-86.

Nigel, B., Perez-Padilla, R., & Albalak, R. (2000). Indoor air pollution in developing countries: a major environmental and public health challenge. *Environment and Health*, 78(9), 1078-1092.

O

OCHA (2003). *Angola country report*.

OCHA/IRIN & UN-HABITAT. (2007, September). Dhaka: Reaping the whirlwind. In *Tomorrow's crises today: The humanitarian impact of urbanization*. Nairobi: Authors. Retrieved 1 May, 2008, from http://www.irinnews.org/InDepthMain.aspx?InDepthId=63&ReportId=74973.

Ofori-Amoah, B. (2007). *Beyond metropolis: Urban geography as if small cities mattered*. Lanham, MD: University Press of America.

Olds, K. & Yeung, H. (2004). Pathways to global city formation: A view from the developmental city-state of Singapore. *Review of International Political Economy*, 11(3), 489-521.

Organisation for Economic Cooperation and Development (OECD). (2007). *Ranking port cities with high exposure and vulnerability to climate change*. (Environment Working Paper No.1). Paris: Author.

Overman H.G. & Venables, A. (2005, July). *Cities in the developing world*. (LSE series, CEP Discussion Papers Discussion Paper No. 695). London: Centre for Economic Performance.

Oxford Policy Management (OPM). (2004a). *DFID rural and urban development case study – India*. London: DFID.

Oxford Policy Management (OPM). (2004b). *DFID rural and urban development case study – Nigeria*. London: DFID.

Oyelaran-Oyeyinka, B. & Gehl Sampath, P. (in press). *Innovation in late development, India and China within global reach?* Cambridge, MA: MIT Press.

Oyelaran-Oyeyinka, B. & Rasiah, R. (2008, July). *Uneven paths of development: Learning and innovation in Asia and Africa*. Cheltenham, U.K.: Edward Elgar.

P

Palat, R.A. (in press). A new Bandung? Economic growth vs. distributive justice among emerging powers. *Futures*.

Palczynski, R.J. (2002, July). Study on solid waste management options for Africa. Abidjan, Cote D'Ivoire: African Development Bank. Retrieved 1 May, 2008, from http://www.afdb.org.

Pandey, D. (2002). *Fuelwood studies in India: Myth and reality*. Jakarta: Centre for International Forestry Research.

Pantelic, J. (2000, March). *Urban-rural synergies and poverty alleviation: The case of Bangladesh*. Washington, D.C.: The World Bank Group.

Park, A., Wang, D., & Cai, F. (2006, December). *Migration and urban poverty and inequality in China*. Institute of Population and Labor Economics, CASS. Retrieved 10 July, 2008, from http://iple.cass.cn/file/Migration and Urban Poverty and Inequality in China.pdf.

Parnell, S. & Robinson, J. (2006). Development and urban policy: Johannesburg's city development strategy. *Urban Studies*, 43(2), 337-355.

Parr, J.B. (1999). *Growth-pole strategies in regional economic planning: A retrospective view*. Urban Studies, 36(7) 1195-1215.

The People's Government of Lu'an. (n.d.). *Approaching to Lu'an*. Retrieved 20 July, 2008, from http://www.luan.gov.cn/english/.

Persson, T. & Tabellini, G. (1994). Is inequality harmful for growth? *American Economic Review*, 84(3), 600-621.

Petersdorff, C., Boermans, T., Stobbe, O., Joosen, S., Graus, W., Mikkers, E., & Harnisch, J. (2004, February). Mitigation of CO_2 emissions from the building stock: Beyond the EU directive on the energy performance of buildings. Cologne, Germany: Ecofys. Retrieved 1 May, 2008, from http://www.eurima.org/downloads/ecofys report final 160204.pdf.

Peterson, G.E. & Muzzini, E. (2006, 10 September). Decentralizing basic infrastructure services. *Economy*, 209-236.

Philippines Department of the Interior and Local Government, UN-HABITAT & UNDP. (2007). *State of cities of the Philippines* [CD].

Policy Research Initiative (PRI). (2005, September). *Social capital as a public policy tool*: Project report. (Report commissioned by the government of Canada as part of the Social Capital Project). Retrieved 10 July, 2008, from http://www.policyresearch.gc.ca/doclib/SC Synthesis E.pdf.

Prüss-Üstün, A. & Corvalán, C. (2006). *Preventing disease through healthy environments: Towards an estimate of the environmental burden of disease*. Geneva: World Health Organization.

Public Administration and Development. (2005). *Special issue on metropolitan governance reform*, 25(4), 275-364.

Putnam, R. (1993). *Making democracy work: Civic traditions in modern Italy*. Princeton: Princeton University Press.

Putnam, R. (2000). *Bowling alone: The collapse and revival of American community*. New York: Simon & Schuster.

Q

Qadeer, M.A. (2000). Ruralopolises: The spatial organisations of residential land economy of high density rural regions in South Asia. *Urban Studies*, 37 (9), 1583-1603.

Qiao, M. (2004, November). Strengthening building energy efficiency, constructing a beautiful homeland. *Proceedings of the International Mayors Forum on Sustainable Urban Energy Development, Kunming, Yunnan Province, China*. Retrieved 19 May, 2008, from http://www.gobrt.org/China Conference 12 2004-MF BriefingBook EN.pdf.

Qin, P. (2005). Suicide risk in relation to level of urbanicity: A population-based linkage study. *International Journal of Epidemiology*, 34, 846-852.

R

Rabinovich, J. (1996). Innovative land use and public transport policy: The case of Curitiba, Brazil. *Land Use Policy*, 13(1), 51-67.

Ravallion, M. & Chaudhuri, S. (2006). Partially awakened giants: Uneven growth in China and India. In L.A. Winters & S. Yusuf (Eds.), *Dancing with giants: China, India and the global economy*. Washington, D.C.: World Bank.

Rees, W. (1992). Ecological footprints and carrying capacity: What urban economics leaves out. *Environment and Urbanization*, 4(2), 121-130.

Regmi, C. & Tisdell, T. (2002). Remitting behaviour of Nepalese rural-to-urban migrants: Implications for theory and policy. *Journal of Development Studies*, 38 (3), 76-94.

Reilly, J., Robinson, P., Vaggione, P., Fernandez-Maldonado, A.M., Gossop, C., Jain, B.K., Moustafa, A., Viana, I., & Wright, T. (2008). *Planning for harmony*. Framework document for the World Urban Forum 2008 prepared for UN-HABITAT by the International Society of City and Regional Planners (ISOCARP).

Robinson, P. (2005). Durban: The Cato Manor experience. In W. Ng & J. Ryser (Eds.), *Making spaces for the creative economy. ISOCARP Review No. 1*. The Hague: International Society of City and Regional Planners.

Rodriguez, F. (2002). *Inequality, economic growth and economic performance*. Unpublished note for the World Bank development report. University of Maryland.

Rodriguez, J. (2007). Urbanización y desarrollo en América Latina y el Caribe: Revisando la experiencia. *EL Reporte Mundial de FNUAP*. Santiago, Chile: CEPAL.

Rodriguez, J. (2008, January). *Spatial distribution of the population, internal migration and development in Latin America and the Caribbean*. Paper prepared for the United Nations Expert Group Meeting on Population Distribution, Urbanization, Internal Migration and Development. New York: United Nations.

Rojas, E. (2007). The metropolitan regions of Latin America: Problems of governance and development. In E. Rojas, J. Cuaudrado-Roura, & J.M.F. Guell (Eds.), *Governing the metropolis*. Washington, D.C.: Inter-American Development Bank.

Rojas, E., Cuadrado-Roura, J., & Guell, J.M.F. (Eds.). (2005). *Gobernar las metropolis*. Washington, D.C.: Inter-American Development Bank.

Rosenberg, D. (2002). *Cloning Silicon Valley: The next generation high-tech hotspots*. London: Reuters/Pearson Education

Rosenfeld, A. (2004, November). *Saving energy, money, and pollution with building standards in California. Proceedings of the International Mayors Forum on Sustainable Urban Energy Development, Kunming, Yunnan Province, China*. Retrieved 19 May, 2008, from http://www.gobrt.org/China Conference-12-2004-MF BriefingBook EN.pdf.

Rosero-Bixby, L., (2006). Social capital, urban settings and demographic behaviour in Latin America. *Population Review*, 45(2), 24-43.

Royal Government of Bhutan. (2000). Bhutan national human development report. Planning Commission Secretariat.

Royal Town Planning Institute. (2007). *RTPI Good Practice Note 7*. Retrieved 10 July, 2008, from www.rtpi.org.uk.

Rustiadi, E. & Panuju, D.R. (n.d.) *A study of spatial pattern of suburbanization process: A case study in Jakarta suburb*. (HDP-Indonesia, Laboratory of Land Resources and Regional Planning). Retrieved 20 July, 2008 from http://hdp-ina.net/?p=ur.

S

Salehi-Isfahani, D. (2006, March). *Revolution and redistribution in Iran: Changes in poverty and distribution 25 years later*. (Working Paper, Department of Economics, Virginia Tech University). Retrieved 10 July, 2008, from http://siteresources.worldbank.org/INTDECINEQ/Resources/1149208-1147789289867/IIIWB_Conference_Revolutio&Redistribution_Iran.pdf.

Santamouris, M., Kapsis, K., Korres, D., Livada, I., Pavlou, C., & Assimakopoulos, M.N. On the relation between the energy and social characteristics of the residential sector. *Energy and Buildings*, 39(8), 893-905.

Satterthwaite, D. (2000, April). *Seeking an understanding of poverty that recognizes rural-urban differences and rural-urban linkages*. Paper commissioned by The World Bank, first draft presented at the World Bank's *Urban Forum on Urban Poverty Reduction in the 21st Century*, Washington, D.C.

Satterthwaite, D. (2007, September). *The transition to a predominantly urban world and its underpinnings*. (Human Settlements Discussion Paper, Urban Change: 4). London: International Institute for Environment and Development.

Satterthwaite, D., Huq, S., Reid, H., Pelling, M., & Lankao, P.R. (2007). *Adapting to climate change in urban areas: The possibilities and constraints in low-and middle-income nations*. London: International Institute for Environment and Development.

Scarpaci, J.L. (2002). Havana: The dynamics of local executive power. In D.J. Myers & H.A. Dietz (Eds.), *Capital city politics in Latin America: Democratization and empowerment* (pp. 163-92). Boulder, CO: Lynne Rienner.

Schaefer-Preuss, U. (2008, June). *Managing Asian cities for sustainability*. Speech delivered at the 2008 World Cities Summit: Launch of Managing Asian cities, Singapore. Retrieved 20 July, 2008, from http://www.adb.org/Media/Articles/2008/12511-ursula-shaefer-preuss-speeches/.

Shaktin, G. (2002). Working with the community: Dilemmas in radical planning in Metro Manila, The Philippines. *Planning Theory & Practice*, 3(3), 301-317.

Shanghai Research Institute of Building Sciences (SRIBS) & Politecnico di Milano (BEST). (2006). Feasibility study for renewable and low-energy applications in Shanghai building sector.

Sharpe, L.J. (Ed.). (1995). *The government of world cities: The future of the metro model*. Chichesterm U.K.: John Wiley & Sons.

Shin, D.C. (2006, March). *Shrinking coal mining cities in Asia: A comparative study*. Paper presented at the International Symposium, Coping with City Shrinkage and Demographic Change - Lessons from around the Globe, Dresden, Germany.

Simms, A., & Reid, H. (2006, August). *Up in smoke? Latin America and the Caribbean: The threat from climate change to the environment and human development*. London: New Economics Foundation.

Simon, D., McGregor, D. & Thompson, D. (2006). Contemporary perspectives on the peri-urban zones of cities in developing countries. In D. McGregor, D. Simon & D. Thompson (Eds.), *The peri-urban interface: Approaches to sustainable natural and human resource use* (pp. 3-17). London: Earthscan.

Singhal, A. & Rogers, E.M. (2001). *India's communication revolution: From bullock carts to cyber marts*. New Delhi: Sage Publications India Pvt. Ltd.

Sitar, S. & Sverdlov, A. (2004, February). *Shrinking cities: Reinventing urbanism*, a critical introduction to Ivanovo context from an urban perspective. (Working Paper). Leipzig, Germany: Federal Cultural Foundation.

Slack, E. (2007). *Managing the coordination of service delivery in metropolitan cities: The role of metropolitan governance*. (Finance Economics and Urban Development, Urban Development Unit, Policy Research Working Paper # 4317). Washington, D.C.: The World Bank.

Smith, K.R. & Mehta, S. (2000, May). The burden of disease from indoor air pollution in developing countries. In the proceedings of the USAID/WHO Global Technical Consultation on the Health Impacts of Indoor Air Pollution and Household Energy in Developing Countries. Washington D.C.: World Health Organization.

Society for International Development (SID). (2004). *Pulling apart: Facts and figures on inequality in Kenya*. Nairobi.

Society for International Development (SID). (2006). *Readings on inequality in Kenya: Sectoral dynamics and perspectives*. Nairobi.

Sood, D. (2004, February). *Solid waste management study for Freetown, Sierra Leone: Component design for the World Bank*. (Draft Report Project No. P078389). Washington, D.C.: World Bank. Retrieved 12 March, 2008, from http://www-ds.worldbank.org.

Sorensen, A. (2001). Subcentres and satellite cities: Tokyo's 20th century experience of planned polycentrism. International Planning Studies, 6(1), 9-32.

South African Cities Network. (2006). *State of the cities report 2006*. Braamfontein: Author.

Southern African Regional Poverty Network. (2008). *Socio-economic progress or regression?* Retrieved 10 July, 2008, from http://www.sarpn.org/documents/d0000164/page1.php.

Spring, M. (2008, 10 May). Memories of urban renewal: When a community embraces both progress and heritage. *The Boston Globe*, pp. A11. Retrieved 20 July, 2008, from http://www.boston.com.

State of Food and Agriculture (SOFA). (2002, January). *Special chapter on urbanization: Linking development across the changing landscape*. Rome: FAO.

The State University of New York Regional Institute. (2002). *State of the region*. Retrieved 10 July, 2008, from http://regional-institute.buffalo.edu/sotr/Indicator.cfm?Indicator=301087fd-b756-4899-8bf9-00d6c341817b.

Statistics Canada. (2001). *A profile of the*

Canadian population: Where we live, 2001 census. Retrieved 20 July, 2008, from http://www.statcan.ca.

Statistics New Zealand. (1999a). New Zealand: A regional profile – Auckland region. Retrieved 20 July, 2008, from http://www2.stats.govt.nz/.

Statistics New Zealand. (1999b). New Zealand: A regional profile – Otago region. Retrieved 20 July, 2008, from http://www2.stats.govt.nz/.

Statistics Norway. (2004, December). Energy balance and energy accounts 2002 and 2003: Large decrease in electricity consumption. Retrieved 1 May, 2008, from http://www.ssb.no/energiregn_en/arkiv/art-2004-12-06-01-en.html.

Statistics South Africa. (2002, November). Earning and spending in South Africa: Selected findings and comparisons 1995-2000. Pretoria, SA: Author.

Stern, N. (2006, October). Stern review on the economics of climate change. London: UK Government, Office of Climate Change. Retrieved 1 May, 2008, from http://www.hm-treasury.gov.uk/independent reviews/stern review economics climate change/sternreview index.cfm.

Stren, R. (2007). Urban governance in developing countries: Experiences and challenges. In R. Hambleton & J. Gross (Eds.), Governing cities in a global era: Urban innovation, competition, and democratic reform. New York: Palgrave Macmillan.

Sutton, K. & Fahmi, F. (2001). Cairo's urban growth and strategic master plans in light of Egypt's 1996 population census results. Cairo: University of Helwan.

T

Tachibanaki, T. (2005). Confronting income inequality in Japan: A comparative analysis of causes, consequences and reform. Cambridge, MA: MIT Press.

Tacoli, C. (1998a). Rural-urban interactions: A guide to the literature. Environment and Urbanization, 10 (1), 147-166.

Tacoli, C. (1998b). Bridging the divide: Rural-urban interactions and livelihood strategies. (Gatekeeper Series No 77). London: IIED. Retrieved 13 August, 2007, from http://www.iied.org/pubs/display.php?o=6144IIED.

Tacoli, C. (Ed.). (2006). The Earthscan reader in rural-urban linkages. London: Earthscan.

Tata Institute of Social Sciences. (n.d.). The maker of modern cities. Retrieved 13 June, 2007, from http://www.tiss.edu/news056.pdf.

Thanh, L.V. (2006, November). Migrants and the socio-economic development of Ho Chi Minh City. Proceedings of the NIE-SEAGA conference, Sustainability and Southeast Asia, Singapore. Retrieved 20 July, 2008, from http://www.hsse.nie.edu.sg/Staff/CHANGCH/SEAGA/seaga2006/proceedings.

Tibaijuka, A.K. (2005). Report of the fact-finding mission to Zimbabwe to assess the scope and impact of Operation Murambatsvina by the UN special envoy on human settlements. New York: United Nations.

Tiebout, C. (1956). A pure theory of local expenditures. The Journal of Political Economy, 64(5), 416-24.

Tokyo Metropolitan Government. (2003). Living standards survey. Tokyo.

Tostensen, A. (2004). Rural-urban linkages in sub-Saharan Africa: Contemporary debates and implications for Kenyan urban workers in the 21st century. (CMI Working Paper WP 4). Bergen, Norway: Chr. Michelsen Institute.

U

U.K. Department for Business, Enterprise and Regulatory Reform. (2007). The U.K. fuel poverty strategy: 5th annual progress report. Retrieved 1 September, 2007, from http://www.dti.gov.uk/energy/fuel-poverty/index.html.

U.K. Department for International Development (DFID). (2005). People, place and sub-national growth. London: Author.

Ullmann-Margalit, E. & Sunstein, C. (2001). Inequality and indignation. Philosophy and Public Affairs, 30(4), 337-362.

UNCTAD. (2007). Least developed country report: Knowledge, technological learning and innovation for development. Geneva: Author.

U.N. Department of Economic and Social Affairs (DESA). (2006). World urbanization prospects: The 2005 revision. New York: United Nations.

U.N. Department of Economic and Social Affairs Population Division (DESA). (2007a, March). World population prospects: The 2006 revision – highlights. New York: Author.

UN-DESA. (2007b). Industrial development for the 21st century: Sustainable Development Perspectives. New York: United Nations. Retrieved 10 July, 2008, from http://www.un.org/esa/sustdev/publications/industrial_development/full_report.pdf

UNDP (1998). Overcoming human poverty: UNDP poverty report. New York: Author.

UNDP. (2001). Human development report 2001 (Viet Nam). New York: Author.

UNDP. (2003). National human development report 2001 (India). New York: Author.

UNDP & Center for Economic Research. (2005). Linking macroeconomic policy to poverty reduction in Uzbekistan. Tashkent: Authors. Retrieved 10 July, 2008, from www.cer.uz/files/downloads/publication/LMPPR_en.pdf.

UNDP & China Development Research Foundation. (2005). China human development report 2005. Beijing: UNDP. Retrieved 10 July, 2008, from http://www.undp.org.cn/downloads/nhdr2005/NHDR2005_complete.pdf.

UN Economic Commission for Europe. (2004). Poverty in Eastern Europe and the CIS. Economic Survey of Europe. Retrieved 10 July, 2008, from http://www.unece.org/ead/pub/041/041c7.pdf.

UNEP Regional Office for Latin America and the Caribbean and SEMARNET (Secretaria de Medio Ambiente y Recursis Naturales. (2006). El cambio climático en América Latina y el Caribe. Retrieved 1 June, 2008, from http://www.pnuma.org/El%20cambio%20Climatico_r.pdf.

UNESCO World Heritage Centre. (n.d.). Success stories. Retrieved 20 July, 2008, fromhttp://whc.unesco.org/en/107.

UNFPA. (n.d.). Demographic trends by region. Retrieved 20 July, 2008, from http://www.unfpa.org/intercenter/upshort/demograp.htm.

UNFPA. (2007). State of world population 2007: Unleashing the potential of urban growth. New York.

UN-HABITAT. (in press). State of the African cities report 2007. Nairobi.

UN-HABITAT. (2006a). State of the world's cities 2006/7. London: Earthscan.

UN-HABITAT (2006b). UrbanInfo database. Nairobi.

UNIDO. (2006). Industrialization and poverty alleviation: Pro-poor industrialization strategies revisited. (UNIDO Research Programme, Combating Marginalization and Poverty through Industrial Development). Vienna.

United Nations. (2007). The millennium development goals report 2007 New York.

United Nations Economic and Social Council. (1997, February). Report on the thirtieth session of the UN Commission on Population and Development. New York: United Nations.

United Nations Environment Programme. (2005).

Dhaka City state of environment 2005 report. Nairobi: Author.

United Nations Environment Programme. (2007a). *Buildings and climate change: Status, challenges and opportunities*. Nairobi: Author.

United Nations Environment Programme. (2007b). Global environment outlook: *Environment for development (GEO-4)*. Nairobi: Author.

United States Census Bureau. (2007). *Population change and distribution 1990-2000*. Washington, D.C.: Author.

United States Environmental Protection Agency. (2000). *Greenhouse gases from small-scale combustion devices in developing countries: Phase IIa, household stoves in India*. (Report No. EPA/600/R-00/052). Washington, D.C.: Author. Retrieved 1 May, 2008, from http://www.epa. gov/nrmrl/pubs/600r00052/600r00052.htm.

V

Vargas, L. (2001, June). Maquiladoras: Impact on Texas border cities. *The border economy*, *Federal Reserve Bank of Dallas*, 25-29.

Veni, L.K. (2005). Demographic profile of urbanization in India: A special focus on slums. *The ICFAI Journal of Public Administration*, 1(2), 61-75.

Vergara, W. (2005, October). *Adapting to climate change: Lessons learned, works in progress, and proposed next steps for the World Bank in Latin America*. (Sustainable Development Working Paper No. 25). Washington, D.C.: The World Bank, Latin American and the Caribbean Region, Environmentally and Socially Sustainable Development Department. Retrieved 1 May, 2008, from http://ncsp.va-network.org/section/ resources/adaptation.

Vijayakumar, L., Nagaraj, K., & Sujit, J. (2004, June). *Suicide and suicide prevention in developing countries* (Working Paper No. 27). Disease Control Priorities Project. Retrieved 1 May, 2008, from http://www.dcp2.org/file/41/ wp27.pdf.

Villa, M. & Rodriguez, J. (1996). Demographic trends in Latin America's metropolises, 1950-1990. In A. Gilbert (Ed.), *The mega-city in Latin America*. Tokyo: United Nations University Press.

W

Wackernagel, M., & Rees, W. (1996). *Our ecological footprint: Reducing human impact on the earth*. Philadelphia: New Society Publishers.

Warah, R. (2005). Divided city: Information poverty in Nairobi's slums. In U. Carlsson & C. von Feilitzen (Eds.), *In the service of young people?*

Studies and reflections on media in the digital age. Göteborg, Sweden: NORDICOM.

Warah, R. (2008, 14 January). Kenyans are fighting inequality, not ethnicity. *Daily Nation*, Nairobi, Kenya.

Weber, E.D., B. Bridier, & R. Fiorentino. (1997). *Rural agro industry in Latin America: An evaluation of the PRODAR network*. Ottowa, CA: International Development Research Centre. Retrieved 20 August, 2007, from http://www.idrc.ca/en/ev-9305-201-1-DO_TOPIC.html.

Webster, D. (2004). Bangkok: Evolution and adaptation under stress. In J. Gugler (Ed.), *World cities beyond the west* (pp. 82-118). Cambridge, MA: Cambridge University Press.

Weiding, L., Ting, Z., & Beihong, Z. (2004). China: The issue of residential air conditioning. (Bulletin 2004-4). International Institute of Refrigeration. Retrieved 1 May, 2008, from http://www.iifiir.org/ en/doc/1056.pdf.

Weiding, L. & Wei, B. (2006, January). The impact of air-conditioning use on Shanghai's energy situation in 2010. China Sustainable Energy Program. Retrieved 15 September, 2007, from http://www.efchina.org.

Wells, H.G. (1902). *Anticipations of the reaction of mechanical and scientific progress upon human life and thought*. London: Chapman & Hall.

WHO Centre for Health Development. (2007, July). *Our cities, our health, our future: Acting on social determinants for health equity in urban settings*. Report to the WHO Commission on Social Determinants of Health for the Knowledge Network on Urban Settings, Kobe, Japan.

Wiechmann, T. (2006, March). *Types of shrinking cities – Introductive notes on a global issue*. Presentation prepared for the International Symposium, Coping with City Shrinkage and Demographic Change - Lessons from around the Globe, Dresden, Germany. Retrieved 20 July, 2008, from http://www.schader-stiftung.de/ wohn_wandel/966.php.

Williamson, J. (1965). Regional inequality and the process of national development: A description of patterns. *Economic Development and Cultural Change*, 13(4), 1-84.

Wines, M. (2005, 25 December). Shantytown dwellers in South Africa protest sluggish pace of change. *The New York Times*.

Winkler, H., Borchers, M., Hughes, A., Visagie, E., & Heinrich, G. (2005). *Cape Town energy futures: Policies and scenarios for sustainable city energy development*. Cape Town: Energy Research Centre. Retrieved 1 May, 2008, from http://www. erc.uct.ac.za/publications/CT%20energy%20

futures.pdf.

Woolcock, M. (2000). *Friends in high places? An overview of social capital*. Washington, D.C.: The World Bank.

Woolcock, M. (2005). Calling on friends and relatives: Social capital. In M. Fay (Ed.), *The urban poor in Latin America* (pp. 219-239). Washington, D.C.: The World Bank.

The World Bank. (n.d.). *Meeting the Millennium Development Goals in Europe and Central Asia*. Retrieved 23 April, 2008, from http://www. worldbank.org.

World Bank. (2001). *World development report 2000/2001: Attacking poverty*. Washington, D.C.

World Bank. (2004a). *The little green data book*. Washington D.C.

World Bank. (2004b). *World development report, 2004: Making services work for people*. Washington, D.C.

World Bank. (2005, 16 June). Majority of Indonesians see public services improving decentralization says new survey. Retrieved 10 July, 2008, from http://go.worldbank.org/ Z8O9ZU4XY0.

World Bank. (2006). *World development report 2006: Equity and development*. New York: Oxford University Press.

World Bank. (2007a). *World development indicators 2007*. Washington, D.C.: Author.

World Bank. (2007b). *World development report 2009*. Outline draft. Washington, D.C.

World Bank. (2007c, November). *Growth and CO_2 emissions: How do different countries fare?* (Environment Working Paper, No. 41760). Washington, D.C.

World Bank. (2008). *Fighting poverty: Findings and lessons from China's success*. Retrieved 10 July, 2008, from http://go.worldbank.org/QXOQI9MP30.

World Energy Council. (2006, April). *Alleviating urban energy poverty in Latin America*. London: Author. Retrieved 1 May, 2008, from http://www. worldenergy.org/publications/310.asp.

World Health Organization. (2007, May). *Health conditions in the Occupied Palestinian Territories, including east Jerusalem and the occupied Syrian Golan: Fact-finding report of the sixteenth World Health Assembly*. Geneva.

Wright, L. &Montezuma, R. (2004, June). *Reclaiming public space: The economic, environmental, and social impacts of Bogotá's transformation*. Paper presented at Walk21, Cities for People, Copenhagen, Denmark. Retrieved 1 June, 2008, from http://www.walk21.com/.

Wu, F. (2004). Urban poverty and marginalization under market transition: The case of Chinese cities. *International Journal of Urban and Regional Research*, 28(2), 401-423.

Wu, X. & Perloff, J.M. (2004, February). *China's income distribution over time: Reasons for rising inequality*. (CUDARE Working Paper 977). Berkeley, CA: University of California.

X

Xinhua News Agency. (2006, 19 October). China publishes *"harmonious society" resolution*. Retrieved 2 October, 2007, from http://www.china.org.cn.

Xue, J. (1997). Urban-rural income disparity and its significance in China.*Hitotsubashi Journal of Economics*, 38(1), 45-59.

Y

Yuanzhu, D. (2005, 10 June). *A strategic move towards social harmony*. Beijing: Academy of Macro-Economic Research, State Development and Reform Commission. Retrieved 20 July, 2008, from http://www.china-embassy.org/eng/gyzg/t215185.htm.

Z

Zhang, X. (2004, November). Implementing "scientific development" and advancing building energy efficiency: A report on Beijing's building energy efficiency progress. *Proceedings of the International Mayors Forum on Sustainable Urban Energy Development, Kunming, Yunnan Province, China*. Retrieved 19 May, 2008, from http://www.gobrt.org/China_Conference-12-2004-MF_BriefingBook_EN.pdf.

Zhao, S.X. & Zhang, L. (2005). Economic growth and income inequality in Hong Kong: Trends and explanations. *China: An International Journal*, 3(1), 74-103.

Zhu, Y. (2003). Changing urbanization processes and in situ rural-urban transformation: Reflections on China's settlements definitions. In A.G. Champion, G. Hugo, & T. Champion (Eds.), *New forms of urbanization: Beyond the urban-rural dichotomy*. Hampshire, U.K.: Ashgate.

Zhu, Y. (2006). Patterns of population and employment change in Shanghai in the 1990s. *International Development Planning Review*, 28(3), 287-310.

Zhu, Y. (2007). China's floating population and their settlement intention in the cities: Beyond the *Hukou* reform. *Habitat International*, 31, 65-76.

Zin, R.H.M. (2001). Improving quality of life after the crisis: New dilemmas. *Malaysian Journal of Economic Studies*, 38(1&2).

Zunino, H.M. (2006). Power relations in urban decision-making: Neo-liberalism, "techno-politicians" and authoritarian redevelopment in Santiago, Chile. *Urban Studies*, 43(10), 1825-1846.

Index

Note: Page numbers in *italics* refer to maps, figures, tables, boxes and illustrations. Those followed by 'n' refer to notes.